Improving Mental Health and Wellbeing Through Bibliotherapy

Antonio Cortijo Ocaña
University of California, Santa Barbara, USA

Vicent Martines Peres
University of Alicante, Spain

Veronica Orazi
Università degli Studi di Torino, Italy

A volume in the Advances in
Psychology, Mental Health, and
Behavioral Studies (APMHBS)
Book Series

Published in the United States of America by
IGI Global
Medical Information Science Reference (an imprint of IGI Global)
701 E. Chocolate Avenue
Hershey PA, USA 17033
Tel: 717-533-8845
Fax: 717-533-8661
E-mail: cust@igi-global.com
Web site: http://www.igi-global.com

Library of Congress Cataloging-in-Publication Data

CIP Pending
ISBN: 979-8-3693-4244-2
EISBN: 979-8-3693-4245-9

British Cataloguing in Publication Data
A Cataloguing in Publication record for this book is available from the British Library.

All work contributed to this book is new, previously-unpublished material.
The views expressed in this book are those of the authors, but not necessarily of the publisher.

For electronic access to this publication, please contact: eresources@igi-global.com.

Advances in Psychology, Mental Health, and Behavioral Studies (APMHBS) Book Series

Harish C. Chandan
Argosy University, USA
Bryan Christiansen
Southern New Hampshire University, USA

MISSION

ISSN:2475-6660
EISSN:2475-6679

The complexity of the human mind has puzzled researchers and physicians for centuries. While widely studied, the brain still remains largely misunderstood.

The **Advances in Psychology, Mental Health, and Behavioral Studies (APMHBS)** book series presents comprehensive research publications focusing on topics relating to the human psyche, cognition, psychiatric care, mental and developmental disorders, as well as human behavior and interaction. Featuring diverse and innovative research, publications within APMHBS are ideally designed for use by mental health professionals, academicians, researchers, and upper-level students.

Coverage

- Addiction
- Anxiety
- Cognition
- Counseling & Therapy
- Eating Disorders
- Emotional Health
- Socialization

IGI Global is currently accepting manuscripts for publication within this series. To submit a proposal for a volume in this series, please contact our Acquisition Editors at Acquisitions@igi-global.com or visit: http://www.igi-global.com/publish/.

The (ISSN) is published by IGI Global, 701 E. Chocolate Avenue, Hershey, PA 17033-1240, USA, www.igi-global.com. This series is composed of titles available for purchase individually; each title is edited to be contextually exclusive from any other title within the series. For pricing and ordering information please visit http://www.igi-global.com/book-series/advances-psychology-mental-health-behavioral/110200. Postmaster: Send all address changes to above address.

Titles in this Series

For a list of additional titles in this series, please visit: www.igi-global.com/book-series

Machine and Deep Learning Techniques for Emotion Detection
Mritunjay Rai (Department of Electrical and Electronics Engineering, Shri Ramswaroop Memorial University, India) and Jay Kumar Pandey (Department of Electrical and Electronics Engineering, Shri Ramswaroop Memorial University, India)
Medical Information Science Reference • copyright 2024 • 313pp • H/C (ISBN: 9798369341438) • US $265.00 (our price)

The Climate Change Crisis and Its Impact on Mental Health
Debabrata Samanta (Rochester Institute of Technology, Kosovo) and Muskan Garg (Mayo Clinic, USA)
Information Science Reference • copyright 2024 • 301pp • H/C (ISBN: 9798369332726) • US $245.00 (our price)

Using Machine Learning to Detect Emotions and Predict Human Psychology
Mritunjay Rai (Department of Electrical and Electronics Engineering, Shri Ramswaroop Memorial University, India) and Jay Kumar Pandey (Department of Electrical and Electronics Engineering, Shri Ramswaroop Memorial University, India)
Medical Information Science Reference • copyright 2024 • 313pp • H/C (ISBN: 9798369319109) • US $240.00 (our price)

Promoting Mindfulness and Well-Being with Indian Psychology
Anuradha Sathiyaseelan (Christ University, India) and Sathiyaseelan Balasundaram (Christ University, India)
Information Science Reference • copyright 2024 • 337pp • H/C (ISBN: 9798369326510) • US $245.00 (our price)

IGI Global
PUBLISHER of TIMELY KNOWLEDGE

701 East Chocolate Avenue, Hershey, PA 17033, USA
Tel: 717-533-8845 x100 • Fax: 717-533-8661
E-Mail: cust@igi-global.com • www.igi-global.com

Table of Contents

Detailed Table of Contents

The reading of the series of die-cut stories Greek Stories on Papyri can help us to open us to express emotions and to better understand human nature. The collection comprises five volumes: *The Adventures of Calligone and the Amazons; Ninus; The Adventures of the King of Nineveh; The Papyrus of the Sailor Sinuhe;* and *The Martyrdom of Saint Parthenope*. Ninus is an Assyrian prince and the action begins in Mesopotamia. Calligone is the daughter of the king of Boristhenes and her ship is wrecked in the country of the Amazons. Sesoncosis is a Pharaoh who that travels to the Iberian Peninsula. Finally, Parthenope is the protagonist of a martyrdom. Both the texts and the illustrations on each page are based on data of a literary, historical, iconographic, and archaeological nature. By means of the corresponding adaptations, this documentation is made available to an audience from children to adults. It could be a tool for interactive, enjoyable and relaxed exchange of knowledge and experience between readers of different generations within the same family.

The biography or memory book of Kandinsky written by his wife Nina refers to the years in which the great painter devoted himself to teaching Roman law, and highlights certain aspects of the subject that particularly appealed to him. She refers to the logical precision and modes of argumentation in which the Roman jurists—according to the artist—would have excelled. The authors have examined the type of Roman law that was taught in Czarist Russia, the milieu in which he lived and the sources from which it was derived. It seems that the influence of German Pandectistics was decisive, particularly at the end of the 19th century. Several Russian scholars were trained in Germany, and not only in Roman law, so the influence of Pandectistics was greater than previously thought. This work of research into the context in which the painter moved during his years as a jurist enables the authors to explain what he understood by the logical precision and ways of legal argumentation in the case of the Roman jurists.

This chapter deals with the possible impact that reading Goethe had on Paul Klee and his trip to Italy, which marked his life and his growth as an artist. It takes into account Klee's diaries, as edited by his son Felix, and compares Goethe's vision of Neohumanism with Klee's approach to classical art and to Neohumanism itself in general, with the distances that exist between the two with respect to this movement and their similarities, particularly in the study of nature. The authors are not going to deal with Goethe's most obvious influence on Klee, which is his theory of light and colour, on which much has been written and about which the painter himself was very explicit in the pedagogical works he published for the Bauhaus.

This chapter explores the transcultural and transhistorical conversation between Henry David Thoreau's *Walden* and Byung-Chul Han's philosophy, offering a bibliotherapeutic perspective on navigating modern society's challenges. Han's analysis of late capitalism's impact on individual subjectivity resonates with Thoreau's call for deliberate living and connection with nature. Through introspective exercises aligned with Walden, readers are prompted to reflect on values, cultivate authenticity, and resist societal pressures. By merging Thoreau's timeless wisdom with Han's contemporary critique, the chapter provides practical strategies for personal resilience and growth in the face of modernity's demands. This dialogue illuminates a path towards fulfillment and purpose, inviting readers to embody authenticity and lead lives aligned with their values.

In this study, the author focuses attention on some theatrical texts written by Juan Mayorga, especially, *El traductor de Blumemberg, Himmelweg, La paz perpetua,* and *La lengua en pedazos* in order to observe some influences ——mainly philosophical——, with which the author works in his dramaturgy. In this sense, this studies the concept of translation developed by Walter Benjamin regarding the metaphor of the broken vessel; the act of reading as a non-ending one, thanks to intertextuality, and the face of the Other conceived by Lévinas. On the one hand, we understand memory, reading, listening and silence as a kind of unit, especially, in the authors' historic dramatic plays. On the other hand, we see how Mayorga's writing becomes an endless rewriting.

The chapter proposes a critical analysis of educational discourses and practices related to gender emancipation and the education of the younger generation. Through the centuries, it highlights how male chauvinist principles and a distorted view of sexuality, influenced by theology and morality, dominated women's education. The need for a profound change in the way these issues are dealt with is emphasised through conscious education that promotes mutual respect and human emancipation. Current projects, aimed at fighting gender-based violence and hatred, are also discussed by underlining the importance of a transversal and inclusive educational approach that actively involves families, communities and institutions. Finally, the debate is raised on the need for greater autonomy of schools in addressing these issues, instead of adopting projects imposed from above, in order to foster a real cultural transformation towards gender equality and respect for human relations.

The chapter outlines the theoretical foundations and methods of autobiographical pedagogy and its importance in the current context. The centrality of the narrative method for care settings in general and specifically for the care of the elderly is highlighted. With reference then to the medical humanities, the importance of the community dimension among individuals is underlined, also in order to recover a global perspective able to counteract the current fragmentation of knowledge. The fundamental contribution comes from the humanistic tradition, from arts to literature, that gives great weight to the 'story' and to the process of writing of them.

Contemporary medicine makes a radical epistemological shift indispensable, one that brings out the human dimension and the active participation of the subject in building prevention processes, care, and well-being. From this perspective, listening to patients' stories, re-evaluating the care relationship, and using narrative based medicine instead of exclusively evidence-based medicine are of crucial importance. Placed in the realm of medical humanities, the chapter intends to present, investigate, and discuss the potential of narrative medicine, with particular reference to bibliotherapy as a tool for prevention, educational care, and well-being. Furthermore, the contribution reconstructs the historical-pedagogical pathway that has led to the outlining of such innovative training approaches and tools. In conclusion, the 'Dialogic Literary Gathering' model is presented as an educational empowerment strategy, in the field of mental health promotion and psychosocial support (MHPSS) in LGBTQIA+ adolescent victims of minority stress.

In narrative medicine practices, emotional education and reading represent two intrinsically connected elements for the countless reasons that describe the potential of reading in promoting well-being and quality of life, self-realization and planning of one's future. The chapter starts from some theoretical references that trace the reasons for the importance of reading from early childhood and takes a deliberately methodological turn when the discussion on emotions is addressed precisely to bring to light a possible educability and management of them to encourage well-being and interpersonal relationships. The contribution intends to reflect on the development of emotional education through the practice of reading to give a meaningful orientation to our human form, to our formation, to our taking care of ourselves to build together answers for the future starting from the reflection on the actions to be taken to re-plan existences from an inclusive and transformative perspective.

In the twentieth century, aesthetics gained central importance in the philosophical debate. Croce viewed aesthetics as the first form of knowing, rooted in feeling and intuition. This challenges traditional methodologies that prioritize formalistic and intellectual aspects over intuition and aesthetics. Heidegger and Gadamer reinforced the significance of aesthetics in contrast to a technicist view of epistemology, emphasizing its intrinsic connection to truth, promoting a holistic understanding of art and expression. These ideas inform pedagogy's reflections on reading education, emphasizing narration as vital for education. Reading, storytelling, and writing are seen as tools that can enhance resilience and well-being, especially when approached within a narrative framework. Bibliotherapy and narrative based medicine are highlighted for their therapeutic and humanizing benefits in healthcare, emphasizing the importance of professional guidance for effective therapeutic results.

The burgeoning intersection of bibliotherapy and technology presents a dynamic frontier for mental health intervention and personal development. This chapter explores the evolving means and tools within bibliotherapy, emphasizing the integral role of technology in enhancing its accessibility, efficacy, and range. The authors delve into the foundations of bibliotherapy as a therapeutic modality, employing literature for emotional and psychological healing, and transition to a comprehensive examination of contemporary technological advancements that have transformed traditional practices. Key focal areas include digital platforms for literature access, such as e-books and audiobooks; online bibliotherapy sessions facilitated by professionals; and the utilization of algorithms for personalized reading recommendations based on psychological profiles. The chapter also highlights the importance of interactive applications that combine cognitive-behavioral techniques with literary exposure, offering users a multifaceted therapeutic tool.

This research addresses the therapeutic effects of creative writing for population segments aged over 50. In recent years, the author has taught story and micro-story writing workshops as part of the University of Alicante's training programmes for senior citizens, and this experience provides the starting point for the study. The study has focused on the creation of micro-stories (stories up to 10-12 lines in length), useful in developing writing skills due to the concision and precision needed to meet the length requirements. Thus, workshop participants of this age group have to be creative and innovative, improve their concentration and experiment with creative structures. With these objectives, several techniques have been employed to combat ageism: looking for diverse voices and experiences, exploring ageing-related issues, challenging standards of beauty and success, promoting empathy and understanding, and avoiding stereotypes and clichés.

Traditionally, comics were undervalued and relegated to being childish and immature. This situation began to change in the 20th century, when they gradually gained more social prestige and had a place in new circles, among them medicine. This is partly because of the growth of graphic medicine, a form of bibliotherapy and an emerging area that challenges traditional methods and offers a more inclusive perspective on medicine. Consequently, comics are no longer considered as mere entertainment, but as mediums that allow a new approach to medicine and the construction of safe spaces to talk about what is never talked about. This chapter explores the ways in which comics can be used as an effective and empowering tool of therapeutic storytelling through the representation of eating disorders in comics from a cross-cultural perspective, thus contributing to the consolidation of Graphic Medicine.

This chapter describes how two teacher educators incorporated children's poetry in their undergraduate children's literature courses. The preservice teachers participated in course invitations that exposed them to well-written children's poetry that focused on tenets of the collaborative for academic, social, and emotional learning (CASEL) framework. Poetry can be read and enjoyed by everyone to help navigate complex emotions while developing empathy and understanding. This chapter also includes suggestions to incorporate social and emotional poetry with readers of all ages. Professionals from all fields can utilize poetry to facilitate social and emotional learning within their respective contexts.

Preface

The activity of reading has always been seen as calming and soothing. In fact, in Classical Antiquity, Stoics such as Seneca and Cicero conceived of it as a relaxing evening conversation with friends. Quevedo, a famous Renaissance Spanish poet, followed suit by describing it as a casual and intimate "conversation with the dead". Only recently, the medical profession has rediscovered the therapeutic effects of books, reading, and sharing the emotions and feelings that reading fiction elicits.

In *Improving Mental Health and Wellbeing Through Bibliotherapy*, we aim to delve deeply into the therapeutic potential of reading. By bringing together a comprehensive list of specialists from various disciplines, ranging from literary studies to psychology and education, we explore the manifold ways in which literature can serve as a balm for the soul. The term "bibliotherapy" has emerged to encapsulate this profound connection between reading and healing.

The relevance of this work has been underscored by the current COVID-19 pandemic. The isolation brought about by lockdowns and suburban living conditions, especially among the elderly, highlights the importance of literature as a source of solace and connection. In times of unprecedented global stress, the healing aspects of reading have become more apparent than ever, providing an invaluable contribution to our overall well-being.

Our target audience is diverse, encompassing university professors, graduate and undergraduate students, the reading public at large, health professionals, psychologists, stress management specialists, educators, neurologists, and more. This broad spectrum reflects the interdisciplinary nature of our exploration and the wide-reaching impact of bibliotherapy.

As editors, we are honored to present this volume as a resource for those seeking to understand and harness the power of literature for therapeutic purposes. We hope that it will inspire further research and practice in the field of bibliotherapy, and ultimately, contribute to the enhancement of mental health and well-being across diverse populations.

Chapter 1: Open it that you may know wonders: Keys to Improve Mental Health and Wellbeing Through Fiction in Papyrus

María López Martínez, Universidad de Alicante, Spain
Olimpia López, University of Alicante, Spain

This chapter explores the therapeutic potential of reading ancient Greek stories preserved on papyrus. The die-cut series "Greek Stories on Papyri" comprises five volumes, including "The Adventures of Calligone and the Amazons," "Ninus, the Adventures of the King of Nineveh," "The Papyrus of the Sailor Sinuhe," and "The Martyrdom of Saint Parthenope." These stories, set in diverse historical and mythological contexts, are enhanced with rich illustrations based on literary, historical, iconographic, and archaeological data. By adapting these ancient narratives for modern audiences ranging from children to adults, the authors suggest that such stories can facilitate an interactive, enjoyable, and relaxed exchange of knowledge and emotional expression across generations.

Chapter 2: A Glimpse into Roman Law by Kandinsky

Aránzazu Calzada, Universidad de Alicante, Spain

This chapter examines the unexpected intersection between Roman law and the life of the painter Kandinsky, as chronicled in a biography written by his wife, Nina. Focusing on the period when Kandinsky taught Roman law in Tsarist Russia, the chapter highlights his appreciation for the logical precision and argumentation techniques of Roman jurists. The author investigates the type of Roman law education prevalent in Kandinsky's milieu, particularly the influence of German Pandectistics. This exploration provides insights into the intellectual environment that shaped Kandinsky's views and his subsequent contributions to art and legal theory.

Chapter 3: The Journey to Italy in Paul Klee's Diary: In the Footsteps of Goethe?

Carlos Sánchez-Moreno Ellart, University of Valencia, Spain

This chapter delves into the impact of Johann Wolfgang von Goethe's writings on Paul Klee, particularly focusing on Klee's transformative journey to Italy. By comparing Klee's diaries, edited by his son Felix, with Goethe's vision of Neohumanism, the chapter examines Klee's approach to classical art and his philosophical alignment with Goethe's ideas. Although Klee's theory of light and color is well-documented, this chapter aims to uncover deeper influences of Goethe on Klee's artistic development, especially in their shared study of nature and aesthetics.

Chapter 4: Reinterpreting Walden. A Bibliotherapeutic Perspective through Dialogue with Byung-Chul Han's Philosophy

Alfonso Fernández-Manso, Universidad de León, Spain

In this chapter, the author presents a bibliotherapeutic analysis of Henry David Thoreau's "Walden" through the lens of Byung-Chul Han's philosophy. By juxtaposing Thoreau's call for deliberate living and connection with nature against Han's critique of late capitalism's impact on individual subjectivity, the chapter offers strategies for personal resilience and growth. Readers are encouraged to reflect on their values, cultivate authenticity, and resist societal pressures through introspective exercises inspired by Thoreau. This dialogue between Thoreau and Han provides practical tools for navigating modernity's challenges and achieving a fulfilling and purposeful life.

Chapter 5: Translation, Memory, and the Face of the Other in Juan Mayorga's Theatre: Reading as a Commitment

Robert March Tortajada, Universitat d'Alacant, Spain

Focusing on the theatrical works of Juan Mayorga, this chapter explores the philosophical influences underpinning his dramaturgy. The study examines concepts such as Walter Benjamin's metaphor of the broken vessel in translation, Emmanuel Levinas' notion of the face of the Other, and the interplay of memory, reading, listening, and silence in historical dramas like "El traductor de Blumemberg," "Himmelweg," "La paz perpetua," and "La lengua en pedazos." Mayorga's writing is portrayed as an endless act of rewriting, emphasizing the continuous engagement with past and present texts, and the ethical commitment involved in reading and interpreting his plays.

Chapter 6: Educational, Cultural, and Social Conditioning: The Role of Education and Pedagogy in Human Emancipation

Giorgio Crescenza, Università degli Studi della Tuscia, Italy

This chapter critically analyzes the historical and contemporary educational discourses surrounding gender emancipation and the education of young generations. It highlights the persistent influence of male chauvinism and distorted views of sexuality, shaped by theological and moral principles, on women's education. The author advocates for a transformative approach to education that promotes mutual respect and human emancipation. The chapter discusses current projects aimed at combating gender-based violence and hatred, emphasizing the need for inclusive and community-driven educational strategies to foster cultural transformation towards gender equality and respect for human relations.

Chapter 7: Well-being and Health through Autobiographical Pedagogy: Theoretical Foundations and Perspectives

Fabrizio Manuel Sirignano, Università degli Studi Suor Orsola Benincasa, Italy
Gabriele Borghese, Università degli Studi Suor Orsola Benincasa, Italy

This chapter outlines the theoretical foundations and methods of autobiographical pedagogy, emphasizing its significance in contemporary care settings, particularly for the elderly. The narrative method is highlighted as central to care practices, fostering a sense of community and holistic understanding. The authors argue that autobiographical storytelling and writing, rooted in the humanistic tradition, are essential for countering the fragmentation of knowledge and promoting overall well-being. The chapter underscores the therapeutic and educational value of autobiographical pedagogy in enhancing resilience and personal growth.

Chapter 8: Medical Humanities, Narrative Medicine, and Bibliotherapy: New Pedagogical Frontiers to Build Health and Promote Well-Being

Fabrizio Sirignano, Suor Orsola Benincasa University, Italy
Valerio Ferro Allodola, Mediterranea University of Reggio Calabria, Italy
Antonio Di Grigoli, University of Florence, Italy

This chapter explores the epistemological shift in contemporary medicine towards integrating the human dimension and active patient participation in health and well-being. The authors emphasize the importance of Narrative Based Medicine (NBM) and bibliotherapy as tools for prevention, care, and well-being, contrasting them with the traditional Evidence Based Medicine (EBM). The chapter presents the historical-pedagogical evolution of these innovative approaches and introduces the "Dialogue Literary Gathering" model as an empowerment strategy for mental health promotion, particularly for LGBTQIA+ adolescents experiencing minority stress.

Chapter 9: Narrative Medicine Practices: Emotional Literacy and Inclusion Through Reading

Gianluca Amatori, European University of Rome, Italy
Maria Buccolo, European University of Rome, Italy

This chapter examines the intrinsic connection between emotional education and reading within the framework of narrative medicine practices. The authors discuss the theoretical underpinnings of reading's importance from early childhood and propose a methodological approach to emotional literacy. By highlighting the educability and management of emotions through reading, the chapter aims to promote well-being and enhance interpersonal relationships. The authors advocate for the development of emotional education to foster resilience and inclusivity, offering practical reflections on the transformative potential of reading in personal and communal contexts.

Chapter 10: The Aesthetic Dimension as a 'Lost Paradigm' of Reading: Education for Resilience Through Bibliotherapy

Maria Federica Paolozzi, Università degli Studi Suor Orsola Benincasa, Italy
Stefania Maddalena, University of Chieti-Pescara, Italy

This chapter revisits the centrality of aesthetics in 20th-century philosophical debate, drawing on the works of Croce, Heidegger, and Gadamer. It challenges traditional methodologies that prioritize formalism over intuition and aesthetics, promoting a holistic understanding of art and expression. The authors argue that reading, storytelling, and writing, approached through a narrative framework, are essential tools for enhancing resilience and well-being. The chapter underscores the therapeutic and humanizing benefits of bibliotherapy and Narrative Based Medicine, highlighting the need for professional guidance to achieve effective therapeutic outcomes.

Chapter 11: Means and Tools of Bibliotherapy: The Help of Technology

Christos Lalos, University of Alicante, Greece

This chapter explores the dynamic intersection of bibliotherapy and technology, highlighting the ways in which technological advancements have enhanced the accessibility and efficacy of bibliotherapy. The author discusses digital platforms for literature access, online bibliotherapy sessions, personalized reading recommendations, and interactive applications that combine cognitive-behavioral techniques with literary exposure. The chapter emphasizes the potential of technology to transform traditional bibliotherapy practices, offering multifaceted therapeutic tools for emotional and psychological healing.

Chapter 12: Creative Writing: Creating Micro-Stories to Combat Ageism

Carles Cortés Orts, Universitat d'Alacant, Spain

This chapter addresses the therapeutic effects of creative writing for individuals over 50, focusing on the creation of micro-stories. Drawing from workshops conducted at the University of Alicante, the author highlights the benefits of micro-story writing in developing writing skills, enhancing creativity, and improving concentration. The chapter explores techniques to combat ageism through diverse voices and experiences, challenging stereotypes, and promoting empathy and understanding. By engaging older adults in creative writing, the chapter advocates for a more inclusive and empowering approach to aging.

Chapter 13: An Oncology Patient's Reading: Between Evasion and Knowledge

Flavia Amar, Universidad de Cádiz, Spain
Víctor Amar, Universidad de Cádiz, Spain

This chapter presents a narrative study of an oncology patient's relationship with reading as a means of seeking evasion and knowledge. The authors explore the patient's journey of reading for personal satisfaction and the desire to share information with other patients. The chapter highlights the transformative power of reading in providing knowledge, emotional support, and a sense of community among oncology patients. The narrative approach reveals how the patient's engagement with literature evolves through different stages of the illness, emphasizing the therapeutic value of committed reading.

Chapter 14: The Therapeutic Value of Reading Graphic Medicine: Visual Narratives of Eating Disorders in Comics

María José Mompeán Mejías, University of Alicante, Spain

This chapter examines the therapeutic potential of graphic medicine, particularly the use of comics to address eating disorders. The author discusses the historical evolution of comics from being considered childish to gaining social prestige and their role in medical discourse. By analyzing visual narratives of eating disorders in comics, the chapter highlights the empowering and inclusive nature of graphic medicine. The author argues that comics provide a unique medium for therapeutic storytelling, offering safe spaces to discuss stigmatized issues and contributing to the field of bibliotherapy.

Chapter 15: Poetry as a Vehicle to Support Social and Emotional Learning

Mary Napoli, Penn State University, Harrisburg, United States
Deanna Day, Washington State University, United States

This chapter explores the use of children's poetry in promoting social and emotional learning (SEL). The authors describe their experiences incorporating poetry into undergraduate children's literature courses, focusing on the tenets of the Collaborative for Academic, Social, and Emotional Learning (CASEL) framework. The chapter provides practical suggestions for using poetry to navigate complex emotions, develop empathy, and foster understanding across all age groups. By highlighting the versatility of poetry, the authors advocate for its use as a tool for SEL in diverse professional contexts.

As editors of *Improving Mental Health and Wellbeing Through Bibliotherapy*, we are profoundly grateful for the diverse contributions and insights presented in this volume. The journey through these chapters has revealed the multifaceted and transformative power of literature, highlighting its capacity to soothe, heal, and connect individuals across various contexts and life stages.

The collective work encapsulated here underscores the timeless relevance of reading as a therapeutic practice, harkening back to Classical Antiquity while addressing contemporary challenges exacerbated by the COVID-19 pandemic. The interdisciplinary approach of our contributors—spanning literary studies, psychology, education, and beyond—reflects the broad scope and profound impact of bibliotherapy.

Each chapter provides a unique perspective on how literature can serve as a balm for the soul, offering practical tools and theoretical foundations for enhancing mental health and well-being. From ancient Greek stories on papyrus to the therapeutic use of poetry and graphic medicine, the chapters explore the myriad ways in which reading can foster emotional resilience, intellectual growth, and social connection.

In the context of unprecedented global stress and isolation, the importance of literature as a source of solace and connection cannot be overstated. The chapters within this volume collectively advocate for the recognition and integration of bibliotherapy in various professional practices, aiming to inspire further research and implementation in the field.

We extend our deepest appreciation to the scholars, practitioners, and educators who have contributed their expertise and passion to this work. It is our hope that this volume will serve as a valuable resource for all those seeking to harness the healing power of literature, ultimately contributing to the enhancement of mental health and well-being across diverse populations.

As we conclude this preface, we invite you, our readers, to explore the rich and varied content of this book with an open heart and mind. May it inspire you to further appreciate the profound connection between reading and healing, and to consider how the stories we read and share can enrich our lives and the lives of those around us.

With gratitude and anticipation,

Antonio Cortijo Ocaña
University of California, Santa Barbara, United States

Vicent Martines
University of Alicante, Spain

Veronica Orazi
University of Torino, Italy

Acknowledgement

This research has been carried out within the Institut Superior d'Investigació Cooperativa IVITRA [ISIC-IVITRA] (Programa per a la Constitució i Acreditació d'Instituts Superiors d'Investigació Cooperativa d'Excel•lència de la Generalitat Valenciana, Ref. ISIC/012/042), and within the frame of the following projects, research groups and networksy: Ministerio de Ciencia y Universidades del Gobierno de España (MICINUN), Ref. PID2021-128381NB-I00; *Red Internacional de Investigación COVID19-Literary Training via ICT for Higher Education Improvement, Behavioral Coaching and Discomfort Management during the CORONA-VIRUS Pandemics [COVID19 LiTraPan].* Co-directors: V. Orazi, V. Martines & A. Cortijo. Università degli Studi di Torino / Universidad de Alicante / University of California at Santa Barbara. 2020-present; Institut d'Estudis Catalans-IEC, ref. PRO2018-S04-MARTINES; Grup d'Investigació VIGROB-125 at the Universidad de Alicante; Grup d'Investigació en Tecnologia Educativa en Història de la Cultura, Diacronia lingüística i Traducció (Universitat d'Alacant, ref. GITE-09009-UA]); Seu Universitària de la Nucia; and Grup d'Investigació en Tecnologia Educativa en Història de la Cultura, Diacronia lingüística i Traducció (Universitat d'Alacant, ref. GITE-09009-UA).

Chapter 1
"Open It That You May Know Wonders": Keys to Improve Mental Health and Wellbeing Through Fiction in Papyrus

María Paz López Martínez
https://orcid.org/0000-0002-8564-7780
University of Alicante, Spain

Olimpia Navarro López
University of Alicante, Spain

ABSTRACT

The reading of the series of die-cut stories Greek Stories on Papyri can help us to open us to express emotions and to better understand human nature. The collection comprises five volumes: The Adventures of Calligone and the Amazons; Ninus; The Adventures of the King of Nineveh; The Papyrus of the Sailor Sinuhe; and The Martyrdom of Saint Parthenope. Ninus is an Assyrian prince and the action begins in Mesopotamia. Calligone is the daughter of the king of Boristhenes and her ship is wrecked in the country of the Amazons. Sesoncosis is a Pharaoh who that travels to the Iberian Peninsula. Finally, Parthenope is the protagonist of a martyrdom. Both the texts and the illustrations on each page are based on data of a literary, historical, iconographic, and archaeological nature. By means of the corresponding adaptations, this documentation is made available to an audience from children to adults. It could be a tool for interactive, enjoyable and relaxed exchange of knowledge and experience between readers of different generations within the same family.

DOI: 10.4018/979-8-3693-4244-2.ch001

INTRODUCTION

Love, war and travel are fundamental ingredients in adventure novels, the last literary genre to be born in Greece. The manuscript tradition managed to bring down to our days five complete texts that fit the scheme of what we could consider novels: *Callirroe* by Charito, *Ephesian Tale* by Xenophon of Ephesus, *Daphnis and Chloe* by Longo, *Leucipa and Clitophon* by Achilles Thacius and *Aethiopica* by Heliodorus.

Other works of prose fiction can also be considered novels: is the case of some of Lucian's short works; the picaresque biographies of the young Lucius, metamorphosed into an ass; the live of the fabulist Aesop or of some philosophers. As well as the *Alexander Romance*, which is also a novel biography but of a more serious nature.

We also have the summaries of the plots of two other novels written in Byzantine times by the patriarch Photius: *Babylonian History* by Jamblichus and *The Wonders Beyond Thule* by Antonius Diogenes.

Finally, three Latin novels: *Satiricon* by Petronius, *The Golden Ass* by Apuleius and the anonymous *History of Apollonius King of Tyre*.

A synthetic definition is that they consist of prose accounts of the adventures and dangers faced separately by the members of a heterosexual couple until the happy ending, which consists of the lovers' reunion. Despite the beauty, youth and aristocratic background of both protagonists, the girl is usually a more interesting and mature character than her partner.

Who are the characters in the novels? Beautiful, heterosexual young men are usually the main characters. Usually, both partners come from a good family. There can be two types of parents: natural and adoptive. Foundlings, at the end of the play, are recognised by the natural parents. This gives rise to a scene of anagnorisis with Homeric and tragic echoes. There are homosexual characters and the novel, in this sense, is a school of tolerance towards sexual diversity. There are aristocrats, tyrants and rulers of Eastern peoples, such as Assyrian kings, satraps and pharaohs. There are also intellectuals, poets, philosophers, magicians and priests. There are exotic characters, such as eunuchs, ghosts and many characters from the underworld: rogues, villains, pirates, brothel treasurers, pimps, among others. The women are especially interesting and brave: brides, wives, widows, mothers, wet nurses. They undertake the search for their partners and travel alone, take the initiative in love affairs and some even harass the protagonist. There are also women with intellectual concerns who travel, not in search of a husband but in search of knowledge, educated women who defy the pedantry of their companions. There are powerful, "empowered" women, we would now say: queens who organise and lead armies or build public works and exercise matronage. There are also witches, freedwomen, wealthy prostitutes who pay for the sexual first fruits of young boys?

What events take place in the action of these novels? Travel is fundamental: overland expeditions and the raids of bandits. There are also sea voyages, of course, interrupted by storms, after which there is the corresponding shipwreck.

Eros plays a central role: we find tender loves, which arise in childhood between cousins, or crushes and love at first sight, vows of fidelity and weddings, but also paraphilias, such as zoophilia or necrophilia. Alongside the god Eros, Tyche, of course, Fate, turned into a capricious divinity that shakes up the lives of the protagonists and gives rise to changes of fortune. Besides Eros and Tyche, of course, the divinities of the classical Olympian pantheon, especially Aphrodite or Artemis. There are also many foreign and exotic divinities, the result of the spread of Greek culture to the East: Egyptian, Syrian and Phoenician gods: Serapis, Isis and Astarte.

Magic plays a fundamental role and brings with it scenes of sacrifice, apparent death, anthropophagy rituals... Other scenes include courts and wars. Scenes of abduction, letters, poisons and potions are also very frequent.

Alongside the novels we have just listed, there were others that were lost as early as Antiquity or the Byzantine period. They remained hidden under the desert sands in Egypt. They were preserved in precise conditions of humidity and temperature until the archaeological campaigns of the 19th century. Thanks to the excavations, we have been able to recover papyrus fragments containing some fifty other texts, which are now in libraries all over the world and in the hands of private collectors. From the number of papyri novels we have we can deduce that the genre was very successful throughout the Roman Empire.

María Paz López Martínez is a pioneer in the study of these papyri and has been researching them for decades.As a result, the *Ficción en papiro* (Fiction in papyri) team, of which she is a part, can develop the project on the basis of good editions, translations and commentaries of the texts.

The collection *Greek Tales on Papyrus* comprises a collection of written tales inspired by lost Greek novels known from papyrus fragments. Five volumes have already been published: *The Adventures of Calligone and the Amazons* (2021a), *Ninus, the Adventures of the King of Nineveh* (2021b), *The Papyrus of the Sailor Sinuhe* (2022a), and *The Martyrdom of Saint Parthenope* (2023), written by the expert on Greek novels, María Paz López Martínez. There is a fifth volume, *Partenope* (López Juan, López Martínez and Navarro López 2022c), in the same format and aimed at adult readers, although it is suitable for all types of readers.

The volumes are available in paper version and online version free through the platform *Ficción en papiro* (www.ficcionenpapiro.es). We have described the characteristics of the collection in several previous publications (López Martínez 2023b and 2023c; López Juan, López Martínez and Navarro López 2022a and 2022b; Navarro López 2023a and 2024b).

Both the texts and the illustrations on each page of the tale are based on data of a literary, historical, iconographic and archaeological nature. By means of the corresponding adaptations, this documentation is made available to an audience that, while trying to be as broad as possible, ranges from children to adults with cultural concerns, so that the final product manages to be attractive and comprehensible to all. We refer you to the corresponding section of the website where you will find all the philological, literary, iconographic, archaeological and historical documentation on which the texts and images are based, as well as our comments on each page of the corresponding story: *Transferencia-Cuentos-Nino/Calígone/El papiro del marino Sinuhé/Parténope* (López Martínez 2023d).

The aim of this contribution is to explain the mechanisms by which the philological, literary, archaeological, historical and the knowledge of the classical tradition has been implemented in order to make this fascinating fictional world more widely known in an attractive way and to demonstrate that the reading of these ancient stories can help us to open us to express emotions, unblock feelings, be more condescending with our faults, forgive our own and others' mistakes and, in short, to better understand human nature.

OBJECTIVES

The aim of this contribution is to explain the mechanisms by which the philological, literary, archaeological, historical and the knowledge of the classical tradition has been implemented in order to make this fascinating fictional world more widely known in an attractive way and to demonstrate that the reading of these ancient stories can help us to open us to express emotions, unblock feelings, be more condescending with our faults, forgive our own and others' mistakes and, in short, to better understand human nature. We are also particularly interested in highlighting its usefulness as a tool for interactive, enjoyable and relaxed exchange of knowledge and experience between readers of different generations within the same family.

METHODOLOGICAL APPROACH

The starting point is the texts of the five stories that have so far been published in the collection, based on an in-depth study that allows us to get to know the old material.

The activity will take place in the quiet and familiar setting of the family home. The aim is that the activity can be enriching but also restful and rewarding for both readers. As an example, we will refer here to some of the pages of each die-cut.

Through QR codes and with the help of a mobile phone or tablet, the reader can access the text translated into various modern languages but also the documentation used by the author, María Paz López Martínez. We we also going to pay special attention to a case of shared reading in which a child and an adult can read together.

Ninus, the Adventures of the King of Nineveh

The two papyri of this lost novel date from the 1st century BC and the 1st century AD (*P.Berol.* 6926 + *P.Gen.* 85 and *PSI* 1305, respectively) and are in rhetorical and learned Greek, full of references to the earlier literary tradition. The characters are familiar figures in Greek sources, notably Diodorus of Sicily, more or less a contemporary of the novelist.

Ninus is an Assyrian prince, but he is a fully Hellenised character, according to the ideal of the Greek paideia. The action begins in Mesopotamia, during the Assyrian empire, and narrates his adventures and vicissitudes of love and war. The adventures of Rodan and Sinonis, the main characters of the Babylonian (written between 164 and 180 AD, more than a century after Nino) also take place in Mesopotamia.

The Greek novel could be based on a very ancient millenary tradition, around the legend of King Tukultī-Ninurta I (1243-1207), whose epic was written during the monarch's lifetime, which takes place in the middle of the Bronze Age and is therefore more or less contemporary with the Trojan War. From an oral and written tradition, a native legend based on several historical Assyrian kings was born.

We do not know if the work records the birth of the character; the testimonies we have show him as an adolescent. The *Cyropedia* is the fundamental model. Ninus is brought up in the palace of Nineveh, in the family and with his aunt and cousin. He receives a careful education, as befits a crown prince, while he matures physically and psychologically, until, one fine day, new feelings awaken in him, he discovers that he is in love with his cousin and that she loves him back. In principle, Nino's cousin could be none other than the Assyrian queen Semiramis, but the novelist is not interested in giving us this information. In the fragments the beloved is an anonymous character, "the girl", "the maiden" and "the girl". In contrast, in Diodorus' *Assyrian history*, Semiramis is the main figure in Book II, the real founder of Assyria and a kind of Amazon.

Meetings and exchanges of oaths of eternal love follow one after the other, until disturbing news from the front reaches the palace. Nino must accompany or replace his father on this campaign. Like Telemachus, the time has come for him to assume his role as heir to the throne. Nino sets out on a land expedition against Armenia at the head of a powerful army. Because of the ice, it is difficult for them to cross the mountain passes and rivers, until they reach a plain where Ninus orders them to set up camp. The Assyrian allows ten days for both soldiers and animals to rest and then sets out on the attack, but not before delivering a prayer to the gods or a fiery harangue to boost the morale of his troops. Back at the palace, now victorious, a court scene ensues. Impatient to be married, he delivers a speech to his aunt Dercia that has been exhaustively studied for its quality and literary interest. The young woman also tries to verbalise her feelings to Tambe, but modesty prevents her from speaking. The difference between the girl's mental and physical blockage in expressing her feelings and the young man's naturalness, ease and freedom of speech inevitably lends itself to a gendered reading. Finally, the sisters meet and probably give their consent to the wedding.

The scene in the second papyrus tells of a voyage across the Euxine Pontus, perhaps motivated by the desire to extend the Assyrian kingdom after the conquest of Armenia. Archaeological evidence shows the existence of trade routes from Urartu to the Colchis for the exchange of luxury goods. Despite the captain's great experience, the ship was stranded on sandbanks and shipwrecked on the banks of the Hipo River, now Kodori, in Georgia (or Abkhazia). They have reached a beach near a lush forest that combines the usual ingredients of locus amoenus: shade and a freshwater spring. This is the mythical Colchis, a recurring destination in Greek literature. A despondent crew abandons the ship trying to save all their belongings. Nino feels even more desperate than his own sailors and curses his fate. The changes of fortune are typical of the novel's vicissitudes. The account of the shipwreck is presented in the third person, along the lines of the messenger rheseis so frequent in tragedy. The narrator could be a member of the ship's crew or Nino himself, as a homodiegetic narrator, for which we have precedents in *Odyssey* IX-XII.

At the end of the parley, the text of the papyrus and the testimonies of the text of the novel come to an end and we have to speculate: either both lovers have followed parallel paths, while the narrator keeps the focus on both itineraries until the happy reunion, or the bride stays in the palace without intervening until the end of the work, as in the Life of Apollonius.

The landing on the Colchis invites us to think of characters such as the Amazons, recurring figures in Greek literary tradition, who have left their mark on other literatures, such as Egyptian literature. They are associated with both military conflicts and erotic encounters, such as those between Alexander and Candace, Thalestris, or Tomiris, or even, in demotic literature, Prince Pedikhons and Queen Serpot.

Both the *Life of Alexander* and Nino and Parthenope, to which I will refer shortly, were read and spread to other provinces of the empire, including Syria. This is evidenced by the mosaics of the 2nd and 3rd centuries AD, which depict scenes that could be related to the plots of these novels.

The Adventures of Calligone and the Amazons

Calligone, Καλλλιγόνη, 'born beautiful', is set on the Black Sea. The character may have been inspired by real Ukrainian women, in whose tombs arrows, bows and other objects related to horse training (4th-3rd century BC) have been found, or by Hypsicratea herself, the last wife of Mithridates VI.

What has come down to us of the original text has been preserved in two papyrus fragments now in the Sackler Library and the Archaeological Museum of Alexandria, dating from the 2nd-3rd century AD, so that the writing of the work must have been earlier, probably before the beginning of the Imperial period.

The protagonist is the daughter of the king of Boristhenes, the historic Milesian colony located in Pontus at the mouth of the Dnieper River, near the site now referred to by local archaeologists as Olbia. Eubiotus was to be the king and father of Calligone. Beset by problems, the nature of which we do not know, perhaps a Scythian attack or a conspiracy by members of his own court, he takes his sons away from Boristhenes, embarking them on several ships. Caligone is shipwrecked in the country of the Amazons, whose queen, Themisto, receives her at her court and is impressed by the beauty and stature of the shipwrecked woman. Calligone has arrived in peace, perhaps sent by her father to ask for help. She gains the trust of these warriors who are at war with the Scythians. She helps them to organise and expand their army, incorporating soldiers from other peoples, Maeots and perhaps Sarmatians and Alans, on condition that they are all ruled by women. Later, Eubiotus also arrives on the battlefield. Calligone, enraged and cursing the goddess Artemis and a certain Erasinus, with whom she is probably in love, enters his tent and takes a weapon. Eubiotus has entered the tent with her and, when he manages to make sure that the princess is unarmed and they are left alone, he probably consoles her and helps her to calm down.

The Papyrus of the Sailor Sinuhe

It is one of the best documented lost novels, as five papyri have been recovered from the original Greek text (*P.Oxy*. 2466, *P.Oxy*. 3319, *P.Oxy*. 1826, *P.Oxy*. 5262 and *P.Oxy*. 5263). All come from the city of Oxyrhynchus and date from the 2nd to 4th centuries AD. The protagonist is inspired by a historical figure, the Pharaoh Sesonchosis of the 12th Dynasty, a period during which important literary texts were composed, such as the *History of Sinuhé* or the *Instructions of Amenemhat*, fragments of which have come down to us from the Pharaonic and Demotic periods, involving characters related to those in the novel.

Sesostris presumably acquired military training from his father, who also gave him useful advice and warnings about possible treachery and intrigue that he could expect from the people of the court, as occurs in The *Teachings of King Amenemhat.* Also, Diodorus Siculus, I BC, relates that Amenhemhat I himself educated Sesonchosis in fasting, military training, hard physical exercises, hunting, etc.

While Sesonchosis was still a child, the Arabs attacked Egypt under the command of a certain Webelis. Reinforcements arrived on the battlefield from all over the kingdom, both from Upper and Lower Egypt. His friend Temo tells Sesoncosis that many enemies are falling and that the Arabs have fled in fear. The protagonist decides that one day he will conquer Arabia. We do not know that the Arabs in general or a certain Webelis in particular invaded Egypt. Perhaps the author invented this Arab attack as a provocation in order to justify the Egyptian attack. After his disastrous campaign, he tries to seal an alliance with the enemy by giving his own daughter Meameris in marriage. The pharaoh sends his son to Arabia and then to Libya, accompanied by his adviser and faithful friend Pamunis. Both Diodorus of Sicily (I.53.5-6) and demotic fragments from the library of the temple of Tebtunis speak of this mission of Sesoncosis, during which the historical Amenemhet I dies, so that Senwosret must have ruled alone from then on. Sesoncosis would return to Arabia, now allied territory, incognito, like Ulysses to Ithaca.

From the mention of the Red Sea, we could situate the action of the shortest papyrus of all in this enclave, which would be followed by the text of the following fragment, in which the author introduces an erotic episode that takes place in Arabia, near the tent of Webelis, where the Arab leader is holding a banquet or feast attended by his daughter Meameris. The protagonist hides near a fountain in the company of his faithful friend Pamunis. Meameris goes for a walk. He stops by the water fountain, right next to where Sesoncosis is standing. At that moment, their gazes meet and Meameris is captivated by the beauty of the protagonist. Quite disturbed, she returns to the tent. Later, the handsome young man would make himself known to Webelis, marry his fiancée Meameris and return victorious to Egypt where, after his campaigns in Arabia and Libya, he would be proclaimed Pharaoh.

It is at this point that we place the action of the following papyrus. Sesoncosis embarks on a sea voyage, after returning to Egypt, victorious after the campaigns in Arabia and Libya and after being proclaimed pharaoh. Departing from the port of Alexandria, the ship would take a route that would have two destinations by sea, firstly westwards to Italy and Hispania, and secondly northwards through Dacia and Germania. But just as the ship was about to dock in Italy, something unexpected happened. It becomes night in the middle of the day, perhaps because of a storm at sea, an eruption of Vesuvius, a total eclipse, or some other unknown phenomenon. After this, they continue their journey to the "untrodden" places, where they enter until they see rocks that emit fire and plunge into the sea and even the descent to earth of the mythical Phoenix bird. Everything suggests that, from this point onwards, the story moves into the realm of science fiction, connecting Sesonchosis' journey with Alexander's itinerary in the biography of Pseudo-Callisthenes or with the journeys of the protagonists of another lost novel, Incredible *Wonders Beyond Tule*, but, unfortunately, at this point the papyrus is interrupted.

The Martyrdom of Saint Parthenope

Another historical novel is the daughter of the tyrant Polycrates of Samos, the famous tyrant of the 6th century BC, of whom we have three papyri from between the first half of the 2nd and the 3rd century AD (*P.Berol.* 9588 + *P.Berol.* 7927 + *P.Berol.* 21179, *P.Oxy.* 435, *P.Mich.* inv. 3402v). We also have an ostracon, related to the plot of the novel and dated to the 1st century AD (*O. Bodl.*2175), which shows that the novel was already known at that time.

In the novel the daughter of the tyrant of Samos is called Παρθενόπη "who has the face or look of a maiden", although Herodotus does not give the name of this character: "Her father threatened her that, if she returned without mishap, she would remain unmarried for a long time, but she implored the gods that the threat should be carried out, for, rather than be deprived of her father, she preferred to remain unmarried for a longer time" (III.124).

From various Greek sources and from a Persian epic poem of which only 380 verses survive, we know that the heroine was highly educated and that she played sports or conducted war like a man. The poem is entitled *Vāmiq u dhrā* (The Virgin and the Lover), was written in the 11th century by 'Un ʋrī and seems to follow quite closely the plot of this novel.

In the novel, Parthenope is interested in Methiocus, also mentioned by Herodotus and son of Miltiades, who was an eponymous archon of Athens, governor of the Thracian Chersonese and hero of Marathon in 490 BC, so Methiocus' relationship with Parthenope is anachronistic, as it is with other characters in the novel, such as the philosopher Anaximenes and the poet Ibicus.

The novel tells us that Metiochus comes to Samos, to the court of Polycrates, fleeing from the intrigues of his stepmother Hegesípila, who wants to benefit her sons in dynastic rights. The longest surviving papyrus is of a banquet in Polycrates' palace, which he offers to his guest and blood relative, Methiochus, like the one offered to Odysseus by the Phaeacians in *Od.* 8-12. Polycrates interrogates Metycoccus, who informs him of the reasons for his arrival on Samos. This is followed by a philosophical-rhetorical debate on the nature of love, in the manner of Plato's banquet. After Methiocus' lengthy intervention, Parthenope takes an active part in the banquet, indignantly rejecting the young man's words, quite the opposite of Ninus's cousin. Parthenope will help to construct a narrative pattern that we will see in later novels. The papyrus is then interrupted, but everything suggests that this discussion does not prevent the young people from falling in love.

In the Persian version, what follows is a nocturnal wandering of the lovers through the palace and a subsequent enemy invasion of Samos, which leads to the flight or capture of Methiochus, so that Parthenope must set out in search of him across the Mediterranean. Itinerant journeys by the two men, stories of suitors and unwanted marriages will follow. The second papyrus is very short and in very poor condition. It may refer to one of Parthenope's journeys through the islands, in this case Corsica, an island that plays an important role in Thucydides' *Histories*, the ancient home of the Phaeacians. The scene that can be reconstructed is probably set in a theatre where the assembly of the Corsicans is gathered, who, in high spirits, pay Demoxenos for the talent (with article, according to the text) and appoint him guardian of Parthenope. The text also mentions a certain Euphranias, who is to organise the wedding ceremony. We do not know whether Parthenope marries a local suitor, for example, a nobleman from Corcira, as Callirhoe marries Dionysus, after having been bought in exchange for a talent, or as Antia is to marry Perilaus in Xenophon's novel. Echoes of our novel probably reach as far as Heliodorus' Cariclea. Another character named Alexander must take care of the rest of the affairs, because of his friendship and loyalty, according to the terms used by the papyrus, as happens in Chariton, when Chereas commissions an Egyptian philosopher named Demetrius to accompany the Persian queen to her country, who, as the text itself says, "surpassed the other Egyptians in education and virtue" (8.3.10).

After the episode of the Corcyrians, and we do not know if there were any other incidents, Parthenope resumed her search for her partner and, from Greek and Persian sources, we know that she wandered as far as Persia. In the novels we know, we have the examples of Psyche from Apuleius' *Metamorphoses*, who acts as a seeker of her husband, as well as Cariclea. Metyoco, for his part, could also marry another in Persia, as does Callirroe in Chariton. Furthermore, Herodotus links the story of Methiochus to that of Darius, who protected the young man and gave him Persian estates and a Persian wife.

In the end, the lovers are most likely reunited and Parthenope returns to Samos to regain her father's power or "throne", aided by Methiocus, as we see in some other similar Persian poems and in love novels, such as the Aethiopics, which would count Parthenope among their narrative models.

There was also a Christian reading of the novel and we have the martyrdom of St. Parthenope, set in the 4th century, a saint who never existed. IV, a saint who never existed, of which an unabridged version is preserved in Arabic and a Coptic manuscript from the 9th century, which undoubtedly traces back to a Greek original. In this story, human love has become divine love and the young woman would lose her life to defend her virtue.

As in the case of Alexander and Ninus, we also have two mosaics from Syria and quotations from Lucian, from whom we know of the great success of *Parthenope* in the 2nd-century pantomime.

PARTICIPANTS

As an example, we will refer here to some of the pages of each die-cut. Through QR codes and with the help of a mobile phone or tablet, the reader can access the text translated into various modern languages but also the documentation used by the author, María Paz López Martínez. We we also going to pay special attention to a case of shared reading in which a child and an adult can read together.

DESCRIPTION OF THE EXPERIENCE

Briefly, we will give some examples that can serve as a reading guide. This is one hypothetical approach to the subject among many possible ones. Among these explanations, there are also those referring to the proper names of the characters in the stories. If you wish to go deeper into this subject, you can consult López Martínez (2019b), where a scientific bibliography on this issue is also indicated. Among the motifs to be commented on could be the following:

Ninus, the Adventures of the King of Nineveh

We will focus on page four, the text of which is based on what is preserved in one of the original papyri that have transmitted the text of the novel to us. The beginning is in a very poor state of preservation; we can read only the second half of the writing column, but the rest is quite legible:

Between games and quarrels, both children are growing up and have now reached adolescence. They spend a lot of time together and lately they have started to see each other somewhat differently. One day Ninus whispers into his cousin's ear: "If you promise not to laugh I'll tell you a secret. I love you!" The girl replies that she has feelings for him also. From then on they spend more time in each other's company, exchanging poems and kisses. One afternoon finds them lying on the divan. They exchange caresses until they end up arguing as the girl is annoyed by her cousin's impulsiveness. The young prince goes over to the rose bush and cuts a flower and offers it to her and asks her to forgive him and declares his love for her. Finally they are reconciled. The maiden places herself in the care of the goddess Isthar and they spend the night together. (Translation into English by Carlos Sánchez Moreno)

The illustration accompanying the text of this page is available on the website at https://ficcionenpapiro.es/index.php/es/papiros/cuentos/nino,-rey-de-ninime/página-4

The scene reflects one of these dates of the very young protagonists and we have set it in one of the quintessential spaces of Persian culture: the garden. The testimonies that we have present the protagonist as an adolescent, who is beginning to mature physically and psychologically, until one day he discovers that he is in love and that his beloved loves him back. Nino, at first, behaves like an impetuous lover, but the girl does not like to be rushed. Patience, respect, delicacy, like the protagonists of the novel, the readers will learn to contain their instincts and that haste is not a good advisor in matters of love.

The website presents the image of the reference papyrus and information on other details of the image: Persian gardens, as well as the mythical hanging gardens of Babylon. Also some classical Persian poetry and information on the goddess Isthar.

Focusing now on page nine. Some themes stand out: the Black Sea where the river Phasis is found and the Colchis, the destination of the mythical Argonauts. The episode of the shipwreck in Pontus Euxinus also corresponds to the text of the papyrus:

Now that he had conquered Urartu and is now King, Ninus considered that the time had come to establish trading relations with other kingdoms. The Assyrians have tin and the splendid fabrics woven by their women. In return, pottery, wine, purple and other exotic goods will be traded in exchange.

One day, the King, together with a crew of experienced sailors, set sail from a Black Sea port with a cargo of valuable goods.

A few days later they are caught in the middle of a tremendous storm. The ship is adrift, despite the experience of the captain. After a while the sun appears and the lookout is heard calling, "Land ho!"

They manage to come ashore as shipwrecked sailors on the mythical Colchis. It is a beautiful spot, close to a shady forest where they find a freshwater spring. Despite the beauty of the place, fear and foreboding spread among the sailors. (Translation into English by Carlos Sánchez-Moreno).

During the naval expedition, Ninus does not seem to be accompanied by his fiancée, perhaps they are married, but it is not certain. The Assyrian prince and his crew have reached the shore of the river Hippus, the mythical Colchis. The beach is near a lush forest, a *locus amoenus*: with shade and a freshwater spring. Needless to say, the fundamental intertext or reference of this episode is, on the one hand, the shipwreck of Odysseus on the island of the Phaeacians and, on the other, Jason's voyage to the Colchis.

The sailors abandon ship in an attempt to save their belongings. Ninus, in keeping with the character's impetuous character, is even more desperate than his own sailors.

Fear and helplessness are emotions inherent to the human condition. Even the rich, the powerful, the successful can fall from grace, any of us, by a stroke of fate, by a reversal of fortune (what the Greeks called μεταβολή τ ς τύχης), can fall from grace. These ancient and dismembered texts speak to us of our vulnerability.

The Adventures of Calligone and the Amazons

Given that the novel revolves around the myth of the Amazons, it seems important to us, first of all, to make a few considerations on the novel as a whole. It is important to situate the Black Sea on a map. Comment on its archaeological richness, review the location of the ancient cities mentioned in the text, as well as that of some present-day cities.

Moreover, at such a delicate time as we have been experiencing worldwide in recent years, Calligone helps us to reflect on the linguistic and archaeological heritage of the Black Sea. Knowing that among younger readers, unfortunately, many of them will have come into contact with the geographical enclave in which the novel is set after the conflict of the Ukrainian war, it would be interesting to highlight the value of the region in terms of cultural heritage, apart from the conflict.

The story of Calligone invite us to look for present a nearby example of the presence of Amazons in ancient iconography. For example, the impressive piece from the Municipal Archaeological Museum of Ecija (Seville), the ancient Astigi, known as the Amazon of Ecija. Depending on the circumstances, a visit to the museum itself could be planned.

We can also compare this piece with other ancient representations of these women. It also allows us to take a look at the presence of Amazons in 21st century art and, especially, the superheroine Wonder Woman.

Calligone also offers us a great opportunity to comment on the coincidence of the name of this village of women with the name of the Amazon River, also place it on the map and try to find out the origin of this coincidence. It would also be a good way of connecting the survival of Greco-Latin culture, demonstrating that our link with the classical tradition is not limited to Europe, but that the umbilical cord connects us with America.

Finally, it can be observed that the leadership of the female characters presented in the tale, Caligone or Themisto, as women with social prestige, prepared and capable of making strategic decisions in their communities, could be inspired by some kind of real woman who existed in the cities of the Black Sea coast. In the Kurgans of Pokrovka, south of the Urals, in Kazakhstan, tombs of Saurgan women from the 6th to 4th centuries BC and Sarmatians (4th to 3rd centuries BC) have been found with arrows, gorythos (gorythos) and gorythos (gorythos).) with arrows, gorytos, swords, daggers and pierced fang amulets among their grave goods and, around the same time, graves of women with bows, arrows and objects related to horsemanship have also been found in Ukraine. These remains could be the basis of the legend of the Black Sea Amazons.

Focusing on the contents of page four, we provide below the text of the story which includes the famous *Hymn to Artemis*:

"Calligone has grown into a lanky, strong and cheerful young woman. Together with other girls her age, she often goes to the temple to sing hymns and make offerings to the hunter-goddess Artemis, mistress of the forests and animals:

«*We come to sing to Artemis, she of golden arrows,*
the venerable and noisy maiden, the huntress of deer,
The sister of Apollo, who traverses the shadowy mountains
and climbs the windswept peaks.
She amuses herself by drawing her bow and throwing painful darts.
The top of the high mountain shudders and the thick forest groans
at the cry of the animals, but she is unmoved.
She goes to the abode of Apollo, her beloved brother,
to the fertile land of Delphi, to prepare
a beautiful chorus of Muses and Graces.
Once there, leaving the bow and arrows hanging,
she dresses and begins to conduct the chorus and to sing to her mother,
to Leto, the one with the beautiful ankles». (Translation into English by Olimpia Navarro).

The illustration accompanying the text of this page is available on the website at [https://ficcionenpapiro.es/index.php/es/papiros/cuentos/cal%C3%ADgone] and [https://ficcionenpapiro.es/index.php/es/papiros/cuentos/cal%C3%ADgone/pagina-4-caligone].

Here are some aspects of the page that can be commented on:

1) The goddess Artemis, as protector of the Amazons, according to the myth, and her main attributes.
2) The statue of the goddess Artemis of Gabios, attributed to Praxiteles, which presides over the scene and is currently kept in the Louvre Museum.
3) The vignette in the story presents a procession of girls, carrying offerings to the goddess: explain the role of the goddess in accompanying them in their transition to adolescence. Compare the girls in the vignette with the statues of girls in the Archaeological Museum of Brauron in Greece, which will soon be available on the corresponding page of the story's own website. The cult of the goddess Artemis Brauronia in Attica was linked to a female initiation rite called arkteía (ρκτεία). This was a festival in which young women dressed up as bears and mimicked the animal (ρκτεύω). It is also worth mentioning that, at present, in the Archaeological Museum of modern Braurona, a small and very old wooden

image of this goddess is exhibited, which is dated to about 500 BC, and which was found in the area to which Euripides could have referred.

4) Locate on the map the archaeological site of Brauron and explain the connection of the place with the myth of Iphigenia and with the tragedy of Euripides, entitled *Iphigenia in Thauride*. Recall that Agamemnon's daughter Iphigenia, about to be sacrificed by her own father, is miraculously saved by the goddess Artemis who takes her to Thauride in Pontus (present-day Crimea), where she will serve as a priestess of her cult. On the other hand, her brother Orestes, pursued by the Erinias, must travel to the Taurid to bring the image of this goddess to Attica. He is reunited with his brother Orestes, helps him to steal the statue of the goddess and, with the help of Artemis, they manage to flee and reach Brauron in Attica, where they deposit the xomanon, the wooden statue, and build the temple according to the instructions of the goddess herself (1446-67). In the Archaeological Museum of Brauron, near Athens, there is a display case with various offerings, including a small wooden Artemis found in the sanctuary, which is displayed in a glass case in the Archaeological Museum of Brauron and is dated to between the 6th and early 5th century BC. Interested adults can further explore these and other aspects of the myth relating to the survival of classical culture in universal culture, by listening to a passage from the opera *Iphigenia in Thauride*.
5) Colouring and cut of the peplos: The short peplos is typical in the iconography of the goddess and the saffron colour, in imitation of the bear's fur, as the virgin maidens, during the feast of the arkteia were dressed in a saffron-coloured robe, the krokotós, (κροκωτός), from krókos (κρόκος), "saffron".
6) Draw attention to the image of the hind, comment on it from a zoological point of view, its historical and current distribution, its role in myth and its connection with the goddess Artemis.
7) Analyse the characteristics of the Ionic column.
8) The prayer intoned by Calligone and the other girls is not a literal translation of the Greek text, although it is based on the so-called Homeric Hymn to the goddess Artemis.
9) Depending on the age of the child, you can ask them to read aloud, suggesting that they pay attention to pronunciation and modulate intonation and volume. You can ask them questions about vocabulary: terms they do not understand, suggesting other vocabulary to replace that which appears in the text. You can consult a dictionary with him/her and play together to find more familiar alternatives.

Finally, in the case of a girl or adolescent girl and an adult woman reading together, the vignette lends itself to an exchange of concerns and doubts, on the part of the former, and experiences and memories, on the part of the latter, regarding the arrival of the first menstruation in a woman's life.

The Papyrus of the Sailor Sinuhe

La viñeta de la página dieciséis presenta una escena de despedida, cuyo texto es el siguiente:

Once he had achieved a certain degree of prosperity, Sesoncosis wished to establish commercial contacts in the Mediterranean: "It is my wish to make known the talent of Egyptian artists and the quality of our products, especially perfumes and papyrus scrolls". Together with Meameris, Pamunis and a group of artists, scribes and priests set sail for Alexandria. Once the cargo was stowed, taking special care with the ibis cage, the expert crew raised the stone anchor and set sail, heading east: "We will sail first to Hispania, to visit the temple of Isis, and then to Ostia.

From there, we will embark on a land expedition through Dacia and Gemania, where we will meet peoples with exotic languages and customs," exclaims the pharaoh from the bow.

As the astronomers had predicted, a few days later, a total eclipse occurred, which Sesoncosis and Meameris were particularly excited about, as they were still very young and had never witnessed such a spectacle. (Translation into English by Olimpia Navarro).

The expectation of a journey is full of emotions: excitement for the journey, curiosity for new discoveries, sadness for the farewells... The image allows us to comment on several interesting elements, of which we will limit ourselves to three. Firstly, the port of Alexandria. It is impossible to list here all the rich history of the city founded by Alexander the Great in 331 BC and which became the cultural center in Antiquity. Ships loaded with valuable goods from all over the world arrived at its docks. The scene invites to connect present and past with the reading of *Ithaka* by C. P. Cavafy:

Hope your road is a long one.
May there be many summer mornings when,
with what pleasure, what joy,
you enter harbors you're seeing for the first time;
may you stop at Phoenician trading stations
to buy fine things,
mother of pearl and coral, amber and ebony,
sensual perfume of every kind—
as many sensual perfumes as you can;

and may you visit many Egyptian cities

to learn and go on learning from their scholars. (Translated into English by Edmund Keeley)

The presence of the Ibis is also very interesting. In Egypt itself, this bird was considered a benefactor. Both the ibis and the flamingo are migratory birds, or partially so: from North Africa and even from the eastern Mediterranean, they reach the Iberian Peninsula and disperse to different wetlands. Both, βις and φοινικόπτερος, are cited by Greek sources, such as Herodotus (2.67, 75, 76) and Aristophanes (*Birds* 273), among others, but unfortunately the *Ibis Eremita* is currently in danger of extinction.

Lastly, we will stop at the stone anchor, one of the most interesting materials that we have learned about underwater archaeology and which provides a great deal of information about trade routes in the ancient world.

The Martyrdom of Saint Parthenope

Absolutely all of us, at some point, will be faced with the experience of the loss. The text of the vignette on the page describes the moment when the nuns of the convent of Parthenope say goodbye to her, in this case forever, by singing.

Thus, as if asleep, Parthenope crosses the atrium again. The sisters listen to the astonishing story of the Persian messenger. A clamour of bells breaks the monastic silence and the excited voices of the nuns pierce the thick walls of the convent singing in unison:

"*Salve Regina, Mater misericordiae, Vita, dulcedo, et spes nostra, salve.*

Ad te clamamus, exsules filii Hevae.

Ad te suspiramus, gementes et flentes

In hac lacrimarum valle.

Eia, ergo, Advocata nostra, illos tuos misericordes oculos ad nos converte.

Et Jesum, benedictum fructum ventris tui,

Nobis post hoc exilium Ostende

O Clemens, O pia, O dulcis Virgo Maria." (Translation into English by Carlos Sánchez).

The death of a loved one is a very painful experience for anyone and, if it happens, difficult for a child to understand. Sharing the grief, remembering the loved one (it could be a pet) in happy moments and paying tribute to them by doing those things that made them happy is something we can do to ease some of the pain. In this case it is a rather famous piece of Gregorian chant known as the *Salve Regina*. It is a prayer expressing devotion to the Virgin Mary. The scene also provides a suitable context for commenting on *P. Ryl.* 470. This is a Greek papyrus dated to around the 3-4th century AD which preserves a prayer to the Virgin Mary and became an important hymn in the Roman Catholic and Orthodox traditions, known in Latin as *Sub Tuum Praesidium*.

CONCLUSION

In conclusion, that is here described is only a small sample of the interest of reading the picture book, to work on emotions. In particular, in the case of these volumes of stories inspired by the papyri of lost Greek novels. The therapeutic function of this experience can even be considered. By adapting the language and content of the original, the story becomes a platform for the promotion of shared reading and between readers of different ages: children, adolescents, and even young people and adults and even for deepening one's own feelings. The picture story encourages the exchange of experiences, memories and knowledge, whether at home or at school, between readers of different ages.

Reading is cathartic. Through language, we identify with the emotions of the anonymous authors of these fictional stories where there is so much wisdom contained about the human condition. Classics always come to rescue us from our anger, frustration, feelings of helplessness, loneliness, sadness and fear but also to accompany us when we awaken to love and courageously face new paths.

ACKNOWLEGEMENTS

This work has been carried out within the framework of the project *Los papiros de la “Vida de Alejandro”: edición y estudio literario del texto en el contexto de la narrativa de ficción en griego antiguo (PAVIDAL) (PID 2022-138853NB-100)* of the Spanish Ministry of Science and Innovation

REFERENCES

Kavafis, K. (n.d.). *Ithaka*. [trans. Edmund Keeley]. Poetry Foundation. [https://www.poetryfoundation.org/poems/51296/ithaka-56d22eef917ec]

López Juan, A. (2024). *Amazonas, creación de una nueva iconografía a través de la computación actual*. In: *Carolina Flores Lueg and Marcos Gómez Puerta, Conocimiento compartido y educación*. Dykinson.

López Juan, A., López Martínez, M. P., & Navarro López, O. (2022a). Ficción en papiro: nuevas aplicaciones didácticas de la investigación en humanidades. In *D. Gavilán Martín, y G. Merma Molina, Investigación e innovación en el contexto educativo desde una perspectiva colectiva* (pp. 171–179). Dykinson.

López Juan, A., López Martínez, M. P., & Navarro López, O. (2022b). 88. Cuentos griegos en papiro: Un nuevo tipo de aplicación didáctica de la investigación en Filología Griega. En R. Roig-Vila (Coord.), V. Martines y J. Antolí (Edd.), *Proceedings.I International Congress: Education and Knowledge I Congres* (p. 148). Octaedro, S.L.

López Juan, A., López Martínez, M. P., & Navarro López, O. (2022c). *Parténope*. Editorial Turpin.

López Martínez, M. P. (2021a). *Las aventuras de Calígone y las amazonas*. Editorial Turpin.

López Martínez, M. P. (2021b). *Nino, las aventuras del rey de Nínive*. Editorial Turpin.

López Martínez, M. P. (2022a). *El papiro del Marino Sinuhé*. Editorial Turpin.

López Martínez, M. P. (2023a). *El martirio de Santa Parténope*. Turpin Editores.

López Martínez, M. P. (2023b). Un tópos literario apto para todos los públicos: los nombres de los personajes de los papiros de novelas griegas perdidas. In *Esther Chiner e Iván Sánchez-López, Nuevas tendencias interdisciplinares en educación y conocimiento* (pp. 331–346). Editorial Tirant lo Blanch.

López Martínez, M. P. (2023c). Docere delectando: Las aventuras de Calígone y las amazonas. In: Rosabel Roig-Vila, Fabrizio Manuel Sirignano y Jordi M. Antolí Martínez Actas / *Proceedings 2nd International Congress: Education and Knowledge*. Octaedro.

López, M. P. (Dir.). (2023d). *Ficción en papiro* (Fiction in Papyri). [Website]. [https://www.ficcionenpapiro.es/index.php/es/]

López Juan, A., López Martínez, M.P., y Navarro López, O. (2022a). *Ficción en papiro: nuevas.*

Navarro López, O. (2023). La lectura del cuento troquelado como instrumento de intercambio generacional. *Proceedings 2nd International Congress: Education and Knowledge*. Ediciones Octaedro.

Navarro López, O. (2024). La lectura compartida como espacio de intercambio generacional: a propósito de la página cuatro de «*Las aventuras de Calígone y las amazonas*». In: *Conocimiento compartido y educación*. Universidad de Alicante.

Chapter 2
A Glimpse Into Roman Law by Kandinsky

Aránzazu Calzada
University of Alicante, Spain

ABSTRACT

The biography or memory book of Kandinsky written by his wife Nina refers to the years in which the great painter devoted himself to teaching Roman law, and highlights certain aspects of the subject that particularly appealed to him. She refers to the logical precision and modes of argumentation in which the Roman jurists—according to the artist—would have excelled. The authors have examined the type of Roman law that was taught in Czarist Russia, the milieu in which he lived and the sources from which it was derived. It seems that the influence of German Pandectistics was decisive, particularly at the end of the 19th century. Several Russian scholars were trained in Germany, and not only in Roman law, so the influence of Pandectistics was greater than previously thought. This work of research into the context in which the painter moved during his years as a jurist enables the authors to explain what he understood by the logical precision and ways of legal argumentation in the case of the Roman jurists.

DEPARTING POINT: NINA KANDINSKY

Sometimes, reading favours certain findings that are a priori far removed from the reader's field of study, or even from his interest or taste. It could be said that reading has an attractive quality that can lead to unusual paths. This is the case: Nina Kandinsky's memoirs have served as a spur, for an unexpected legal research, which in some cases had already attracted the attention of legal scholars, but which, in our opinion, deserves a more contextualised study. Jacques Lassaigne, an art critic

DOI: 10.4018/979-8-3693-4244-2.ch002

and expert on Kandinsky, said that Nina Kandinsky's memories of her husband's portrait show that love is the best way to know and recognise each other deeply.

Nina de Andreewsky, a descendant of an aristocratic family from Tula, was originally Kandinsky's "unknown voice", not only the muse who inspired the watercolour in which the painter captured the impression made by her voice on the other end of the telephone during their first conversation. Thus, came to truth what a marriage oracle had prophesied on New Year's Eve: she would marry a man called Wassily, with whom she would be very happy. "With our marriage, spring began in the autumn of his life," says the author, in this delightful account of their life together (Kandinsky, N., 1976, p. 26).

Nina no doubt wrote this book to record their shared life, to emphasise Kandinsky's qualities and to divulge his work, a task to which she devoted herself wholeheartedly, especially after the painter's death. It is only fair to point out its decisive role in the recognition and fame of Kandinsky, as well as in the care, protection and promotion of his work. Nina met a tragic end: she was the victim of a robbery, known to have treasured priceless jewellery, and was murdered at Villa Esmeralda, her Swiss residence, in September 1980. Kandinsky's paintings remained untouched.

KANDINSKY AND THE UNIVERSITY

As far as this chapter is concerned, the book gives a brief but illustrative account of the young Kandinsky's thorough school and university education; he went to school in Odessa and studied there for nine years of high school. During his student years, Wassily always had the desire to return to Moscow, which he finally achieved at the age of eighteen. In 1886 he moved there permanently to enrol at the university. There, Kandinsky did not confine himself to the study of his speciality; as an outstanding student, his thirst for knowledge led him to take an interest in other fields of study, particularly law (Kandinsky, N., 1976, p. 29).

According to Nina Kandinsky, in 1889, the Society of Natural Sciences, Anthropology and Ethnography commissioned him to travel to the Vologda province to study the criminal law of the peasants and to investigate the remains of the pagan religion of the Syrian fishing and hunting people. The Society was so satisfied with Kandinsky's work that he was admitted as a member almost at the same time as he became a member of the Jurisprudence Society. In 1892, he passed his official examination, was admired for his thesis on the problem of wages, and shortly afterwards was appointed as assistant professor. He now had a promising academic future, and the doors of the University were open to him to develop a brilliant academic career, perhaps at the University of Dorpat, where he was offered a professorship that Kandinsky turned down. The decision had already been made. On the threshold of his academic life, at the age of thirty, his artistic vocation finally won out over his scientific career. (Kandinsky, N., 1976, p. 29)

Kandinsky and the Fascination for Roman Law

However, Nina herself mentions Kandinsky's fascination with Roman law:

"Das römische Recht", so bekennt er, "das mich durch die feine, bewußte, hochraffinierte "Konstruktion" bezauberte, das mich, den Slawen, aber als eine viel zu kalte, viel zu vernünftige, unbiegsame Logik nicht befriedigen konnte, das Kriminalrecht (das mich besonders und vielleicht zu ausschließlich durch die damals neue Theorie Lombrosos berührte), die Geschichte des russischen Rechtes uns das Bauernrecht (das als Gegensatz zum römischen Recht mich als Befreiung und glückliche Lösung des fundamentalen Gesetzes in große Bewunderung versetzte und meine tiefe Liebe gewann), die diese Wissenschaft berührende Ethnographie (von der ich mir anfänglich die Seele des Volkes versprach), nahmen mich in Anspruch und verhalfen mir zum abstrakten Denken." (Kandinsky, N, 1976, p. 27).

(""Roman law", he confesses, "which enchanted me by its fine, deliberate, highly refined "construction", but which could not satisfy me, the Slav, as a logic far too cold, far too reasonable, inflexible, criminal law (which touched me especially and perhaps too exclusively through the then new theory of Lombroso), the history of Russian law and peasant law (which, as a contrast to Roman law, filled me with great admiration as a liberation and happy solution of fundamental law and won my deep love), ethnography, which touches on this science (from which I initially expected to gain the soul of the people), occupied me and helped me to think abstractly).

Who knows whether this attraction to Roman law would have led him, even remotely, to his original aesthetic conception, which would have given rise to a *forma mentis* capable of revolutionising the art of the time. Perhaps juridical abstraction favoured the path towards pictorial abstraction.

Romanists' Interest for Kandinsky

At least that has been the common desire of notable Romanists, (Garofalo, 2003 and Paricio, 2003), i.e. to give evidence of these links. Paricio also reports on his personal inclination for painting and establishes a comparison between their respective trajectories, his own and Kandinsky's, "resolved in exactly the opposite direction" (Paricio, 2003, p.328).

It is precisely on this subject that we should refer to Garofalo's work on an article published on 31 March 2003 in the *Corriere della Sera* by Sebastiano Grasso under the title "E Kandinsky si ritrovò in Wagner", in which he alludes to the teaching of Roman law at Dorpat by the famous Russian artist, despite which he resigned from the university and moved to Germany to study painting.

With this as a starting point, Garofalo develops in detail the painter's career, his links with the University and his interest in Roman law, and qualifies Grasso's assertion: "Non risulta, dunque, un Kandinsky docente di diritto romano, né a Dorpat né altrove. Risulta, invece…un Kandinsky che, prima di consacrarsi totalmente all'arte, aveva provato un forte interesse per questa materia". (Garofalo, 2003, p. 49 and 50, (n.1 to 3) with an abundance of literature, draws on the painter's autobiographical texts, the work of his friend Will Grohmann, and the memoirs of his second wife, Nina von Andreewsky).

According to the Italian Romanist, the study of Roman law, to which the painter had devoted himself with enthusiasm, would, by his own admission, contribute to the development in him of abstract thinking, which was a particularly important acknowledgement coming from someone who "colloca l' 'abstraktes Denken' tra i valori primi del suo patrimonio interiore". Garofalo (2003, p. 51) based on the authors cited initially, and later referring to artistic evolution, which will lead him to experiment and theorise in his famous and influential writings, which are well known. It does seem pertinent to reproduce here the words of Philippe Sers quoted by the author:" il metodo e la riflessione rigorosa, ma non i paraocchi, sono quelli del professore di diritto *in spe"*.

Garofalo (2003, p. 55) summarises the background of the legal landscape in which, in his opinion, Kandinsky was immersed during the ten years (1886-1896) that he spent in contact with the legal world and particularly with Roman law, as follows: "verosimilmente mostratogli all'interno della splendida cornice sistematica elaborata dalla pandettistica".

The legal training of young Russians in Berlin under Savigny and in Leipzig under Puchta, as well as the privileged place where some of them also received training in Berlin from 1887 onwards: the Russisches Seminar für römisches Recht (Russian Law Seminar), is noteworthy in this respect. (Garofalo, 2003, pp. 53-55, describes the legal scenario in which foreseeably a Muscovite interested in this field would operate at the end of the 19th century). In short, the teaching of Roman law conceived as an introduction to civil law that the students retained on their return to Russia (Garofalo, 2003, p. 55).Therefore, the perception of Roman law as an ""elegante edificio concettuale connodato da una fredda logica" (Garofalo, 2003, p.56) is not at all strange.

Similarly, Paricio, in the article he wrote about Kandinsky in response to Garofalo's article, after an unusual coincidence, underlines what the artist said about Roman law: "which subjugated him by its construction, so subtle, so clear-sighted, so refined, but whose logic, too cold, too rigid, could not satisfy a Slavic soul like his". Paricio (2003, p. 326) recalls this perception of the author in Rückblicke, his memorable autobiographical work, and in the same vein, Garofalo, (2003, p. 50), gives details of the painter's personal life and academic and musical training, supported by a voluminous literature.

According to Paricio, since the middle of the 19th century, Roman law has had an influence in Russia through German Pandectists, especially because many Russian students studied in German universities. This could explain why, despite Kandinsky´s admiration for Roman law, he found it too cold, rigid and strict (as anybody would, not only those with Slavic souls) (Paricio, 2003, p. 327).

The Influence of Pandectists on the Study of Roman Law

We agree with the idea already put forward that Kandinsky's view of Roman law was that it was a jurisprudence of concepts derived from Pandectists, which constructs such general concepts on the basis of the formulations of each specific case. Pandectists, as we have already indicated, had a strong influence in Russia and the brilliant painter was immersed in that paradigm.

To address this question, we must refer both to the nature of the system in Roman law and to studies of Roman jurisprudence at the time of its development. This theme, to which we have already briefly alluded, undoubtedly determines Kandinsky's admiration for Roman law. Perhaps a jurist focused on criminal law could make a similar point about his interest in the criminal sociology of Cesare Lombroso.

Bearing in mind that a genius is a fruit of his time, we shall briefly describe the context in which the painter moved during his years as a law student and doctoral student, although we shall deal with this point in more detail in the last part of this chapter.

Thus, even a superficial knowledge of Tsarist Russia clarifies many dimensions of Kandinsky's appreciation of certain areas of legal studies. From the reign of Alexander II onwards, politics took a more Europeanist direction, and law and the study of law was no stranger to this; this is the conceptual framework in which Kandinsky referred to Roman law. If we reflect on the influence of Pandectists in 19th and early 20th century Tsarist Russia, we will come to the conclusion that its presence is related to the codification movement, which in its origin, at least in Germany, is not exactly the case. In Italy, on the other hand, the role of Pandectists is different, because its cultivation (Ferrini) or the annotated translations of Windscheid or Arndts (Fadda, Bensa, Bonfante, Serafini) are activities subsequent to the first codification. In this case, the study of the sources according to Pandectists method, aims to make a critique of the law in force (Torrent, 2007 y 2015): it is a work, in a certain sense, *de lege ferenda*.

Roman Law and Legal Logic

Now, what role does logic play in Roman law and how does the author understand it? First of all, the emphasis should be placed on the logical studies of the time. Pandectists, even the later of its manifestations, is built on a conceptual logic and wants in turn to create a jurisprudence of concepts, in a sense paradoxically contrary to the approach of the Roman jurists. If they went from the case to the general rule, the treatment of the sources that characterises this paradigm is the opposite: constructing general concepts from the particular cases dealt with in the Digest (*Vid.* e.g. D. 50.17.1 *Paulus libro 16 ad Plautium. Regula est, quae rem quae est breviter enarrat. Non ex regula ius sumatur, sed ex iure quod est regula fiat. Per regulam igitur brevis rerum narratio traditur, et, ut ait Sabinus, quasi causae coniectio est, quae simul cum in aliquo vitiata est, perdit officium suum).*

The most significant and innovative aspect of the study of logic (Frege's propositional logic) was not going to influence the Romanists of the time, nor, therefore, Kandinsky's teachers, for in Russia, as we shall see, a conceptual study of law was followed. Therefore, the logic that Kandinsky thinks he sees is that of Pandectists, not that of the classical jurists. In any case, we must remember that there is a very obvious link between Pandectists and the Historical School, although it is not usually cited by a large part of the doctrine. Andreas B. Schwarz, in a now classic article published in 1921, showed that there is a continuity between the 17th century naturalists, the Pandectists and the Historical School. Puffendorf's schema, for example, is present in Savigny and is taken over by the Pandectists of the 19th century (Torrent, 2016).

This has an important consequence for the study of Roman law as possibly conceived by the Russian University of the time, which we will' deal with later. As far as we are concerned here, the logic in the reasoning of the jurists is considered by all of them, in von Savigny's phrase, to fall within "the 'fungibility of the Roman jurists", that is to say, that there is an error of perspective:

In the first instance, general concepts are extracted from a casuistic ordering: this phase is part of the pandectists' approach and is justifiable in a context in which the Roman sources must be applied to a social and economic reality, that of the 19th century, which is very different from their original framework. It is therefore necessary to rely on those general rules that underlie the resolution of concrete cases, but this attitude inevitably generates an uncritical treatment of the sources. This is what Kandinsky rightly considered "too cold", "too rigid", "too strict", and does not correspond, as Paricio warns, with the conception of the Roman jurists of the last century of the Republic and of the Principate (Paricio, 2003, p. 327).

In a second stage, the internal logic of this construction is considered and a certain conception of logic and certain concepts are deduced from it, which the Roman jurists did not define in a clear-cut way either (Martini, 1966, pp. 7-11).

Lastly, the Roman jurists are credited with a logical construction that did not characterise them, which does not imply that logic was not relevant in their reasoning, but it was relevant in a different sense and in different ways according to each jurist. It could therefore be concluded that Kandinsky always moved within this paradigm: Pandectists, which in turn was influenced by the other two schools.

The logic of the Roman jurists, however, was studied later, precisely when the results of propositional logic were developed and some of its methodological aspects were revealed. In particular, (Mates, 1953) highlighted the parallelism between propositional logic and Stoic logic, which signifies the beginning of the first rigorous study of the role of logic in Roman jurists.

Consequently, this should allow us to contextualise Kandinsky's further study of the subject with its subsequent development. When Kandinsky was no longer engaged in this profession, the debate between jurisprudence and rhetoric began, which today perhaps deserves a different assessment (Schulz, 1950; Carlos Sánchez-Moreno, 2013), and the study of the jurists themselves as individuals, although it began earlier (Krüger, 1888), did not make its way into classroom explanations until much later. It was only from the sixties and seventies of the last century that the influence of logic on specific authors was studied.

Torrent (2021) traces the argumentative techniques in Julian's *Liber Singularis de Ambiguitatibus*, which goes back to Aristotle's Sophistici Elenchi and the extraordinary tradition of the Stoa philosophers, observing in Julian's texts the influence of Stoic logic that modern authors have tried to explain in a symbolic-mathematical key; Armgardt, Krampe, Miquel or Elmar Bund, reviewed by Armando Torrent, where the author stresses the interest of the subject not only because of the rigid logical structures of his thought, but also as a codifier of the *Edictum perpetuum*. Torrent recalls that in order to study the classical Roman method, there are two possible directions: one of them consists of understanding the approaches to legal structures with the formal relations between their elements, and the other, following Viehweg, which dispenses with axiomatic mental categories, in order to try to arrive at a topical character through the analysis of aporetic legal constructions. Likewise, in Bund's work, he highlights an exemplary exegesis of texts, but more than a textual legal criticism, Torrent understands that he carries out a study of the logical structures of the language used by Julian; in another order of things, regarding the method by similarities, he emphasises the precision that the analogy is not systematic but sporadic.

Legal Studies in Russian Universities of the Period

Recent contributions by Hamza and Avenarius can provide us with an understanding of the context in which Kandinsky was trained as a jurist and, specifically, the meaning of the subject of Roman Law in the curriculum of the Russian Empire; in other words, the value of this discipline as a formative element of the future jurist, which, until now, has not been reflected in the doctrine given the impossibility of pronouncing on the subject or subjects on which he taught in Moscow and the content of the teaching post offered to him at Dorpat.

Garofalo (2003, p.51) is sceptical about the painter's alleged teaching work and states categorically that he made no scientific contribution in this field, and Paricio (2003, pp. 326 and 327), for his part, states his ignorance of the university curricula of Russia a century and a quarter ago and considers it unlikely that there were any professorships in Roman studies at that time, although he supposes that there are some documents on Kandinsky's specific teaching work during those years in the legal field and on the specific call of the University of Dorpat. Certainly, with the bibliography consulted (which was not small,) it was impossible to specify anything else, the author concludes.

The Byzantine Legal Tradition: Russia a Third Rome?

As widely known, in Russia the knowledge of Roman law was due to relations with Byzantium, to the influence of the Orthodox Church and to ideological reasons put forward by the tsars, such as the *renovatio imperii*, which, as a consequence of Caesaropapism, cannot be clearly separated from ecclesiastical influence.

In fact, Byzantine legal texts had already reached the Russian cultural sphere through the writings of John Scholasticus (Synagoge) and Photius, who in his Nomocanon directly transmitted fundamental texts of Byzantine law such as the *Procheiron* or the *Ecloge*. In any case, as Hamza himself points out (Hamza, 2013, p.600):

"El Derecho Romano-Bizantino (ius Graeco-Romanum) tuvo su impacto y se sintió incluso en los reinados rusos de los zares. Iván IV ordenó la traducción al ruso del Codex Iustinianus. La obra legislativa del zar Alexis Mihailovich (1649-1676) de 1649 titulado Sobornoe Ulozhenie contenía textos realizados por los Padres de la Iglesia, las órdenes (ukazy) de los zares y Derecho Romano-Bizantino. Como compilador Nikita Odolevski a quien habían ordenado seleccionar las disposiciones más adecuadas del derecho privado surgidas por los emperadores bizantinos y revisar las normas rusas concordantes. Esta obra legislativa está ampliamente basada en las normas consuetudinarias rusas y en el Tercer Estatuto Lituano de

1588. El impacto del Derecho Romano-Bizantino puede sentirse sólo en la esfera del derecho penal e incluso ahí vagamente".

In other words, much of the Byzantine tradition is applied by the ecclesiastical courts and is related in a complex way to this Russian tradition. The time of its real relevance is in the 18th and 19th centuries, during the codification work and under the influence of the University. This places us in a system more akin to Greco-Roman law (such as that found in the *Hexabiblos*, the cornerstone of Greek civil law today). The parallelism between Greek law and Russian law is suggestive, since the common Roman and Byzantine origin and the influence of the Orthodox Church are joined by the lesser influence of the Napoleonic Code and the much greater imprint of German Pandectists (Yiannopoulos, 1993, p. 7).

As Hamza himself notes, it is difficult to establish boundaries between the political and religious spheres in the context in which we move. Significantly, the Hungarian jurist explains, the title of Tsar of Russia was first used in international relations by Ivan III (1462-1505) in 1473 when he married Sophia Palaeologa, niece of Constantine XI Dragases (1448-1453), the last Byzantine emperor. It was a monk named Philotheos of Pskov (Pleskau) in the early 16th century who devised the theory that the tsar was subrogated to the rights of the Roman Emperor of the East, which was also done by the Sultan of the Ottomans, who retained this title until 1921. The basis of this theory is Justinian's Novel VI, from which Philotheus derived the principle of the unity (symphonia or in Russian sviashchennaya sugubitsa) of ecclesiastical power (*sacerdotium* or hierosyne) and political power (*imperium* or basileia) which entailed the subordination of the Church to the emperor, thus titled "Pair of the Apostles". The title of tsar was already recognised by the Holy Roman Emperor Maximilian I during the reign of Basil III (1505-1533), but the Byzantine patriarch made the coronation of the Byzantine form of Ivan IV, "the Terrible" (1533-1584) necessary as a precondition for his legitimacy.

The Russian Legal System: The Codification

According to Hamza (2013, 602):

"corresponde a MM Speranski y al jurista húngaro nacionalizado ruso Mihály Balugyánszky [Michael Balugianski] el mérito de haber iniciado el proceso de consolidación del sistema jurídico del Imperio Ruso. La labor codificadora es uno de los empeños del zar Alejandro III, quien estableció una comisión que habría de preparar los proyectos de Código Civil ruso en 1899 y 1903. Es significativo que la estructura del Proyecto de Código Civil ruso siguiera el sistema elaborado por los pandectistas alemanes. La Escuela de Derecho Pandectista puede observarse

también en el Código Civil de la Rusia soviética redactado por AG Gojkbarg en 1922, y lo mismo se aplicará a los Principios (Fundamentos) de la legislación de derecho civil de la Unión Soviética promulgada en 1961. El Código Civil de la República Federal de Rusia de la Unión Soviética promulgado en 1964 se basa tanto en su estructura como en la regulación de la mayoría de las instituciones jurídicas en la tradición jurídica pandectista. El nuevo Código Civil ruso (1995-2007), que entró en vigor gradualmente, al igual que el nuevo Código Civil holandés, refleja principalmente la influencia del BGB alemán y del nuevo Código Civil holandés".

Hamza (2013, p. 604) considers that the Dutch Civil Code is of mediocre technical quality, far from the level of the Dutch jurists of the 17th and 18th centuries and even of the old code of 1838, but it takes up, although in an unoriginal but clear and systematic way, a whole important tradition expressed today in the dynamic Roman-Dutch law of South Africa (G. Meijer and S. Y. Meijer, 2002). This is the real reason why Russian jurists took it into account. It is not for nothing that Zimmermann's historical and at the same time systematising work must be understood in this context, that of his years of teaching in Cape Town.

With regard to the teaching presupposed in a system conceived under these methodological requirements, it is not surprising that at the University of St Petersburg the official examination syllabus of 1885 stated that "A sound theoretical knowledge of Russian law, generally taught according to the Pandektensystem and the historical-dogmatic method, will be required..." (Avenarius, 2005, p. 51).

The Russian Codification was forged on this basis and this logically conditioned Kandinsky's teaching approach. It is in our opinion significant how Hamza (2013, p.603) summarises this period, in which both Byzantine roots and the influence of French iusnaturalism prior to the Code Napoleon (Pothier), local tradition and - above all - the method of Pandectistics are mixed. The role of studies at German universities was decisive:

"A comienzos del siglo XIX varios estudiosos, G.A. von Rosenkampf (1764-1832), M.M. Speranski (1772-1839) y el húngaro Mihály Balugyánszky [Michael Balugianski] (1769-1847), profesor en la Academia de derecho de Nagyvárad en Hungría (hoy Oradea en Rumania) se les encomendó la consolidación, por ejemplo, resumen del derecho privado ruso, pero el Zar no estuvo satisfecho con sus proyectos. Hacia 1832 una revisión sistematizada del derecho anterior todavía se estaba preparando y surgió en quince volúmenes bajo el título Svod Zakonov Rossijskoj Imperii (Colección de Leyes del Imperio Ruso). Varias instituciones jurídicas de su sección de derecho privado (volumen X) estaban basadas en el Código civil francés y en las ideas de Robert-Joseph Pothier (1699-1772). Por lo que se refiere a los derechos reales, la influencia de la ciencia jurídica alemana se dejó sentir.

El Derecho Romano-Bizantino en el Imperio Ruso sobrevivió exclusivamente en lo que se refería al derecho de familia y de matrimonio. La Escuela Pandectista dejó sentir su impronta en Rusia desde la década de 1820, cuando los estudiantes rusos de derecho comenzaron a estudiar en las universidades alemanas, en Heidelberg con Anton Friedrich Justus Thibaut (1772-1840), en Berlín con Friedrich Carl von Savigny y en Leipzig con Georg Friedrich Puchta (1798-1846)".

One of the most influential Pandectists in Russia (and curiously, in Italy, through Serafini's translation) is Heinrich Dernburg (1830-1907), who even directed a seminar on Russian law at the University of Berlinand who trained several students who translated his work and that of other Pandectists into Russian.

A number of Russian jurists were trained at this seminar. Commenting on Dernburg's influence, he mentions that:"Entre sus estudiantes D.D. Grimm y I.A. Pokrovski se convirtieron en profesores de Derecho Romano, L. Petrazhitski (1867-1931) se dedicó a la filosofía jurídica y W. von Seeler al derecho privado en Rusia"(Hamza (2013, p. 604). Hamza lists several names of Russian jurists who introduced different areas of German legal science to the Russian university: Pandectists was developed as a general theory of private law by Pokrovsky and Hvostov; Jhering's jurisprudence of interests was dealt with by S. A. Muromtsev.

CONCLUSION

However, this was not the field in which Kandinsky developed as a student, as by this period law had ceased to be his main interest. It is mentioned here as further evidence of the influence of Pandectists on Russian legal studies, which conditioned the painter's appreciation of logic as one of the attributes of Roman jurisprudence.

The recent paper by Avenarius to which we have alluded helps us to reconstruct that context from the teaching point of view. The author focuses on the University of St. Petersburg at the end of the 19th century, on the eve of the Codification, but his conclusions are certainly similar to the program that Kandinsky studied, since the University of St. Petersburg, one of the three in the capital, was the paradigm of the entire system of higher education in the Russian Empire (Avenarius, 2005, p. 52).

In any case, what interests us most in understanding the words of the eminent painter is his knowledge of the syllabus; thus, as we have already mentioned, Avenarius looks at the instructions for the final examination of 1885, where the requirements of a solid prior classical training were in keeping with the German University of the time. Within this influence of Germanic culture, the text condemns Hegel's Theory of Law, precisely because of its confrontation with the Historical School (Avenarius, 2005, p. 54 and n.17), and we have already referred to its links with Pandectists, which are those of rationalist iusnaturalism; consequently, this ideological bias is coherent with the option chosen.

Moreover, as far as Roman law is concerned, its study is compulsory, particularly its history and the institutions of private law (Avenarius, 2005, p. 54 y 55). Russian civil law must be studied, as we have already specified above, according to the system of the Law of Pandectas and the historical-critical method. The oral and written examinations included the commentary on Gaius and Justinian's Institutions in Latin, and it is significant that the History of Philosophy, especially ancient philosophy, was also mandatory (Avenarius, 2005, p. 55).

Another point to consider is that the teaching of civil law was carried out by Romanists. Avenarius cites, among others, the case of Nikolai Djuvernua, author of a manual according to the Pandectists outline and of a booklet on the value of Roman jurists in the work of Russian jurists, a book to which we do not have access, but which may have been one of our author's readings (Avenarius, 2005, p. 62).

Perhaps encouraged by an exacerbated optimism, we Romanists try to link Kandinsky's talent with the teaching of our discipline, or simply with his fascination for it, considering Roman law as the prima ratio of the genius precursor of abstraction. Just as his work and his aesthetic thought are inseparable from music and the spiritual, we try to glimpse the pictorial transposition of his legal mentality.

Be that as it may, perhaps a mere - and happy - coincidence in a double mastery: Romanism and painting, Nina Kandinsky has been the starting point for tracing the line from Roman law to abstraction, guiding our hand in this particular 'Romanist brushstroke'. Our gratitude to her: the memory of Kandinsky.

REFERENCES

Armgardt, M. (2008). Zur Bedingungsdogmatik im klassischen römischen Recht und zu ihren Grundlagen in der stoischen Logik. *TR, 76*, 219-235.

Avenarius, M. (2005). Das pandektistische Rechtsstudium in St. Petersburg in den letzten Jahrzehnten der Zarenherrschaft. Wojciech Dajczak y Hans-Georg Knothe (eds.) *Deutsches Sachenrecht in polnischer Gerichtspraxis. Das BGB-Sachenrecht in derpolnischen höchstrichterlichen Rechtsprechung in den Jahren 1920-1939: Tradition und europäische Perspektive,* Berlin.

Bund, E. (1965). *Untersuchungen zur Methode Julians (Forschungen zum römischen Recht, 20. Abhandlung).* Böhlau Köln-Graz.

Frege, G. (1884). *Die Grundlagen der Arithmetik.*

Garofalo, K. "Kandinsky e il diritto romano", (2003) Labeo 49, 1 pp. 49-60.

Hamza, G. (2013). Derecho Romano y el desarrollo del Derecho privado en Europa del Este. *AFDUC, 17,* 595-604.

Kandinsky, N. (1976). *Kandinsky und ich.* Kindler.

Kandinsky, W. (1996). *De lo espiritual en el arte. Contribución al análisis de los elementos pictóricos.* Genoveva Dieterich, Barcelona.

Krüger, P. (1888). *Geschichte der Quellen und Litteratur des Römischen Rechts.*

Martini, R. (1966). *Le definizioni dei giuristi romani.* Giuffrè.

Mates, B. (1953). *Stoic Logic.* University of California Press.

Meijer, G., & Meijer, S. Y. (2002). Influence of the Code Civil in the Netherlands. *European Journal of Law and Economics*, 14(3), 227–236. 10.1023/A:1020780914470

Miquel, J. (1970). Stoische Logik und römische Jurisprudenz. *SZ, 87*, 85-122.

Paricio, J. (2003). Mirada al pasado. A propósito de Kandinsky y de un artículo de Luigi Garofalo. *Labeo*, 49(3), 323–328.

Sánchez-Moreno, C. (2013). *Law and Oratory. The Encyclopedia of Ancient History.* Editorial Biley Blackwell.

Schulz, F. (1950). *History of Roman Legal Science.*

Schwarz, A. (1921). Zur Entstehung des modernen Pandektensystems. ZSS.

Torrent, A. (1996). *Zur Bedingungsdogmatik im klassischen römischen Recht und zu ihren Grundlagen in der stoischen Logik*. AHDE.

Torrent, A. (2007). *Fundamentos del Derecho europeo. Ciencia del Derecho: Derecho romano-Ius Commune-Derecho comparado*. Edisofer.

Torrent, A. (2015). La Pandectística del siglo XIX, último gran andamiaje teórico de los fundamentos del derecho europeo. *SDHI*, 8, 469–514.

Torrent, A. (2016). *El iusnaturalismo racionalista de los siglos XVII y XVIII. Precursor de los códigos en la secuencia de fundamentos del Derecho europeo, Madrid, Edisofer, Torrent, A. (2021), Retórica, dialéctica, lógica en Juliano. Liber Singularis de Ambiguitatibus, Madrid, Edisofer. Krampe, C. (1970), Proculi Epistulae. Eine frühklassische Juristenschrift*. C. F. Müller.

Yiannopoulos, A. (1993). Historical Development., in K. D. Kerameus y P. J. Kozyris (eds), *Introduction to Greek Law*, (2nd ed), Kluwer/Sakkoulas, Deventer.

Chapter 3
The Journey to Italy in Paul Klee's Diary: In the Footsteps of Goethe?

Carlos Sánchez-Moreno Ellart
University of Valencia, Spain

ABSTRACT

This chapter deals with the possible impact that reading Goethe had on Paul Klee and his trip to Italy, which marked his life and his growth as an artist. It takes into account Klee's diaries, as edited by his son Felix, and compares Goethe's vision of Neohumanism with Klee's approach to classical art and to Neohumanism itself in general, with the distances that exist between the two with respect to this movement and their similarities, particularly in the study of nature. The authors are not going to deal with Goethe's most obvious influence on Klee, which is his theory of light and colour, on which much has been written and about which the painter himself was very explicit in the pedagogical works he published for the Bauhaus.

INTRODUCTION

As reading and its healing value in difficult times is the subject of this book, we originally thought of discussing the books Klee talks about in his diary, just as others have talked about the music which appears everywhere in it. We shall see how important the impact of literature was on Klee's formative years and consequently on his work, but we shall concentrate above all on Goethe's *Italienische Reise*, which the painter read during his own journey to Italy. Klee's contact with the art of antiquity and the Renaissance is influenced by his reading of Goethe, but at the same time he distances himself in important respects from the Weimar genius.

DOI: 10.4018/979-8-3693-4244-2.ch003

But what does literature mean in Klee's work in general? The answer at first glance seems easy, but sometimes too much information makes it hard to put into words. There are painters who have left works of a highly suggestive literary nature, be it the poetic work of Michelangelo or the satirical prose of Solana. Paul Klee was, to say the least, a remarkable essayist, and the publications he produced around the time of his teaching years are good proof of this. However, although his written work is abundant and his readings, as we shall see, diverse and rich, the main value of his writings is to understand the creative process of his pictorial work.

In fact, much can be said about Klee's literary work. All of it reflects on his own condition as an artist and is therefore, as stated above, a privileged window onto the evolution of his plastic work. This reflection is clearly exemplified in his diaries, which cover the long period from 1898 to 1918, and which were published by his son Felix in 1957. We can also find this meditation in texts of an essayistic nature, such as the works he published during his time at the Bauhaus (Klee 1976).

One of Klee's first observations on rereading his notebooks, almost at the beginning of them, is that a diary is not a product of art but of time (170). The paragraphs from Klee's diary are quoted from his son's edition, mentioned in the bibliography. We quote, therefore, paragraphs, not pages.

During the painter's formative years, these notes offer us a multitude of comments on painting, both his own and that of his colleagues or that which he viewed in the museums he visited, but also on his various readings and on what was his second vocation: music. We could draw from the copious references to operas and musical pieces he cites, an article on Klee's music and how it influenced his pictorial vocation. But this, apart from the fact that it is not the subject of this book, is already the work of others (Sopeña 1974 pp. 40-52).

We have already noted that it is easy to choose a classical author Klee would have read and highlight his influence on him. Klee starts from a diverse list of Cervantes (he calls Don Quixote his bedside book: 768), Aristophanes, Plautus, Ibsen, Chekhov, Hebbel, Gogol, and his preferences are therefore clear and frank. For example, his appreciation for Heine is higher than for Lord Byron (569), with whom he declares he feels no affinity (782), although in reading Childe Harold he also values his poetic talent (550).

Nevertheless, we believe that, because of the significance of Goethe's work for German-language culture - something to which Klee is by no means oblivious - and the circumstances in which the painter organised his journey, The Italian Journey would be the most appropriate reading for a brief commentary.

If the subject of this book is reading therapy, it is worth examining what therapeutic effect reading this book had on Klee's soul and what it meant in terms of his personal development and growth as an artist.

Italienische Reise and Klee's life context

Just to contextualise the time of the journey, it should be remembered that Klee, in the preceding pages of his diary, recalls certain memories, especially what might be called his childhood traumas in Bern. The texts, almost dreamlike in nature, are fertile ground for some psychoanalysts, and we will not go into their description, let alone the veracity of these interpretations. We suggest that Klee himself is indirectly influenced by his reading of Freud in his account of them, as has been claimed (Sopeña 1974 p. 148) but, to the best of my knowledge, never studied in depth. Of course there are exceptions, for example Perkins' psychoanalytic study of Klee's childhood and sexuality (Perkins 2008), but the extent to which the first pages of Klee's diary reveal an influence of his reading of Freud in the way he narrates certain experiences of his childhood has not been studied.

Among these memories, which the author labels according to the years in which they occurred, we find -as pointed out above- some of a sexual nature, others of a terrifying nature, as they refer to death and the fear it produced in him, others transcribe the caricatured features of the characters of the Bern of the time. The story continues with thc painter's adolescence in Basel. His fascination with music, and especially with opera will appear again and again throughout these pages.

Admittedly, far from being an outstanding student, as a teenager Klee, by his own admission, only enjoyed the forbidden: poems and drawing. It was in these circumstances that Klee began to study painting in Munich (63). This is one of the starting points for dealing with Goethe's influence on Klee. Certainly, the author, immersed in the Germanic cultural world, must have studied the author of Faust in high school, but it is his interest in nature, in which a certain pantheism can be seen from the outset, which probably brought him closer to him. A trip to Italy as part of an artistic training project brought him back into contact with his work.

Throughout this period, Klee showed a love of nature which linked him, without forcing his texts too much, to Goethe. It is generally accepted that Klee was as much a naturalist (in the sense of his time) as he was a poet. Stefan Bollmann has recently drawn our attention to many of the characteristics of this well-known passion, particularly his theory of colour, so influential in Klee's case, for whom colour unites our brain and the world. In fact, Bollmann begins his book with a quotation from the naturalist Kaspar Maria von Sternberg, who identifies Goethe as a researcher of nature who also wrote poetry. Recently, Bollmann (2021 pp. 5-30), has tackled Goethe's relationship with Alexander von Humboldt in terms of speculation on the laws of nature.

Klee goes so far as to humanise nature (54) when he states that nature loves him after all. Or he draws parallels between his unhealthy state and the morbid quality he attributes to the violet light of the landscape (56). However, also in the same fragment in which he speaks of his fondness for writing and drawing, he refers to the fact that at the time he enjoyed showing contempt for humanism. This is the element that separates him from Goethe, as we shall see, at least in some features.

It can be said that Klee's reading of Goethe's *Italienische Reise* had a great influence on his view of nature, which led him to take an interest in other works by Goethe, but at the same time it is obvious that the painter received the humanist vision of art conveyed by this book in a very relative way.

Personal crisis as a student in Munich

The personal crisis that shook Klee's soul is related to his first experiences and disappointments in love in Munich and his courtship with the woman who was to become his wife. Some recent authors, such as Clemenz, a connoisseur of the painter, have attributed a certain misogyny to Klee's words in the pages before his trip to Italy. In fact, without going into this interpretation, it is possible to observe in his work a very different, or even opposite, treatment of the erotic theme to that of Franz von Stuck, who would represent an idealised vision of this subject. Some of Klee's works from this period were considered scandalous and his concept of eroticism was tainted with satire. The feminine, on the other hand, is presented as being associated with the fateful (Clemenz 2016 pp. 26-27.). As Clemenz points out, the correspondence of those years also has a bearing on this degraded, negative, and materialistic view of women. In a letter to Bloesch he states:

"Verachte die Weiber ein wenig. Das thut heillos gut. Betrachte sie als Butterbrot, als einen guten Trunk Wein, wenn Du willst Champagner".

("Despise the women a little. It's hopelessly good for you. Think of them as sandwiches, as a good drink of wine, champagne if you like ").

Clemenz also emphasises a fact which may go unnoticed on first reading the diaries, namely that Klee's dull life in Munich was in fact more complex than is apparent from the pages of the diary, at least as far as conflicting and failed relationships with women are concerned. He mentions them, at least in a couple of cases, but gives hardly any details, so it is legitimate and reasonable to believe that the impact on his sensibility was even greater than he expresses.

Even if we remember only the stories Klee tells succinctly about his relationships with women, the reality of their sinister and obscure nature becomes apparent. He has a relationship with Cenzi, whom he remembers with desire for a long time. She is a woman who, at least in appearance (Klee's version is unclear), does not demand love from him (127):

" Dies Verhältnis zu Cenzi dauerte nur bis zum 10. Januar 1901. Als ihr früherer Herr aus den Weihnachtsferien zurück war, kehrte sie treu in seine Arme. Mir war das zuerts recht schmerzlich, denn die Sache hatte ganz meinem Geschmack entsprochen. Cenzi verlangte gar keine Liebesschwüre, sie nannte mich sogar 'Sie'."

("This relationship with Cenzi only lasted until 10 January 1901, when her former master returned from the Christmas holidays and she faithfully returned to his arms. At first this was quite painful for me, because the affair had been entirely to my liking. Cenzi didn't ask for any vows of love, she even called me 'Sie'")

We believe that Klee's assessment of his own feelings is ambiguous and may conceal precisely the opposite. At a time when his relationship with Lily, whom he was later to marry, was not at its best, as this slightly later text (128) shows:

"Anfang Januar 1901. Das Abenteuer mit Cenzi hatte mich erstens etwas von Lily abgelenkt. Es war eine Art Erholung von jener Unklarheit."

("At the beginning of January 1901, the affair with Cenzi had diverted my attention from Lily. It was a kind of respite from that ambiguity ").

The link between the two stories does not seem to fit in with what Klee remembers or wants to convey. The first seems to have been more important than he wants to admit and is part of his uneasiness, which will lead him on the journey.

In his correspondence we also find allusions to his excessive alcohol consumption, his enthusiasm for Nietzsche's work and various ailments, probably of a psychosomatic nature. All this suggests a period of severe depression.

The journey to Italy

In the following lines we shall analyse Klee's relationship with Goethe, dealing only tangentially with the enormous influence that the Weimar genius's colour theory had on Klee's teaching at the Bauhaus and on his pictorial theory as a whole, but focusing on the influence that Goethe's work left on the painter's formative years, as he himself records in his diaries.

There is nothing like Klee's reading of one of his favourite works, Goethe's Italian Journey (*Italienische Reise*). In it the Weimar genius recounts his long journey through Italy from 1786 to 1788 and, together with Poetry and Truth (Dichtung und Wahrheit), it is one of his main autobiographical writings.

Although there are hardly any direct references to Goethe in Klee's diaries, his influence can be glimpsed on more than one occasion in the diary of his journey to Italy. Apart from this, there are occasional mentions of other works by Goethe.

It is difficult to assess exactly what Goethe's imprint was on Klee in organising his journey. One of the fundamental differences is that Winckelmann and his revival of antiquity is an essential feature of Goethe's journey, but not very characteristic of Klee's, or at least very slightly so. References to Winckelmann in this book are relatively frequent, cf e.g. 3 December, in Rome:" Winckelmanns Kunstgeschichte, übersetzt von Fea, die neue Ausgabe, ist ein sehr brauchbares Werk, das ich gleich angeschafft habe und hier am Orte in guter, auslegender und belehrender Gesellschaft sehr nützlich finde". They are not, however, to be found in Klee.

Let us remember how in his teenage years he disavowed humanism, which may have predisposed him against that project so characteristic of Goethe and of German culture in the 18th and 19th centuries:

"Dann fing ich an, mich als Landschafter zu fühlen, und beschimpfte den Humanismus. Vor der Sekunda wäre ich gern durchgebrannt, was aber der Eltern Willen verhinderte."

("Then I started to feel like a country bumpkin and insulted humanism. I would have liked to have eloped before secondary school, but my parents prevented me from doing so.")

The context for this serious assertion is the Neohumanism which, among others, Goethe himself contributed to create. We can easily reconstruct what Italy, and especially Rome, represented for Neohumanism. These ideas, with references for example to Winckelmann, are present throughout the Journey to Italy.

As widely known, the Latin word '*humanitas*', as is well known, dates back to Cicero (*pro Archia*) or even earlier, in the anonymous *Rhetorica ad Herenium*, wherethis word means 'gentle

behaviour', for example when used in conjunction with the terms *clementia*, gentleness, and *misericordia*, compassion, or when it is said of the truly brave man that it is his duty to treat the defeated like human beings (Lefevre 1998 5-6).

It is difficult to speak out more radically against 'Bildung' and Classicism as essential basis of human life.

"Denn wenn wir uns dem Alterthum gegenüber stellen und es ernstlich in der Absicht anschauen, uns daran zu bilden, so gewinnen wir die Empfindung als ob wir erst eigentlich zu Menschen wurden " (Goethe 2016 n. 660).

("For when we face antiquity and look at it seriously with the intention of educating ourselves about it, we gain the impression that we have only just become human beings ")

Klee's reaction, however, is not so inexplicable if we bear in mind that access to the intellectual training advocated by Neohumanism has always been associated with particular difficulties. The fact that the old Latin school with its predominant focus on the learning of languages was not perhaps the best way to arouse enthusiasm for antiquity as an intellectual phenomenon. This fact was already mentioned by no other than Christian Gottlob Heyne, one of the great teachers in the field of antiquity (Lefevre 1998 23).

There is, however, one feature that unites the two authors, and that is, apart from their interest in plastic art, their fixation on nature. Later, as we have already mentioned, Goethe's other writings on colour and light exerted a considerable influence on Klee, but the wealth of details on mineralogy and botany that pepper the pages of the Journey to Italy also encouraged the painter to read it.

The presence of music in both books is very varied. In Goethe we find the discovery of Palestrina or Allegri and his visits to concerts, sometimes accompanied by his friend, the musician Philipp Christoph Kayser. Klee's attendance at concerts is attested to throughout his diaries. Another factor which unites and at the same time disunites the two authors is their appreciation of art. Goethe was interested in antiquity and the Renaissance and largely disregarded medieval and baroque art, while Klee was open to everything the eye could see. Goethe's relationships with artists during his journey are also remarkable: Johann Heinrich Tischbein, Angelika Kauffmann and Antonio Zucchi, among others, since there are many other artists with whom Goethe met in Rome: Friedrich Bury, Philipp Hackert....

Klee's journey to Italy, which began after a stay in Bern, lasted from October 1901 to May 1902. Significantly, when he has just returned from his sojourn (411/412), he wonders whether this experience was for him nothing less than a reason to rethink his training as an artist. He considers that the result was not very encouraging and recounts how he destroyed some of his works. He goes so far as to say that his hope is that his harsh self-criticism is the result of his true spiritual growth. Art, he concludes, does not arise from a set of principles that regulate it, but grows as a product of nature. It is reminiscent of Vicente Huidobro's determination in the creationist manifesto: to make a poem as nature makes a tree.

In the very context of the beginning of the journey (295) there is a strange double allusion to Goethe. The first in a poem, an epigram, in which he says:

"In solchen Zustand gibt
es schöne Mittel.
Gebete um Glauben
und Kraft.
Auch Goethe Italienische
Reise gehört hierher.
Aber vor allem ein glücklicher
Stern. Ich sah ihn oft.
Ich werde ihn wieder entdecken".
("In such a state

there are beautiful remedies.
Prayers for faith
and strength.
Goethe's Italian Journey
Journey also belongs here.
But above all a lucky
star. I saw him often.
I will discover him again")

He then concludes:

"An der pantheistischen Ehrfurcht Goethes kann man sich wohl stärken. Zur Genußfähigkeit stärken einmal ganz sicher."

("You can probably fortify yourself with Goethe's pantheistic awe. To fortify one's capacity for enjoyment, certainly.")

After vowing a happy journey, he refers to the Journey to Italy as something that also belongs (gehört) to it. This epigram is the only statement of Goethe's influence on his conception of the journey, at least the only indisputable one. Were it not for it, everything connected with the Weimar poet would be merely hypothetical.

In Klee's view, Goethe is an example of pantheism. The issue itself is not a peaceful one, for Goethe is confused in his expression and, moreover, the term was even novel at the time. John Toland, an Irish disciple of Locke coined the term 'pantheist', but it is in the context of German Idealism that Goethe can be understood to be so interpreted. Friedrich Heinrich Jacobi in 1786 accuses various thinkers of the time of pantheism: Hegel, Schelling and specifically Goethe for his poem Prometheus. explains that the resurgence of Spinoza and Bruno at that time led to the discovery of pantheism (Goedewaagen (1971 p. 172).

In this context and in debate with Jacobi, Goethe confined himself to stating that he sought God in stones and plants, although in Eckermann he is attributed with more explicit phrases (550)[1].

Perhaps "Gott und Natur" is a more explicit quotation for understanding what Klee is referring to:

"Was wär ein Gott, der nur von außen stieße,
Im Kreis das All am Finger laufen ließe!
Ihm ziemt's, die Welt im Innern zu bewegen,
Natur in Sich, Sich in Natur zu hegen,
So daß, was in Ihm lebt und webt und ist,
Nie Seine Kraft, nie Seinen Geist vermißt".
("What would a God be who only pushed from the outside,
Let the universe run in circles on his finger!

It behoves Him to move the world within,
To cherish nature within Himself, Himself within nature,
So that what lives and weaves and is in Him,
Never misses His power, never misses His spirit".)

God appears as incardinated in the world, not situated outside of it. God, for Goethe, moves in nature and is all that lives and beats in it.

Klee also refers in other passages to Jacob Burkhardt's Der Cicerone as a guide to his journey, a book which, as is well known, gave rise to the well-known expression and was widely read in the Germanic world at the time. The comparison between Goethe (and secondarily, the same could be said of Burkhardt) in Klee's travelogue is less idealistic and passionate in tone than in Goethe's, in keeping with his disagreement with the humanist project. Goethe is not able to sleep before he enters Rome because of the emotion that grips him, nor does he believe he is living in reality when he enters it through the Porta del Popolo. Klee, however, maintains a more humorous tone, referring to the hives he gets from his vaccinations, his early drunkenness and the most trivial domestic details.

Before inserting this epigram, Klee meditates on the role of classical and Renaissance art, both in his own time and in his own work. The commentary is ambivalent if we take into account the enthusiasm he felt for certain works, as he remarks in other passages. The painter shows admiration for Burckhardt (sometimes Klee also refuses Burckhardt's criterion e.g., 290; 294), but at the same time expresses something that would fit neither with this author nor with Goethe's *Italian Journey*. The quotation is important because it helps us to understand Klee's relationship with the humanism vindicated by the German culture of the time. Significantly, the text precedes the mention of Goethe and pantheism (294):

"So weit bin ich jetzt, daß ich die große Kultur der Antike und ihre Renaissance überblicke. Nur zu unserer Zeit kann ich mir kein künstlerisches Verhältnis denken. Und unzeitgemäß etwas leisten zu wollen, kommt mir suspekt vor.

Große Ratlosigkeit

Deshalb bin ich wieder ganz Satire. Sollte ich mich noch einmal ganz drin auflösen? Vorläufig ist sie mein einziger Glaube. Vielleicht werde ich nicht positiv? Jedenfalls werde ich mich wehren wie eine Bestie".

("I have now come so far that I have an overview of the great culture of antiquity and its Renaissance. But I can't imagine an artistic relationship to our time. And to want to achieve something out of time seems suspicious to me.

Great perplexity

That's why I'm all satire again. Should I dissolve completely into it again? For the time being, it's my only faith. Maybe I won't become positive? In any case, I will fight back like a beast".)

After acknowledging that he was getting a bird's eye view of the great ancient and renaissance culture, he confessed that he was unable to see its relationship to the art of his time, and even seemed suspicious of wanting to do something outside it. This also marks a difference with Goethe's culturalist project. It is important to note that Klee refers to satire as something which is characteristic of his character and that, when he mentions Goethe in the following section, it is in the context of a satirical poem. Admiration coexists with a certain distance, for satire, he confesses, is something he can blend into, for it is his only faith. The last mention of Goethe in the diary of the journey to Italy is in a strange passage dedicated to an acquaintance of his, Schmoll:

"Ein Pietist ist er, ein Schönheitsfrömmler, verkennt das Salz der Wahrheit, kann keine Grenze mit Humor überschreiten. Er glaubt, deutsch zu sein. Fragezeichen, ob in guten Sinn. Und wenn, dann soll man nicht deutsch sein, denn es gab Griechen, Römer und Päpste. Selbst in der Gegenwart gibt es höhere Werte. Überhaupt ist Goethe der einzige erträgliche Deutsche (so deutsch möchte ich vielleicht selber ganz gern sein)".

("He is a pietist, a bigot of beauty, misjudges the salt of truth, cannot cross borders with humour. He believes he is German. Question mark, whether in a good sense. And if so, then you shouldn't be German, because there were Greeks, Romans and Popes. Even in the present there are higher values. In general, Goethe is the only tolerable German (I would perhaps like to be that German myself)".)

In this text Klee contrasts the creation of culture with devotion to culture. Schmoll stands, it is true, for a part of what Goethe represents, the worship of culture which the Germanic humanist project presupposes. Goethe, however, is creation, as it appears in other spheres outside German: Greeks, Romans, Popes. For Klee, the Weimar poet is a model German, and in this sense, he would like to be considered as such.

CONCLUSION

The aim of these pages is a rather humble one, to reflect the influence which reading *The Italian Journey* may have had on Klee's diary, but at the same time it is an arduous task, for it is difficult to pinpoint Goethe's influence on the aspects which Klee might have valued. The brilliant painter appreciates Goethe's relationship with nature, which he affirms at a time when his artistic status is growing, but he distances himself from the cult of culture for its own sake. This part of Goethe's work does not sit well with his tendency towards satire, as he himself acknowledges.

The reading of *The Italian Journey* was undoubtedly one of the reasons for Klee's journey and serves to define artist's mentality of his time, someone who values the past but, loyal to his status as an avant-garde artist, perceives a certain discontinuity with it. His admiration for Goethe and the pantheism he displays are also consistent with his studies of colour and his experience of natural inner growth.

References

Bollmann, St. (2021). *Der Atem der Welt. J. W. Goethe und die Erfahrung der Natur*. Klett-Cotta.

Goedewaagen, T. (1971). Hegel und der Pantheismus. *Hegel-Studien*, 6, 171–187.

Goethe, J. W. v. (2011). *Italienische Reise*. Deutscher Klassikerverlag.

Goethe, J. W. v. (2016). *Maximen und Reflexionen*. Verlag der Contumax.

Klee, P. (1957). *Tagebücher 1898-1918. Herausgegeben und eingeleitet von Felix Klee*. Cologne (M. Dumont).

Klee, P. (1976). Schriften: Rezensionen und Aufsätze. Colonia (M. Dumont).

Lefevre, E. (1998). Humanismus und humanistische Bildung. In *Humanismus in Europa* (pp. 1–43). Heidbollmelberg.

Perkins, J. (2008). Childhood and Eros: Parallels between Klee and Freud. *Source (New York, N.Y.)*, 27(2/3), 32–39. 10.1086/sou.27.2_3.23208134

Sopeña, F. (1974). El diario de Paul Klee: un pintor músico. In *Música y Literatura* (pp. 145–151). Rialp.

Chapter 4
Reinterpreting Walden: A Bibliotherapeutic Perspective Through Dialogue With Byung-Chul Han's Philosophy

Alfonso Fernández-Manso
Universidad de León, Spain

ABSTRACT

This chapter explores the transcultural and transhistorical conversation between Henry David Thoreau's Walden and Byung-Chul Han's philosophy, offering a bibliotherapeutic perspective on navigating modern society's challenges. Han's analysis of late capitalism's impact on individual subjectivity resonates with Thoreau's call for deliberate living and connection with nature. Through introspective exercises aligned with Walden, readers are prompted to reflect on values, cultivate authenticity, and resist societal pressures. By merging Thoreau's timeless wisdom with Han's contemporary critique, the chapter provides practical strategies for personal resilience and growth in the face of modernity's demands. This dialogue illuminates a path towards fulfillment and purpose, inviting readers to embody authenticity and lead lives aligned with their values.

THOREAU AND HAN: AN UNEXPLORED DIALOGUE BETWEEN THEIR PHILOSOPHIES

Despite their similarities, the possible dialogue between the philosophies of Han and Thoreau, we can affirm that this relationship has not been studied to date. This chapter proposing a conversation between Thoreau and Han invites us to contemplate the intersection between two thinkers separated by more than a century

DOI: 10.4018/979-8-3693-4244-2.ch004

and vast cultural differences, but united by their penetrating critique of the social dynamics of their respective eras (Furtak, et al. 2012).. Thoreau, in *Walden* offers a philosophical account of his experiment in living in solitude near Walden Lake, seeking the essence of life through simplicity and connection with nature, and resisting the pressures of modern society. Han, on the other hand, analyzes in depth the challenges of contemporary society, marked by late capitalism and the technological paradigm, highlighting how social structures and norms affect human subjectivity, interpersonal relationships and our existential orientation.

Walden is a magnum opus by Henry David Thoreau, in which he offers a philosophical account spanning the two years, two months and two days he had to spend inside his self-built cabin in the woods near the shore of Walden Lake, located in Concord, Massachusetts. From a bibliotherapeutic point of view, *Walden* can be understood as a self-reflective guide toward awareness of one's own slowing down and reconnection with the essence of life, offering important lessons about simplicity, nature, and resistance to the pressures of modern society (Harding, 1982).

Byung-Chul Han (Seoul, 1959) is a South Korean philosopher and essayist who carries out a philosophical inquiry launching a look at contemporary society, which has solid roots in the mechanisms of late capitalism and the technological paradigm that coexists with it. His analysis unfolds a meandering narrative that reveals the nuanced and often insidious ways in which social structures and norms have evolved, cascading impacts on human subjectivity, interpersonal relationships, and our collective existential orientation. The very idea of the "subject of achievement," around which Han's discourse evolves, is an idea that determines the change of the individual into a self-exploiting entity.

In this sense, Han argues that such a paradigm shift is ascertained from external alien subjectivity to an internal self-compulsion for constant optimization and achievement (Han, 2022). Man, now master and slave, has to negotiate a terrain free of traditional class antagonism but, paradoxically, stabilizing the neoliberal system by means of control mechanisms implanted in the psyche of the individual. Hence the cascade of neural disorders: depression, ADHD, burnout, etc., which Han poignantly calls, in the best existentialist tradition, "not infections but infarcts, not derived from immunological negativity, but from an excess of positivity". Here, then, is the big question of this chapter: How to survive in today's society?

What can a German philosopher born in Korea at the beginning of the 21st century and an American transcendentalist thinker from the 19th century have in common, when more than a century and very different cultural contexts separate their lives and philosophies? In any case, this work is quite critical of the prevailing social dynamics of the times in which they lived, and sets out to reclaim the need for great reflection and resistance in the face of the thought and currents of lifestyle domination. And yet, Thoreau's work could be a historical antecedent to Han's concern to offer an intertemporal dialogue concerning the search for meaning in an age increasingly accelerated toward change. Both demonstrate - in their lives and works - the path to recovery, leading to a more leisurely and reflective existence (Han, 2022).

Thoreau's work can be seen as a historical antecedent to Han's concerns, offering an intertemporal dialogue on the search for meaning in a fast-paced age. Both, through their lives and works, demonstrate a path to recovery leading to a more leisurely and reflective existence. Despite the lack of studies directly connecting Thoreau and Han, the intersection of their ideas about society, nature, technology, and individualism provides fertile ground for comparative analysis. Both authors critique the contemporary way of life and propose a return to more deliberate and contemplative forms of existence as antidotes to the pressures of their respective eras.

As we have mentioned, no specific study has been found that directly analyzes the connection between Han and Thoreau. The intersection of their ideas about society, nature, technology, and individualism, however, offers a rich field for comparative analysis. Both authors provide penetrating critiques of the contemporary way of life and propose a return to more deliberate and contemplative forms of existence as antidotes to the pressures of their respective eras. Exploring their works through this prism can reveal valuable insights into how to meet the challenges of modern life from philosophical perspectives that transcend time and space.

The analysis of Thoreau's *Walden* from Han's perspective leads us to a profound reflection on the practices of kindness and resistance to the neoliberal rationality that dominates our age. Thoreau, in his retreat to Walden Pond, prefigures what Han would describe as a "praxis of delay" and a rejection of the model of society based on performance and competition. Thoreau's life at Walden is an act of rebellion against the acceleration of time and the commodification of existence, elements that Han criticizes in his analysis of contemporary society.

Thoreau embarks on a life experiment that seeks the essence of the contemplative vita, confronting the performance society by prioritizing experience over the accumulation of goods and efficiency. This quest reflects Han's proposal to rebel against neoliberal rationality through the revolution of time, proposing a life more attentive to the "praxis of delay," that is, an existence that values pause, reflection, and depth of experience over the immediacy and superficiality imposed by the performance model.

The connection between Thoreau and Han becomes even more apparent when we consider Han's critique of the digitalization of society and how this leads to a way of life where everything is measured in terms of efficiency and productivity, leaving little room for contemplation and genuine encounter with the other. Thoreau, in retreating to Walden, seeks precisely that space for authentic encounter with himself and with nature, rejecting the logic of optimization and life mediated by technologies that alienate the individual from his environment and his own inner experiences.

Likewise, Han's "praxis of delay, (Han, 2017) " which revitalizes the contemplative vita in opposition to digital neoliberal rationality, finds a parallel in Thoreau's practice of living deliberately, of taking time to observe and learn from nature, and of questioning the value and purpose of routine human activities. Thoreau, through his life in Walden, performs a form of resistance that Han might describe as a systemic subversion, a refusal to participate in the performance society and a search for alternatives based on kindness, contemplation, and authentic connection with the world.

Finally, it is important to note how Thoreau anticipates Han's critique of the lack of depth and erosion of human bonds in contemporary society. Thoreau's decision to live in Walden is an act of affirmation of the importance of solitude, silence, and deep reflection, elements that are fundamental to resisting the pressures of a society that privileges speed, efficiency, and productivity above all else. In this sense, Thoreau not only anticipates Han's concerns, but offers a practical example and inspiration for those who seek to resist and subvert the dominant logic of our time (Han, 2017).

The chapter "Reinterpreting *Walden*: Bibliotherapeutic Perspectives through Dialogue with the Philosophy of Han" aligns the cross-cultural and transhistorical conversation of visions between Thoreau and Han, opening enriching pathways toward personal resilience and refounded discovery within the demands and challenges of modernity. Merging the bibliotherapeutic insights advanced by *Walden* with contemporary critical studies on late capitalism and its effect on the individual and society, this chapter offers insightful information on how the works of both thinkers could be used to navigate this stormy sea of our time and provide a practical and reflective treatment aimed at personal development (Han, 2022). This approach takes the reader through an introspective journey of transformation and healing that highlights the timeless relevance of Thoreau's quest for a simply simplified life and Han's critical eye for the pitfalls of self-optimization and alienation. Ultimately, the dialogue with *Walden* and Han's philosophy illuminates the way and shows avenues for those trying to follow in actualizing modernity to be in the world and be their authentic selves, thus experiencing the essence of how to lead a life of fulfillment and purpose. In this chapter we will use the depth of Han's thought to analyze the genesis of the sources of mental illness in our society and Thoreau's praxis to overcome these sources of mental alienation.

BYUNG-CHUL HAN: DIAGNOSIS OF A SICK SOCIETY

Han stands as one of the most outstanding philosophers in the landscape of contemporary thought. His work stands as an incisive critique of our age, a voice that accurately unravels the complexities and contradictions of contemporary society. Han examines with an insightful eye the foundations on which Western modernity rests, exposing the dynamics of power, technology and economics that shape our reality. Through his work, he articulates a narrative that illuminates how social structures and norms have evolved, profoundly impacting human subjectivity, interpersonal interactions, and our collective existential orientation.

Central to Han is the figure of the "achievement subject," an entity that self-exploits under the illusion of freedom, marking a paradigm shift from external subjugation to a compulsion for self-optimization and achievement. This phenomenon, explored in detail in *The Burnout Society* (2015), reflects an era where depression, ADHD and burnout are not aberrations, but the result of excessive positivity and a constant pressure to perform. Han extends his analysis to the sphere of desire and relationships in *The Agony of Eros* (Han, 2012), where he laments the erosion of the "Other" and the superficiality of human connections in a culture inundated by narcissism and self-referentiality.

In *Topology of Violence* (Han, 2018) and *Psychopolitics* (Han, 2017), he delves into the forms of violence and control that characterize modern society, distinguishing between negative violence, direct and physical manifestations, and positive violence, more insidious and destructive because of its fusion with the notion of freedom. This latter form of violence manifests itself through performance overload, hyperactivity and excessive communication, making it difficult to identify and resist.

In *The Transparency Society* (Han, 2015) Han criticizes the obsession with total visibility, arguing that it erodes essential spaces of intimacy and mystery, promoting a culture of uniformity and superficiality. Meanwhile, in "In the Swarm" (Han, 2017), Han reflects on the effects of digitalization on social cohesion, highlighting how hyperconnectivity leads to a form of isolation and the loss of the "other."

Han not only diagnoses the ailments of our time; he also proposes avenues of resistance, such as the recovery of rituals, which he suggests in several of his works, to find meaning and structure in a desacralized life. These acts, according to Han, have the potential to reconnect the individual to the community and to broader traditions, offering an antidote to the destructuring of modernity (Han, 2021).

Han's critique of today's society focuses, as we have seen, on how contemporary social and economic structures profoundly influence the mental and physical well-being of individuals. His analysis provides an interesting framework for understanding the growing mental health problems in societies such as the United States.

In the United States, the prevalence of mental disorders has been a growing concern, with an increase in cases of depression, anxiety, and other stress-related disorders. The current state of mental health in the U.S. reflects Han's growing concern about contemporary social and economic structures and their impact on the well-being of individuals. In 2019-2020, 20.78% of adults experienced some mental illness, which equates to more than 50 million Americans. In addition, 15.35% of adults had a substance use disorder in the past year, and of these, 93.5% received no treatment at all. Other highlights include that 55% of adults with a mental illness did not receive treatment and 5.44% of adults experience a serious mental illness. More than 12.1 million adults (4.8%) reported having serious thoughts of suicide, and this figure doubles among adults who identify with two or more races (Mental Health America, 2023).

The prevalence of mental illness is on the rise, and barriers to accessing mental health care are becoming even more difficult, especially among marginalized groups (NextStep Solutions, 2023).. For example, more than 40% of Americans reported symptoms of anxiety and depression in 2020 compared with only 11% in 2019, evidencing the huge role that uncertainty and fear around the pandemic played in this increase. In addition, nearly 11% of adults reported abusing alcohol, while 6.82% reported abusing illicit drugs, of which less than 7% were seeking treatment for their substance use disorder.

These figures are a clear reflection of how current social dynamics are negatively impacting the mental health of the population, aligning with Han's critique of self-exploitation and constant pressure to be efficient, which can eventually lead to a range of mental disorders (Han, 2021). The difficulty in accessing adequate mental health care and the increasing prevalence of mental illness and substance use disorders underscore the urgent need to rethink and restructure our social and economic norms to improve collective mental well-being (Han, 2022).

Han's vision offers a critical lens for examining how the demands of the performance society, along with digitization and the erosion of community and family relationships, may be contributing to this phenomenon. He suggests that to effectively address mental health issues, the social and economic norms that underlie how we live, work, and connect with others need to be reconsidered and restructured.

Han's work is, in essence, a call for introspection about our contemporary existence, urging us to reconsider our aspirations for efficiency, achievement, and self-optimization. He invites us to imagine less self-centered and more reflective ways of living that rekindle our capacity to love, think and make genuine human connections. In an increasingly homogenized world, his books are a critical reminder of the importance of seeking spaces of freedom and authenticity. His work, ranging from cultural criticism to philosophical reflection, is an invaluable contribution to understanding the dilemmas of our time and encourages us to find paths to a more authentic and satisfying existence (National Institute of Mental Health, 2023).

BOOKS THAT HEAL

The history of bibliotherapy begins almost from the beginning of humanity, with the use of verbal and written materials to guide and teach others how to live and behave socially, ethically, spiritually, and to foster emotional well-being. (Hawley & Spillman, 2003). The ancients used spoken words (such as parables, myths, fables and legends) and written words as influential tools to heal and change the human condition. These stories, passed down orally from generation to generation, carried with them the heritage of the ancestors and a code of conduct for life (Berthoud & Elderkin, 2013).

The practice of inscribing statements at the entrances to libraries provides an early historical example of the recognition of the healing power of books. The library founded in Alexandria around 300 B.C. had an epigraph that read, "Medicine [or remedy] for the Mind." The library at Thebes in ancient Greece was dedicated to "Healing of the Soul" as related by Hecataeus of Abdera, a historian of the 3rd century BC. This inscription was found in the sacred library of the funerary complex of Osymandyas (also known as Ramses II). This quotation is mentioned in Diodorus Siculus' work, "Library of History" (Biblioqhks Istorikhs) (Ouzts, 1991).

Throughout history, there have been important developments, each reflecting a growing interest in bibliotherapy as a therapeutic tool. In the Middle Ages, books were used in medical and institutional correctional facilities to help people cope with mental and physical ailments, based on an attempt to maintain a moral foundation. The practice of therapeutic reading became more institutionalized in 18th century Europe, advocating humane methods of treatment for the "mentally unsound" and classifying treatment into physical and moral categories. Reading became one of the most popular forms of recreation prescribed within the "moral" method. By the end of the 18th century, libraries were established in many psychiatric hospitals in Europe. During the 19th century, the use of books for treatment purposes spread to the United States, with reading being recommended as part of the treatment plan for patients by figures such as Dr. Benjamin Rus (Sarah & Kevin, 2008)

Throughout the 20th century, especially after World War I, the therapeutic use of books received a major boost, with the establishment of libraries in army hospitals and the recognition of books as a therapeutic tool for both veterans and the general population (Gregory, 2004). This period also marked the beginning of bibliotherapy with children, with publications advising the use of books to treat behavioral and personality disorders in young people (Hebert & Kent, 2000).

Bibliotherapy offers an alternative to conventional treatments through literature, available in bookstores, libraries or electronically. Using a vast collection of texts, from works by Beckett to Proust, bibliotherapists prescribe readings that not only entertain, but also heal. This approach, though popularized recently through self-help books, is centuries old, with literature historically serving as a means to alleviate emotional distress. The therapy relies on fiction's unique ability to transport readers to other realities, providing new perspectives and comfort.

André Gide emphasized the transformative power of reading, suggesting that we embark on a journey with the author that changes our perception. Regular reading of novels is recommended for all types of emotional ailments, with administration varying from individual reading to the use of audiobooks or group sessions. The key is to complete the "treatment" for optimal impact.

Today, bibliotherapy has spread beyond the hospital setting, being applied in educational and community contexts as an effective method to address personal challenges. Although its definition and scope are still debated, the practice encompasses a wide range of techniques that utilize literature for therapeutic purposes, positively impacting emotional and psychological well-being.

Bibliotherapy allows for emotional catharsis, helping to process feelings in a healthy way. It can offer new perspectives through identification with characters, decrease isolation and teach useful strategies for coping with personal problems. It stimulates the imagination, fosters creativity, improves self-esteem and facilitates personal growth. In addition, it provides comfort in times of loss or grief and helps reduce stress and anxiety, improving quality of life and promoting peace of mind.

WALDEN AND BIBLIOTHERAPY

Walden by Henry David Thoreau is a testament to the transformative power of nature and reflection on life (Thoreau, 2008)., where the author immerses himself in simplicity and isolation in his cabin by Walden Lake. Seeking more than a minimalist existence, Thoreau embarks on a philosophical journey toward self-knowledge and a sharp critique of contemporary civilization. His experience becomes a living laboratory for examining the essential conditions of human life and its dynamic interaction with the environment (Walls,1995).

Early on, in the chapter "Economy," he lays out his motivations for this isolated life, explaining how he designed his dwelling and adopted a lifestyle that prioritizes fundamental needs-food, shelter, clothing and warmth-over the hoarding of material goods. This section not only criticizes consumerist society but also suggests that the simplification of life can free up space for personal growth and introspection (Walls, 2012)..

Progressing through the text, in "Where I Lived and What For," Thoreau elaborates on the importance of living intentionally and purposefully, valuing personal growth over the hoarding of material wealth. The work also highlights the relevance of literature and learning in the chapter "Reading," where he advocates the essential role of deep reading and exploration of meaningful works for the enrichment of the soul (Walls, 2000)

Thoreau examines solitude and social interactions through the chapters "Solitary" and "Visits," contrasting these aspects of life and arguing how they contribute to enriching the human experience. "The Beans" narrates his experience growing this vegetable, using it as an analogy to discuss self-discipline and connection to the land. In "The Pond in Winter," he reflects on the seasons and the flow of time, using the pond as a mirror to meditate on life and change (Friedrich, 2009).

The work concludes with "Conclusion," where Thoreau recaps his experiment in nature, explaining why he chose to end it and sharing lessons learned about living meaningfully. He urges readers to embrace life with determination and seek their own path to self-fulfillment (Channing, 1902).

Walden goes beyond being a simple story about living independently in nature; it is a profound philosophical reflection that combines detailed observations of the natural environment with thoughts on how we manage our economic lives, our relationship with society, and the search for spiritual meaning. Thoreau invites readers to reconsider what they really need and how they can satisfy these needs in a way that is more genuine and less tied to the demands of a consumer-oriented society (Sanborn, 1917). In this sense, *Walden* becomes a call to live with intention and in harmony with the environment, while being mindful of the challenges presented by modern life. It provides a cogent critique and an inspiring message to seek purpose in life that continues to motivate people today (Cain, 2000).

Thoreau's choice to reside at Walden Pond reflects his dedication to transcendentalism and self-formation, influenced by the self-cultivation ideas of figures such as Goethe and Humboldt. This decision marked a departure from his mentor, Ralph Waldo Emerson, and represented a crucial shift in his philosophy toward a more tangible and concrete understanding of existence. Immersing himself in the life of the forest, Thoreau found a balance between the material and the spiritual, offering a holistic view of the human being and his place in the universe (Walls, 2017).

Walden rises above autobiography or nature study to assert itself as an essential text in Western philosophy, whose relevance to modern thought, especially with regard to ecosystem-centered visions and the formulation of a new cultural paradigm that integrates the human with the natural, is extraordinary (Richardson,1988).. By relating *Walden* to contemporary thinkers such as Han, we discover a work that inspires us to face the challenges of modernity through a more authentic existence, marked by simplicity, wonder at nature and a profound ethical reflection on our life in community (Krutch, 1976).

WALDEN AND ITS USEFULNESS IN BIBLIOTHERAPY

Based on the evidence in the article on the efficacy of bibliotherapy in improving mental health, I believe that using Henry David Thoreau's *Walden* could be an extremely promising therapeutic strategy. This is due to the book's in-depth exploration of themes such as living in touch with nature, self-reliance, simplicity, and personal reflection, all of which can be incredibly beneficial to an individual's psychological well-being. By incorporating *Walden* into therapy sessions, patients could be encouraged to reflect on their relationship with nature and themselves by reading specific passages that promote introspection about their own lives, values, and connection to the natural environment (Rossi, 2000). In addition, by encouraging connection with nature, patients could be encouraged to spend time outdoors and practice mindfulness in natural settings, which would help improve their mood and reduce stress. Thoreau also advocates simple, minimalist living, which could be explored in therapy to see how adopting a simpler lifestyle can contribute to mental health, helping patients reduce sources of material stress (Walls, 2013).

Self-sufficiency, being a key theme in *Walden*, can serve to foster autonomy and self-efficacy in patients through practical exercises inspired by the book, such as gardening or crafts, thus boosting their skills and self-esteem. In addition, the book can be an excellent starting point for group discussions, allowing the sharing of personal insights and experiences that foster a sense of community and mutual support, crucial aspects for mental health recovery (Harding, 1958). Writing and creativity exercises inspired by Thoreau's reflections can encourage patients to write about their own experiences, offering a means for creative expression and a powerful tool for catharsis and self-exploration (Sattelmeyer, 2000). The incorporation of *Walden* into a bibliotherapy program should be careful and personalized, ensuring that the themes of the book resonate with each patient's individual experiences and needs, always under the accompaniment of mental health professionals who guide the reflection and learning derived from the reading (Monroy-Fraustro, 2021).

Both Han and Thoreau seem to make an explicit call for the need to revisit the foundations on which our contemporary social construct is based and built: our values and the way we relate to the Other and to each other (Higgins, 2017). His ideas interrogate us about the cost of our constant pursuit of efficiency, achievement and self-optimization, and push us to reflect anew on what it might mean to be truly free, connected and human in an age governed by the imperatives of late capitalism and technological progress. Han, through his philosophical lens, echoes Thoreau in pointing out the ailments that afflict humanity in the modern era. Han invites us to ways of being more reflective and less self-centered, so that we can rekindle our capacity to love, think and truly connect with others through his philosophical perspective. (Burbick, 1987).

From Han's philosophical point of view, *Walden* can be seen as a critique of the modern social structures of the time, but also as a compass for how one should resist and give depth to one's life. In their own way, Thoreau and Han change our attitude toward the life we live. In turn, they encourage us to change our perspective to seek another meaning beyond production and performance, but also in rediscovering the value of reflection, nature. and the genuine.

If not from an economic and financial point of view, then certainly in the light of today's society, *Walden* seems a manifesto of low-productivity living and self-study as a way to stay afloat. What "deliberate living" means is to temper this speed and productivity-disconnection with the demands of our times. This would make it easier for one to sink deeper in one's relationship with the environment and with oneself, but it would also facilitate openness toward reflection and creativity. At the same time, the suggestion is somewhat fundamental to do the opposite with respect to the invasion of noise and digital surveillance of our private lives: that is, to value silence and protect our privacy from the above, to further avoid living a less authentic life centered on true self-knowledge.

Conversely, a much more focused idea allows us to accept negativities and challenges as an intrinsic part of the human experience. This helps to face reality from a much truer and more compelling perspective. *Walden* encourages the recovery of the value of ritual and the appreciation of diversity as both productive and creative, as well as pointing to the importance of holistic care and balance between individual and community life. All this, together with the encouragement of the development of critical thinking and the search for authenticity, is presented as part of what is essential to survive and succeed in the present times despite the pressures towards homogenization and superficiality imposed by the very context of the digital and representation.

Finally, this book urges us to rediscover *Walden* not only as a literary work, but as an essential manual for achieving a fuller understanding of ourselves and the world around us, something that resonates with particular importance in our age of disconnection and environmental crisis. Thoreau offers us a window into his experience, but also a mirror to reflect on our own existence, encouraging us to live more richly, ethically and in conscious connection with the natural environment.

HOW TO SURVIVE IN TODAY'S SOCIETY BY RELYING ON WALDEN'S STRENGTH?

From a Stoic perspective, surviving today's society by relying on "Walden strength"-an allusion to Henry David Thoreau's quest for simplicity and nature in Walden-implies a return to authenticity and autarky, concepts dear to Stoics such as Epictetus and Marcus Aurelius.

The Stoics teach that we should focus on what is within our control, ignoring what we cannot change. The power of Walden, in this context, encourages us to divest ourselves of the incessant demands of modern society and seek refuge in voluntary simplicity. This includes not only a reduction of our material possessions, but also a distancing from the external distractions and preoccupations that flood our day to day lives. (Tauber, 2012).

Adopting the Stoic philosophy here involves practicing inner reflection and cultivating emotional resilience. This allows us to face adversity with equanimity and maintain our moral center, without getting swept away by consumerism or social pressures. For example, Marcus Aurelius reminds us that it is not external events that disturb us, but our perceptions of these events. By periodically retreating into our own version of Walden, either literally or metaphorically, we can reevaluate these perceptions and align ourselves more closely with our core values.

This chapter offers Han's top ten answers to the question "How to survive in today's society?" and outlines, as some of the most important priorities, the need to "follow your heart, be true to yourself, use every part of your body, and have a premium lifestyle." The prescription that our study would imply as a bibliotherapeutic treatment with Henry David Thoreau's *Walden* is holistic, involving reading with reflective and practical activities that are designed to foster growth and well-being. This organized method interconnects selected chapters of *Walden* with exercises that would prompt meditation and mindful practice in a broad scope of life, from learning and practicing procrastination and cultivating silence to preserving intimacy, negativity, and regaining meaning in rituals. Activities will include keeping a reflective writing journal, establishing daily rituals, exploring new cultures, caring for others and the environment, balancing life, developing critical thinking and authenticity. This treatment will foster the reader's connection to the principles set forth in *Walden* living a life more deliberate and reflective of the personal values one believes in, thus making this type of personal transformation a daily practice away from simply reading.

Practice the Art of Procrastination

Han argues that living at a fast pace acts as a form of aggression that limits our ability to think and feel deeply. In response to this situation, he advocates adopting the art of delay, which involves pausing our fast-paced lives to focus on truly meaningful aspects. This intentional pause gives us space to reflect, to be creative, to enjoy life and to resist the constant demand to be productive.

Walden, meanwhile, celebrates the idea of living at a more leisurely pace and with full awareness. Henry David Thoreau, its author, retreats to live alone in the woods as an act of resistance against the speed of society, seeking a more deliberate and meaningful existence. This retreat, according to Han, is crucial to combat the violence inherent in the speed of modern life. By slowing down, we can achieve a deeper connection with ourselves and with nature, creating a space away from the pressure to be constantly productive.

In particular, in the "Sounds" chapter of *Walden* Thoreau meditates on the importance of pausing to listen to the sounds of the natural environment. He argues that these moments of mindfulness take us away from the frenetic speed of human time and bring us closer to natural time, which flows more slowly and deliberately. This observation underscores how the practice of slowing down and focusing on the here and now can free us from the chains of haste and open us to richer, deeper experiences of existence.

Cultivate Silence

Han emphasizes the importance of fostering silence, both within ourselves and in our environment. For him, silence is not just the absence of noise, but a necessary precondition for listening to our own inner voice, engaging in meaningful dialogues with others and capturing the beauty that surrounds us. Furthermore, promoting silence acts as a form of protest against the constant bombardment of noise and distractions that characterize our age, which often hinder our ability to concentrate and reflect deeply.

Henry David Thoreau's *Walden* reflects a parallel quest to simplify life, which involves not only a reduction of material possessions but also the pursuit of physical and inner silence. For Han, this silence that Thoreau seeks and values is crucial; he sees it as a tool to combat the sensory and cognitive overload of modern life, facilitating a space for introspection and true appreciation of the beautiful.

In particular, in the "Solitude" chapter of *Walden* Thoreau extols solitude and silence not as a lack of companionship, but as the opportunity to be fully present with oneself and one's surroundings. This perspective on solitude and silence emphasizes its value not as emptiness, but as a state full of potential for self-knowledge and deep connection with nature. Thoreau and Han agree in considering silence not only as an escape from external noise, but as a path to a more reflective and enriching life, where solitude becomes a rich source of introspection and connection.

Protect Your Privacy

Han and Henry David Thoreau offer critical and insightful perspectives on contemporary society, particularly with regard to transparency and privacy. Han argues that we live in a "transparency society," where total visibility and public scrutiny have become the norm. This transparency, far from being liberating, acts as a control mechanism that infringes on our privacy. Han warns us about the dangers of indiscriminately exposing our lives on social media platforms and being subject to the design and monitoring of algorithms that not only monitor but also shape our behavior.

For his part, Thoreau, in his work *Walden*, celebrates solitude and privacy as essential values for introspection and self-knowledge. Through his experience in nature, living in a cabin away from society, Thoreau highlights the importance of preserving our private sphere in the face of intrusion and constant surveillance, elements that are increasingly prevalent in today's digital environment. The connection between the two thinkers lies in their shared concern for the erosion of privacy in modernity. While Thoreau invites us to protect and value our privacy in the face of external invasions, Han delves into a critique of how digital technologies and the culture of transparency seriously compromise our personal and collective autonomy. In the "Visitors" chapter of *Walden* Thoreau reflects on the importance of selecting how and when we interact with others, highlighting the relevance of safeguarding our personal space and time from unwanted intrusions, an echo of current concerns about how social networks and algorithms impinge on our ability to maintain privacy and control over our own lives. These reflections invite us to critically reconsider our relationship with technology and the culture of transparency, underscoring the imperative need to defend our privacy and intimacy in an increasingly interconnected and observed world.

Embrace Negativity

Han invites us to reflect on a dominant trend in today's society: the compulsion towards constant positivity. We face a social pressure that pushes us to always appear happy, optimistic and successful, a mandate that paradoxically can trigger stress, anxiety and depression when we feel that we do not meet these expectations. According to Han, this insistence on positivity ignores a fundamental dimension of human experience: negativity. The ability to accept aspects of life that are considered negative-pain, failure, grief-is essential, not only because they are unavoidable, but because they offer profound opportunities for learning and personal growth.

Henry David Thoreau, in his solitary wilderness experience recounted in *Walden* also faces challenges and adversity that reflect this negativity. Far from being an obstacle, Thoreau shows that facing these difficulties is an integral part of an authentic life rich in learning. In the chapter "The Ponds," Thoreau not only celebrates the beauty of nature but also suggests we look beyond the surface, to recognize that the true depth of life includes the coexistence of beauty with adversity.

To accept negativity, then, is not to resign ourselves to pessimism, but to adopt a more realistic and comprehensive approach to life. Han and Thoreau teach us that facing and accepting the negative aspects of our existence allows us to better understand our human condition and to find meaning and value in our struggles. This approach not only makes us more resilient but also enriches our life experience, allowing us to grow in a genuine and profound way.

Reclaim Ritual

Han invites us to reconsider the value of rituals in our lives. He sees them as deeply rooted symbolic practices that connect us to essential dimensions of human existence: the sacred, the communal and the historical. Rituals offer us a way to make sense of our existence, allowing us to celebrate significant moments, honor our traditions and transmit our values. Beyond their social or spiritual function, rituals provide us with a respite from the frenzy of modern life, marked by linear and accelerated time, and immerse us in an experience of circular and contemplative time.

In *Walden* Henry David Thoreau illustrates how life can be imbued with simple yet profound rituals that reconnect us with natural rhythms and the seasons. This approach to ritual, as Thoreau demonstrates in preparing his home for winter in the chapter "House-Warming," transcends the merely practical and becomes a celebration of the changing seasons and a deep connection to the cycle of life. This act, though personal and simple, resonates with Han's proposal to seek a return to a more circular and reflective time, where rituals act as an antidote to the linear and accelerated perception of time.

To recover ritual, then, is to rediscover an essential tool for finding meaning and belonging in our lives. It allows us to pause, reflect and connect more deeply with ourselves, with others and with the world around us. In an era defined by speed and efficiency, reintegrating rituals into our daily existence emerges as a vital path to a more balanced and meaningful life.

Value The Different

Han challenges us to reflect on a disturbing feature of contemporary society: its tendency toward uniformity and the elimination of diversity. This "cultural homogenization" not only impoverishes our experience of life, but also blunts the rich dimensions of creativity and dialogue that arise from encounters with the different. For Han, the different is not a barrier, but a bridge to a deeper and more enriching understanding of the world. He encourages us to embrace and value diversity, whether in cultures, perspectives, or ways of life, as a vital source of learning and enrichment.

Henry David Thoreau, in his immersion in nature that he documents in *Walden* celebrates this diversity, finding in it an inexhaustible source of richness and learning. Through his observations and experiences, from tending a bean field to the changing of the seasons, Thoreau shows us how diversity in nature and in human practices opens paths to self-exploration and discovery.

In the chapter "The Bean-Field," Thoreau takes us through his experience growing beans, an act that may seem mundane, but for him becomes a powerful metaphor for life and a reminder of the importance of attending to small differences. This cultivation is not only a means of sustenance; it is a practice that connects Thoreau to the land, the seasons, and the life cycle, allowing him to appreciate the subtle variations in nature and, by extension, in life itself.

Han and Thoreau's vision invites us to question the tendency toward uniformity and to open ourselves to the richness that diversity offers. Recognizing and valuing what is different is essential to fostering a culture of creativity, respect and dialogue, crucial elements for a more understanding and enriched society.

Practice Care

Han presents care as an essential practice, extending it beyond mere personal attention to encompass our environment and the people with whom we share our world. This concept of care goes beyond self-care; it becomes an act of deep love, responsibility and solidarity towards others and our planet. In this vision, care is understood as an ethical and compassionate response to the alienation and heightened individualism that characterize our age, especially in the digital context.

Similarly, Henry David Thoreau, in his work *Walden* embodies this practice of caring not only for oneself but also for the surrounding natural environment. In the chapter "Higher Laws," Thoreau delves into reflection on personal and collective ethics, food and our relationship with nature. This approach to care and respect is manifested in his consideration of all forms of life, promoting harmonious and sustainable coexistence.

Han's proposal, like Thoreau's experience, invites us to adopt a holistic perspective of care. It encourages us to recognize our interconnectedness with others and with the natural world, reminding us of the importance of acting with empathy and consideration. By practicing care in these broad terms, we not only improve our quality of life and that of those around us, but also contribute to the creation of a more sustainable and compassionate world.

Seek Balance

Han raises a pertinent critique of the dynamics of contemporary society, which tends to force us into a state of permanent imbalance. This dynamic manifest itself in the constant pressure to surpass our limits and in the difficulty of finding moments of true rest. Faced with this scenario, Han suggests the search for balance as a solution. This balance refers to the need to harmonize the different facets of our existence: the physical, the mental and the spiritual, as well as achieving coherence between the work, family and personal spheres. Achieving this balance is essential to live a healthy, peaceful and joyful life.

Henry David Thoreau, in his work *Walden* embodies this quest for balance in an exemplary manner. His life reflects a harmony between retreat and community interaction, between work and rest, offering us a model of how to live a balanced life. In the chapter "Economy," Thoreau lays the groundwork for his existence in Walden, illustrating how he seeks to balance his material needs with his spiritual needs, as well as work with leisure time.

Han's perspective, in keeping with Thoreau's experience, invites us to reconsider our priorities and ways of life. He encourages us to find a point of balance that allows us to live more fully and authentically, moving away from the inordinate demands of a performance-focused society. This approach to balance is not only key to a healthy and fulfilling life, but also constitutes an act of resistance against the dehumanizing tendencies of modernity.

Develop Your Critical Thinking

Han urges us to cultivate and develop our critical thinking, understood as the ability to analyze, question and rigorously evaluate both the information we receive and the beliefs we hold. This process of critical reflection is essential for constructing our own judgment, defending our rights and participating actively and consciously in society. Moreover, critical thinking acts as a shield against manipulation, disinformation and alienation, phenomena that are especially prevalent in the digital age.

Henry David Thoreau, in his immersive wilderness experience recounted in *Walden* stands as a model of how critical thinking can be applied to reflect on society, the individual and their interaction. Thoreau's decision to live at Walden Pond is itself an act of social and personal critique, seeking a life that is deliberate and conscious, removed from automatic social pressures and conventions.

In the chapter "Where I Lived, and What I Lived For," Thoreau invites us to question social norms and expectations, promoting a life lived with intention and purpose. Similarly, Han highlights the importance of critical thinking as a vital tool for navigating and resisting the currents of superficiality and manipulation that characterize our digital culture. Developing critical thinking, then, is not just an academic exercise, but a vital practice that enriches our participation in society, affirms our autonomy, and empowers us to live more authentically and consciously.

Be Authentic

Han's invitation to be authentic finds a resonant echo in the "Conclusion" chapter of Henry David Thoreau's Walden. Both texts, although separated by time and context, weave a profound reflection on the importance of authenticity in the life of the individual. Thoreau, in *Walden* not only narrates his experiment in simplified living connected to nature, but also presents a philosophy of life that challenges the social norms and expectations of his time. This philosophy crystallizes in the chapter "Conclusion," where Thoreau distills the essence of his experience and the importance of following one's own path, being true to oneself, and living according to one's own values and desires, beyond the pressures of society.

This call for authenticity, as Thoreau describes it, is a resistance against conformity and homogenization. It suggests that each person has a unique path to travel, one that does not necessarily align with social conventions or the expectations of others. It is a reminder that true satisfaction and fulfillment come from living a life that is authentically our own, not one that has been dictated or unduly influenced by external factors.

Han, in advising us to be authentic, reinforces this message, warning against the dangers of getting lost in the sameness and superficiality that often characterize modern life. For Han, as for Thoreau, authenticity is an act of resistance and a path to personal freedom. He encourages us to recognize and embrace our individuality, our passions, and our inner truths as a means of resisting the forces that seek to homogenize us.

In essence, the "Conclusion" chapter of *Walden* serves as a powerful reminder and source of inspiration for those who seek to live authentically. Thoreau and Han, through their works, offer a shared vision of the importance of staying true to oneself in a world that constantly seeks to shape us. They remind us that in authenticity lies not only our freedom, but also the very essence of what it means to be human.

CONCLUSION: PRESCRIBING WALDEN FOR THE BETTER. PSYCHOSOMATIC HEALTH

The application of Henry David Thoreau's book Walden in bibliotherapy is an exceptional example of how classic literature can serve as a therapeutic tool on the path to self-reflection, self-knowledge and emotional healing. Walden, a work that chronicles Thoreau's experience living in nature, away from the distractions and demands of society, offers profound introspection about life, simplicity, and the importance of living with purpose.

In the context of bibliotherapy, which employs literature as a means of facilitating emotional and mental well-being, Walden presents itself as a rich source of reflections on autonomy, minimalism, and the importance of connecting with the natural environment. Thoreau articulates throughout his work a critique of the complexity and materialism of modern life, promoting a simpler lifestyle focused on the essentials. This perspective may be particularly resonant for those seeking to escape the pressures and constant noise of the contemporary world, offering a literary refuge in which to reflect on their own lives and find peace of mind (Sullivan & Strang, 2002).

Drawing on the evidence from the article on bibliotherapy and using Henry David Thoreau's *Walden* as a basis, here I present to you a therapeutic prescription designed to improve the mental health of patients. This plan focuses on tapping into the themes of introspection, connection with nature, simplicity, and self-sufficiency that Thoreau explores in his work.

The main goals for a Walden prescription would be to (1) Encourage reflection and self-awareness, (2) Stimulate connection with nature, (3) Promote a simpler, more mindful lifestyle, and (4) Develop self-reliance and empowerment.

Thoreau's Walden experience is not only a physical retreat, but also an introspective journey that invites the reader to question his or her own choices and the meaning of happiness. In the search for a purposeful life, Walden serves as a mirror that reflects the reader's concerns, encouraging him or her to contemplate the possibility of a path less traveled, more authentic and in harmony with nature. This reflection can be particularly therapeutic for individuals facing existential crises, depression, or anxiety, as it provides a space to reconsider the priorities and values that guide their lives.

A possible bibliotherapy program based on *Walden* for mental health improvement, inspired by Han's advice, can be divided into two main categories: activities focused on reflection on the book and activities involving concrete actions and changes in real life.

Activities focused on reflecting on the book

a. Practice the art of delay: Reflect on how *Walden* invites a slower, more deliberate life, comparing this to one's own life. Consider how speed affects the ability to think and feel deeply.
b. Cultivate silence: Discuss the importance of both inner and outer silence, as presented in *Walden*. Reflect on how silence contributes to introspection and appreciation of the world.
c. Accepting Negativity: Analyze passages from *Walden* that show Thoreau's acceptance of pain, failure, and negativity. Consider how these aspects are essential to personal growth.
d. Develop critical thinking: Reflect on how Thoreau critiques society and the individual in *Walden*. Discuss the importance of critical thinking in resisting manipulation and superficiality.
e. Being Authentic: Explore the concept of authenticity in *Walden* and how Thoreau lives by his values. Reflect on the importance of being true to ourselves and our values in today's society.

Activities involving concrete actions and changes

a. Stimulate contact with nature: Motivate participants to spend more time outdoors, emulating Thoreau's connection with nature. This can be a concrete action such as organizing walks or moments of observation in nature.
b. Protect your privacy: Take concrete actions to protect the private sphere, such as limiting exposure on social networks or practicing periods of digital disconnection, inspired by the privacy and solitude Thoreau sought in Walden.
c. Reclaim ritual: Implement simple but meaningful rituals in daily life that connect with nature and the seasons, inspired by Thoreau's practices in *Walden*. This could include morning or evening rituals that help us connect with our environment and ourselves.
d. Value what is different: Engage in actions that promote appreciation of diversity and cultural richness. This can translate into exploring different cultures through food, art or literature.
e. Practice mindfulness: Initiate practices of self-care and care for others that reflect a commitment to collective well-being and the environment. Concrete actions may include volunteering in community or environmental initiatives, or simply practicing mindfulness in caring for oneself and loved ones.

f. Seek balance: Conduct a life inventory to assess where a better balance can be found between work, leisure and personal obligations. This could lead to concrete changes in time management and priorities.

Ultimately, adopting *Walden* in bibliotherapy not only offers a doorway to introspection and deep meditation, but also fosters an environment of healing and personal growth through simplicity and connection with nature. This holistic approach to improving psychosomatic health emphasizes the importance of reducing external noise and valuing the essence of our lives. By encouraging individuals to rediscover and realign their core values with everyday practices, *Walden* acts as a beacon of calm in an often tumultuous world. The strength that can be drawn from Thoreau's work is a testament to the enduring power of literature to touch the deepest aspects of being human, guiding us toward a more reflective and ultimately more fulfilling life.

REFERENCES

Berthoud, E., & Elderkin, S. (2013). *The Novel Cure: An A-Z Of Literary Remedies*. Canongate Books.

Burbick, J. (1987). *Thoreau's alternative history: Changing perspectives on nature, culture, and language*. University of Pennsylvania Press. 10.9783/9781512819779

Cain, W. E. (Ed.). (2000). *A historical guide to Henry David Thoreau*. Oxford University Press. 10.1093/oso/9780195138627.001.0001

Channing, W. E. (1902). *Thoreau: The poet-naturalist*. C.E. Goodspeed.

Friedrich, P. (2009). *The Gita within Walden*. SUNY Press.

Furtak, R. A., Ellsworth, J., & Reid, J. D. (Eds.). (2012). *Thoreau's importance for philosophy*. Fordham University Press. 10.5422/fordham/9780823239306.001.0001

Gregory, R. J., Canning, S. S., Lee, T. W., & Wise, J. C. (2004). Cognitive bibliotherapy for depression: A meta-analysis. *Professional Psychology, Research and Practice*, 35(3), 275–280. 10.1037/0735-7028.35.3.275

Han, B. C. (2015). *The burnout society*. Stanford University Press. 10.1515/9780804797504

Han, B. C. (2015). *The transparency society*. Stanford Briefs. 10.1515/9780804797511

Han, B. C. (2017). *In the swarm: Digital prospects*. MIT Press. 10.7551/mitpress/11055.001.0001

Han, B. C. (2017). *Psychopolitics: Neoliberalism and new technologies of power*. Verso Books.

Han, B. C. (2017). *The agony of Eros*. MIT Press. 10.7551/mitpress/11054.001.0001

Han, B. C. (2017). *The scent of time: A philosophical essay on the art of lingering*. Polity Press.

Han, B. C. (2018). *Topology of violence*. MIT Press. 10.7551/mitpress/11056.001.0001

Han, B. C. (2021). *Capitalism and the death drive*. Polity Press.

Han, B. C. (2021). *The palliative society: Pain today*. Polity Press.

Han, B. C. (2022). *Hyperculture: Culture and globalisation*. Polity Press.

Han, B. C. (2022). *Infocracy: Digitization and the crisis of democracy*. Polity Press.

Han, B. C. (2022). *Non-things: Upheaval in the lifeworld*. Polity Press.

Han, B. C. (2022). *The philosophy of Zen Buddhism*. Polity Press.

Harding, W. (1982). *The days of Henry Thoreau: A biography*.

Harding, W., & Bode, C. (Eds.). (1958). *The Correspondence of Henry David Thoreau*. New York University Press.

Hawley, S. W., & Spillman, C. V. (2003). *Literacy and Learning: An Expeditionary Discovery Through Children's Literature*. Scarecrow Press.

Hebert, T. P., & Kent, R. (2000). Nurturing social and emotional development in gifted teenagers through young adult literature. *Roeper Review*, 22(3), 167–172. 10.1080/02783190009554027

Higgins, R. (2017). *Thoreau and the language of trees*. University of California Press. 10.1525/california/9780520294042.001.0001

Krutch, J. W. (1976). *Henry David Thoreau*. Greenwood Press.

Mental Health America. (2023). *The State of Mental Health in America*. Mental Health America. https://www.mhanational.org/issues/state-mental-health-america

Monroy-Fraustro, D., Maldonado-Castellanos, I., Aboites-Molina, M., Rodríguez, S., Sueiras, P., Altamirano-Bustamante, N. F., de Hoyos-Bermea, A., & Altamirano-Bustamante, M. M. (2021). Bibliotherapy as a non-pharmaceutical intervention to enhance mental health in response to the COVID-19 pandemic: A mixed-methods systematic review and bioethical meta-analysis. *Frontiers in Public Health*, 9, 629872. 10.3389/fpubh.2021.62987233796496

National Institute of Mental Health. (2023). *Transforming the understanding and treatment of mental illnesses*. NIMH. https://www.nimh.nih.gov/health/statistics

NextStep Solutions. (2023). *The State of Mental Health in America 2023: Adult Prevalence and Access to Care*. NextStep Solutions. https://www.nssbehavioralhealth.com/nss-blog-the-state-of-mental-health-in-america-2023-adult-prevalence-and-access-to-care/

Ouzts, D. (1991). The emergence of bibliotherapy as a discipline. *Reading Horizons*, 31(3), 199–206.

Richardson, R. D. (1988). *Henry Thoreau: A life of the mind*. University of California Press.

Rossi, W. (2000). Thoreau's Transcendental Ecocentrism. In Schneider, R. J. (Ed.), *Thoreau's*. 10.2307/j.ctt20q20hz.8

Sanborn, F. (1917). *The Life of Henry David Thoreau*. Houghton Mifflin & Co.

Sarah, J. J., & Kevin, R. R. (2008). Bibliotherapy. Practice and research. *School Psychology International*, 29(2).

Sattelmeyer, R. (2000). Depopulation, Deforestation, and the Actual Walden Pond. In Schneider, R. J. (Ed.), *Thoreau's Sense of Place: Essays in American Environmental Writing* (pp. 235–243). University of Iowa Press. 10.2307/j.ctt20q20hz.22

Sullivan, A. K., & Strang, H. R. (2002). Bibliotherapy in the classroom: Using literature to promote the development of emotional intelligence. *Childhood Education*, 79(2), 74–80. 10.1080/00094056.2003.10522773

Tauber, A. J. (2012). Thoreau's Moral Epistemology and Its Contemporary Relevance. In Furtak, R. A. (ed.), *Thoreau's Importance for Philosophy* (pp. 127–142). Fordham University Press. 10.5422/fordham/9780823239306.003.0008

Thoreau, H. D. (1906). *The Writings of Henry D. Thoreau (20 vol.)*. Houghton Mifflin & Co.

Thoreau, H. D. (2008). *Walden*. Oxford University Press. 10.1093/owc/9780199538065.001.0001

Walls, L. D. (1995). *Seeing new worlds: Henry David Thoreau and nineteenth-century natural science*. The University of Wisconsin Press.

Walls, L. D. (2000). Believing in Nature: Wilderness and Wildness in Thoreauvian Science. In Schneider, R. J. (Ed.), *Thoreau's Sense of Place: Essays in American Environmental Writing* (pp. 15–27). University of Iowa Press. 10.2307/j.ctt20q20hz.7

Walls, L. D. (2012). Articulating Huckleberry Cosmos: Thoreau's Moral Ecology of Knowledge. In Furtak, R. A. (Eds.), *Thoreau's Importance for Philosophy* (pp. 91–111). Fordham University Press. 10.5422/fordham/9780823239306.003.0006

Walls, L. D. (2013). Walking West, Gazing East: Planetarity on the Shores of Cape Cod. In Specq, F., (ed.), *Thoreauvian Modernities: Transatlantic Conversations on an American Icon* (pp. 21–42). University of Georgia Press.

Walls, L. D. (2017). *Henry David Thoreau: A Life*. The University of Chicago Press. 10.7208/chicago/9780226344720.001.0001

Chapter 5
Translation, Memory, and Face of the Other in Juan Mayorga's Theatre: Reading as a Commitment

Robert March Tortajada
University of Alicante - IIFV, Spain

ABSTRACT

In this study, the author focuses attention on some theatrical texts written by Juan Mayorga, especially, El traductor de Blumemberg, Himmelweg, La paz perpetua, and La lengua en pedazos in order to observe some influences mainly philosophical, with which the author works in his dramaturgy. In this sense, this studies the concept of translation developed by Walter Benjamin regarding the metaphor of the broken vessel; the act of reading as a non-ending one, thanks to intertextuality, and the face of the Other conceived by Lévinas. On the one hand, we understand memory, reading, listening and silence as a kind of unit, especially, in the authors' historic dramatic plays. On the other hand, we see how Mayorga's writing becomes an endless rewriting.

BOOKS AND READING IN JUAN MAYORGA'S PLAYS

In Juan Mayorga's dramaturgy, the presence of books and references to literature appear continuously, as well as Philosophy does. In this sense, the importance the author offers to words and silence draws an atmosphere where thought, especially the Benjaminian one, becomes a kind of *echo*, a dialectic image in which a text lights the rest of Mayorga's production, as a constellation would. For that reason,

DOI: 10.4018/979-8-3693-4244-2.ch005

the words in his words are like magic, since the author is conscious of how they offer the possibility to name. At the same time, the writer's usage of dramatic words allows us to imagine the other side of things, and then the act of reading links with pleasure, thanks to Mayorga's writing, always in movement, opened to the reader's suture. The reader or the theatrical spectator becomes a type of writer, specifically, because it will be thanks to his reading and to his interpretation that the meaning of the work can be completed.

In this way, the playwright is conscious of the theatre's power. A relationship between the representation of memory and translation can be sometimes seen in his plays. Moreover, the author examines his texts constantly. In fact, he rewrites them again and again. According to Mayorga, any word is crossed by time; and time –as we have heard from him– is the one who finally writes. Memory, reading and listening appear as a kind of unity in most of his plays, where his characters usually show us the strength of their fragilities too. Besides, intertextuality acts as a compass to read his literature. Mayorga's plays wish to be inhabited by the Other. He puts a strain on fiction, just as the ancient did, to establish a dialogue even with the dead, with the intention to speak about our past from a historical or literary perspective, but, of course, because the past can be read from different perspectives, just as the sides of a prism can be seen. However, it does not mean the author is a nostalgic of the past and decides to rewrite his works continuously, it is no like that. In fact, the idea that can be found in Mayorga's texts is the author approach to the past to open a kind of closed door that offers a new point of view for reading, obviously, thanks to the theatre possibilities. If we take, for instance, *Himmelweg*, a dramatic play set in a concentration camp, we observe how it is due to the distribution of the theatrical scenes and the strategies used, and of course by the use of metateatrality, that one of the characters, Gottfried, a Jew, can shout at another one, concretely, a Nazi Commander, which would be a difficult, perhaps impossible, thing to imagine in real life. In other words, it is thanks how the play is structured, but also thanks to the text conceived as a dispositive, that the Jew and the Nazi can rehearse a play inside a play, and then, the prisoner is able to contradict his guard, because of the dramatically words contained in the text. In any case, regardless of whether the work is presented as a device, the final sense, as we have mentioned above, depends on the reader's interpretation.

However, there is another example of the same play that has to do with silence, which belongs to the ending. In this sense, the strategy designed by Mayorga is thought for the reader or the spectator, so both of them can approach the silence, specifically here, that of a world that does not exist, precisely because of horror. Then, in *Himmelweg*'s ending, a young girl called Rebeca, sings a song, while we know her life no longer exists. In other words, we already know that the characters that appear after the first monologue are dead or just alive thanks to fiction. The montage of the entire work goes from the present backwards, and yet, the text is presented as a mechanism in which past presents itself with different time jumps and repetitions. In fact, the present time described is the one of the Second World War:

"Les deja el libreto. El Hombre intenta memorizar sus nuevas frases, Gottfried se dirige a la Niña. Ella está sentada en el suelo, con la cabeza entre las manos y las piernas. A sus pies, tirado, el muñeco. Gottfried acaricia la cabeza de la niña.

Tenemos que seguir esperando un poco más. Tenemos que seguir esperando hasta que ese hombre aparezca. Cuando ese hombre aparezca, coges a Walter y dices: (Toma el muñeco.) «Sé amable, Walter, saluda a este señor.» No sabemos cómo es, ni cuándo va a venir, nadie lo sabe, así que tenemos que estar preparados en cualquier momento. «Sé amable, Walter, saluda a este señor.» Si lo haces bien, volveremos a ver a mamá. Ella va a venir en uno de esos trenes. Si hace os lo que ellos nos piden. No vamos a perder la paciencia, ¿verdad, Rebeca? Lo haremos tantas veces como sea necesario hasta que mamá vuelva, ¿verdad que lo vamos a hacer tantas veces como haga falta? Si tú puedes, yo también podré. Y si yo no pudiese, si yo perdiese la paciencia, tú no la perderías. Tú vas a seguir hasta el final. Por mamá y por mí, si yo pierdo la paciencia. «Sé amable, Walter, saluda a este señor.» Y luego, una canción. Quieren que cantes unacanción.Bueno, no está mal, ¿no?, que nos manden cantar. ¿Te acuerdas de aquella que mamá te cantaba para dormir? Una canción para acabar.

Canta a la Niña la canción. La Niña se pone en pie, coge el muñeco y le canta," (Mayorga 2015, 332)

In an example like this, and in many others, Juan Mayorga deals with the traumatic wounds of history, but it does not mean his theatre does therapy with the spectator or the reader. He presents us the possibility of reading as a tool. In other words, we cannot affirm than reading heals, but, for sure, that possibility can happen. In any case, the author's main goal is to make the silence of those who are no longer here resonate, a matter in which he invests not only in his most profound theatre, but in those works in which he offers us his different views of what theatre is like for him or, at least, where the good theater should go.

EL TRADUCTOR DE BLUMEMBERG, A KIND OF BABEL'S TOWER

In our opinion, *El traductor de Blumemberg* is one of his most interesting dramatic theatrical plays. In fact, Juan Mayorga centred his creative capacity in a huge tension, which is presented in interspersed scenes that take place either in the compartment of a train without a driver that runs through Europe, or in a basement. An impossible journey, according to César Oliva's point of view, that serves Mayorga to denounce fascism (2004: 248-249). The playwright presents the possibilities of stopping that train. Ultimately, *El traductor de Blumemberg*'s intention is to break the *continuum* of history, the one that Walter Benjamin talks about offering the present as a messianic time, full and profane, just as Reyes Mate (2009) would say, to fill the needs of the fallen ones. And Mayorga does it by taking into account all the possibilities of language he knows:

Calderón: Tiene que ser jodido, usted perdone. Trabajar de representante en esas condiciones. ¿O no es usted ciego al ciento por ciento? (Calderón toma una de las pistolas, la apunta contra Blumemberg. Éste no reacciona.) Y ahora va a...

Blumemberg: Berlin.

Calderón: Qué casualidad. Yo también. ¿Ya conoce el jodido lugar?

Blumemberg: Pas encore.

Calderón: Yo tampoco. Dicen que es guapo, sobre todo el Este. Supongo que no puede dejar indiferente a un francés. ¿Cuántas veces les han frito el país?

Blumemberg: Trois ou quatre.

Calderón: Gente siniestra esos alemanes. Son como robots con deseo. Yo los defino así.

Blumemberg: Des robots désirants?

Calderón: Exacto. Un alemán es un robot que conoce el deseo. No crea que me hace gracia. Berlín, digo. Un trabajo bien pagado, que si no... (Aparta un poco la cortina.) Hace un día magníf...

Blumemberg: (Interrumpiéndole.) S'il vous plait (Mayorga 2014: 114-115).

The attention Mayorga dedicates to Walter Benjamin does not end there, it expands itself to a complex relationship, concretely, the one that links Blumemberg and Calderón, the two characters of *El traductor de Blumemberg*. The first one acts as a blind, whereas the second one, at least at the very beginning, presents himself as the future translator of a book that does not exist –the book of the Evil–, or it only does thanks to memory, because it could be written by a dictation. Besides, in a certain way, dictation is also present in different Mayorga's plays, like *Animales nocturnos*, where Hombre Bajo asks Hombre Alto, a foreigner, to write a diary; in *Cartas de amor a Stalin,* where the Russian dictator dictates the letters to Bulgákov that he must write to fulfil his wishes: to leave his country. Or even in *Silencio*, but, of course, from a very different point of view. In this case, through a kind of translation in which the author himself takes the speech he pronounced in his RAE's admission on May 19, 2019, and transfers it into a dramatic text that has been performed by Blanca Portillo. Both the RAE's speech and the theatrical play share the same title. In any case, in *Cartas de amor a Stalin*:

Bulgákov: (*Distante.*) No lo había visto. No sabía que estaba usted aquí.

Stalin: ¿No te alegras de verme?

Bulgákov: Es sólo que he pasado una mala noche. ¿No podríamos tomarnos un día de descanso?

Stalin: ¿Un día de descanso, con todo lo que tenemos que hacer? (Pone ante Bulgákov la pluma y el papel.) ¿Por dónde íbamos? Léeme por dónde íbamos.

Bulgákov: «La respuesta que dio a Eugueni Zamiatin me permite albergar la esperanza de que…».

Stalin: Quita «esperanza». Pon «certeza». ¿Cómo queda?

Bulgákov: «… me permite albergar la esperanza de que también yo seré escuchado».

(Mayorga 2015, 245).

However, as regards *Silencio*, we offer two different fragments of texts. The first one, in which intertextuality is presented and «silence» is understood as a knot. However, the second one, about the dramatic ending in which silence must be assumed by the reader or the spectator, or even by the hearer, in the case of those who attended Mayorga's speech at RAE. The first one:

No hay tragedia sin silencio, pero en ninguna este ocupa el centro como en Antígona, donde se representa el antagonismo entre la voz del tirano y todas las demás, cuyo rumor la heroína dará a oír a costa de su vida. Por eso, la escena más reveladora sobre el sentido de la pieza es una en la que su protagonista no aparece: el encuentro de Creonte y Hemón. Se trata de un diálogo en que cada palabra es agónica, palabra de combate, y donde el lenguaje es medio y objeto del conflicto; el cual plantea Creonte cuando ve acercarse al menor de sus hijos y prometido de Antígona, condenada a muerte por haber enterrado a su hermano Polinices y –esto es esencial- haber dado publicidad a ese acto (Mayorga 2022, 28-29).

The second one:

Yo siento ahora la tentación de fingir un blanco. Tentación de fingir que he olvidado lo que no nunca he sabido. Pero más vale que simplemente me calle. No abusaré más de la vanidad de la palabra y de su paciencia. Es un momento de liberarles de su silencio y de guardarlo. Muchas gracias (Mayorga 2002: 46).

As we have already seen, in *El Traductor de Blumemberg,* at the time the train goes on, Blumemberg speaks a different language from the one is spoken in each country that he visits without leaving the train. Mayorga invites the reader to actively pay attention, and gives us the possibility, but also the difficulty, to come into the translation's world, whether we understand what Blumemberg transmits or we finally get the meaning of Silesius' replies. According to Claire Spooner, our author's dramaturgy presents «une opacité qui voile la réalité […] et qui en réleve en même des aspects nouveau» (Spooner 2013, 112). Thus, as the playwright confesses to the researcher, *El traductor de Blumemberg* presents itself as Babel: «un tren que atraviesa lenguas, tradiciones, que atraviesa el lenguaje [...] el viaje hacia Berlín, y el viaje de un hombre a otro. Entonces el viaje en tren dura tanto cuanto es necesario para que se produzca esta transmisión» (Spooner 2013, 112).

La lengua propia se alumbra a la sombra de la que no comunica; se torna otro lenguaje (distinto de sí mismo, o por fin él mismo, nuevo otra vez después de tanto usarlo); de modo que ninguna de sus palabras pase desapercibida; porque ninguna dejará de ser traducida, salvada de otro modo, en escena [...] Varios viajes constituyen la obra: el viaje en que Blumemberg regresa a Berlín; el viaje en que el traductor descubre esa ciudad; el viaje del fascismo, que cambia de lengua... Pero el viaje principal se desarrolla entre el alma de Blumemberg y el alma de su traductor. Ni Blumemberg ni el traductor protagonizan El traductor de Blumemberg; el protagonista es el «de» que los vincula y los separa: el túnel por el que transitan sus imágenes como entre dos espejos, cada uno de los cuales refleja al opuesto hasta que del reflejo infinito resulta no lo idéntico, sino precisamente lo otro (Spooner 2013, 497-498).

Indeed, the author proposes a dramatic game in which he considers communication and language in order to establish a reflection on its reverse, but also to suggest the uncomfortable place of thinking about how evil would not have stopped throughout history: the will by which Calderón translates the words Blumemberg can remember, but just little by little, phrase by phrase: «Satz für Satz». In *El traductor de Blumemberg* translation does not come from a book, but from a character's memory. The way that exists from translation to betrayal presented in the well-known expression *traduttore traditore.*

Furioso, Blumemberg se pone la pierna y se viste. Calderón saca la máquina de escribir.

Calderón: Bien. ¿Dónde está el libro?

Blumemberg: «Der Feind ist unsere einzige Frage als Gestalt».

Calderón: ¿Perdón?

Blumemberg: Der erste Satz.

Calderón: ¿La primera frase?

Blumemberg: Es wird so gemacht werden: Satz für Satz.

Calderón: Acostumbro leer el libro entero antes de traducir una pala...

Blumemberg: (Interrumpiéndole, haciéndole gesto de que escuche un ruido.) Folgt ein Wagen den Zug?

Calderón: (Mirando por la ventana.) No, no nos sigue ningún automóvil.

(Blumemberg cierra la ventana.) Le decía que sólo cuando la contemplo como un todo, sólo entonces puedo traer la obra a mi idioma. Hágame el favor. (Tiende la mano, como pidiendo el libro.)

Blumemberg: Ich wieder hole: «Der Feind ist unsere einzige Frage als Gestalt».

Calderón: Está bien, si cree que es lo justo, tampoco usted lo leyó entero antes de escribirlo. Lo haré frase a frase. ¿Ni siquiera me dejará verlo por fuera?

Blumemberg: Du siehstes jetzt (Mayorga 2015, 124).

THE BENJAMINIAN BROKEN VESSEL AS A SAMPLE OF TRANSLATION

For Walter Benjamin irony resides in any kind of translation, at least, when paying attention to how the aura moves from the original to a more definitive linguistic text: «puesto que de él ya no es posible trasladarlo, valiéndose de otra traducción y sólo es posible elevarlo de nuevo a otras regiones de dicho ámbito sin salir de él» (Benjamin 1971, 136). The philosopher from the Frankfurt School differentiates between the translator and the literary writer, which, in turn, in our opinion, has a relation to the kind of *echo* we have already mentioned. Along these lines, the figure of translator would approach his activity in order to enter the original, looking for that *echo* in each place, the reflection that unites every translation to the language of the origin. However, a different matter arises if we look to the relationship between the literary writer and the playwright, and in Mayorga's case, we cannot forget that being a playwright he thinks of himself as a cartographer (March 2019, Mayorga 2016, 325-335; 2022, 59), especially, from his theatrical work *El cartógrafo*.

Furthermore, if we consider *Himmelweg*'s creative process, we can say that Mayorga acts as a translator, for sure because he created his poetics having in mind *Alguien vivo pasa*, but also considering a conference he heard dedicated to Claude Lanzmann, the French director of the amazing *Shoa* (1995). In any case, as a writer, Mayorga distances himself from writing a play of historicist temptation.

Juan Mayorga, si bien consultó el texto de Lanzmann, se interesó por aquello que en sí le despertó complejidad en favor de la teatralización: el artificio y la figura de un Delegado y de un Comandante que no dejan de interpelar al público de hoy, al de cada representación. O lo que es lo mismo, una poética que dejaría de lado el teatro historicista en busca de una actualización, en este caso, a través de una palabra que haga resonar el silencio. Ahora bien, entre la mirada de Lanzmann y la de Mayorga –la verdad buscada por Lanzmann en la figura inabarcable del testigo y la mirada por la ficción por parte de Mayorga– se genera una distancia, un vuelo creativo. Es decir, las estrategias dramatúrgicas que Mayorga traduce en otro tipo de interpelación con tal de desestabilizar al lector-espectador a la par que sumergirlo en un mundo ficcionalizado (March 2014, 28).

There is another interesting aspect we would like to convey here, because it can help us understand both translation and the reflection which Mayorga invites us to by reading *El Traductor de Blumemberg*. We talk about the Benjamin's metaphor of the broken vessel thanks to which the philosopher establishes his idea about what a translator does, aspect that, for us, Mayorga considers in his writing.

Walter Benjamin compared translation to the intention of putting together the fragments of a broken vessel, so that the pieces -the details- could fit together even if inexactly. For this reason, instead of identifying the translation itself with the original meaning, the philosopher thinks it is preferable to reconstitute the smallest details, which finally are those a person has in his own language. Then, both languages –the original and the translated one– could be recognized as fragments of a higher language (Benjamin 1971, 139). If we understand properly, Walter Benjamin seems to tell us that access to every meaning is perhaps the one of its impossibility: the sum of singularities to construct new interpretations could not be, at least, immediately translatable, and, at the same time, that immediately translatable meaning becomes the most important meaning to translate (Benjamin 1971, 139). Moreover, this thought connects with that of Giorgio Agamben (2010), when impossibility of experience appears where communication is prevented by its own communicability.

Todos los seres vivos están en lo abierto, se manifiestan y resplandecen en su apariencia. Pero sólo el hombre quiere apropiarse de esta apertura, aferrar la propia imagen, el propio ser manifiesto. El lenguaje es esta apropiación, que trasforma la naturaleza en rostro. [...] La revelación del rostro es revelación del lenguaje mismo. Precisamente por eso no tiene ningún contenido real, no dice la verdad sobre tal o cual aspecto del hombre o del mundo: es sólo apertura, sólo comunicabilidad. Caminar en la luz del rostro significa ser esta apertura, padecerla (Agamben 2010, 79).

We consider Mayorga's plays act, especially in *El traductor de Blumemberg,* in a way as the pieces of Benjamin's vessel do too. In any case, later we will return to the idea of the face presented by Agamben, specifically, based on Lévinas' postulates (1974).

READING AND TRANSLATION AS A COMMITMENT

In one of the final passages of *Los Hundidos y los salvados,* Primo Levi goes so far as to speak of translation as a synonym of commitment. This concept also appears in Joan-Carles Mèlich's *La lección de Auschwitz,* where he talks about how the anthropology of approaches would be the contrary of that of the distance: neighborhood, multilingualism and the demand of the other, compared to monolingualism and its effectiveness (Mèlich 2004, 15). Taking these parameters into account, Mèlich studies the reading act, and his conclusions, if we are not wrong, are similar to those we have expressed thanks to Walter Benjamin's point of view and, by extension, with the idea of responsibility and memory presented in Mayorga's theatre:

El acogimiento de una palabra que viene de lejos, es la respuesta a una demanda, a la apelación de un ausente. [...] la lección es el aprendizaje de un acontecimiento en la lectura de un relato. [...] «Dar una lección» quiere decir dar a leer y, por lo tanto, abrir la interpretación, mantener viva la pregunta, la lectura infinita, el interrogante, el deseo (Mèlich 2004, 21).

As we see it, the idea developed by Joan Carles Mèlich connects with the experience Juan Mayorga constructs through fiction: «ser capaz de transmitir la experiencia del otro, el recuerdo de los otros, y volver a leer y leer, y a releer, infinitamente» (Mèlich 2004, 32). Mèlich talks about the experience of evil as a place, and, aware of the danger of sacralising Auschwitz, considers ethics as the philosophical discipline that must come in regarding responsibility, without forgetting that memory also gives rise to oblivion.

En toda rememoración existe un trabajo de recuperar el pasado pero siempre filtrado por el olvido, porque el olvido es una de las formas de la finitud humana. Pretender mantener vivo un recuerdo sin la erosión del olvido no solo es un modo de sacralizarlo sino también de canonizarlo, de inmunizarlo [...] «Auschwitz» ha sido sacralizado hasta tal punto que es imposible extraer una lección de este acontecimiento, porque para que algo pueda convertirse en lección es necesaria su actualización, es decir, que el acontecimiento no permanezca inmóvil en su pasado, en su singularidad, sino que sea posible convertirlo en presente y en futuro (Mèlich 2004, 32).

A dialectical update, irremediably linked to the idea of translation, allows Juan Mayorga to offer a kind of writing where damage cannot be undone. Now, that does not mean that the playwright does not try to heal it, as happens in *Himmelweg*, where, as we have already said, the dramatic play sets in a concentration camp with some connections with Lanzman's *Alguien vivo pasa*, above all, because of a member of the Red Cross who visited the camp and did not discover what the Nazis were really doing there, due to the fact that everything was prepared as a disguise, that Juan Mayorga transformed into a theatrical play. Indeed, the author invites us to become translators, reading that *echo*, the play's silence: «El teatro arte del cuerpo, puede hacer visible su ausencia. El teatro, arte de la memoria, puede hacer sensible el olvido» (García Barrientos 2011, 42). Regarding the monologue's goal, and more precisely, silence, in De la Parra's opinion:

> *Hay que escribirlo pensando en que no se podría hacer otra cosa que decir eso, que es lo único posible, que hablar es un acto fatal, que se corre un peligro inminente. Eso es lo más bello del monólogo. De tanto hablar convierte sus silencios en manantiales solares, rayos de luz que atraviesan la caverna. Cada silencio debe oler a peligro, a dolor infinito, a lento movimiento de un animal malherido. Hasta el del comediante debe dejar que la risa quede suspendida en el aire. Debe entrenar el peligro del silencio (De la Parra 2010, 21).*

In fact, we talk about a political poetics of absence (March and Martínez, 2011), where Mayorga conceives his writing as open as possible, but ready for the non-negotiable. According to Josep Lluís Sirera, a theatrical word for a stage where memory does not belong to any past.

> *Els records no són només d'experiències viscudes, sinó també de les empremtes que altres fets han deixat en nosaltres a través de múltiples mecanismes de transmissió, en especial mitjançant un procediment sovint no menyspreat sinó oblidat: la transmissió de les emocions... El teatre sí pot... fer-nos viure i fer-nos sentir el que uns altres van viure i sentir al seu moment: el passat efectivament viscut dels personatges que, així, es fan una mica (o un molt) nosaltres mateixos... Una opció que en definitiva, recupera la història (tal com s'entén a hores d'ara, és clar) com a matèria teatral i posa al descobert una cosa que als setanta potser no es va saber explotar com calia: la seva potència dramàtica a partir de l'interior mateix dels personatges (Sirera 2005, 45-51).*

LOOKING FOR ANOTHER TYPE OF HUMANISM: THE FACE OF THE OTHER

In relation to translation, but mostly about memory, we think of *Cartas de amor a Stalin* or *El cartógrafo*, where Mayorga narrows down the distance between us –the spectators–, where the wounds, the own wounds, look for and care for the others' wounds (March and Martínez 2011: 126) And, however, if we return to the idea of reading established by Mèlich, there is still another nuance that can be equated again as regards Benjaminian's metaphor of translation: the face of the Other established by Lévinas (1974). This image brings us closer to Mayorga's writing, where the playwright, like a poet does, knows we are crossed by time, and, as Lévinas thinks, time is the other. Memory needs time and, for Juan Mayorga, «el tiempo lee, el tiempo reescribe, subraya, tacha» (Vilar & Artesero 2010, 5). However, a theatrical text is full of holes, gaps, and «el texto teatral sabe cosas que el autor no sabe» (Vilar & Artesero 2010, 5).

Emmanuel Lévinas talks about experience as meaning. He questions sameness, looking for an approach to others in openness. He wonders how one is responsible for the other, for his demands. And for Lévinas this is how the being is discharged from itself, and, in this way, he understands that the concordances of the representation of the present are disarranged to, thus, embark on the meeting of the otherness of the neighbour: «ese hueco de no lugar en el que el rostro se ausenta ya sin promesa de retorno y resurrección» (Lévinas 1974: 13-14). In this sense, for us, that meaning is close to Juan Mayorga's theatre, at least, if we read it from a political point of view:

> *El sujeto que está presente frente al ser para «recibir el reflejo», está también del lado del ser para realizar la reunión. Esta ubicuidad es la encarnación misma, la maravilla del cuerpo humano. [...] Pero es el sujeto encarnado el que, reuniendo al ser, va a levantar el telón. El espectador es actor. La visión no se reduce a la recepción del espectáculo; simultáneamente, opera en el seno del espectáculo que recibe (Lévinas 1974, 28).*

Juan Mayorga's theatre coincides with the thought the Lithuanian philosopher developed in *Humanismo de otro hombre,* where criticism links together to any utopia. Emmanuel Lévinas desires a future where listening to others can be possible. And we relate that idea to the point Juan Mayorga thinks there is nothing neutral in theatre, as there is not in a map's drawing, even if we talk about it as a metaphor. In other words, in theatre, metaphor becomes also a political act, as reading and the approach to knowledge is. In this sense, metaphor relates itself with true like in Friedrich Nietzsche's philosophy:

Una hueste en movimiento de metáforas, metonimias, antropomorfismos, en resumidas cuentas, una suma de relaciones humanas que han sido realzadas, extrapoladas y adornadas poética y retóricamente y que, después de un prolongado uso, un pueblo considera firmes, canónicas y vinculantes; las verdades son ilusiones de las que se ha olvidado que lo son; metáforas que se han vuelto gastadas y sin fuerza sensible, monedas que han perdido su troquelado y no son ahora ya consideradas moneda sino como metal (Nietzsche 1980, 9-10)

Lévinas talks about how is in the face of the Other, the visage, where representation «se resiste de tal forma que ni su resistencia se convierte en contenido de conciencia» (Lévinas 1974: 69). In fact, in *Razón del teatro* –the speech Mayorga read in the possession of his place in the Sección de Arquitectura y Bellas Artes (Real Academia de Doctores de España)– there is an especial mention to the Emmanuel Lévinas' thought, which the playwright adopts in his reflection on theatre:

En el escenario todo lo informativo ha de ser poética. Distancia y rodeo. Elipse. En el escenario todo es inmediatamente metáfora. Cada acción, cada objeto es metáfora. Lo es cada palabra. Pero la metáfora, enseña Lévinas, no es una desviación del lenguaje, sino su centro: el lenguaje es metáfora, desplazamiento que crea sentido. Entonces, en el escenario la palabra es doblemente metáfora. En el escenario, el silencio es metáfora. Dice por ejemplo, soledad (Mayorga 2022, 60).

REWRITING AS A WAY OF WRITING AND INTERTEXTUALITY AS A NON-ENDING READING

As we have noted previously, Juan Mayorga consciously subjects his texts to constant rewriting from the very beginning of his career as a playwright (March 2014, 377). In *Siete hombres buenos*, his first play, or even in *El jardín quemado,* the playwright had applied some revisions, to actualize a «realidad enrevesada», specifically, to rewrite about memories, but not considering them as simple phantasmagorias or not only like that, but understanding memory as a kind of inheritance (Guzman 2010: 89-94). Even, understanding it, we insist again, as a kind of guide or compass with which to delve deeper into the reading of Juan Mayorga's theater.

Although we cannot now pay attention to all the pieces that the author has rewritten, there are different aspects that we would be interested in bringing up, since they help us address again everything described above regarding translation, because, in our opinion, the author himself becomes a translator of his own work, at least, under the Benjaminian postulates we have exposed. Now, the rewritings we will refer to below have references or influences from other texts and other authors. In fact, sometimes there is even a kind of game that, as a mirror, shows different relationships between the texts, as for example occurs between *581 mapas* and *El cartógrafo* (March 2019, 240-251). In any case, what it is really interesting is the way Mayorga thinks how the dramatic writing can become a map, and, of course how this can string it together with hope, as the Anciano tells his granddaughter in *El cartógrafo*:

Anciano: Colores, puntos, flechas, nos vale cualquier signo con tal de que hable claro. El mapa debe hablar a primera vista. No lo hacemos para nosotros, sino para alguien que algún día lo mirará, quizá dentro de mil años. ¿Qué queremos que él vea? Ahí aparece la cuestión de la escala. Las cosas importantes sólo se ven a pequeña escala. Dos ejércitos a punto de entrar en combate: es fácil representar el número de soldados, su ubicación, su armamento… Pero ¿y las razones de unos y otros para morir?, ¿y el valor y el miedo de un soldado? Es fácil dibujar una calle, pero su olor, sus sonidos, un instante de vida en esa calle… Vamos a empezar por Nowolipie. Cuando lleguemos a la esquina de Smocza, vamos a torcer a la derecha (Mayorga 2015, 615).

La paz perpetua takes us directly to the Kantian text, where the philosopher of the Illustration refers to peace that can only be found in the cemetery, and, little by little, he thinks how countries can relate to each other in order to avoid wars, something that today would take place through trade relations. However, the issue that interests us here goes further, since the plot of the play presents three dogs that have to compete to see which of them is able to get a man's collar. In other words, they must discover who is a friend and who is not. However, at the end, one of the dogs, Emmanuel (a German shepherd), thanks to his morality, but also due to his idea of God, dies without any resistance. As far as we know, this play has had at least three rewritings, and has been published in different media with some differences, especially in relation to the ending. For example, in the version the author brings together his theatre (*Teatro 1989-2014*):

Enmanuel: Déjeme habar con ese hombre. Encontraré las palabras.

Humano: ¿Cuántas vidas está dispuesto a sacrificar a sus palabras? Inocentes como Isabel. Isabel. Isabel estaría viva si hubiéramos sabido que el peligro estaba allí, esperándola. Usted no vio el peligro a tiempo. ¿En qué estaba pensando, mientas Isabel se acerca a la muerte? Piense en ella, Enmanuel.

Enmanuel: No dejo de pensar en ti. Sé que a ti te daría vergüenza. Tú sentirías vergüenza.

Humano: Kant se avergonzaría de usted. Kant estaría a nuestro lado. Trabajamos para que todos puedan leer a Kant, pensar en libertad, vivir en libertad. Pero la libertad tiene un precio. Ese precio lo pagamos nosotros, en nuestros corazones. Y lo seguiremos pagando hasta que llegue la paz. Al mundo y a nuestros corazones. Es nuestro sueño: la paz perpetua.

Hace una señal a John-John y a Odín, que van hacía la puerta B. Pero Enmanuel les cierra el paso, protegiendo la puerta. John-John y Odín amenazan a Emmanuel, que no cede. John-John y Odín atacan a Enmanuel. Enmanuel muere (Mayorga 2014, 544-545).

However, in *La Lengua en Pedazos*, there is a very interesting intertextual aspect. We talk about the relationship the author establishes with *Los Hermanos Karamazov*, by Dostoievski, specifically, as far as the chapter of *El Gran Inquisidor* is concerned, where Iván tells Alyosha about Jesus Christ's appearance in the 16th century Seville.

El viejo querría que el otro le dijera algo aunque fuese amargo y terrible. Él, de pronto, sin decir una palabra, se le acerca y le besa dulcemente los exangües labios nonagenarios. Esta es toda mi respuesta. El viejo estremece, algo tiembla en los dos extremos de sus labios; se dirige a la puerta, la abre y dice: «Vete y no vuelvas más... no vuelvas nunca... ¡nunca, nunca!». Y le deja salir a las «oscuras plazas y calles de la ciudad». El prisionero se va. -¿Y el viejo? -El beso le quema el corazón, pero el viejo persiste en su idea. -¿Y tú con él? ¿También tú?- preguntó con amargura Aliosha (Dostoievski 2010: 46).

Although the story does not tend to be wasted and it has become one of the best-known passages of the Russian novelist, what interests us here is, on the one hand, to consider the setting of the play and, on the other, the *translation* Juan Mayorga carries out. In this sense, if Iván's story refers to the time of the Spanish Inquisition, that context is also drawn in Mayorga's piece, but not in relation to the Christ's coming or the kiss that Jesus gives to the inquisitor, but through the dialogue Saint Teresa of Jesus (named just Teresa in Juan Mayorga's play) maintains with her Inquisitor. In other words, how imagination takes shape in the convent of San José, in a kitchen, where, at the very end, the impotent religious man cannot condemn the woman.

Teresa: Que dudo, decís. Que dudo cada instante. Si miro esta casa, me da contento haberlo contentado. No por lo que yo haya hecho, pues solo en su poder se puede, sino porque me es regalo que me haya tomado por instrumento. Mas al poco viene el demonio a revolverme. Dice, riendo, que todo ha sido astucia suya para robarme el alma. La oración de años la quita mi enemiga de un soplo. La fe queda suspendida y yo sin fuerza para defenderme de sus golpes, y en el alma la oscuridad más honde. Así es esta vida de miserable, no hay contento sin mudanza. Tan pronto no me cambiara por ninguna como no sé qué hacer de mí. Y el único que podría socorrerme, ahora se me oculta. Dios se esconde del alma y hace al alma no saber de sí. ¿Dónde estás? ¿Por qué me dejas sola? ¿O es que estuve sola siempre? ¿Quién soy, si siempre estuve sola? Dudo, sí, dudo cada instante. Pero siempre podrá el ángel Bueno más que el malo. Siempre acaba venciendo el ángel del Señor. Lo veo a mi izquierda pequeño, el rostro que hunde en mi corazón. Es tan grande el dolor que me hace dar quejidos. Dolor del espíritu que corta el cuerpo. Y la lengua, en pedazos, se niega a dar palabras. Sólo da gemidos, porque más no puede. Es gran pena, pero tan dulce que no hay deleite que más contento dé. Dios aprieta al alma con abrazo que nunca querría salir de él. Cautiva de quien ama, consciente el alma que se la encarcele. Y no anhela sin la muerte, que solo en ella podría gozar su bien. Ni puede la palabra recoger tanto amor, pues, como fuego que arde demasiado, no cabe a la palabra contener la llama. Se levanta en el alma un vuelo porque, loca, no ve diferencia a Dios y habla desatinos. La lengua está en pedazos y es solo el amor el que habla. Pero nadie puede hablar de ellos. Es mejor no decir más.

Silencio. Teresa corta cebolla. El Inquisidor sale (Mayorga 2014: 571-572).

CONCLUSION

When we approach Juan Mayorga's plays we have the feeling we go back to school, but one where things are not in their place and we are the ones we have to construct the meaning. However, Mayorga's writing does not present like a mess, it is the opposite, but the task is not easy. His plays are in motion, neither they are photographs nor they want to be. He would like to present them as a possible history, for instance, like the photo that no photographer could capture.

Memory, reading and listening appear as a possible unity, thanks to intertextuality and, of course, bearing in mind that content and form cannot coincide perfectly, as it happens in life. However, it does not mean that Mayorga's plays and thoughts do not try to look for a kind of map in which that realization can occur, at least for a while. In fact, his writing offers us to think about a fairer, more habitable world: to think about the origin, the words, the power of words; and about silence, translation, reading and the other's wounds.

Juan Mayorga's theatre invites us to question whether we are the true protagonists of our life, the true actors, or if our words are written by others. His theatre is that of the conflict of his characters: our conflict. Their problems are ours: violence, law, terrorism, torture, threat, horror, and the perversion of words. Nevertheless, in his theatre, there is still room for hope, although this, as Juan Mayorga once told us, is not for us, but for the ones who will come. A hope like the playwright desires for Rebeca, thanks to the song she sings in the concentration camp.

In most of Mayorga's plays memory presents itself as a guide to read, almost, the complete author's dramaturgy. Memory, but also silence (that which the reader-spectator has to give meaning), appears as a network that takes us to other places. In his dramaturgy, Juan Mayorga pays attention to the same concerns to which he has dedicated his study as a researcher. Walter Benjamin's thoughts are palpable. The idea of translation is fundamental. It allows the playwright to get closer to the origin, to the authenticity. When Juan Mayorga writes has in mind to do it to each spectator, just to build a present, so the pieces of the broken vessel could approach each other, if not to heal the wounds of our past, at least to evoke a silence that can attempt to do so.

REFERENCES

Agamben, G. (2010). *Medios sin fin. Notas sobre política*. Pre-textos.

Benjamin, W. (1971). *«La tarea del traductor». AngelusNovus*. La Gaya Ciencia.

Dostoievski, F. (2010). *El gran inquisidor y otros cuentos*. Siruela.

García Barrientos, J. L. (2011). El Holocausto en el teatro de Juan Mayorga. M. Brizuela (ed.), *Un espejo que se despliega. El teatro de Juan Mayorga*. Universidad Nacional de Córdoba, Argentina.

Guzmán. (2010). Memoria y fantasía de la guerra civil española en *Siete hombres buenos* y *El jardín quemado* de Juan Mayorga. *Estreno*, 36(2), 82–97.

Lévinas, E. (1974). *Humanismo del otro hombre*. Siglo XXI.

March, R. (2014). *Memoria y desmemoria, pensamiento y poética en la dramaturgia de Juan Mayorga*. [Tesis Doctoral, Universitat de València].

March, R. (2019). La elipse, una figura para leer su dramaturgia. In Puertas, D. (Ed.), *Poliedro. Acerca de Juan Mayorga*. Antígona-Serie de Estudios Teatrales RESAD.

March, R. & Martínez, M. Á. (2012). Poéticas de la ausencia en *El cartógrafo. Varsovia. Stichomythia, 13.*

Mate, R. (2009). Medianoche en la historia. Comentarios a las tesis de Walter Benjamín. In *Sobre el concepto de historia*. Ed. Trotta.

Mayorga, J. (2009). *Teatro para minutos*. Ñaque editora.

Mayorga, J. (2015). *Teatro 1989-2014*. Ediciones La uña rota.

Mayorga, J. (2016). *Elipses*. Ediciones La uña rota.

Mayorga, J. (2022). *Silencio. Razón del teatro*. Ediciones La uña rota.

Mèlich, J. C. (2004). *La lección de Auschwitz*. Herder.

Nietzsche, F. (1980). Sobre verdad y mentira en sentido extramoral, Teorema. Levi, P. (2010). *Trilogía de Auschwitz*. Aleph Editores. Lévinas, E. (1974). *El humanismo del otro hombre*. Siglo XXI.

Oliva, C. (2004). *La última escena (Teatro español de 1975 a nuestros días)*. Cátedra.

Sirera, J. L. (2005). *«La memòria no té passat (Per a una contextualització del teatre històric català actual)». I Simposi Internacional sobre Teatre Català Contemporani (de la transició a l'actualitat)*. Diputació de Barcelona-Institut del Teatre.

Spooner, C. (2013). *Le théatre de Juan Mayorga: de la scèneau monde à travers le prisme du langage*. [Thèse doctorale de l'Université de Toulouse].

Vilar, R. & Artesero, S. (2010). Conversación con Juan Mayorga. *Pausa,* 32.

Chapter 6
Educational, Cultural, and Social Conditioning:
The Role of Education and Pedagogy in Human Emancipation

Giorgio Crescenza
https://orcid.org/0000-0001-6704-8314
Università degli Studi della Tuscia, Italy

ABSTRACT

The chapter proposes a critical analysis of educational discourses and practices related to gender emancipation and the education of the younger generation. Through the centuries, it highlights how male chauvinist principles and a distorted view of sexuality, influenced by theology and morality, dominated women's education. The need for a profound change in the way these issues are dealt with is emphasised through conscious education that promotes mutual respect and human emancipation. Current projects, aimed at fighting gender-based violence and hatred, are also discussed by underlining the importance of a transversal and inclusive educational approach that actively involves families, communities and institutions. Finally, the debate is raised on the need for greater autonomy of schools in addressing these issues, instead of adopting projects imposed from above, in order to foster a real cultural transformation towards gender equality and respect for human relations.

DOI: 10.4018/979-8-3693-4244-2.ch006

INTRODUCTION: THE WEIGHT OF CONDITIONING

One issue is certain: the primary problem is not the emancipation of women, but the emancipation of men, indeed.

The male chauvinist principles of women's education are mainly expressed in the negative: "woman shall not read, woman shall not write, woman shall not leave the house, woman shall not dare to etc., etc." or their equivalents: "woman shall obey, woman shall work, woman shall pray, woman shall love chastely etc.". What meaning can there be in all these and the other endless commandments, repeated for millennia, which presuppose opposite commandments or no commandment for the male? Can love chastely be commanded to one and not to the other of the two partners? Yet, for millennia we have been pleased and fed on such golden sentences. This has been the pagan, and especially Jewish and Christian thinking for millennia. To obey and remain different, to have a model and not be able to imitate it! Can one think of a more radical negation of the values of humanity, both male and female?

Can one think of more sinister sadism, more gloomy pessimism about human fortunes?

Plato rarely considered women as subjects, and this was not an accident. However, he was more correct when he made Aristophanes tell the extravagant myth of the originally bisexual man, i.e. either doubly male or doubly female, or male on one side and female on the other, in which sexual differences did not entail any value judgement either in relation to the two sexes or in relation to the multiple possible uses of that sexuality, as male or female homosexuality, and as heterosexuality (cf. Convivio, 189c-193e) (Brisson, 1998).

This serene Aristophanean mentality has been contrasted for centuries by the conception of chastity as a choice in itself superior to any sexuality, even heteronomous and monogamous: a conception that distorts or rejects any natural justification (which should also appear divine) of sex, and that forgets how the pursuit of chastity often, if not inevitably, turns into its opposite, i.e. the obsession of sexuality, that is, of that very human component that one would like to exorcise.

This is testified to by the recurring cliché in the lives of saints who, in order to get rid of sex, only ended up thinking about sex, thus deserving paradise. Nor can it be said that this discourse is also about depriving sex: the fact is that all pious discourses on women's instruction and education, on the family, work, society and politics start from sex and arrive at sex, having it as their initial and final referent (Strano, 2010; D'Addelfio, 2017; Lopez, 2017; Ulivieri, 2023). And so, they also force us to talk about it.

For centuries in all theological treatises, sexuality has been presented as a sin: rather, as the sin par excellence, alongside stealing and killing. That's right: love-making as well as killing and stealing. Furthermore, stealing was always and only the individual's illegitimate taking away, and never that social "legitimately" taking away that was gradually the immediate plundering in war, the exploitation of slave, servile or proletarian labour, colonialist exploitation, etc.: to all of this was opposed, at most, by the duty to give the "right wages", without ever being able to say what it was. Killing, as well, if it was done en masse in wars, was permitted, and even blessed, especially if it involved that most human and peaceful thing that are wars of religion and the burning of heretics. On the other hand, love was always a sin, unless it was practised in matrimony, i.e. allowed heteronomously from without, and surrounded by all those cautions - so far yes, further no; do this, don't do that - that would make any amorous transport perplexing and obnoxious, making it akin to the sexually phobic obsessions of the lives of saints and holy women. Sacred theology, these are your glories!

I am not exaggerating. The identification of the three "sins" is constant among theologians. Here they investigate the *mala voluntas furandi, fornicandi, occidendi*, the stealing, the making love, the killing, to discuss, for example, to what extent those *impudicitiae praecurrentes copulam* are a sin in themselves, in addition to copulation. As if to say: copulate quickly, "*na benedizionaccia lesta lesta*", as the poet Belli said it, and let's talk no more about it: this is truly human, indeed theological.

Yes, behind the obsessive education of women to chastity, at least to chaste love, there was all this wise and unchaste chastity. Within the education of women, indeed, one moves from the sinful triad of stealing-fornicating-killing to the monad of just fornicating (McIntosh, 2013; Obaizamomwan-Hamilton *et al.*, 2024).

Behind the many commandments, prohibitions and prescriptions - the home, the family, mothers and wives and sisters, housework, sewing, embroidering, the spindle, not reading, not writing, the lives of the saints, devotions, modest dress, obedience, etc. - sex is always the only issue (McIntosh, 2013). Why be surprised by this? What does firstly distinguish woman from man? And is it not from this that pious interventions must begin, and then end? The main issue is that behind this sexual *primum* we can recognise that other social *primum* which - as we have already seen - is the exploitation of women's labour. It is realized in women the first historic example of the transformation of the natural division of labour from a technical division, which distinguishes, to a social division, which subjugates.

If the real enemy is always material oppression and exploitation, the ideal enemy is immaterial oppression and ideological conditioning: which, at its peak, is always moralistic and theological, like all the eternal discourses on women's education and upbringing (Borruso, Gallelli & Seveso, 2022), which continue to consider them as mere objects of man's decisions.

THE ROLE OF WOMEN IN WESTERN PEDAGOGY: BETWEEN CULTURAL STEREOTYPES AND EMANCIPATIONIST MOVEMENTS

Indeed, the assertion of the existence of a natural difference between the two sexes, from which differences of a cultural nature are derived, is widely present in the numerous attempts to demonstrate and justify the undisputed predisposition of women to play a socially marginal role that their natural characteristics would have assigned them, even before history. This argument, recurring throughout the history of Western thought, is further developed, starting with the 18th century Enlightenment, based on new axioms, laden with ancient prejudices.

“The male is male only for a few moments, the female is female for life,” wrote J.J. Rousseau in 1762, drawing from this unshakeable certainty pedagogical consequences, already rooted in common sense and destined to last: “Thus all women's education must be in function of men. Pleasing and being useful to them, being loved and honoured by them, bringing them up when they are young, caring for them when they are old, advising them, consoling them, making their lives pleasant and sweet: this is the duty of women in every age of life and this must be taught to them from childhood” (Rousseau, 1969, pp. 544-550). Therefore, education has the task of realising that idea of femininity that does not originate in the terrain of pedagogical reflection but is the consequence of the social implications of a precise conception of the relationship between the two sexes.

From the point of view of the development of pedagogical theories, Rousseau, Pestalozzi and Froebel represent the most significant examples of the re-proposition of the educational importance of the maternal function. Beyond the theoretical and pedagogical differences, there is no doubt that the mother figure takes on previously unseen connotations and spaces in their thought.

From *Emilio* to *Come Gertrude educa i suoi figli* to *Canti e carezze materne*, there will be constant attention devoted to the problem of proper child-rearing from a hygiene point of view and from the point of view of the importance of the mother-child relationship, especially in the very first years of a child's life, for its emotional, linguistical and intellectual development.

The mother's caresses, free body and clean clothes are proof of a new love for the young child. However, to ensure these attentions, the mother must devote her life to the child. The woman disappears in favour of the good mother who will henceforth see the field of her responsibilities widen more and more (Banditer, 1981).

The culture of motherhood therefore has a precise historical origin. In the field of pedagogical theories, at the end of the 18th century, the figure of the woman mother represented an instance connected to the new social demand for the rearing and education of the new generations (in Pestalozzi. This theme is combined in a very significant way with a pedagogical spirit of a welfare and humanitarian type). In the following century, the focus will shift to how to educate women in this function that seems to belong naturally to them, protecting them from everything - including excessive intellectual commitment – that could divert them from their task. The theme of educating women destined to educate obsessively invades treatises, manuals, moral operettas (sometimes even written by women), giving rise to a boundless literature on the subject (Riva, 2013; Covato, 2014; Ulivieri & Biemmi, 2020).

"That the mission of woman is an eminently educational fact" wrote the pedagogue L. Marini in 1879 "is not a fact to be debated, but to be held in its evidence, and accepted for the benefit of every useful effect" (p. 22). This undisputed certainty also pervades medical books and anthropological studies of positivist inspiration. The example of P. Mantegazza (1891) who, in the context of a study on the physiology of women, states: 'Motherhood is the primary and essential mission of woman, and she can only become a mother through love, which stands to motherhood as the flower stands to the fruit' (p. 141). Education and culture do not seem to be indispensable. These are the years in which Lombroso theorises the intellectual inferiority of women, based on anatomical observation of the brain, according to quantitative criteria.

In the same period, an interdependence between the organs of reproduction and those of reason is hypothesised. Education, according to this theory, would dry up the ovaries of women, irreparably leading to the extinction of the race, or of its best part.

Even without carefully analyzing the historiographical and cultural evaluation of the emancipationist movement of those years, which reflects the contradictions and inhomogeneities of civil society at the time, one cannot underestimate the importance, in the years from the Unification of Italy to Fascism, of the experiences of women's movements, whose presence was asserting itself at a European and world level, despite the heterogeneity of their objectives and political and cultural implications (Pironi, 2010).

MARIA MONTESSORI AND EARLY 20TH CENTURY FEMINISM: EDUCATION, WORK AND AUTONOMY

However, the battles for the right to vote, to work, for divorce and for education have groups of women as their protagonists who, courageously challenging a composite but almost always unequivocally hostile cultural front, operate a breaking action against traditional power relations and pose the problem of women's emancipation as a political and social issue, proposing a new, historically unprecedented female image.

Even in the early 20th century, the fight against female illiteracy which, reached values of 60 per cent, the defence of those few women who were beginning to attend university, the criticism of a cultural differentiation of female education from male education are themes that are always present in their analyses and stances, matured in a cultural climate that was still very distrustful and persecutory.

In the first decade of the century, education and sex education becomes in our country and throughout the old continent "one of the problems most agitated by [...] pedagogy". In this regard, you can think of Maria Montessori.

Montessori participated intensively in the initiatives of the women's movements of the early 20th century: in 1896 she took part in the International Women's Congress in Berlin and brought the subject of child illiteracy and the economic inequality of working women to the attention of the Congress; in 1899 she went to the one in London as a representative of Italian women; at the National Conference in Padua in 1899 she gave a paper focused on the concept of 'scientific feminism' and was very determined in supporting the importance of women being involved in the path of education and achieving high levels of education. Montessori emphasised that a woman's cultural preparation did not interfere with her commitment to her family, but rather enabled her to be a more knowledgeable mother.

As many claim, it is not true that she [the woman] causes in this way [by her work] the disintegration of the family and that it is therefore opportune to limit her transition to the social environment by forcing her into home. Wanting to bring her back into the now narrow family circle means failing to understand the true, positive side of the matter: namely, that the same economic fatalities which came to disintegrate the old family order are now pushing women outside the old domestic walls. [...] The evolution of woman and her present issue must be studied together with the transformations of the family (Montessori, 1902, p. 203).

These were Maria Montessori's words at the 1902 Congress in Rome that reiterated the need to support women's non-domestic work in order to guarantee women autonomy and independence in their life choices, i.e. to be able to engage in a marriage relationship that was not based on calculation or on a patriarchal/economic system. We are dealing with a scholar who well understands and analyses the close correlation between industrial capitalism and different forms of the family, anticipating by as much as fifty years the transformations that would go through Italian families in a century of profound changes such as the twentieth one (Volpicella, 2017; Ulivieri, 2019, p. 146). However, Montessori's exceptionality lies in a feminism that identifies precisely in the body - understood as sexuality and motherhood together - the possibility of a re-appropriation of a femininity that means one's own and personal individuality in order to emerge from the binomial and destiny of wives and mothers. Not women as equals of men but women recognised in their competences and capacities, not homologation to the male model but valorisation of 'feminine gifts' and 'domestic virtues' to be engaged, as Maria Montessori said, in social life, for works of assistance and prevention. In this vision of the new woman there is all of her 'scientific feminism' to be understood not only as the need to disseminate scientific progress by educating and opening women's minds, but also 'as the need to encourage women to pursue intellectual professions and devote themselves to scientific studies'. According to Montessori, only in this way women's participation would "be active and bring benefits to science itself, which would be enriched by the critical and vigilant gaze of the female world" (Babini, Lama, 2010, p. 86.).

"Every day the literature on the subject grows more and more", even without seeing the state directly committed, even in Italy, to find a solution to the sexual issue through the educational key. There was no lack of proliferation of publications on the subject nor of associationist, political and cultural activism of which certainly one of the most significant moments was the Florentine conference organised by Prezzolini's *Voce* at the end of 1910 and dedicated to the issue, indeed.

From so many essays and so much debate, often bitter and polemical, a number of little divergent pedagogical proposals came, thus uniting rather distant ideological starting points. Apart from the more extremist and traditionalist fringes, which wanted to perpetuate at all costs the regime of total silence about sex, and the extreme peaks of feminism and the rare small groups of difficult cultural and political positioning, in any case of anarcho-socialist extraction, in favour of a more or less accentuated liberalisation of sexual customs, "all the most diverse tendencies found themselves in agreement on the appropriateness of sexual pedagogy for young people", all or almost all "also agreed that it would be preferable for such teaching to be given in the family, but that, given the incapacity or negligence of most of these, the school should make up for it", which without the use of special teachers would "carefully incorporate" sex education "into the existing subjects of study".

At some point, the didactics of "silence" and "ethical alarm" won out.

SCHOOL AS A PLACE OF HUMAN RESILIENCE: REFLECTIONS ON KNOWLEDGE, EDUCATION AND THE FUTURE

Certainly the school has rediscovered itself as a place of encounter and reworking of experiences of particular value: there acceptance can take place in direct narratives (Demetrio, 2013; Crescenza, 2024) and the meeting is promoted through the juxtaposition of literary works and cultural reflections or in the engagement of a project, in dealing with issues, in redesigning problems (Anastasija & Jelena, 2021).

A difficult dance of relationships and reciprocity, of willingness and responsibility, of interactions, rendered services and cooperation has accompanied this school, between common moments both in person and remotely, or solitary personal re-elaborations. And even comparisons, integrations and deepenings, in a decisive and carefully curated continuous referral between: study and research around cultural objects, about problems, languages, the reflective work on oneself, personal experience, the assumption of one's own task of growth, of development (Dewey, 1933; Schön, 1987; Cambi, 2014). All of the above in the awareness that must be clear to teachers and to be made to blossom in pupils that to collect a question (an object of study, a problem, etc.) in us is always to welcome its charge and expectation of meaning, the adventure of the human being that is at stake in it: it is to collect oneself in it. To enter it, somehow becoming part of it (Manghi, 2004; Bruzzone, 2012).

For years one will have to deal with thresholds of personal and social suffering, that are already well known to those who have always tried to do school in the social and existential peripheries (Fiorucci, 2020).

Indeed, School is built around 'pedagogical rights': that of activation, of observation, of participation; that of maturation, of re-motivation, of the valorisation of potential and interactive support in difficulties; that of cooperative capacity, of critical sense, of the experience of dialogue and research (Swartz, 1996; Nussbaum, 2012); that of the exercise of responsibility, of service, of planning. It will be necessary to organize all this, in responsible presence and at a distance, with shared and meaningful expositions. That in the places of a school that is more widespread in the community and in its times, in its concrete experiences, which are connected to the world.

Because of the pandemic, for instance, the experience of knowledge has to be redesigned and not only because knowing as operating a cognitive and technical grasp on the world has passed from the fire of the crisis being thus demythologised, re-emerging as a place of confrontation with the limit and as a place of positioning in responsibility (Crescenza & Fiorucci, 2024).

To know is to question and grasp, cultivate meaning, regard, mystery; to know is the humility of a thought that dares to seek without presumption and rigidity. Through the pain, knowledge has above all become an experience of co-birth, between adults and minors, and between them and reality, the world.

We could underwrite to what Paul Ricoeur's pupil Philippe Secretan (1969) argues: "The sense and relation of co-birth/knowledge through which the world becomes human and the human being familiar with the world" (p. 247). By way of formation and co-formation, learning about the human and non-violence is a practical way of exercising coexistence.

To know is to change, to change by knowing. Today it is important to find each other by stemming loneliness and abandonment; to keep girls and boys in touch with each other thanks to school; bringing them into contact with literature, mathematics, art, getting them out, making them protagonists of understanding and searching, of discovering and choosing; discovering parts of oneself by cultural rebound, as Franco Lorenzoni (2019) indicates, and also by working in a learning community.

In a certain way, School is a place of 'human resistance', of encounter and dialogue, but also of desire: desiring as imagining together, creating, thinking and devoting oneself to what is valuable. Today, girls, boys and children have a great need to face big, deep and difficult issues, to pause in their questions and to go deeper; not to retrieve content and programmes, but to do less and go deeper with reflection and confrontation. It is necessary to think well and find cultural objects for this age, probe memories and heritages to exchange, investigate (Pasta & Rondonotti, 2020). We are all educated by vulnerability, by a loving and responsible knowledge, by capacities to hold open and generative co-designs and interactions.

Making feel the link between generations and diversity; the openness of the possible, of life; the roots of the origin of reality: this could be a good path to follow in order to leave behind those educational conditionings that continue to subjugate a multitude of young people. Yet this utopian dimension is not often accompanied and supported by educational policies (Baldacci, 2019).

At a press conference in Italy, Minister Valditara presented the experimental "Relationship Education" project aimed at secondary schools and designed to set up discussion and self-awareness groups among students about gender-based violence subject.

The implementation of the project will see the involvement of the order of psychologists, who among other things will collaborate with INDIRE for the training of teachers, "qualified" experts and well-known influencers in the world of young people. A teacher will take on the role of moderator, within the discussion groups, corresponding to the class. The activities will take place during extracurricular hours and will aim to promote preventive behaviour against all forms of discrimination and violence, while also investigating the legal and criminal consequences of violations.

It is undoubtedly important to address issues such as gender respect and awareness-raising against abuse in the school *curricula* by focusing on education as the key to a real and lasting cultural change (Loiodice, 2014; Deluigi & Stramaglia, 2020; Lopez, 2018). It points out, though, the absolute need to generalise transversal educational paths, with defined and contextualised objectives, addressed to pupils of all ages, starting from childhood when the structuring and consolidation of personality and relational life is still in its early stages (Loiodice, 2023).

Above all, it is necessary to act synergistically, involving all the agencies that play an educational role, starting with families and territorial communities, avoiding to discharge onto schools the entire responsibility for an intervention that must be structural and ongoing. This is a "specialized" rather than educational approach in which the focus is on phenomena rather than on their causes and prevention, with a focus on sanctions, in line with the policies implemented by this government with regard to male and female students and outside the school's own role.

It is believed that equal opportunity education and respect for relationships does not require a binding regulation, much less a project dropped from above and imposed as ad additional subject. On the contrary, there should be the creation of conditions that always allow schools – while forced to operate in a limited number of staff, time and resources - to fully exercise their autonomy and planning faculty, and not to respond to a news emergency, also in terms of the "new narrative" of gender.

CONCLUSION: THE IMPORTANCE OF EMOTIONAL AWARENESS

By proceeding from an original positivist matrix, the clearest indication of the connection between feeling and thinking comes today from neuroscience which opens the way to the recognition of the inseparable link between brain and emotions. Antonio Damasio states that the legacy of philosophical thought has given us a view of emotional life considered an interference, 'an excess mental faculty, an unwanted companion - that nature has imposed on us - of our rational thought' (Damasio,1995, p. 95). It is precisely neuroscience that refutes this conception and affirms that emotions and feelings are by no means 'intruders within the walls of reason' (Ibid., 18), but are indispensable for implementing rational behaviour.

The first necessary step is to let oneself be challenged by feelings, listen to them, not to deny them or run away from the unpleasant, uncomfortable, difficult to accept (feelings are not just 'good feelings'). Being poor in certainties means recognising oneself in need of "learning to inhabit even the negative, to accept and understand even the dark sides of one's life" (Rossi, 2006, 109).

Having overcome the mistrust or fear of what we feel, the next step is to give voice to emotional life. As we name our moods, we make them exist. It is therefore necessary to learn how to name feelings. Today's impoverished lexicon has either lost the words for emotions or reduced them to a few standardised expressions. Younger people rely on emoticons, as if there were no more words available to them.

Naming moods is the necessary step towards being able to understand them. Emotional awareness is about being honest with us in questioning the meaning of what we feel. Awareness removes us from the temptation of homologising or routine behaviour and returns us to the question of meaning.

From authentic understanding it is possible to open up to acceptance: this is the most difficult step because the 'calculating thinking' in which we are immersed makes problematic to accept our limits and frailties, pushing us rather towards the illusion of controlling everything. Letting be, where we cannot change, does not express an attitude of renunciation or indifference, but one of wisdom. By accepting our emotional dimensions, we can take the next step: sharing them with others. Sharing increases our emotional awareness and feeling becomes the 'knowledge of feelings' that is not built in isolation or solitude, but in relationship with others. The burden of processing difficult emotions is lightened when shared: emotional overload, feelings of loneliness and helplessness are thus alleviated, recovering security and serenity.

Finally, the decisive step on the path to emotional life awareness is the ability to distinguish what we feel from what we do about the feeling we have. When we have named, understood, accepted, shared it, we must be able to take responsibility for the consequent choice. The choice that involves me and puts personality at a stake does not arise from an abstract and universal principle of value, but from the face of the other who looks at me because his or her destiny is not foreign to me but 'concerns me' (Lévinas, 1980, p. 48). First of all, cultivating emotional competence means learning to recognise the motions of the soul, to name them, to let them be, to accept them, to express them and, what is most important, to take responsibility for the behaviour resulting from what we feel.

It is therefore not by denying the emotional life that education takes place, but by fully and consciously assuming it as a constitutive dimension of human existence.

In this regard, in the last part of *The Anger and Forgiveness* Marta Nussbaum (2017) addresses the issue of Nelson Mandela as a prisoner, victim of injustice and moved by anger. From his autobiography emerges a Mandela who deals with sorting out himself, his interiority and his representations of the other to prepare for future. He does this by disciplining himself, by weaving attitudes and gestures that educate him to be open, attentive and dialoguing although he does not yet feel he is and within himself he still feels anger.

This is a humble and practical work for women and men who discovered to have a lot of aggression within. Such women and men who are not innocent but who, nevertheless, can manage to deal with anger because they are stubborn, even against the evidence, till to read the signs of the gift of beauty around them, to experience generous closeness that makes life better. Thus, even the corrosion of time, the rigidity and banality of marked destinies and routine, the separations can be crossed, provided they feel they have nothing to lose, and therefore that they want, that they can, that they have energy.

It deals with a maturing of the days, of the encounters, of the gaze that is caught by what is valuable, that calls and destines you, by the long breath of passion and desire. There is pain, sweat and expectation, but you can only live a life that is not easy, that opens but also closes unknown chances, that takes different paths, sometimes incomprehensible. Sometimes promising and open to good horizons.

REFERENCES

Anastasija, M., & Jelena, M. (2021). The role of action research in teachers' professional development. *International Journal of Cognitive Research in Science. Engineering and Education*, 9(3), 301–317.

Babini, V. P., & Lama, L. (2010). *Una donna nuova. Il femminismo scientifico di Maria Montessori*. FrancoAngeli.

Badinter, E. (1981). *L'amore in più. Storia dell'amore materno*. Longanesi.

Baldacci, M. (2019). *La scuola al bivio. Mercato o democrazia?* FrancoAngeli.

Borruso, F., Gallelli, R., & Seveso, G. (Eds.). (2022). Dai saperi negati alle avventure della conoscenza. *Esclusione ed emancipazione delle donne nei percorsi educativi tra storia e attualità*. Edizioni Unicopli.

Brisson, L. (1998). *Plato the myth maker*. University of Chicago Press.

Bruzzone, D. (2012). *Farsi persona. Lo sguardo fenomenologico e l'enigma della formazione*. FrancoAngeli.

Cambi, F. (2014). La formazione dell'insegnante oggi: la funzione della riflessività. In Mariani, A. (Ed.), *L'orientamento e la formazione degli insegnanti del futuro* (pp. 31–36). Firenze University Press.

Covato, C. (2014). *Idoli di bontà: il genere come norma nella storia dell'educazione*. Unicopli.

Crescenza, G. (2024). *Ritratti di maestri. Suggestioni pedagogiche sulla professione docente*. Ed. Conoscenza.

Crescenza, G., & Fiorucci, M. (2024). Enfoques innovadores, retos formativos y vías pedagógicas plurales en la educación contemporánea. Reflexiones introductorias sobre un texto coral. In Crescenza, G., & Fiorucci, M. (Eds.), *Educación e Innovación al servicio de la mejora del Conocimiento* (pp. 15–26). AulaMagna.

D'Addelfio, G. (2017). La nostra epoca tarda. In Bellingreri, A. (Ed.), *Lezioni di pedagogia fondamentale* (pp. 75–92). La Scuola.

Damasio, A. R. (1995). *L'errore di Cartesio*.

Deluigi, R., & Stramaglia, M. (2020). Projectuality and education, between learning objectives and political-cultural dynamics. *Form@ re-Open Journal per la formazione in rete, 20*(2), 103-116.

Demetrio, D. (2013). Educare è narrare. Le teorie, le pratiche, la cura. *Mimesis*.

Dewey, J. (1933). How We Think: A Restatement of the Relation of Reflective Thinking to the Educative Process. In Boydston, J. (Ed.), *John Dewey: The Later Works, 1925-1953* (Vol. 8, pp. 105–352). Southern Illinois University Press.

Fiorucci, M. (2020). *Educazione, formazione e pedagogia in prospettiva interculturale*. FrancoAngeli.

Lévinas, E. (1980). *Totalità e infinito*. Jaca Book.

Loiodice, I. (2014). *Formazione di genere. Racconti, immagini, relazione di persone e famiglie*. FrancoAngeli.

Loiodice, I. (2023). Prevenire la violenza contro le donne attraverso l'educazione di genere. A partire dall'infanzia. *Civitas educationis. Education. Política y Cultura*, 12(1), 43–57.

Lopez, A. G. (2017). *Decostruire l'immaginario femminile. Percorsi educativi per vecchie e nuove forme di condizionamento culturale*. ETS.

Lopez, A.G. (2018). *Pedagogia delle differenze. Intersezioni tra genere ed etnia*. ETS.

Lorenzoni, F. (2019). *Il dialogo euristico. Orientamenti operativi per una pedagogia dell'ascolto nella scuola*. Carocci.

Manghi, S. (2004). *La conoscenza ecologica. Attualità di Gregory Bateson*. Raffaello Cortina.

Mantegazza, P. (1891). *Fisiologia della donna*. Treves.

Marini, L. (1879). *L'educazione conveniente della donna*. Paravia.

McIntosh, M. (2013). The state and the oppression of women. In *Feminism and Materialism (RLE Feminist Theory)*. Routledge.

Nussbaum, M. C. (2012). *Creare capacità. Liberarsi dalla dittatura del Pil*. Il Mulino.

Nussbaum, M. C. (2017). *Rabbia e perdono. La generosità come giustizia*. Il Mulino.

Obaizamomwan-Hamilton, E., Norris, A., Elsinbawi, M., Paley, M., & Cohen, A. (2024). Femmenoir pedagogies: Rescripting the reproduction of Black women's marginalization in education. *Race, Ethnicity and Education*, 1–23. 10.1080/13613324.2024.2327110

Pasta, S., & Rondonotti, M. (2020). Competenze mediaeducative e tecnologie di comunità. Nuove direzioni per il lavoro socioeducativo territoriale. *Rivista Italiana di Educazione Familiare*, 17(2), 377–398.

Pironi, T. (2010). *Percorsi di pedagogia al femminile. Dall'Unità d'Italia al secondo dopoguerra*. Carocci.

Riva, M. G. (2013). The role of the traumatic 'transgenerational unsaid'-historical, social, educational, psychological-in life histories. *Pedagogia oggi, 2*, 51-79.

Rossi, B. (2006). *L'educazione dei sentimenti*. Unicopli.

Rousseau, J. J. (1969). *Emilio [1762]*. Armando.

Schön, D. A. (1987). *Educating the Reflective Practitioner: Toward a new design for teaching and learning in the professions*. Jossey-Bass.

Secretan, P. (1969). *Autorité, pauvoir, puissance. Principes de philosophie politique réflexive*. L'Age d'Homme.

Striano, M. (2010). *Pratiche educative per l'inclusione sociale*. FrancoAngeli.

Swartz, E. (1996). Emancipatory Pedagogy: A postcritical response to 'standard' school knowledge. *Journal of Curriculum Studies*, 28(4), 397–418. 10.1080/0022027980280402

Ulivieri, S. (2019). Il femminismo di Maria Montessori. Educazione, emancipazione per un nuovo modello di donna. In Baldacci, M., & Zabalza, M. A. (Eds.), *L'utopia montessoriana. Pace, diritti, libertà, ambiente* (pp. 137–152). Erickson.

Ulivieri, S. (2023). Identità di genere, femminismo e educazione. *Civitas educationis. Education. Política y Cultura*, 12(1), 109–122.

Ulivieri, S., & Biemmi, I. (Eds.). (2020). *Storie di donne. Autobiografie al femminile e narrazione identitaria*. Guerini Associati.

Volpicella, A. M. (2017). *L'aprirsi delle famiglie alla comunità. Mito-Realtà-Utopia*. Pensa Multimedia.

Chapter 7
Well-Being and Health Through Autobiographical Pedagogy:
Theoretical Foundations and Perspectives

Fabrizio Manuel Sirignano
https://orcid.org/0000-0002-9072-9342
Università degli Studi Suor Orsola Benincasa, Italy

Gabriele Borghese
Università degli Studi Suor Orsola Benincasa, Italy

ABSTRACT

The chapter outlines the theoretical foundations and methods of autobiographical pedagogy and its importance in the current context. The centrality of the narrative method for care settings in general and specifically for the care of the elderly is highlighted. With reference then to the medical humanities, the importance of the community dimension among individuals is underlined, also in order to recover a global perspective able to counteract the current fragmentation of knowledge. The fundamental contribution comes from the humanistic tradition, from arts to literature, that gives great weight to the 'story' and to the process of writing of them.

DOI: 10.4018/979-8-3693-4244-2.ch007

FOUNDATIONS AND METHODS OF AUTOBIOGRAPHICAL PEDAGOGY

Autobiography has taken on an important role as an educational methodology that enables the achievement of elevated-level educational objectives starting from the enhancement of experience and subjectivity. This theory and the practices connected to it make it possible to overcome the crisis of the positivist paradigm from a methodological point of view, thus putting the purposes of education back at the centre, revaluing a hermeneutic approach capable of practicing the understanding of the phenomenon, going beyond its simple explanation-description (Sirignano, 2003: 48-60).

This has led to the emergence of a more complex approach, able to integrate the two research methods, in the awareness that it is not possible to describe and explain without understanding. The adult training process is thus managed as a dynamic process, so as to guide the person's training pathway by fostering his or her growth, and also accommodating self-training needs. Life experiences, previous training experiences and work history strongly influence training.

As Pierre Dominicé has pointed out, knowledge of the earlier stages of the individual's educational biography is very useful for accurately identifying the individual's learning possibilities (Dominicé, 2000). The dynamics that have contributed to the subject's formation emerge from the life stories, also highlighting the social dynamics in which the individual is immersed, the pressures he or she is subjected to, also showing possible paths to liberation and emancipation. The education biography approach can be used nearly anywhere adult learning takes place including places not usually devolved to education, health care places for example. According to Duccio Demetrio (2000), every autobiography is characterized by variations, different shades, that the author imprints on it, showing the importance of choices, marks the journey of growing up, the process of becoming an adult, which begins before the start of adult life from a stadial point of view, and is indeed distinguished by the fact of being challenged in the face of life's choices. The strong pedagogical value of the reflexive and narrative techniques inherent in autobiography make possible for the subject to elaborate new ways of learning and knowing, to discover the dynamics of learning processes, with strong reflects in terms of personal growth.

These dynamics make it clear that knowledge is the result of an interweaving of moral, emotional and cognitive dimensions. By retracing their formative experiences and narrating them, the subject elaborates their own 'theory', organizing their search for meaning in a particular way. The autobiography method can be effectively employed from an intercultural perspective, as the subject, by reflecting on his or her own life experience, prepares to recognize stories that are 'other' than his or her own, activating a path of knowledge of the other based on empathy. Already from here one can clearly see the point of this practice to enhance in the medical field the ability to create stories and empathy through narratives.

This approach puts the learner at the center of the learning process, thus distinguishing it from classical adult education methodologies, which focus on tutoring by the teacher. It also represents a reversal of the teacher's perspective, which helps the learner to become aware of his or her own capacity to change, thus becoming a guide and not an 'instructor'. From this point of view, the reflections carried out by Paulo Freire (1968), Gaston Pineau (1973), Peter Alheit (1995) and by Dominicé, find their meeting point in the valorization of the personal experience of the subjects, of their experiences, also in relation to the social dynamics of emancipation.

The purpose of these narrative practices is the pursuit of well-being, practiced through self-reflection, in search of meaning in the choices made and to be made, in order to live one's life in a better way.

Freire’s work intended to promote a global approach to education, not only in the sense of a broader concept of education, but also capable of connecting peoples. It is clear that Freire's intent is to pull people out of oppression, to bring them out of the domination in which they are subjugated, in search of a better life, viable through the practices of humanity that come from emancipation, conscientization and emancipation by creating and re-creating relations between people. Pineau sees education as a path that leads the subject to take ownership of his own personal growth process. He put training for the subject at the center, making him better able to understand himself in depth, in such a way that he can better organize his life, through the understanding of the past, of the personal story. Alheit also believes that quantitative approaches are incapable of understanding the complexity of social reality. The biographical approach thus, through its narrative component, understands several variables that in human life have a decisive weight.

According to Bruner (1986, 1996), the human mind possesses the capacity to elaborate a particular form of reasoning, the *narrative thought*, that can construct stories that make possible the interpretation of reality and the elaboration of the individual’s identity. Proceeding in narrative thinking, the mind ties together the events that come to mind through a network of relationships, trying to fit them into a unitary design endowed with meaning. The calculative thinking, marked by mere representation of empirical data, would fail to do this. Thus, in the construction of a story, facts are immersed in a dense fabric of intentionalities, causes, emotions, whose warp is the subjectivity of the narrating *ego*. In his 1996 book *The Culture of Education*, Bruner underlines the importance of narrative processes in education, highlighting their potential in helping individuals construct their identity and find their role within society. Also allows for the enhancement of human experience through a reinterpretation and reinterpretation of the concepts of memory and forgetting, construction and loss of self, old age and youth, life and death, in a transformative way. At the end of the tale, a unitary design appears, which is the interpretation given to one's own life. The autobiographical account is not a faithful chronicle of the past, it is instead a reconstruction of the life story filtered through the narrator's interpretation of it by telling himself.

The transition from oral storytelling to the drafting of a written text is fundamental in the adult learning process because the effort to translate strong emotions and feelings into writing is a source of further reflection and could create frustration in those who do not possess adequate lexical and syntactic tools. It is the specific task of the trainer to support the adult in this difficult task of representing in his or her own words, as freely as possible, moments of life that still arouse emotion in him or her when remembering. The autobiographical approach identifies the subject's reference knowledge by helping him reflect on the experiential paths through which he has learned what he knows, highlighting the contribution to constructing his own knowledge. Thus, is the text of the life that emerges, in her weavings, offering a plastic representation of the sense of *Bildung*. These approaches prove particularly fruitful when related to the medical humanities, which provide a privileged role for narrative, highlighting the various types of narratives and storytelling.

The activity of telling one's story allows personal experiences to be re-elaborated within their social context, making it possible to grasp the subjectivity of the individual. This method can be an interesting tool to investigate the institutions of society, as well as health conditions, coming into contact with the living conditions of those individuals.

Also, the humanities, including the educational sciences, assume that change is an intrinsic aspect of human experience. They view the study of life stories as a fundamental tool for exploring the formative value of individual events experienced, analyzing their ability to influence and modify behavior, knowledge, and skills in relating to one's surroundings. Contemporary pedagogical reflection highlights the crucial importance, at every stage of life, of autobiography and life stories as educational tools capable of achieving high cognitive and educational goals, starting from the enhancement of individual subjectivity. If we adopt this principle as an interpretive paradigm for reinterpreting the meaning of our life experiences, we realize how autobiography can serve as a meaningful interpretive space that can connect the present, past and future in a complex temporal dimension.

The importance of constructing a narrative of care contexts that places the configuration of the individual at the center and respects the complexity of everyday life is evident. In this context, literature, especially literature open to childhood experiences, can become a resilient device and a new paradigm of reference. It can serve as an effective formative and transformative tool for children and young people through a historical-pedagogical interpretation of the works of various writers.

Contributions from various disciplines and research perspectives, ranging from pedagogy to sociology, from philosophy to medicine, from literature to the arts (music, painting, cinema), outline educational pathways that can promote risk prevention (both medical and marginality), transformative, formative and self-formative processes. It is fundamental to deepen the problem of transdisciplinary teaching, stimulating future research and hoping for a full inclusion of Narrative Medicine in the undergraduate and postgraduate pathways of health care personnel. This process aims at improving medical treatment, the therapeutic relationship between patient and health care provider, more accurate clinical assessment, and deeper understanding of the patient. Topics of considerable relevance include those related to pain and suffering, for which there is an increasing need for specific training for health care professionals as well, so that they can deal with them in a more prepared way, benefit personally, understand themselves better, and facilitate generative expressive channels of sharing.

It is therefore crucial to understand how new technologies can also assist the operation of medical instruments, particularly without losing sight of the human wholeness that characterizes medical humanism. In this context, therapeutic writing in the context of Narrative Medicine emerges as a powerful tool for exploring the transformative potential of life stories affected by suffering and illness, bringing them to a level of systemic reflection. These stories can relate to both patients and professionals working in the field of medical care. Valuing the history of the patient not identifying him with the disease, but with his experiences, memories, thus ultimately is helpful to put pedagogy at the service of the person.

USE OF AUTOBIOGRAPHICAL PEDAGOGY FOR WELLNESS AND THE ELDERLY

The importance of narrative methods, which originated from the humanities, can be dropped into the context of care. Because of its relationship with the past and with the enhancement of the past in the form of narrative, we can investigate its significance as a tool of care for the elderly.

Contemporary pedagogical reflection brings out the centrality, in every season of life, of *autobiography* and *life stories* as pedagogical devices capable of achieving *high* cognitive and educational goals starting from the enhancement of the individual's subjectivity. If we use this assumption as an interpretive paradigm for re-reading and re-interpreting the meaning of one's life experiences, we realize how much autobiography can represent that hermeneutic space capable of posing itself as a meaningful place capable of connecting in a single complex temporal dimension the present, the past and the future.

The analysis around autobiography and life stories is intertwined, in our hypothesis, with the theme of educational care that from childhood to old age accompanies any educational journey.

The narrative shows old age in its usefulness (Rossiello, 2016), giving presence to a past that would be lost as it is deemed useless to a more superficial and utilitarian view. Biographical narratives highlight the strong pressure that the social group to which the individual belongs exerts on each individual, aimed at determining behavior that conforms to unwritten but binding rules; they also highlight how individual growth paths necessarily pass through a conflictual relationship with such a system of rules and expectations, the natural outcome of which is the conquest of an autonomy of thought and thus the development of an adult individuality.

The trainer using the biographical procedure with the elderly can therefore, through knowledge of the subject's life frame of reference and his or her *liberating* path, identify the most effective intervention tools to complete the individual training process. The formative value of the biographical approach is confirmed by Dominicé (2000) who, reflecting on today's society subject to sudden changes, dominated by the demands of the globalized economy, wonders what the guidelines might be for adult education in the near future. He glimpses the possible answer in a development of the biographical method which, starting from the knowledge of the mechanisms of modification of the mental attitudes of adults, is used to trace a training path adequate to make the subject acquire an autonomous position with regard to modernity. From this point of view, autobiographical reflection fits fully within the educational landscape with a highly motivating value because it allows the elderly person to gain confidence in his or her own abilities, to initiate autonomous processes of meaning-making by reflecting on the events of his life, retracing the choices made and rediscovering the motivations that determined them.

Autobiographical reconnaissance helps the subject to identify the dynamic connections existing between the cognitive, affective, moral, and emotional dimensions of knowledge. Reconstructing one's training history is an opportunity for change because it occurs through a constant connection between experience and explanation, between lived experience and narration, producing processes of searching for meaning, and constructions of theories (Formenti 1998). In fact, every story told involves the construction of a *theory*, that is, a particular way of organizing a temporal succession of events.

It seems evident how the autobiographical method, being aimed at grasping the uniqueness of the subject and his or her trajectories of life, self-expression and attribution of meaning, can be usefully employed in old age: in shared narratives, the elderly are led to the awareness that life, however singular and different for each person, can present a common background, a social and relational construction, and when the old age, through self-telling, comes to such awareness, it feels less of a sense of loneliness (Rossiello, 2016). In addition to bringing about an awareness of one's own changes, self-narrative is itself an incitement for further change as it is a *laboratory* for the construction of meanings and opportunities for growth (Schettini, 2000).

The life experience gained acts on the memories by modifying them; therefore, in rethinking the past in the light of the present, the subject performs a work of re-interpretation of the events experienced sometimes accomplishing, in order to create a coherence between past and present, a kind of *prophetic* reading of one's history in which some past events seem to foreshadow events that subsequently occurred. The autobiographical approach not only makes it possible to grasp the subjectivity of the individual in all its complexity but, through the activity of telling one's self, allows for a reworking of personal experiences within their socio-historical context. Thus, autobiography is also "testimony to the structures of a society, an historical time, a culture, a mentality, a process of formation" (Certini, 2001). Making autobiography takes the form of a real exercise of those cognitive skills useful for remembering, analyzing and classifying facts and events, figures and circumstances encountered. All this takes on a formative value as through the past one attempts to understand the present and plan for the future. Through storytelling it is possible to develop autobiographical intelligence, which enables the subject to know himself better and is objectified in different forms depending on the age of the storyteller (Demetrio, 2000).

Self-narrative thus becomes a *nonlinear mental path* that allows both the storyteller and the listener to arrive at outcomes that are difficult to achieve with other strategies. The formative value of this methodology can be further traced in the opportunity it offers the storyteller to self-form, reflecting on his own life journey and what has been learned and what he can actually still learn from himself, others and the environment in which he or she is immersed.

In the course of writing, the subject slowly sees the outlines of another self of which he or she had no clear perception, because writing involves unaccustomed activities of introspection and reflection. Once set in motion, the mechanism of self-reflection proceeds along its own path and leads toward different outcomes depending on the subject's ability to question himself, the degree of authenticity of which he is capable. The radical form of autobiography is that which leads to looking at oneself from that position of impersonality that envelops the self, and which is achieved by bringing the self to *spoliation* (Gargani 1990). Demetrio speaks of *bilocation*, of a splitting that allows the autobiographical *self* to become the biographer of that character whom he observes living and who is *self* and *not self*. A creative distancing is brought about that helps the subject consolidate a sense of self through acceptance of what he or she has been. The present gaze, looking at the past from a distance, is able to see it in a different light, understanding previously unclear connections and meanings. According to Demetrio (1994), splitting takes place on three levels. In the first level: *me-he* subject is able to place himself outside himself, observing himself as an outsider. In the second level: *yesterday-today-tomorrow* there is the placement of self in the past and, through the self-narrative, projection into the future. Then the third level: *inside-outside* appears, alongside the outer life, the world of one's inner experiences that resurface and of which the subject becomes aware precisely through the narrative. This discourse leads to the theme of *taking the voice*, the true positioning at the center of the subject in narrative practice, which is also carried out in the methodology of 'life stories'. Speaking can be, for the individual in training, a moment of great emotional intensity, the breaking of isolation, the beginning of a strongly desired growth path.

In the educational field the objective is to activate learning and transformation processes in the recipients of the interventions. Therefore, in this context it is necessary to focus attention on the subject who tells his own life, and on the close connection between the story and its author, the one who gives it shape through connections, contents, meanings, and plots.

In building a life story the listener has an important task; he must establish the right atmosphere, incitate the conversation with questions and interventions aimed at helping the narrator clarify the meanings of his story for himself. The listener must have human sensitivity and knowledge of the defense mechanisms that subjects can activate, to deactivate them and to get emotionally in tune with the narrator; that is, it must establish a constructive dialogue, managing to communicate its sharing of the experience told. This proves particularly useful in the methodologies of the medical humanities because only through an interested and critical participation in the journey of the patient story will the listener be able to help the subject progressively make an important transition: from speaking to thinking, therefore to reconnect the fragments of the story to each other to identify the plot, his own life and vicissitudes of the disease. From this point of view, autobiographical accounts highlight how concretely experienced situations are sources of sometimes more valuable knowledge than that acquired in school desks and books. A category, that of experience, which acquires particular importance in life stories because it can stem that *pedagogical double damage* (Iori, 2012) that deprives the younger generations of the educational, social and cultural heritage that is represented precisely by the experience of *grandparents* and that undermines, in themselves, the meaning of their own existence. The dialectic between experience and action, between memory and oblivion, construction and loss of the self, old age and youth, narrative and thought is the driving force behind any pedagogical activity that chooses to use autobiography and life stories as devices of educational care. Through the path of life stories, in fact, this dialectical game, which opposes an apparent dichotomy, realizes a new process of knowledge toward the other characterized by openness, sharing, and self-awareness, starting from the way the elderly perceive their own subjectivity, endowed with purposes, values, and bonds (Ricoeur, 1983).

In the end, self-understanding in fact turns out to be important with respect to the concept self-representation in illness. A theme investigated by classics of literature itself, but one that appears even more important when one considers that through the book, narrative qualities are externalized, weaving a tale that can truly mark life and relaunch it in a different, transformative perspective.

MEDICAL HUMANITIES, WELFARE, WELFARE STATE, NARRATIVE THINKING

The debate on the Medical Humanities comes to Western Europe from United States of America at a time when the supporting structures of the *welfare state*, on which democratic institutions had been built, is being remade, dismantled. This produces in individuals an overload of responsibility, since in the *liquid society* it is the individuals who have to take charge of their personal security (Bauman 2021). The many cuts to the welfare state for example in Italy in recent years have included cuts to the health care system, which has thus been reduced and with it also the territorial social service that covered needs. Since the late 1980s, therefore, a "real transition phase" occurs, which has impacted management criteria, imprinting them with a rationalistic and managerial character (Conti, Silei, 2022). This should make us question the true practicability of welfare and well-being in Western societies, whether it is possible as outside the economic conditions under which it is being realized. The effort of reflection therefore also focuses today on better focusing on the relationships between health and welfare, recovering tools and forms of knowledge that were not previously understood as related to these areas. As we have seen, pedagogy and its practices, such as the autobiographical one, can bring benefits to health if articulated on a doctor-patient discourse in such a way as to consider that, good communicative practices can be established by exploiting a knowledge that is traditionally elaborated, in the pedagogical field, in a dialectical and interpersonal way.

Those who are therefore concerned with medicine, but in fact with the entire field of care, must be interested in these forms of knowledge that can spread and restructure themselves thanks to the good practices formulated in the pedagogical tradition, and especially in the one concerning recent years, such as autobiographical pedagogy. Autobiographical pedagogy in fact empowers the subject to make a meta-reflection on himself and his journey, so it also concerns his discomforts, his difficulties, his perplexities about his surroundings. What is more, storytelling is itself a practice for liberating oneself, in that the subject provides the happenings about him with a different logic during the narration that he would not otherwise give to the facts of his life. It has a strong pedagogical significance precisely because it is the elaboration of life, through storytelling, not a chronology, not a neutral form of storytelling such as is usually practiced with, but rather can open up new insights and new nuances about the self and the lived experience.

It is not by chance that we speak of lived experience, because it is not only life, but precisely it is the individual and above all subjective form of it, reworked and reorganized from the point of view of the subject who lives it and deals with it on a daily basis, especially in moments of pain and suffering, going through all the stages of his discomfort and feelings, deepening those aspects that would not emerge on a daily basis. This surfacing, this bringing to the surface of experience characterizes the most productive moment of these practices, for it is precisely through this bringing to the surface that the subject emerges, with his ability to put his experience in order and to rework it, in a peculiar way that is his own and that represents the core of his singularity. In addition to this essentiality for the individual of autobiographical experience, which is welded with the narratological turn deepened in recent years. Indeed, it is well known that the narratological turn, which comes up towards the end of the 1980s, also due to Bruner's work. He popularized story as a mean by the identity is created and deepened, coming to understand the importance of story for our lives. From this was developed a pathway that focused on narrative in medicine, thanks to the perspective of narrativists (Chambers, 1999). This leads reflection on the nature of writing, on writing interpreted as a body leaving a written trace, a theme discussed by philosophers since ancient times. It means leaving a trace for another, moving from living expression to a medium, from the animate to the inanimate, from mobility to immobility. The conversion of memory to a medium is not just an act of preservation, it's not pure preservation, but it is transformation of what one chooses to preserve. It is an authorial process that comes into play in this transfer, as if I am telling the story myself, thanks to the creative memory of orality that has its own specific production.

In this sense, it appears the opportunity to implement autobiographical pedagogy by also adopting it in health care settings means making it possible for caregivers to harness the power of storytelling in order to create a patient-centered approach to care. This can be done by training these figures, accustoming them to dealing with patients' stories, also in order to improve communication. This can trigger a paradigm shift as we seek to recover a humanistic component that until now had been left outside the doctor-patient relationship, in which the subjective experiences of patients and caregivers are valued as components of well-being and health itself. Indeed, human health is something complex, and healing itself is something different from physical intervention, encompassing specific emotional dimensions. Therefore, the intersection of medical humanities and autobiographical pedagogy represents a potential fertile ground for investigating personal stories and narratives can broaden our understanding of humans, and the practice of care. Autobiographical pedagogy offers a unique lens through which we can humanize medical education and practice. The theoretical underpinnings of this approach are based on the belief that engaging with patient narratives can counteract the dehumanizing tendencies of modern medicine, which is moving toward a technologization of the physician-patient relationship (Charon, 2006). Better recognize the patient's voice, and also use this methodology to investigate practitioners' experiences, putting in place an empathy-enhancing mechanism (Launer, 2002). This is important when considering the forces of resistance to change within the medical culture that present themselves as obstacles to the implementation of practices that come from the humanistic culture. Charon formalized the ways of narrative knowledge as a set of skills and knowledge parallel to biomedical work, referring precisely to 'narrative competence.' Despite the fact that there may be an inflated use of this word ' competence ', it is understood that with this term we refer to something specific, that can only be obtained by practicing storytelling in such a way that we then become capable of deciphering it.

It is right on these narrative skills that the training that could also be addressed to caregivers, recovering methodologies proper of pedagogy. This turns out to be fundamental if one also intends self-pathographies, (Sirignano, Maddalena, 2023), which are particularly useful to play a fundamental role within the pathways of understanding illness and healing. As mentioned in the opening of the paragraph, the possibility of all this is linked to choices that prioritize well-being as the scope toward which social development should be directed, and this is possible thanks to projects and investments directed in this sense. These concrete activities can also pass through the enhancement of cultural heritage from the perspective of care, framing cultural heritage in the perspective of a true *cultural welfare* (Marone, 2023). In fact, culture can have significant impacts on health, caring relationships and community building. Cultural welfare is precisely therefore based on the enjoyment and activation of people to participate in cultural and creative experiences, which bring into play the very skills we have been talking about so far. In addition to the skills mentioned above, which are predominantly narrative in essence, there are those that have to do with *life skills, soft skills*, as well as *health literacy*, increasing social capital with great spin-offs in positive terms on the well-being of participants (Marone, 2023, 79). As Marone shows, these projects are then targeted at different audiences: the children, the youth, the elderly, the mentally ill and the vulnerable. They are ways to broaden welfare also through new involvement, intercepting new needs of support, and incentivize the search for new practices for territorial institutions. Through the promotion of these initiatives, we also achieve a new synergy therefore between institutions, so as to take coordinated and organized action based on the social needs that comes up.

REVIVING GLOBAL KNOWLEDGE FROM HUMANITIES

It has been seen that narrative expertise, coming from the literary field, also provides physicians with new tools of interpretation to investigate the complexity of emotions and choices that characterize human life. As De Feo (2023) noted, it is also a matter of identifying the differences between an 'evidence-based' medicine and one that uses the narrative device to improve health care. As noted earlier the purely empirical approach to the patient does not allow for the identification of all the shades that have to do with his character, his life choices, and the perspective from which he views the world around him and his past. This empirical approach to illness, which considers the patient as a set of symptoms, evidently comes from the history of medicine, which since the eighteenth century has gradually seen the figure of the Hippocratic physician (whom has a broader horizon) fade away (De Feo, 2023, 226). The use of specific terminology *(disease, illness, sickness)* with which one relates to illness also contributes to fragmenting this experience, and providing an additional reason to elaborate instead a more integrated perspective of approaching illness. Therefore, adopting narrative practices even in the training of medical staff, for example, by noting down patients' stories, also writing down their own state of mind toward what they are feeling, helps to limit that depersonalization that can result from treating the patient from an exclusively clinical perspective. As De Feo (2023, 226-227) writes: “active listening to illness narratives followed by the physician's reflective moment, creates a climate of trust, empathy and mutual respect [...] between caregiver and patient that contrasts with the 'objectifying clinical view' (Bleakley, 2015) and initiates the 'co-construction' of care. There is therefore a need to integrate perspectives on approaching health and illness through the promotion of a dialogue between EBM and Narrative Medicine (NBM).”

The act of writing, investigated thanks to Burner’s insights, possesses specificities that are fruitful from a cognitive perspective, thus takes on various therapeutic meanings (Mortara, 2023): self-disclosure practiced through writing, in that feelings emerge and can be processed later; cognitive processing of information and experiences that emerge during writing, deepening different points of view and broadening perspectives; writing can act as emotional regulation in that the subject becomes aware of and reflects on emotions, strengthening the ability to manage emotional processes; writing is understood as a good memory strategy in the short and long term, as it makes it easier to recall distant events, giving order and meaning to experiences; through writing, stories emerge, as in autobiography, in which the person recounts the events that are fundamental to him or her; one reflects on one's experience as writing objectifies the lived experience, enhancing understanding of it. Thus, practical activities have been designed, such as the shared diary, a writing tool in hospital wards in order to preserve patients' experience and (Mortara, 2023, 289-291). Pathographies as a narrative of the experience of illness by those who have lived through it, aims to reflect on what happened. This contributes to integrating the moment of illness into one's life story, ensuring that it is not a black hole in the experience, but is brought back into the scope of the journey.

As has been pointed out (Maddalena, Paolozzi, 2023, 148-149), the narrative approach also serves to recompose a picture that usually arrives fragmented even to the researcher who is now reduced to a mere specialist, as Morin (2001, 7) noted: "to the researcher is offered the exclusive possession of a fragment of the puzzle whose global vision must slip everyone and everyone". So what is hoped for in this fragmented framework is "a regeneration, a (creative) gaze that is able to regenerate, to offer new possibilities for change that can increasingly cross the needs, desires, and demands for horizons of meaning expressed by increasingly broad and differentiated segments of the population" (Maddalena, Paolozzi, 2023, 151). It would thus be a matter not only of acting in such a way as to make medicine 'humane', but "understanding that in order to confront reality there can be no separate and split visions" (Ibid.), thus grasping the contingent nature of the divisions of knowledge and acting in such a way as to recompose the fragmentation by following the *continuum of* philosophical and literary reflection, capable of orienting the subject in its own way.

In conclusion, to return to Bruner's (1986) remarks, narrative thinking possesses a unifying function capable of orienting in what has been called the 'tower of babel' that is established between physicians, patients and health system workers (Marini, 2016). According to Bruner, the logical-scientific mode seeks to achieve a formal, mathematical system of description. It uses methods, namely categorization and conceptualization, operations by which categories are drawn, thought out, and related in a systematic way. Indeed, it relies on precise rules to hold concepts together, conjunction disjunction, implication, the devices by which general propositions can be distinguished from statements in their contexts. That is, the logical-scientific mode deals with general causes and their determination, to establish verifiable conditions. Imagination combined with narrative skill, on the other hand, leads to stories, accounts that appear credible to us, shining light on the internal dynamics of facts, of passions: "there is an hearthlessness to logic" says Bruner "one goes where one's premises and conclusions and observations take one" (1986, 13). The narrative mode leads to stories, has to do with intentions and actions and is able to explain the human condition, through the combination of action and consciousness. So it is precisely the narrative structure, as we have seen, that opens the door for a different conception of understanding human affairs, particularly important when we reflect about care and on the significance this can have for treating illness, pathology, cure in a better way. Through biographical narrative, a narrative that has to do with one's own life, individuals navigate their journey, articulating fears and hopes, recovering the autonomy they may have lost during their healing journey. The use of narratives in health care serves as a bridge between subjective experiences and the objective pursuit of medical knowledge. This also brings out the transformative power of autobiographical narratives, whereby even students can change their condition after they choose to delve into the motivations behind their specific journey. This is the point of Charon's (Charon, 2006) efforts, who reflected precisely on narrative competence, understanding it as the ability to recognize, absorb and interpret in order to act upon the stories and problems concretely experienced. Literature and the arts can thus be understood as an archive of experiences, of emotions that can have a profound impact on medicine as well. In this sense, Bleakley's work has dwelt on the need to adjust the educational curriculum of young physicians precisely to reevaluate the weight of humanistic culture within their training (Bleakley, 2024). This operation theorized by Bleakley is possible precisely from the pedagogical idea of curriculum, from the theories that have placed social learning and career rethinking models at the center, in such a way as to adapt the path of physicians to the reality of the time in which they find themselves immersed. He in the course of his experience, in which he helped devise changes to the physicians' curriculum, was inspired by the poet Eliot's question, "Where is the wisdom we have lost in knowledge? Where is the knowledge we have lost in information?" (Bleakley, 2024, 37). Through the incitement from cultural fields not directly related to medicine, he reflected on the fact that the idea of *curriculum* has led to the pedagogical contradiction whereby, instead of focusing on the learning process, we focus on the assessment of learning, as if it were now something inert. Hence the impulse to recover pedagogical theory for the training of physicians, in such a way as to recover that focus on the educational process, which prompts one to reflect on the meaning of all one's training and the role one will play in the future when assisting patients. Corroborating his thesis with philosophical references to the concepts of *Wissenschaft* and *Bildung*, he strongly advocated reforming the curriculum to make it a 'curriculum process.' This leads to the idea of bringing knowledge together, adopting a more comprehensive perspective on education and care, bringing together the biomedical sciences and the arts/humanities disciplines, making them translate one into the other but without losing their deep identity. On closer inspection, such a perspective is also evoked by philosophers who have been studying the problem of complexity in contemporary society, such as Edgar Morin, who in one of his seminal works (2000) thematized precisely the mission of teaching as the transmission not of pure knowledge, but of a culture that allows one to help live, to think in an open and free way. Education therefore should involve an attitude aimed at contextualizing knowledge, implementing a capacity of the human mind, to make it exercise itself. It means using even the seemingly insignificant clues to trace the meaning of history through them. Hence Morin's critique of the parcelization of knowledge (which is about to become more and more a parcelization of the curriculum itself), which would go on to compose an inert superficial knowledge, made of disconnected and insignificant elements. This is a perspective that should be vigorously recovered, at a time of crisis such as the present, when it increasingly seems that individuals are losing sight of the concept of well-being as something that should be shared among members of society. From this perspective, it is a matter of returning to the use of the unifying capacity of reason, in spite of scattered individual knowledge, to ensure that comprehensive knowledge is gained even in the medical field, in the design of care pathways and health services in general. This is a perspective that can be embraced, provided that we change course from policies that have progressively focused instead on deeming services, such as territorial medicine, useless or poorly remunerative. In fact, again following Morin, solidarity among individuals has a major role to play, if one assumes that sharing responsibility also means overcoming the individualism that sees everyone as separate monads. In no other context than those aimed at care, however, is the strong value of community perceived, which becomes a community of care and learning together. It is important to link knowledge with each other, thus also providing a basis for dialogue between professional figures, who in their daily lives are indeed dealing with humanity from various points of view, but still referring to an "environment" that unites them. Only learning shaped in such a way as to unite knowledge may be able to grasp the ever-increasing complexity of the world we live in, in which the delegations to machines is increasingly growing. The risk is that if this reliance on machines is poorly controlled, it will exacerbate that tendency toward dehumanization exposed earlier. This is a risk that the medical humanities themselves must face: making sure that the technological development used in the field of bio-medicine is not accompanied by a similarly mechanistic view of man, which, even in light of the most modern theories in the biological and scientific fields, now appear outdated.

REFERENCES

Alheit, P. (1995). *The Biographical Approach in European Adult Education*. Volkshochschule.

Bauman, Z. (2021). *Modernità liquida* [Liquid Modernity]. Laterza.

Bleakley, A. (2005). Stories as data, data as stories: Making sense of narrative inquiry in clinical education. *Medical Education*, 39(5), 534–540. 10.1111/j.1365-2929.2005.02126.x15842721

Bleakley, A. (2024). *Medical Humanities. Ethics, Aesthetics, Politics*. Taylor and Francis Group.

Bruner, J. (1986). *Actual Minds, Possible Worlds*. Harvard University Press. 10.4159/9780674029019

Bruner, J. (1996). *The Culture of Education*. Harvard University Press. 10.4159/9780674251083

Certini, R. (2001). Il metodo autobiografico e la storia dell'educazione. [Autobiographical method and history of education]. *Studium Educationis*, 2, 440–449.

Chambers, T. (1999). *The Fiction of Bioethics: Cases as Literary Texts*. Routledge.

Charon, R. (2006). *Narrative Medicine: Honoring the Stories of Illness*. Oxford University Press. 10.1093/oso/9780195166750.001.0001

Cole, T. R., Carlin, N. S., & Carson, R. (2015). *Medical Humanities*. Cambridge University Press.

Conti, F., & Silei, G. (2022). *Breve storia dello Stato sociale* [Short History of the Welfare State]. Carocci.

De Feo, A. (2023). La formazione dell'operatore sanitario: Dall'approccio biomedico alla 'cura narrativa' [The Training of the Healthcare Professional: from the Biomedical Approach to the 'Narrative Care']. *Medical Humanities & Medicina Narrativa*, 1, 225–234.

Demetrio, D. (1994). La ricerca autobiografica come cura di sé e processo cognitivo [The Autobiographical Research as cure for the self and cognitive process]. *Animazione sociale*, *6/7*, 10-18.

Demetrio, D. (2000). *Raccontarsi. L'autobiografia come cura di sè[Telling the self. Autobiography as self-care]*. Raffaello Cortina.

Dominicé, P. (2000). *Learning from our lives*. Jossey-Bass.

Formenti, L. (1998). *La formazione autobiografica[The autobiographical training].* Guerini Studio.

Frank, A. W. (1995). *The Wounded Storyteller: Body, Illness and Ethics.* University of Chicago Press. 10.7208/chicago/9780226260037.001.0001

Freeman, M. (1993). *Rewriting the Self. History, Memory, Narrative.* Routledge.

Gargani, A. (1990). *L'altra storia[The Other Story].* Il Saggiatore.

Hunter, K. M. (1991). *Doctors' Stories: The Narrative Structure of Medical Knowledge.* Princeton University Press. 10.1515/9780691214726

Iori, V. (2012), Pedagogia dell'invecchiamento e identità di genere [Pedagogy of aging and gender identity], in Corsi, M., Ulivieri, S., *Progetto generazioni. Bambini e anziani due strategie a confronto. [Generations Project. Children and the elderly two strategies compared],* ETS.

Launer, J. (2002). *Narrative-Based Primary Care. A Practical Guide.* Radcliffe Medical Press.

Maddalena, S., & Paolozzi, F. (2023). Complessità, bioetica, resilienza: Tre dimensioni paradigmatiche all'approccio MH e MN nella prospettiva pedagogica [Complexity, Bioethics, Resilience: three paradigmatic dimentions to the MH and MN in a Pedagogical Perspective]. *Medical Humanities & Medicina Narrativa*, 1, 145–164.

Marini, M. G. (2016). *Narrative Medicine. Bridging the Gap between Evidence-Based Care and Medical Humanities.* Springer. 10.1007/978-3-319-22090-1

Marone, F. (2023). Arte, cultural wellbeing e medical education [Art, Cultural Wellbeing and Medical Education]. *Medical Humanities & Medicina Narrativa*, 1, 77–88.

Morin, E. (2000). *La testa ben fatta* [*The 'well-made' head*]. Raffaello Cortina.

Morin, E. (2001). *Il metodo. La natura della natura* [Method: The Nature of Nature]. Raffaello Cortina.

Mortara, C. C. (2023). La scrittura terapeutica nella Medicina Narrativa [Therapeutic writing in Narrative Medicine]. *Medical Humanities & Medicina Narrativa*, 1, 287–295.

Pineau, G., & Marie-Michèle, M.-M. (1983). *Produire sa vie: autoformation et autobiographie* [Producing your life: self-training and autobiography]. Éditions Saint-Martin.

Ricouer, P. (1983). *Tempo e racconto[Time and Tale].* Jaca Book.

Rossiello, M. C. (2016). Gli anziani si raccontano. Alcune riflessioni. [The Elders Tell. Some Thoughts]. *Metis*, 1/6, 322–330.

Sirignano, F. M. (2003). *La pedagogia della formazione. Teoria e storia[Pedagogy of training. Theory and history].* Liguori.

Sirignano, F. M., & Maddalena, S. (2023). L'arte del curare. Nuove prospettive pedagogiche. [The Art of Care. New Pedagogical Perspectives]. *Medical Humanities & Medicina Narrativa*, 1, 15–18.

Chapter 8
Medical Humanties, Narrative Medicine, and Bibliotherapy:
New Pedagogical Frontiers to Build Health and Promote Well-Being

Fabrizio Manuel Sirignano
https://orcid.org/0000-0002-9072-9342
Suor Orsola Benincasa University, Italy

Valerio Ferro Allodola
Mediterranea University of Reggio Calabria, Italy

Antonio Raimondo Di Grigoli
https://orcid.org/0000-0002-1293-2281
University of Florence, Italy

ABSTRACT

Contemporary medicine makes a radical epistemological shift indispensable, one that brings out the human dimension and the active participation of the subject in building prevention processes, care, and well-being. From this perspective, listening to patients' stories, re-evaluating the care relationship, and using narrative based medicine instead of exclusively evidence-based medicine are of crucial importance. Placed in the realm of medical humanities, the chapter intends to present, investigate, and discuss the potential of narrative medicine, with particular reference to bibliotherapy as a tool for prevention, educational care, and well-being. Furthermore, the contribution reconstructs the historical-pedagogical pathway that has led to

DOI: 10.4018/979-8-3693-4244-2.ch008

the outlining of such innovative training approaches and tools. In conclusion, the 'Dialogic Literary Gathering' model is presented as an educational empowerment strategy, in the field of mental health promotion and psychosocial support (MHPSS) in LGBTQIA+ adolescent victims of minority stress.

INTRODUCTION

Numerous important contributions regarding our need to retrieve the sense of narrative and the humanities in medicine have characterized the Italian and international scientific debate in the past few decades. Among the most important ones, it is worth our while mentioning those of Bertolini (1994, 2003), Bert, Quadrino (2002). Campo (2005), Cattorini (2003), Evans (2002), Evand & Greaves (2010), Gordon (2005), Giarelli *et al.* (2005), Giani (2005, 2006), Good (1999), Masini (2005), Pattison (2003), Zannini (2001, 2008). As they consider the healing relation one between several life stories and regard knowledge as a historical construction of a recursive game between formalized notions and tacit notions, they argue that this way of gathering anamnesis and symptom description fosters a better understanding of the illness or disease in question.

In spite of this scientific debate (livelier and more extended in English- and French-speaking countries, for that matter), contemproary western medicine tends to stay disease-centered. Disease is considered

a) a biologic universal that transcends the socio-cultural context;
b) a predictive medicine which, starting from effectiveness tests and through studies based on clinical trials, tries to foresee our likelihood of recovering, falling sick, improving our conditions.

This no doubt entails training and epistemologic consequences, and continues to induce reductionist attitudes towards the disease, which is exclusively limited to its biological factors.

As Galimberti maintained in 1983, the physician is trained to set his/her eyes from one body to another, to reflect on the disease as a clinical entity with a cause, a development, an outcome, a prognosis, but without a sense. The diseased is then an indifferent carrier of the disease. The variables related to it become factors of confusion and as such, they wanted reducing to zero in order to reach the "purity" of knowledge of the disease and allow for a definite acknowledgement and codification of it. The physician's glance does not meet the diseased's, but the disease's - in the body of the sick, the doctor does not read a biography, but a pathology.

Thus, the patient's subjectivity tends to disappear behind the doctor's quest for the objectivity of symptoms which, in their turn, do not refer to a context, a way of living, a series of habits, but a clinical picture where individual differences having their repercussions in the development of the disease annul themselves behind the list of symptoms that the doctor classifies in terms of morbid facts, just as a botanist classifies plants.

The life story of the patient, his/her existential experience, is left outside, the anamnesis becomes a list of objective facts, symptoms and disease, but hardly touches the story of the disease, the patient's biography, or his existential dimension.

In this type of scenario, Medical Humanities, and Narrative Based Medicine (NBM) in particular, can take the challenge to a traditional biomedical knowledge based on effectivenes tests (Evidence Based Medicine, EBM), engaging in the requests for the humanization of treatments and dismantling the medicalization processes rooted in the medical health practices.

According to Villani (2023), Medical Humanities has trodden the path of a closer and closer cooperation between medical and humanistic epistemology. A new alliance between and among the various notional disciplines, with various mergings and contaminations, was promoted in the more and more widespread conviction that diagnosis of the disease and life story of the diseased, science and healing practice, poignant data objectivity and fluid patient (and doctor, for that matter) subjectivity are inseparable. This alliance has been more or less spread through the terrains of narrative medicine.

As Sirignano put it in 2019, the cultural platform that the alliance is based upon consists in the complexity and constructivism perspective which is making the scientific communities more and more aware that learing paradigms are homogeneous and centered on a methodological monism that, unlike in the past, is abreast of the limits, partiality and fallibility of epistemic positions. This monism overcomes the sterile duality between hard or normothetic sciences, alleged depositories of absolute definite truth, and human, social or ideographic sciences which, unlike the former, grasped the world in its individuality and, for this reason, were thought to be unable to formulate laws that would enable us to foresee and rule socio-historical phenomena.

V.i.z., reason is no longer hard and fast, absolute, spendid and non-historical; it undergoes a historicization process and becomes feeble, opaque and problematic. Thus, as Prigogine & Stengers stressed in 1993, reason starts having to

1) confront with irrationality,
2) take into account the plurality of points of view and also
3) accept the aspects relating to singularity and particularity in its studies.

The role and value of science is not under discussion. Science can still give a reading key of the real world through the formulation of representative models of it, which, as such, are now accepted in a partial, probabilistic and fallibilistic sense. Mennato (1999) and Morin (1988) maintained that possibility as a category comes to replace certainty, with the passage through God's absolute and impartial eye myth to man's eye, which is limited, partial and partisan.

Thus, albeit initially arising in the fields of natural, mathematical and geometrical sciences and later spreading in history, philosophy and pedagogy, epistemologic reflection on the validity of the positivistic representation of science inexorably undermines the image of definite objective knowledge and promotes awareness and acceptance of the uncertain and ephemeral nature of the real world, as the image of a hard-and-fast social or natural order based on strictly mechanistic relations has fallen to pieces. In lieu of a stable absolute systematization of knowledge typical of the various reductionistic monisms, the discovery of the dimensions of chaos and disorder introduces to formal natural science features such as problematicness, probability, pluralism, contingency and uniqueness which, up until a few decades ago were considered typical of human and social sciences. Following this new trend, as Frauenfelder, Laporta, Santoianni and Striano pointed out, from 1994 to 2004 respectively, about the bio-educational science model, the quest for connections between pedagogy, educational sciences and experiemental sciences has achieved greater and greater status.

In the aforesaid scenario we can find NBM which has taken so much from constructivist epistemology (albeit breaking away from the empirical quantitative EBM paradigm) and does not mean to oppose it, but to build an integrated inter-acting perspective. So, having its own clinical practice include the *Narrative Based Medicine (EBM)* perspective, developing an attitude towards cognitively listening to the patient and/or considering the history of his/her disease does not mean refusing the EBM paradigm.

Therefore, the constructivist interpretation of medical health training provides the professional in question with some sort of subjective responsibility towards training, not only as to his/her know-how, as Boffo, Zannini, Mortari, Bruzzone, Musi, Contini and Manini pointed out from 2006 to 2014, but also as to those complex dynamics that could activate the drift from "being taken care of" to "taking care of oneself", from "object of treatment" to "subject of the relationship". If it is true that the quality of the treatment depends on the acknowledgement of feelings as attitudes that structure professional identity, then its education should be included in the initial training of operators, who have to garatee its practice while on duty.

Moreover, clinical activity features at least two lines of thought that interact and influence each other: scientific thought (general laws, physio-pathologic mechanisms and pre-defined clinical pictures) and narrative thought, which is linked to the uniqueness, specificity, contingency and contextuality of patient stories. As Zannini stressed in 2001, the hermeneutic part of clinical knowledge first develops from the medical checkup of the patient and the meeting with him/her.

In fact, the movement advocating the primacy of narration in the building of knowledge and interpretation of the world (parallel and on an equal footing with logic) is that of cultural psychology, whose major expositor is Jerome Bruner. In joining the argument against the theories based on 20th-century positivist and cognitivist thought, considering all aspects of human personality, Bruner acquires a holistic view through which he investigates the constructive processes that enable and allow individuals to give sense and meaning to life itself and the world around. These studies are no doubt a breakthrough in psychology and human and social sciences, as they enable and allow the success of a view of man no longer as passive receptor of outer stimuli, but as active selector and builder of experience, thus setting great store by the symbolic, inter-subjective, cultural and contextrual aspects in the construction of the self and the world around. So, as Atkinson pointed out in 2002, we build the real world and personal meaning when exposing and contextualizing our narration; our experiences acquire the shape that we use to describe them, and the stories are the ways in which we order, comprehend and ascribe meaning to the experiences we have made so they can have a sense of continuity.

In his *Actual Minds, Possible Worlds* (1988), Bruner argues against a unilateral concept of the mind and maintains the existence of two different complementary mental worlds: "logical-scientific or paradigmatic thought" and "narrative syntagmatic thought", either one building, shaping and organizing experience according to specific principles and manners. As Groppo *et al.* observed in 1999, Bruner reminds us that people and their own actions cannot exclusively be related to a logica l-paradigmatic-explanation-like analysis, but are specifically comprehended within a view that is connected to those hermeneutic processes which enable and allow the patient to give sense to his/her own events and attitudes as well as those of other people. He/she does so through connecting people's actions with their intentions, wishes, desires, beliefs and feelings.

As they refer to two different ways of relating to, and getting into contact with, the world, these two "mental habits" have each one's own operational principles, validity criteria and testing procedures (Figure 1).

Figure 1. Differences between paradigmetic and narrative thought

Paradigmatic Thought	Narrative Thought
Typical of Scientific Thinking	Typical of Daily Thinking
Vertical Orientation	Horizontal Orientation
Context-Free	Context-Sensitive
Nomothetic and Paradigmatic	Idiographic and Syntagmatic
Validated by Falsification	Validated by Coherence
Builds Laws	Builds Stories
It Is extentional	It Is Intentional

(Smorti, 1994)

As Smorti evinced in 1994, paradigmatic thought (typical of scientific reasoning) consists in always relating a particular case with the general categories according to a vertical process of subordination and superordination, in line with the ideal of a descriptive, explanatory, formal and mathematical system. It is that form of non-contextual thought that implies the construction of theories, laws, postulates which can be hierarchically ordered according to inductive and deductive principles. The features of a subject become residual and are placed in a broader sphere, as priority is given to similarities and analogies with other phenomena. This mentality is characterized by a nomothetic approach, one which tends to provide generalizations and universal context-free theories rather than in-depth analyses of the single case in its uniqueness. In its explanation process, logical-scientific thought uses criteria of truth based on falsifiability and external validation, thus "trying" to eliminate the ambiguities that the experience presents. It leads to unique solutions.

On the contrary, narrative thought deeply focuses upon the features of that particular subject and tries not to explain, but to comprehend the phenomenon in its own specificity and within a context. This way of thinking is often used in everyday life, as it does not need so long and laborious processing as is the case with paradigmatic thought. This condition of continuous uncertainty in which the person has to operate, relate with others and make important decisions, does not allow for an accurate detailed probabilistic analysis by treading a coherent logical route. In professional contexts, as well as in his/her daily life, the subject often has to express himself/

herself through actions in uncertain precarious conditions. In this case narrations have the function of giving the experience concerned a new semantic collocation.

In order to understand the event and grasp its meaning, narrative thought proceeds by historicization and contextualization. As Groppo et al. affirmed in 1999, the purpose of narrative thought is not to test its own arguments, but to produce truthful, plausible and reasonable stories that aim at placing the human experience in the space-time dimension to the single case. It is an interpretive thought having two poles: that of action, i.e. sequence of events, and that of the meaning subjects ascribe to such events. So, narrative thought tries to give an interpretation of human facts by creating a story based on the actors' intentions and the sensitivity of the context. No wonder it is called clinical thinking - in trying the logic of human actions, it operates according to the subject's intended meaning, in an attempt to rebuild the single case on the basis of one single coherent picture. Narrative thought produces topics, themes and collections instead of categories and concepts - it paves the way for multiple interpretive significance. So, telling about something and about ourselves means being aware of ourselves, of the world and of how we are thinking. It is not a simple operation.

As Bruner asserted in 1988, if our own selves were transparent they certainly would not need to talk to ourselves, so he would be positive that we cannot meet with an intuitively evident and essential self that is placidly waiting to be represented in words. Instead, we continuously and continually build and rebuild a self according to what the situations we are in require, under the guidance of our past memories and future hopes and fears. Talking to ourselves about ourselves is like building a story on who and what we are, on what happened and on why we are doing what we are doing. Thus, narrative thought starts from the assumption that healing, curing, treating, being of help to a subject that lives in a disease condition (sometimes a chronical one) means

a) operating on his/her personal experiences and transforming them and, specifically,
b) asking him/her to modify the stories and narrations that rule the meanings he/she ascribes to that experience, to himself/herself, to his/her our body, to the disease, etc.

The structure of existence itself is time-bound. So, as Bruzzone pointed out, telling about something and about ouselves is not merely a sterile repetition exercise whereby we save past events from oblivion by listing them all in chronological order; it is rather some sort of backtracking events, encounters and feelings that emerge from the meanders of the past in a way that is always different in substance and tone. This continual memory-based self-appropriation also turns out to be an opportunity to re-signify the time that has passed and, in so doing, pave the way for new existential possibilities to grow and change.

Thus, NBM envisages the opportunity to re-acquire that narrative competence which seemed to have inexorably diasppeared from medical praxis. The ability to listen, acknowledge, interpret, perceive, grasp are now included not only in disease stories narrated by the patient, but also in those that the doctor tells the others and himself/herself. Moreover, NBM enables and allows the treatment professional to adequately face the clinical meeting as a construction and negotiation of meanings and, in so doing, to foster some sort of therapeutic alliance.

According to Giarelli et al., this orientation tends to humanize medicine on a real patient-centered basis, which enables and allows the doctor to also reflect on his own self, his own journey into his/her profession; it also re-thinks the relationship with medical health colleagues and co-workers, as well as with people and society in general, where he/she has to re-win that trust that seems to become more and more critical. Following this perspective, which connotes medicine as hermeneutic-interpretive activity, oriented towards comprehending what underlies the pathologic event, within a very definite setting such as that of the medical checkup, doctor and patient together delineate and structure the meaning and significance of the disease by telling stories and actively listening to them.

As Zannini stated in 2001, in order to carry out his/her task, the doctor must enact an interpretive activity where he/she must 'read' the patient right from his symptoms and signs, i.e. from the very recounting of the patient's disorder and its concrete manifestations in his/her body.

Albeit adhering to that perspective whereby medicine is a hermeneutic activity, one which interprets signs and symptoms, we have to acknowledge that medical praxis still falls under a well-defined epistemologic realm underlying a reductionist view of disease. The interpretive activity is based on a complex plot which should necessarily include psycho-social and anthropologic dimensions as well, but still in the sense of what is considered a mere "morbid event", characterized by well-defined processes and syndromes that leave no room for listening or analyzing all those aspects concerning the patient's and his/her relatives' life experiences. In spite of the biomedical operators' recalcitrance, however, this interpretive activity is more and more irrelinquishable for the clinical praxis paradigm, not only as regards signs but also as regards meanings. This is carried out through the integration of the two basic components of the medical checkup: the anamnesis, i.e. the dialogue with the patient and with his/her relatives to re-build the story of the disease, and the objective checkup through which the doctor inspects, palpates and auscultates the patient's body.

It is as if western medicine hosted two souls: a biologic one and a clinical one. These two souls mirror the two paradigms of thought mentioned above, which coexist and interact: the logical one and the narrative one (Figure 2), where the clinical soul of medicine seems to be reconnected to narrative thought.

The connection between narrative thought and clinical thought is probably due to the fact that the latter tries to give an interpretation to a disease story, which can be considered the discrepancy par excellence in a life story, an event that still entails a biographic rupture. As any exceptional and unforeseen event, the disease requires an attribution of meaning from the subject that tells the story to insert it in the symbolic cultural system it belongs to.

Figure 2. Differences between paradigmetic and narrative thought in the medical health sector

Medical Health Sector	
Paradigmatic Thought	***Narrative Thought***
Extensional Nomothetic Thought: builds general laws	Intentional Idiographic Thoughts: refers to particular concrete events
Not bound by the context it comes from	Bound by the particular situation it has developed from and by concrete events
Facts are connected according to a linear logic - cause and effect	It has a historical narrative. Events are bound together in chronological order
The subject is body, matter, machine	The intentionality dimension is present, so the subjects of narration have certain aims to pursue through certain actions that want interpreting
Individuals are considered body	Individuals are considered characters
Dimension of Truth	Dimension of Truthfulness
Dimension of Necessity and Causality	Dimension of Possibility
The patient is the context, the situation of the disease	The events are comprehended in relation to the context containing them
The attention is focused on the morbid event in a localized part of the body	Each narration consists of five elements: actor, action, aim, scene and instrument, where the unforeseen circumstance, the discrepancy, intervenes

(Zannini, 2001)

The disease story is part of a broader life story consisting of characters, events, emotions, that characterize the clinical event and enrich it with meanings. This event is a fact that is always built and read from a particular standpoint, which acts as limitation and possibility, still fostering a selective perception of the data related to it.

Thus, as Zannini points out, in clinical praxis the therapist is faced with a story, which needs to be comprehended as such. To do so, he later activates forms of narrative thinking as well. Moreover, not only is medical knowledge closely interrelated with forms of narrative thought, but it reproduces itself in training processes by means of narrations. The doctor listens to the patient, records some data, observes, auscultates, palpates his/her body and turns a single patient's story into a series of data included in a clinical picture, which is another fundamental object of medical health service praxis. The clinical picture is the translation of the patient's story into medical language, into disease story. This takes place through a hermeneutic process whereby the patient's story is used as text. In this perceptive-selective process, however, the doctor obtains data and builds notions, but on the other hand he loses some information which is precious for diagnostic therapeutic aims, information which only the patient can give, certainly not randomized studies or sophisticated technologies. There are obviously some diversities between the story told by the doctor and the story told by the patient.

The doctor's story consists of never neutral formalized knowledge and tacit notions, of a specific intelligence and an instrumental equipment, it is full of emotions, life experiences and influences from the social and cultural context he belongs to (Figure 3). On the contrary, as Zannini points out, the patient's story is the story of his/her illness, which often appears organized and structured in an almost non-scientific manner.

Figure 3. Specificity of the storytelling for doctor and patient

Storytelling	
Doctor	**Patient**
The main aim of his/her contribution is his/her attempt to give a precise shape to a series of events, in a view which is first diagnostic and then therapeutic. This type of contribution sharply separates the disease from the patient's life.	The disease experience is a unique unforeseen event, deeply rooted in the context. The patient's main aim sharing a painful and often unforeseen experience. Recounting the events enables the patient to express his/her feelings and fears originating from his/her disease experience.
As regards his/her aims, the referring paradigm is one which passes through an epistemology of checkup and prescriptions.	As regards his/her aim, the referring paradigm is one that passes through an epistemology of listening and talking.
Relevance of the Object.	Relevance of the life Experience.
Empirical Quantitative Epistemology	Constructivist Epistemology

(Zannini, 2009)

In fact, in clinical praxis, the doctor influenced by tacit notions built on previous life experiences and professional experiences formulates his/her judgement in a manner that is very far away from an aseptically objective analysis of the facts. Doctors do not limit themselves to evaluating the signs and symptoms objectively; they interpret them by connecting single biological facts to a more general historical existential picture. Considering the patient's story from a narrative and not only scientific point of view means, first of all, considering disease a discrepancy in the life story of the individual, a milestone of his/her existence. If the patient uses narration to give sense to this discrepancy, also the operator must take this view and wonder what the symptoms mean to the person involved and his/her relatives not only from a biological point of view, but also within the existential context he/she is in. The narrative register recognizes the psycho-social dimension of the disease and draws our attention on its psychological and social factors which, like biologic variables, are necessary variables for arriving at a comprehension of the single patient's health problem. Thus, the patients' stories are a favorite instrument for building medical knowledge; the disease story, translated into a clinical picture, will become a trace of memory. These translations, however, tend to eliminate the emotional aspects of the stories by turning the patient's subjective and private disease experience into an objective and scientfic story. The more aseptic and science-based the transformation of the patient's disease story, the more disease-centered the interpretation. The biological focus of the disease story and interpretation will consequantly make the relation between doctor and patient more asymmetrical - the former's knwoledge will inevitalby become an instrument of control of the latter.

At this point, the paradigms obviously want revising, the premises of the medical science have actually proved insufficient. As some have found out in the past few years, Descartes' Mechanistic approach is no doubt inappropriate, especially when it comes to

a) chronic, degenerative, highly invalidating pathologies and when
b) therapy consists in totally or mostly modifying the patient' habits.

Here is why medicine features an integrated conjugation of two different approaches, Evidence-Based Medicine and Narrative Medicine.

The narrative perspective is considered not only one of the favorite ways to access the meanings of professional action and of the attribution of sense to events and the real world that the subjects experience and share in their daily experience, but mainly a device that is useful for building new meanings and new practices.

As Striano maintained in 2006, using the narrative device for the analysis and development of professional epistemologies in praxis contexts enables and allows us to effectively evince the transformation factors from the point of view of epistemology, socio-linguistics and psychology. These factors characterize adult situational learning and enables and allows us to trace growth and development processes taking place at a personal and professional level, with a particular focus on the re-definition of meaning perspectives which constitute the interpretive coordinates that socio-cultural-context-bound practices are based upon.

The narration as interpretive construction is practically like a possible explanatory way of explaining intrapersonal, interpersonal and organizational processes for building knowledge and creating and implementing professional actions. The narrative approach starts from the fundamental principle whereby the subject plays an active part in the learning processes involving him/her throughout his/her life, in his/her daily and professional experience. Thus, the subject behaves as an actor, a protagonist in knowledge-building processes, which follow a narration, a story.

As Connelly and Claudinin pointed out in 1997, telling stories becomes an indispensible instruemnt for reflection on personal practical knowledge. Narrations and stories acquire an interpretive constructive function, and enable and allow the subject not only to meet with and rebuild his/her own self, but also to activate reflexive routes and turn practices into texts that can be edited and integrated. These texts can compose and organize the multiplicity of life experiences, evince the implicit hidden meanings and those meanings which are embedded in the actions and enable and allow a continuous and constant process of revision and restructuring of practices. The narration and the story stimulate reflection on actions, thus enabling and allowing the reconstruction of professional experience by ascribing new meanings and engendering a new comprehension of

1) professional actions and situations;
2) themselves as professionals involved in one or more praxis communities;
3) concepts, beliefs, implicit or taken-for-granted theories on the nature of professional practise and on the roles of the elements involved in it.

The story induces us to identify, negotiate, and try to share the meaning of events and past actions with those who belong to the same professional community. The interpersonal dimension of professional experience becames the basis for the prospects of change for the people involved, so that the most significant events that sew the threads of the stories are those they have shared in the relationship with their colleagues.

Right at the very moment when he/she tells his/her own stories to himself/herself and the others, the subject modifies and rebuilds his/her own identity and co-builds the world around him/her. As Groppo et al. pointed out, it gives itself to an active interiority that enacts and builds its own world through a continuous interpretive effort that enables and allows an intersubjective negotiation of meanings ascribed to events and behaviors. The narrative mind, behind which a certain self in continuous evolution hides, leads the indivitual to tell, and signify in the end, all that acquires exceptionality, v.i.z. everything that is not canonical, known and shared. It is through narration, then, that a constant process of interpretive reconstruction of the events of the individual's existence where the turning points acquire particular relevance.

The disease story brings in itself all the potentials for improving the quality of the medical health service, in the direction of an ever-increasing mutual operator-patient comprehension and of a healing relation that meets the subject-patients' complex-health needs. Doctors and patients shared the need to describe and identify the disease as well. Objectivising the disease and its symptoms used to convey a sense of control over it and exerted a remarkable influence on their behavior. The language used to represent the disease was very similar to that used for describing the demon's possession of the subject's body. The disease is represented like an active force which enters the diseased's body and makes its own way through it. It assails, assaults, and/or hits the body, which gives rise to a war between disease and health in the body which becomes the battlefield. As Gentilcore asserted in 2008, People's statements on pain also suggest how the sick body was conceived of. As pain cound not be comprehended objectively, it had to be described in a language that was necessarily metaphoric. During those painful moments, the body became an object and the patient looked down upon it from the outside.

The detailed descriptions of the physical manifestations of the disease, e.g. fever, excruciating pain, convulsion and loss of conscience, evince the powerful violence over the body as the individual perceives it. These symptoms are interpreted as signs of the struggle between the disease and the patient himself/herself, who desperately tries to defend himself/herself and resist its devastating effects.

Thus, the language used to talk of the disease reflects the widespread perception that it is an external malignant threatening force penetrating the human body to destroy it. This concept is rooted in popular culture and representation of health and disease and has deeply influenced the perception and management of disease throughout history.

In conclusion, the language used to describe disease as a hostile invasive force stresses the challenge and fear the individual and people in general perceive and reflects a dualist dichotomic and conflictive view of health and disease. So, disease becomes a story developing through time, with chapters following, and intertwining with, each other as the symptoms and complications that may ensue. The narration enables and allows the individual to give sense and meaning to the disease, explore the origins and causes, as well as reflect on all possible remedies, treatments and strategies for the case in question.

A narration of the disease certainly contributes to creating connections and bridges between the diseased and the people around him, thus fostering the experience of comprehension and empathy. Sharing disease stories can help us face the sense of isolation and solitude they often engender, thus allowing for the creation of support and solidarity networks.

Narrative medicine makes or lets one reconsider medical knowledge through the construction of a common language that starts from the interpretation of one's life experience in order to define personalized meaningful routes. Narration can be considered that moment when one rebuilds vital worlds and orders one's experience so as to be able to creatively connect events and meanings. This operation of sense can lead the researcher and the doctor to understand what the mere objective codification of the real world fails to achieve - an effective comprehension of the diseased in his/her bio-psycho-social malaise, which is what the clinical hermeneutic approach can do quite well, in fact.

Various theoretical approaches in psycho-pedagogy in the past few years have stressed the importance of instruments such as the narration and auto-biography for the construction of the self. Right when the person narrates himself/herself and his/her own personal story, he/she ascribes more meaning to his/her own actions and introduces himself/herself to the other people in the way he/she sees fit for a given performance. Zannini (2021) stressed that narrative-medicine contributions can guarantee promising results, e.g. in the development of communicative relational skills, empathy, medical knowledge, cross-cultural competence, professionality and burnout mitigation.

As Venturini stressed in 2020, a particular declination of Narrative-Based Medicine is Bibliotherapy, whose objective is to make the reader experience the book's great emotional impact, by teaching him/her to find what is looked for in the text. In bibliotherapy, the words the author uses to narrate, describe the character's life experiences and stories, can be useful for recognizing and/or discovering buried or undescribable emotions - the story read becomes a lifejacket to grab in the middle of the sea and try to get ashore. The stories we read provide us with material to write the story of our own life and improve our ability to adapt and the consequent opportunities for personal change and growth. To say it in a way so dear to Bindi (2019), this happens because when we face narrative material we can internalize it and turn it into some sort of vicarious experience that enriches our experiential background.

The term "bibliotherapy" was coined in 1916 by Samuel McChord Crothers in his A Literary Clinic, which appeared in the prestigious American magazine Atlantic Monthly. Crothers considered this practice some sort of self-help book reading to facilitate patient recovery processes. From 1916 (when bibliotherapy was considered to have been founded) up until today, the definitions of this practice have multiplied. On this occasion, it could be useful to concentrate, delimit the scope and focus on the Italian scenario, which features all the necessary premises to promote a positive implementation of bibliotherapy, thanks to the development of Medical Humanities, which is more and more widespread in the healthcare sector. So, we hope that also Bibliotherapy, through the interpretation of the patients' subjective life experience, will become a much more powerful instrument among those that fall under the realm of Medical Humanities, namely that of Narrative Medicine. As Batini & Bertolucci put it in 2016, Bibliotherapy has proved to be much more effective in strengthening particular factors of the patient's physical and moral persona, such as resilience, mindfulness, life quality, socio-relational skills, management of his/her own future, empathy and imagination. Moreover, as Garista stressed in 2017, among the various positive factors of reading, imagination is likely to improve one's health inasmuch as it strengthens the sense of coherence (SOC). From a more pathological standpoint, bibliotherapy contrasts disorders such as depression, general anxiety, that particular condition of psycho-physical inbalance called "chronic stress", medicine-abuse headache and, last but not least, provides its support in facilitating cardiac rehab recovery and in managing some neopastic pathologies more adequately. As Nutbeam, Sørensen et al. and Lorini et al. pointed out in 2008, 2012, 2017 and 2020 respectively, all the aforesaid scenario has obviously been in line with the principles and practices of the more famous Health Literacy, which has been recognized by the World Health Organization as an important empowerment strategy in the promotion of health, starting from school, as Ferro Allodola stressed in 2021. Through the implementation of notions and skills, in line with NBM and Medical Humanities, bibliotherapy aims at stimulating:

1. the individual's ability to make more conscious decisions concerning his/her own health needs,
2. a more adequate knowledge of the major risk factors,
3. his/her adoption of a correct lifestyle,
4. his/her taking an active part in the therapeutic strategies proposed.

As Centonze pointed out in 2018, as one of the causes of malaise that has been most frequently reported in Italy is of a psycho-affective nature, bibliotherapy (even in one of its particular declinations like the illustrated album, within the realm of childhood literature) make its presence in this context strongly felt as one of the simplest, cheapest, most pleasant and most unpleasant-side-effect-free remedies. To best conclude the present paragraph, we must stress that Medical Humanities cannot and does not operate short-term projects, but has to be configured as ordinary long-term practices; that is why it is more and more vital to continue developing more articulated training schemes whereby theory and practice, explanation and comprehension, knowledge and competence can be effectively interrelated to foster a better investigation of the human dimension, the human being and the subject-individual-person.

From the Scientific Method to Medical Humanities: A Historical Pedagogic Route

Maria Montessori's scientific pedagogy and her 20th-century pedagogy-medicine intersections have been the cultural reference platform that the famous Medical Humanity debate rests upon. As Barbara De Serio affirmed in 2022, pedagogic anthropology studies certainly contributed to strengthening Montessori's awareness of the need for a fruitful combination of medical science and pedagogic science. She had grown convinced that medicine was not enough to deal in a precautionary manner with such non-genetically- or non-hereditary-based illnesses and diseases as were the various forms of poverty, misery and despair that she began to face during her post-graduate training in Psychiatric Clinic at the University of Rome, when she came into contact with children that were hospitalized there for being wrongly considered phrenastenic. Thus, in Montessori's view, anthropologic science, medicine supported by pedagogy, should and could have become the promoter of a new morality.

Montessori's first great hypothesis was that the condition children were in at the neuro-psychiatric hospital was pedagogic and not medical. Those children needed educating, not checking up; they needed to play, talk, move, not stand up or sit still; they needed masters, not (only) doctors. Not only did they need to be cured, but also to be cared for. In these respects, as De Serio wonderfully pointed out in 2014, the central role of medical pedagogy in abnormal children therapy had already started making its way through fame even before Montessori came along. Montessori's intuition on the predominantly pedagogic nature of psychic retardation was even a step forward, thus paving the way for a completely different approach to the problem. This is true insomuch as Montessori saw in the mental illness concerned an emotional psychological distress whose source was to be found in the child's life and family habits. Rather than continuing to experiment on the effectiveness of the medical pedagogic method, which was extensively used in treating phrenastenic children, operators should opt for the moral education of these children, who were waiting to be "turned into" better adults.

This epistemologic breakthrough has been fundamental in determining the main points of the argument that we are going to expose - the interaction between

1. evidence-based paradigm and narrative-based paradigm,
2. explanation models (evidence-based medicine) and comprehension models (narrative-based medicine),
3. rationality and reflexivity,

towards the famous Medical Humanities. This Montessorian legacy has also enlightened the methodological debate in pedagogy and education research, which cannot fail to be mentioned and has two main threads.

The open one concerns the amplification of new subjects for investigation, as well as a strengthening of the bond with some research sectors not directly pedagogic (frontier pedagogy) oriented not only towards generating specific knowledge of the real world, but also towards transforming one's own object of inquiry.

The second one is oriented towards a re-interpretation of such qualitative investigation devices as action research, training research, transformational research, participative research, action learning. More specifically, we can say that the most innovative aspects of these devices rest on wondering

1. to what extent results are related to a specific context;
2. if and when these results are considered significant by those who have taken part in the research;

3. to what extent the research process has produced changes in the field of investigation and
4. if the results are shared by the subjects involved.

After making this brief contextual introduction, we must say that it is not our intention to retrace here the evolution of educational research in Italy; we would rather aim at presenting some major breakthroughs that have led pedagogic educational knowledge to intersect healthcare knowledge and then arrive at the Medical Humanities construction.

After cherishing constructivist epistemology, Italian ecucational researchers (strongly influenced by activist school thought, starting from Dewey and Montessori) have realized that individuals never use knowledge in a neutral manner, even when they think they do, but they rather produce concepts whose nature is always personal and singular.

So, from this perspective, we can think of designing a training scheme for health and treatment professionals that is based upon the acknowledgement and recognition of the subjectively constructive and interpretive value of the treatment practice, albeit within pertinence contexts engendered by medical knowledge (Evidence Based Medicine). This knowledge, firm but constantly subject to change, operates in restless cultural milieus, in diversified practice contexts, in relation to singular and specific professional life stories. This context has witnessed a more and more stringent need for a type of training aimed at building a reflexive self-corrective awareness, so as to build prevention and treatment skills which identify the specificities of healthcare professional training. As Schön pointed out in 1993, it is about a reflexive practice that would make trainees capable of facing problems arising from disturbing, problematic, complex, uncertain, situations which are characterized by instability, uniqueness and value conflicts.

On the basis of a reflexive training model is the idea whereby professional knowledge skills stem and spread from the trainees' ability to observe themselves in Personal Practical Knowledge. As Mezirow stressed in 2003, reflexive practice enables and allows trainees to gain access to any professional's personal knowledge, thus producing occasions of conscious reflection and nurturing learning to unlearn, restructuring one's own knowledge and learning styles, showing habitual congnitive schemes, automatic mechanisms and cognitive distortions, exposing the implicit dimensions of treatment practices, by examining and reinterpreting the medical jargon related to a form of "technical rationality" oriented towards a reflexive rationality culture. So, a more and more technical than human and personalized, more specialistic than complex and reflexive, comtemporary medicine requires a radical epistemologic change of medicine itself that would focus on the human dimension. This perspective stresses the crucial importance of listening to the patients' stories, revalorizing the human relation, using qualitative/narrative methods (Narrative Based Medicine) rather than quantitative/statistic ones only. A constructivist (or activist, for that matter) interpretation of healthcare training gives the professional concerned some sort of subjective responsibility to professional training, not only as to his/her own expertise, but also to complex competences whereby he/she could drift from "curing to caring", or the patient could drift "from being an object of the treatment to being the subject of the relation".

In this respect, the pedagogic category of "curing" acquires the features of "educational curing", the center of which is occupied by an emancipating process that could hold and support the subject-patients in the proactive activation of their own resources. Engaging in activating one's own resources means choosing to de-construct and re-comstruct one's own personal (implicit) and professional (expertise) knowledgte determining one's "professional epistemology". Therefore, learning in a transformative manner means becoming aware of professional action, not only in terms of standardized rules and procedures, but of learning to relate with cognitive processes of real practices which define our decisions and subjective choices. Through our attitude to learn from the senses, we should also build a "mind educated to learn while enacting professional action strategies" which acts on our own professional biography and on the fluid complex experience of our own expert practice.

Medical Humanities (MH from now on) started in the 1960s in the USA as an opinion movement consisting of doctors, health operators, spiritual operators, chaplains, who started wondering about the necessary humanization of the bio-medical model and who later founded a new scientific research discipline called "Medical Humanities" (MH).

These were the first steps for MH which, from the 1980s onwards would welcome more and more scholars from various disciplines, like anthropologists, psychologists, language philosophers. As Calabrese, Conti and Fioretti affirmed in 2022, this paved the way for the starting of various research centres and scientific societies (like the Society for Health and Human Values), specialized journals (like the Journal of Medical Humanities, founded 1979) and also several initiatives for the reformation of training routes, like the renewed medical psychology courses held by medical anthropologist Arthur Kleinman at Harvard Medical School. As Kleinman himself maintained in 1998, it was from those classrooms that he signed the essay that methodologically articulated the notions of disease, illness and sickness, on the basis of a new formulation of the curing/caring relation. Initiatives of this type have multiplied in all these decades. Villani asserted in 2023 that, along with the biomedical model, there spread a bio-psycho-social model and, more generally, alternative paradigms directed towards a holistic approach that would stop any form of reductionism.

According to Spinsanti (2006, 2011), the relation between medicine and humanities rests upon their being able and allowed to elaborate man's crucial existential questions, particularly those emerging from suffering, disease, quest for recovery and the limited use of technology. MH mobilizes ethical, philosophical, historical and literary reflections to reconsider the human existence under the impact of modern medicine and is a necessary treatment for medicine itself. We could define MH as being an interdisciplinary field consisting of:

- humanities (literature, philosophy, pedagogy, ethics, history and religion);
- social sciences (anthropology, cultural studies, psychology, sociology);
- arts (literature, drama, cinema and the visual arts) and their application to training and healthcare practices).

Evans (2002) defines the MH features as being an integrated interdisciplinary philosophical approach to record and interpret the human experience of disease, disability and medical intervention - an interdisciplinary investigation into the deep aspects of medical training, research and praxis regarding the human dimension of medicine. As Zannini pointed out in 2008, in the following decades, MH has been generally perceived and regarded as all that which concerns the comprehension of man through human social sciences and has been progressively included in the university curricula, in close connection with bioethics. In international literature, there was no such thing yet as a precise definition of MH: "Medical Humanities as a technical term is still not established in the wider medical, educational and academic communities and there is much confusion as to what comprises Medical Humanities (Campo, 2005). Medical humanities does not yet have a fixed identity and form, nor has it yet been patented or trademarked. Humanities in principle can embrace all disciplines and people (Pattison, 2003).

Donnie (1988), in the United States, pointed out: "only a relatively few years ago medical humanities as a discipline was practically unheard of in medical schools. In the last decade there has been a remarkable growth in this field". Three terms appear in the European context:

- subdiscipline: "for some this did indeed approximate to a new medical subdiscipline, re-establishing and promoting the neglected relationship between medicine and the arts" (Evans & Greaves, 2010);
- approach: "Medical Humanities has been defined as an integrated, interdisciplinary, philosophical approach to recording and interpreting human experiences of illness, disability and medical intervention" (Evans, 2002).

– perspective: "it was a novel interdisciplinary perspective which sought to reunify the arts and sciences in medicine as a whole and so provide a more rounded and humanitarian approach that rejected the notion of a sub-discipline altogether" (Ibidem).

The minimum common denominator is actually the opportunity to combine humanity and science, just as Gordon (2005) observed; "in discussing medical humanities, it can be difficult to avoid emphasising, as the latter definition does, the idea of two opposed sides - the biomedical and the human. It is an opposition that translates too easily into stereotypes: science as cold, unfeeling, and sometimes dangerous, and the humanities as warm-hearted and well-intentioned, but possibly less «scientific»". Greaves e Evans (2000) e Greaves (2001) make a further effort and call MH additive and integrated.

As regards the earlier definition (additive), MH is understood to be a "division of medical knowledge into arts and sciences, the parallel division of medical practice into humanistic and technical components, with priority being given to the scientific and technical aspects" (id.). MH contributes to biomedical sciences towards a humanization of treatment practices. As for the latter definition (integrated), MH is characterized by a "reductionist division of medical knowledge into subdisciplines, and of medical practice into related specialties" (id.). The attention focus here is on the human being rather than on the mere role of arts. Medical knowledge is not understood as being extended to artistic knowledge, but as being generally reconfigured between arts, social sciences and natural sciences. On the other hand, interdisciplinarity seems to be the minimum common denominator in the statutes of the two major MH associations:

- "The American Society for Bioethics and Humanities was established in 1998 to promote the exchange of ideas and foster multidisciplinary, interdisciplinary, and interprofessional scholarship, research, teaching, policy development, professional development, and collegiality among people engaged in all of the endeavors related to clinical and academic bioethics and the health-related humanities" (American Society for Bioethics and Humanities, [ASBH], 2011).
- "The UK Association for Medical Humanities has defined the field as representing a sustained interdisciplinary enquiry into aspects of medical practice, education and research expressly concerned with the human side of medicine" (Evans et al., 2001).

Evans stated that MH is useful for: "reducing the gap between biomedicine and the human sciences, such as philosophy, history, sociology and anthropology; facilitating interdisciplinary teaching and research; promoting a patient-centered and reflective approach to medical care; counteracting professional burnout; reducing biomedical hubris; equipping doctors to meet moral challenges not "covered" by biomedicine".

MH has been included in the curricula of the medical faculties of North America, the United Kingdom and, more recently, Australia.

Bevilacqua stated in 2011 that MH in Italy appears to refer to a scenario which is still undefined and in-fieri, and the Italian healthcare context is characterized by a strong bio-technicist bias. MH experiences slowly start taking part in the core curriculum of some Italian healthcare departments. As Zannini stated in 2009, it does not seem to be a priority to decide whether MH should be included in the curriculum (i.e. be compulsory) or stay optional - what counts the most is to trigger the medical school debate on the meaning of medicine and the deontology related to its praxis. Only in this manner can MH be accepted and valorized, hopefully by deciding to start introducing it more softly within such institutional activities by way of official courses, training stages, etc., i.e. introducing it as a mere educational route. The only rule to be followed is the one which is used in the introduction to MH in the courses for the various operators - integration. A revision of the literature Fieschi et coll. carried out in 2013 about MH in Italy evinced a substantial predominance of NBM (Narrative Based Medicine) and the use of narration as contribution to self-training in the social context, but also as an integral part of healthcare treatment (auto-biographies, auto-patographies, diaries).

MH definitions in the Italian literature can be divided into two main categories: one identifies the fields of knowledge MH introduces in study syllabi, the other is of a teleological nature. As regards the former, many authors agree with Cattorini (2003) on the fact that MH refers to various disciplines and practices ranging from Medical Psychology to Literary Criticism, from Health Anthropology to Health History and Ethics, but also Religion, Drama, Figurative Arts, Music, Law, Phylosophy and Sociology and, more generally, all arts and reflections on them and man, as well as knowledge of Humankind. As for the latter, four different functions of MH can be identified:

1. development of an empathetic attitude;
2. development of interpretive skills;
3. self-comprehension and self-care;
4. acquisition of ethical sense and responsibility sense.

Italian and international pedagogic research has focused on a quest for training devices which support the development of forms of critical thinking and foster types of learning which can put students and professional in a position to transform the prospective meanings through which they interpret social facts (or at least make them more critical). Therefore, reflexivity and reflexive practice are configured as real instruments for changing the facts and social contexts which are closest to us. They obviously promote a conversation with action which is in and of itself problematic, thus interconnecting experience, previous knowledge and the emerging situation to intercept a course of action that would obviously heed the call. Thus, as Rosati pointed out in 2015, this is the meaning of a type of learning that would stimulate, motivate and foster instruments of thinking which are useful for solving problems and, at the same time, would promote transformative routes whereby the person could grasp new logic among possible sequences and innovative connections between facts, notions and life experiences. He went on to say this type of learning implies our ability to grasp the interconnections between processes, mind and culture while elaborating new ones as well. The aim here is to sensitize all the players involved to the problem posed by space, time and power, in a reflexive transition that would allow autonomy and proper management of their own individual resources. Some of the objectives of a potentially transformative type of learning can be identified during the acquisition of the famous life skills (critical reading, intentional and self-directed learning).

As Jones, Wear & Friedman, Charon et al., Charon et al., Atkinson, Macnaughton & Richards, Bleakley, Crawford, Brown and Charise ponted out from 2014 to 2020, the construction of Health Huminities, which, along with those of Narrative Based Medicine and Critical Medical Humanities, is characterized by an evolution of their meanings in the recent literature, emerged from the interdisciplinary debate on Medical Humanities in the past few years. The interconnections between Humanities and Healthcare make Health Humanities spread beyond clinical training to include the promotion of health and well-being by sharing the basic assumption whereby medicine does not need only biological knowledge and competences, especially after the lesson the Covid-19 crisis has taught us. Therefore, Health Humanities are apparently the most useful construction to evince to what extent the environmental and healthcare crisis, the economic crash, the civil, racial and social conflict Covid-19 has caused are no doubt world priorities.
What we must work harder on, however, is

1. the relation between arts and humanities in healthcare training and
2. the use of the system theory of the UNO model on Sustainable Development Objectives.

These two approaches started on parallel roads: Engel's bio-psycho-social model, which developed in the 1970s, and Eric Cassel's contribution in 1982, which re-defined medicine's objectives not exclusively as a battle against disease, but as forces oriented towards the phenomenology of human suffering. Almost 30 years ago,

McWhinney, for instance, exhorted medicine operators to adopt a person-centered approach oriented towards the phenomenological approach, which should aim at comprehending what disease means to the patient, by way of a clinical diagnosis.

Humanist researchers, for that matter, started carrying out more in-depth philosophy, literature, social sciences, political theory, gender and disability studies in their attempt to contrast medical and healthcare reductionism. As Marcum stated in 2008, the integration of phenomenological philosophy with system theory entails that the patient be recognized as a person who occupies a life experience context or a socioeconomic milieu. Although they had a slight impact within health organizations, these studies paved the way for complex interdisciplinary observations all over the world and in Italy, as Kanisza, Scaratti, Bertolini, Massa, Giani, Giarelli and coll., Kanekline and Masini showed from 1994 to 2005 respectively. Another essential point is the fact that Health Humanities does not limit itself to applying Medical Humanities in training health professionals and treating healthcare professionals.

As Garista pointed out in 2020, Health Humanities is a meeting point of arts (and humanities, for that matter) and health and social sciences, for promoting good health and improving professional training in this sector. Health Humanities embraces alternative opportunities to comprehend disease and recovery. As the Arts and Humanities Research Council [AHRC] pointed out in 2017, they include and embrace the arts and offer one of the major routes towards health, well-being, resilience and social connections. As the Ottawa Charter for Health Promotion stressed in 1986, and Clift & Camic corroborated in 2016, promoting health is not the responsibility of the health sector only. As Garista pointed out in 2020, promoting health means wondering about the subjects' stories and turning them into shared co-participated narrations. As a third point, we must say that the term Humanities in Health Humanities includes arts and well-being. As Crawford et al., Brown and Charise affirmed in 2015 and 2020 respectively, Health Humanities is a fast-growing research and practice area which has engendered a more inclusive and attentive approach to socio-cultural aspects aimed at ensuring effective quality treatment. Thus, connecting humanities with healthcare, WHO and UN's Sustainable Development Objectives becomes the challenge that would guarantee the comprehension of the representations of health, sickness, treatment and well-being in the various social groups.

In the aforesaid sense, as the present chapter has evinced, narrative methodologies have shown great prospects of becoming a precious resource to re-orient social healthcare policies precisely because they enable and allow the comprehension of the experiences and representations of health, sickness, and treatment in the various contexts involved. To do so, however, it is necessary to stimulate a fruitful dialogue between humanities (narrative) research and scientific (evidence) research, so that the comprehension models (typical of human sciences) and explanation models (typical of biomedical sciences) can restore complex contextualized research open to the criticism and valorization of differences. Therefore, we advocate a more inclusive and sustainable type of medicine, which is validated by international research results. To say it with Syse & Mueller (2015) and Menton, Larrea, Latorre et al. (2020), it is necessary to start reconfiguring meanings and new lifestyles around the following four interconnected dimensions: sustainability, consumption, well-living and justice.

The Promoting Mental Health and Psychosocial Support (MHPSS) in LGBTQIA+ Adolescents Victims of Minority Stress: Dialogic Literacy Gathering as an Empowerment Educational Strategy

As already mentioned in the previous paragraphs, in the last decades a special attention has been paid to the demedicalization and the depathologization processes of individuals who are living a situation of psychosocial disadvantage. The transition from a disease-centred approach to a patient goals-directed care has been a real paradigm shift, since now the personal experience of the patient was getting more and more importance against the previous and only consideration towards the patient's illness.

Following the remarks proposed by Sirignano and by Ferro Allodola, the interdisciplinary perspective of Medical Humanities relies on the synergic relationship between the narrative and the evidence-based paradigm, so that the rehabilitation process of the person can be supported as a whole. This approach has its centre of gravity in the care relationship and focuses on self-narration, given that there is an enduring interweaving between illness and the story of personal life.

The holistic approach involves different individual dimensions of a person and of people who are around, especially when it takes charge of someone who is living a condition of fragility. If on the one hand, community can be the reason of the suffering of an individual, on the other hand, it can represent a resource for the path of improvement.

In this last part of this chapter, we focus on a specific dimension of psychological distress originated by the context of belonging and involving a group of people, known as minority stress of adolescents who recognize themselves as members of the LGBTQIA+ community. More and more studies show how discrimination, prejudice and, sexual and gender-identity stigma can represent suffering conditions for the psychological well-being of people who are subject to discrimination.

Many LGBTQIA+ adolescents experience forms of discomfort through a number of conditions of persistent emotional stress which can take on chronic and traumatic dimensions (Lingiardi, 2007), causing important consequences in terms of mental health, such as depression, anxiety, self-harm, use of drugs, HIV risk behaviours, suicidal feelings and suicide attempts (Goldbach & Gibbs, 2015; Connolly et al. 2016; Mustanski & Liu 2013; Veale et al. 2017).

According to the report carried out by the European Union Agency for Fundamental Rights (FRA), which aimed at identifying the levels of aversion towards the LGBTQIA+ population, on a sample of 93.079 people, 47% of respondents answered was subject to discrimination for their sexual orientation, gender identity and expression, while 20% was discriminated at the workplace and 18% was discriminated at school or university (Scandurra et al., 2017). On the contrary, on the homo-bi-transphobic violence phenomena, especially at school or university, it can be useful the Italian research carried out by Selmi and Roberti (2021) on a sample of 1.097 female and male students between 13 and 20 years. 46,6% of respondents declared to have experienced an unsafe condition for their sexual preference and 31,4% for their gender identity, regarding the use of a discriminatory language. 80% was victim of sexual harassment for the sexual orientation and 78,6% for the gender expression. Finally, 7,3% said that became subject to physical aggressions for their sexual preference and 8,5% for their gender expression.

As a result of this stress, psychosocial and interpersonal tensions originate above all during violence and abuse events towards those people who society has usually felt (and represented) as individuals with a negative background or more generally story. The homophobic, biphobic, lesbophobic, and transphobic bullying is the form of discrimination affecting LGBTQIA+ adolescents the most, especially in the contexts of onlife dimension . This condition of subjection develops firstly from the building and the internalization of social attitudes, drenched with prejudices and stereotypes caused by difficulty of accepting differences from an individual and a public point of view.

The minority stress model was drafted by the psychologist Meyer (1995) with the purpose of defining the excess stress to which people belonging to stigmatized social categories are exposed, especially for their social and minority position. This model is not based on a single theory, but according to Meyer, it is the result of the elaboration of several sociological and psychological theories. As far as the sociological area is concerned, there are theories formulated by Durkheim (1951) who noticed how much the anomy, that is the lack of social norms, could represent one of the cause of alienation for individuals, to the point of driving them to suicide. On the contrary, according to Merton (1961), society was a stress factor encouraging individuals towards those values contrasting with the social structures of belonging.

Those who are part of a minority are more subject to those conflicts, given that the mainstream culture, the social structures, and the regulations do not represent typically the ones of the minority group. The perspectives of psychosocial matrix focus rather on the inter-group relationships and on the influence that the minority position plays on the mental health of a person. For instance, theories about social identity and self-categorization say that the categorising process (such as the distinction between social groups) triggers important inter-group procedures (the competition and the discrimination) and provides a foothold for the definition of the group and of the self (Turner & Onorato, 1999). On the contrary, theories about the symbolic interaction suggest that a negative consideration of other people leads to a negative consideration of oneself. According to this perspective, prejudice plays some negative effects on those who belong to a minority community, defined by Allport as "traits due to victimisation" (1954).

Albeit with different methods, by the intersection of these two fields of research, Meyer argues that the causes of minority stress are in the process of interconnecting of the "distal and proximal system" proposed by Lazarus and Folkman (1984) . Meyer reports that the factors of distal minority stress can be objective factors, since they do not depend on the perception or the assessment of an individual, even though their relationship relies on the social notion (Operario & Fiske, 2001). On the contrary, the proximal stress factors are more subjective and thus related to the identity of a LGBTQIA+ person.

Prejudice and discrimination are significant and influential sources for the mental health in condition of stress, especially when some social contexts are seen as hostile, adverse, and indifferent. It takes on mainly two aspects definable as consistency and trauma (Lingiardi, 2007).

When the minority stress involves subjects in developmental age, some highly traumatic discomforts may occur for these individuals due to the delicacy of the experiences characterising their existence and involving directly the building of the attitudes, the personality, beyond the perception of themselves. According to Lingiardi (2007) and to Gianola (2015), the condition of minority stress can refer to a series of variables that, interconnected, can represent the source of the psychological and social discomfort previously addressed. Thus, referring to the running of this form of stress a number of dimensions must be taken into account, such as: the social features of the reference environment, the emotional and psychosocial stress condition belonging to the "minorities", and the assumption of the identity considered as minority.

More recent researches have focused on the integration between the theory of minority stress and the intersection theory, useful for shedding some light on the multiple stress of the minorities living different levels of discomfort due to the stigma about the sexual orientation or the gender identity and the racial-ethnical stigma of LGBTQIA+ people. According to these researches, black people who belong to sexual minorities have reported the highest level of racial-ethnical stigma in the LGBTQIA+ contexts, while white men belonging to sexual minorities have reported the lowest levels, and Asians and Hispanic/Latin men placing in the middle (McConnell et al., 2018).

The minority stress model is a useful tool for the understanding of the experiences of LGBTQIA+ individuals, but there are not so many researches on the specific experiences of the development in the social spaces of the adolescents (Goldbach & Gibbs, 2017). Adolescence is a period of the development during which the individuals are not very attentive to feedback received from their peers (Burgio, 2012, 2019; Mancaniello, 2018) and the rejection and the victimisation by the latter can cause high stress (Choukas et al., 2014).

LGBTQIA+ adolescents referring negative reactions against their revelation on the sexual preferences and the gender identity, register higher rates of problems linked to mental health (Heatherington & Lavner, 2008). Parents are important for their children especially during adolescence, for their basic needs and the psychological well-being. Thus, a possible denial towards their children's sexual preference can cause some severe life crisis, increasing moments of depression or the risk of committing suicide (Ryan et al., 2009).

The involvement on the well-being of LGBTQIA+ adolescents requires an approach which may include the dimension of the mental and the social well-being, although we lack of important studies about the correlation between minority stress and the adolescent discomfort for their sexuality. Some researches focus on the action according to the MHPSS model (known also with the acronym Mental Health and Psychosocial Support, introduced in 2007 by the Inter-Agency Standing Committee (IASC), as a way to combine the clinical and the psychosocial approaches, overcoming the attention paid only to psychiatric issues (Jones & Ventevogel, 2021). The MHPSS takes into account beyond the suffering of a person or of a bunch of people, but also the community they belong to. The MHPSS is not limited to a single disciplinary area, but it requires a multi-sectoral approach including the involvement of partners in the health, education, and protection fields.

People who experience any kind of emergency must be taken in charge firstly as active participants of individual and social improvement of their well-being, rather than as passive targets. Thus, the use of an approach based on the community, like is MHPSS, easy families, groups and communities to help and take care for the others encouraging recovery and resilience. The relationship networks and the belonging to a community are fundamental for the definition of the identity of an individual, contributing to the well-being. The networks support people in acquiring knowledge, attitude and skill, as well as strategies on how to address the impact of crises, and they provide protection and sense of belonging.

In the last years, some international organizations, such as UNICEF, have posed the problem of mental health of adolescents with a specific attention to gender issues and to MHPSS actions aimed at supporting them in cases of violations of their rights because of their identity. UNICEF proposes a Gender-transformative MHPSS programming as a support for adolescents victims of gender stereotypes through a path defined "gender continuum" composed of five steps, where from the Gender discriminatory we switch to the Gender blind to get to the Gender aware, up to the Gender responsive and to the Gender transformative dimension (2021, p. 6)

The reference to the MHPSS approach used as a support for LGBTQIA+ adolescents, working with them on the minority stress dimension, involves ad hoc intervention methodologies in the field of education. As previously mentioned, the minority stress concerning LGBTQIA+ people is due to a series of factors rooted in the social context of belonging of those who are considered "minorities" compared to a majority group. An important role is played by educational interventions working on stress lived by marginalized LGBTQIA+ individuals supporting the creation of safe and inclusive spaces.

It is necessary to act by the implementation of approaches involving not only the marginalized individual, but the whole community of belonging. As Sirignano and Ferro Allodola afirm, as an interdisciplinary field composed of arts, literature, cinema, and so on, the Medical Humanities focus on processes triggering considerations of ethical, philosophical, historical, and literary issues, useful for thinking again about the human life under the influence of modern medicine; they represent a necessary care even for medicine itself (Spinsanti, 2011).

Among the educational strategies which gather the sense of promotion of well-being there is the fundamental tool of the Dialogic Literary Gathering (known as DLG) including the dialogic dimension as a moment of co-building of new self-learning. It is a theoretical and methodological construct coming from the dialogic learning theories promoted by Ramón Flecha (2000), and influenced in turn by the considerations on the inter-subjectivity, interactions and dialogues as pillars generating the learning (Bakhtin, 2010; Freire, 1970; Mead, 1934). The dialogic literary gatherings can meet the challenges effectively (Flecha, 2015; Soler-Gallart, 2017). In the DLG, the equal interpersonal dialogue based on the reading of classic literary texts is the core which enables the participants to develop their points of view and skills contributing to change their lives (Flecha, 2000). According to this idea, the process of the knowledge creation is configured as a line of dialogues that are built with on the basis of meanings previously created with other people defined as "dialogic imagination" (Bakhtin, 2010).

The principles guiding the reading gatherings must ensure the co-building of new meanings, starting from the ones already present in the safe space of the literary texts. These spaces are metaphorically felt as places where no one feels judged. According to Flecha, there are seven principles guiding the actions of the DLG, as follows:

1. The equal dialogue where the contributions of the participants are considered on the basis of the value of their arguments and not on their powerful positions.

2. The cultural intelligence, as a criterion that includes the plurality of dimensions of the human interaction: academic, practical, and communicative intelligence. Everyone owns a cultural intelligence, regardless of the cultural and social-educational background, of language, and of identity.
3. The change of relationships between the participants and their contexts.
4. The instrumental dimension, concerning the instrumental learning of the knowledge and the skills that are fundamental to be known.
5. The creation of meanings, thanks to which everyone must be able to dream and to give new meaning to their life.
6. The solidarity, given that during the DLG is important to establish not oppressive relationships. The mediator plays the role of giving the word to all the participants, trying to encourage the most introverted people.
7. The equality of differences. The DLG proceeds from the assumption that the real equality includes an equal right for everyone to live differently their lives (Flecha, 2000).

The psychosocial acts, including the therapies based on the conversation and the narration, can be very successful for the creation of social circumstances conductive to the recovery of the person who experiences a minority stress (Patel et al., 2018).

The encouragement of a collaborative and interpersonal contact is the most effective way to contribute to increase the acceptability of the treatment and to overcome the stigma and the discrimination (Patel et al., 2018), as well as to strengthen social bonds and build up relationships with other people, including those with a condition of mental health, increasing so the possibility to weave a net of social support which will make it easier for patients to continue the activities promoting the healing and, so, making changes in their lives.

At the moment no research has been produced on the use of Dialogue Literacy Gatherings to work with LGBTQIA+ adolescents or adults experiencing minority stress or to prevent the development of it. The studies on the use of this approach have been carried out especially with the purpose of working with people who have experienced stress caused by COVID-19 pandemic, with individuals in the age of development, having a background of migration, or with MSNA people. For instance, the European project REFUGE-ED (2021-2023) reported positive results thanks to the use of DLGs with young girls and boys living in southern Italy with a predominant presence of families with backgrounds of migration (Sordé-Martí et al., 2023).

The DLGs consist in the choice of a book among the classics works of the world literature, with the aim of agreeing with the participants which chapters should be read or which excerpts deserve more attention than others, and finally meet together to comment those chosen underlined paragraphs or sentences (Fernández-Villardón et al., 2021). So, the mediator should not give a lecture on the analysis of a book, but has to ensure mutual respect and interest, making everyone feel at ease and empowered to participate, enriching and widening the talk and the dialogue. The DLGs give the chance to read and to comment a book containing endless themes such as love, war, social relationships and daily challenges concerning every human being regardless the personal and specific circumstances.

This methodology proposed by Flecha may have some limits, especially when the mediator has to face with issues concerning minority stress caused by homo-bi-lesbo-transphobic bullying or other forms of discrimination. The main problem is due to the lack of literary sources considered of "high standards", in the meaning of extraordinary literary works, according to the historical tradition, that address appropriately the problem of discrimination of LGBTQIA+ people. Despite the fact that the principles of DLGs are based on the choice of texts dealing with "universally" issues, such as equality and enhancement of differences, we might face with the problem of the explication of questions causing disparity. The latter may cause some consequences, like the emergence of problems affecting the mental well-being of a person.

In addition, DLG approach should include the use of literary texts going beyond the classic literary canon, in other terms books dealing, for instance, with themes, places, languages and stories about LGBTQIA+ adolescents, if they are the target of this methodology. As a matter of fact, many novels or poems which belong to the classic canon do not address expressly gender identity issues if written or published before the first half of XX century. With a view to promotion of the well-being of LGBTQIA+ adolescents and to reduce and fight the social stereotype, some works could play a pivotal role. In the latest years, for example, several important innovations have been introduced in the global market, starting with the publication of different young adult literary works, such as gender- and sexual-oriented comics and graphic novels up to some large-scale TV and Internet series distributions which promote a queer gaze along with the representation of the daily life of heterosexual adolescents. A prominent example is given by Alice Oseman's Heartstopper, work born as a graphic novel and only after broadcast as a young adult series on the Netflix web platform. It is a production which proposes alternative identity models, through an intersectional dimension that challenges the heteronormative asymmetrical relationships between cisgender and LGBTQIA+ adolescents, and avoids the most common homo-bi-lesbo-transphobic attitudes (Di Grigoli, 2024). As it is known, this different literary and movie works just quoted have been judged sometimes as a "lower popular" production, even though on the other hand, we must recognize that they result more congenial for the intended purposes and objectives than the classic canon proposed by Flecha.

In conclusion, I would like to underline the opportunities and the potentials of the DLGs, especially thanks to the moments of shared readings. First of all, as the Medical Humanities state, literature can ensure promising outcomes, for instance, in the field of the communicative and relational skill, of empathy, of cultural communication (Zannini, 2021). This aspect is fundamental because it lets all the participants to dive into the different stories, to identify with and put themselves in the shoes of other people. DLGs are essentially valuable supports for the knowledge of the others, given that they promote and enhance sexual and gender differences through specific readings on the theme of diversity from the perspective of positivity and inclusion. It is an approach that can focus issues concerning LGBTQIA+ young adults and those who do not identify themselves as those.

Teachers, educators, and trainers play an important role in conducting these learning moments, given that they have to build up situations of exchange of knowledge, of experience, and of creation of new worlds. In accordance with the goals defined by Flecha's DLG approach, another fundamental aspect is the ability of generating and questioning personal points of view with respect to bias and of re-thinking about the concept of diversity as an element of enrichment and not to be devalued a priori.

To work in a MHPSS dimension, according to the Medical Humanities requires an interweaving and intersectional look of methodologies which challenge the cultural canon, acting in a synergic relationship for the whole well-being of the person. DLG can be a possible tool and through literature and the involvement of other current media can contribute and deconstruct the interiorization of gender stereotypes and of homo-bi-lesbo-transphobic devices, creating new dimension of the self and the others.

NOTE

The Chapter is the result of joint work by the three Authors. For scientific evaluation purposes only, Paragraph 1 is attributed to Fabrizio M. Sirignano, Paragraph 2 to Valerio Ferro Allodola and Paragraph 3 to Antonio R. Di Grigoli.

REFERENCES

Allport, G. W. (1954). *The nature of prejudice*. Addison-Wesley.

American Society for Bioethics & Humanities. (2011). *Core competencies for healthcare ethics consultation* (2nd ed.). Author.

Arts and Humanities Research Council. (2017). *Exploring Mental Health and Well-being: The Role of Arts and Humanities Research*. Arts and Humanities Research Council.

Atkinson, R. (2002). *L'intervista narrativa. Raccontare la storia di sé nella ricerca formativa, organizzativa e sociale*. Raffaello Cortina.

Atkinson, S., Macnaughton, J., & Richards, J. (Eds.). (2016). *The Edinburgh Companion to the Critical Medical Humanities*. Edinburgh University Press.

Bakhtin, M. (2010). *Marxism and Philosophy of Language*. HUCITEC.

Batini, F., & Bartolucci, M. (2016). Chi legge ragiona meglio? Abitudini di lettura e funzioni di ragionamento. *Ricerche Di Pedagogia E Didattica.Journal of Theories and Research in Education*, 11(3), 37–45. 10.6092/issn.1970-2221/6444

Bert, G., & Quadrino, S. (2002). *Parole di medici, parole di pazienti. Counselling e narrativa in Medicina*. Il Pensiero Scientifico.

Bertolini, G. (Ed.). (1994). *Diventare medici*. Guerini Studio.

Bertolini, G., & Massa, R. (Eds.). (2003). *Clinica della formazione medica*. FrancoAngeli.

Bevilacqua, A. (2014). Implementing Medical Humanities in Italy: progress of a research. *Formazione & Insegnamento, 9*(2), 101–112. https://ojs.pensamultimedia.it/index.php/siref/article/view/1048

Bindi, R. (2019). *I libri che fanno la felicità*. Vallardi.

Bleakley, A. (Ed.). (2020). *Routledge Handbook of the Medical Humanities*. Routledge.

Boffo, V. (Ed.). (2006). *La cura in pedagogia*. CLUEB.

Bruner, J. (1988). *La mente a più dimensioni*. Laterza.

Bruzzone, D., & Musi, E. (Eds.). (2007). *Vissuti di cura. Competenze emotive e formazione nelle professioni sanitarie*. Guerini e Associati.

Bruzzone, D., & Zannini, L. (Eds.). (2014). Dossier su "Prospettive fenomenologiche della cura di sé nella formazione continua dei professionisti della salute". *Encyclopaideia.Journal of Phenomenology and Education*, 39, 3–5.

Burgio, G. (2012). Adolescenza e violenza. Il bullismo omofobico come costruzione della maschilità. *Mimesis*.

Burgio, G. (2019). Una violenza normale. Maschilità, adolescenza, omofobia. *Education Sciences & Society*, *2*, 222–237.

Calabrese, S., Conti, V., & Fioretti, V. (2022). *Che cos'è la medicina narrativa*. Carocci.

Campo, R. (2005). The Medical Humanities, for lack of a better term. *Journal of the American Medical Association*, 294(9), 1009–1011. 10.1001/jama.294.9.100916145021

Cassel, E. (1982). The Nature of Suffering and the Goals of Medicine. *The New England Journal of Medicine*, 306(11), 639–645. 10.1056/NEJM1982031830611047057823

Cattorini, P. (2003). *Bioetica e cinema. Racconti di malattia e dilemmi morali*. Franco Angeli.

Centonze, V., Palmieri, V. O., Addabbo, F., Palmiotti, G. P., Albano, M. G., Ribatti, D., & Portincasa, P. (2018). *Le nuove frontiere della terapia: la biblioterapia*. Il Pensiero Scientifico Editore.

Charon, R., Sayantani, D., Nellie, H., Craig, I., Eric, R. M., Edgar, R. C., Spencer, D., & Spiegel, M. (2016). *Principles and Practices of Narrative Medicine*. Oxford University Press. 10.1093/med/9780199360192.001.0001

Clift, S., & Camic, P. (Eds.). (2016). *Oxford Textbook of Creative Arts, Health, and Wellbeing: International Perspectives on Practice, Policy, and Research*. Oxford University Press.

Connelly, F. M., & Clandinin, D. J. (1997). *Il curriculum come narrazione*. Loffredo.

Connolly, M. D., Zervos, M. J., Barone, C. J.II, Johnson, C. C., & Joseph, C. L. (2016). The Mental Health of Transgender Youth: Advances in Understanding. *The Journal of Adolescent Health*, 59(5), 489–495. 10.1016/j.jadohealth.2016.06.01227544457

Contini, M., & Manini, M. (2007). *La cura in educazione. Tra famiglie e servizi*. Carocci.

Crawford, P., Brown, B., Baker, C., Tischler, V., & Abrams, B. (Eds.). (2015). *Health Humanities*. Palgrave.

Crawford, P., Brown, B., & Charise, C. (Eds.). (2020). *The Routledge Companion to Health Humanities*. Routledge. 10.4324/9780429469060

de Mennato, P. (1999). *La ricerca partigiana*. Liguori.

De Serio, B. (2014). Help to life. Education from birth. A reflection on early childhood starting from Maria Montessori. *RELAdEI - Revista Latinoamericana de Educación Infantil, 3*(3), 59-66.

De Serio, B., (2022). "Esiste la scienza della guerra, dov'è quella della pace?". Maria Montessori e la sublimazione del materno. (2022). *Medical Humanities & Medicina Narrativa - MHMN, 5*(1), 35-50. https://doi.org/10.53136/97912218007223

Di Grigoli, A. R. (2024). La pedagogia queer e il riconoscimento della non-linearità identitaria. Verso un modello critico della cis-normatività in educazione. In *La pedagogia di genere. Percorsi di ricerca contemporanei* (pp. 205–215). FrancoAngeli.

Donnie, S. (1988). The pedagogy of two different approaches to humanistic medical education: Cognitive vs affective. *Theoretical Medicine*, 9(2), 227–236. 10.1007/BF004894143413709

Durkheim, E. (1951). *Suicide*. Free Press.

Evans, M. (2002). Reflections on the humanities in medical education. *Medical Education*, 36(6), 508–513. 10.1046/j.1365-2923.2002.01225.x12047662

Evans, M., Arnott, R., Bolton, G., Finlay, I., Macnaughton, J., Meakin, R., & Reid, W. (2001). The medical humanities as a field of enquiry. Statement from the Association for Medical Humanities. *Journal of Medical Ethics*, 27(2), 104–105.11314152

Evans, M., & Greaves, D. (2010). Ten years of medical humanities: A decade in the life of a journal and a discipline. *Medical Humanities*, 36(2), 66–68. 10.1136/jmh.2010.00560321393283

Fernández-Villardón, A., Valls-Carol, R., Alcantud, M., & Tellado, I. (2021). Enhancing literacy and communicative skills of students with disabilities in Special Schools through Dialogic Literary gatherings. *Frontiers in Psychology*, 12, 1–13. 10.3389/fpsyg.2021.66263933935921

Ferro Allodola, V. (2021). Costruire una salute sostenibile post Covid-19: verso la Health Literacy nella scuola italiana. *Mizar. Costellazione di pensieri*, 15, 141-149. http://doi.org/10.1285/i24995835v2021n15p141

Fieschi, L., Matarese, M., Vellone, E., Alvaro, R., & De Marinis, M. G. (•••). Medical humanities in healthcare education in Italy: A literature review. *Annali dell'Istituto Superiore di Sanita*, 49(1), 56–64.23535131

Flecha, R. (2000). *Sharing Words: Theory and Practice of Dialogic Learning*. Rowman & Littlefield.

Flecha, R. (2015). *Successful Educational Actions for Inclusion and Social Cohesion in Europe*. Springer. 10.1007/978-3-319-11176-6

Floridi, L. (2015). *Onlife Manifesto*. Springer. 10.1007/978-3-319-04093-6

Frauenfelder, E. (1994). *Pedagogia e Biologia. «Una possibile alleanza»*. Liguori.

Frauenfelder, E., & Santoianni, F. (2002). *Le scienze bioeducative. Prospettive di ricerca*. Liguori.

Frauenfelder, E., Santoianni, F., & Striano, M. (2004). *Introduzione alle scienze bioeducative*. Laterza.

Freire, P. (1970). *Pedagogy of the Oppressed*. Seabury Press.

Galimberti, U. (1983). *Il corpo: antropologia, psicoanalisi, fenomenologia*. Feltrinelli.

Garista, P. (2017). The Health Promoting Schools model. School as a pedagogical setting for generating wellbeing and learning. *Formazione & Insegnamento, 15*(3), 381-390. https://ojs.pensamultimedia.it/index.php/siref/article/view/2651

Garista, P. (2020). Health humanities. Generare salute attraverso le narrazioni in una prospettiva di life-long learning, *Medical Humanities & Medicina Narrativa - MHMN*, 1(1), 65-82. http://dx.doi.org/10.4399/97888255332625

Gentilcore, D. (2008). *Malattia e guarigione. Ciarlatani, guaritori e seri professionisti*. Controluce.

Giani, U. (Ed.). (2005). *Complessità, salute e malattia: Medicina Centrata sulla Persona*. Millennium.

Giani, U. (2006). Enigma. Ragionamento Clinico e Narrative Personali. *Millennium*.

Gianola, M. (2015). *Giovanotti Femmenelle e Signurine Masculone A ognuno la libertà di esprimere la propria identità Gender Nonconformity, ruoli e stereotipi di genere tra un gruppo di minori a rischio in un quartiere della periferia napoletana*. Fondazione Genere Identità Cultura.

Giarelli, G., Good, B. J., Del Vecchio Good, M.-J., Martini, M., & Ruozi, C. (Eds.). (2005). *Storie di cura. Medicina narrativa e medicina delle evidenze: l'integrazione possibile*. Franco Angeli.

Gibbs, J. J., & Goldbach, J. (2015). Religious Conflict, Sexual Identity, and Suicidal Behaviors among LGBT Young Adults. *Archives of Suicide Research*, 19(4), 472–488. 10.1080/13811118.2015.100447625763926

Good, B. J. (1999). *Narrare la malattia. Lo sguardo antropologico sul rapporto medico-paziente*. Edizioni di Comunità. (Original work published 1994)

Gordon, J. (2005). Medical humanities: To cure sometimes, to relieve often, to comfort always. *The Medical Journal of Australia*, 182(1), 430–432. 10.5694/j.1326-5377.2005.tb06772.x15850446

Greaves, D. (2001). Two conceptions of medical humanities. *Nursing Philosophy*, 2(3), 270–271. 10.1046/j.1466-769X.2000.00070.x

Greaves, D., & Evans, M. (2000). Conceptions of medical humanities. *Medical Humanities*, 26(2), 65–66. 10.1136/mh.26.2.6512068906

Groppo, M., Ornaghi, V., Grazzani, I., & Carrubba, L. (1999). *La psicologia culturale di Bruner*. Raffaello Cortina.

Heatherington, L., & Lavner, J. (2008). Coming to Terms With Coming Out: Review and Recommendations for Family Systems-Focused Research. *Journal of Family Psychology*, 22(3), 329–343. 10.1037/0893-3200.22.3.32918540762

IASC - Inter-Agency Standing Committee. (2024, April 05). *About*. IASC. https://interagencystandingcommittee.org/

Jones, L., & Ventevogel, P. (2021). From exception to the norm: How mental health interventions have become part and parcel of the humanitarian response. *World Psychiatry; Official Journal of the World Psychiatric Association (WPA)*, 20(1), 2–3. 10.1002/wps.2080833432770

Jones, T., Wear, D., & Friedman, L. (2014). *Health Humanities Reader*. Rutgers University Press.

Kaneklin, C., & Scaratti, G. (Eds.). (1998). *Formazione e narrazione. Costruzione di significato e processi di cambiamento personale e organizzativo*. Raffaello Cortina.

Kanisza, S. (1994). *L'ascolto del malato*. Guerini e Associati.

Kanisza, S. (1996). *Apprendere nei servizi socio-sanitari*. NIS.

Kanisza, S. (2001). *Pedagogia ospedaliera*. Carocci.

Laporta, R. (2001). *Avviamento alla pedagogia*. Carocci.

Lazarus, R. S., & Folkman, S. (1984). *Stress, Apparaisal and Coping*. Springer.

Lingiardi, V. (2007). *Citizen Gay. Affetti e diritti*. Il Saggiatore.

Lorini, C., Caini, S., Ierardi, F., Bachini, L., Gemmi, F., & Bonaccorsi, G. (2020). Health Literacy as a Shared Capacity: Does the Health Literacy of a Country Influence the Health Disparities among Immigrants? *International Journal of Environmental Research and Public Health*, 17(4), 1149. 10.3390/ijerph17041149320594 96

Lorini, C., Santomauro, F., Grazzini, M., Mantwill, S., Vettori, V., Lastrucci, V., Bechini, A., Boccalini, S., Bussotti, A., & Bonaccorsi, G. (2017). Health literacy in Italy: A cross-sectional study protocol to assess the health literacy level in a population-based sample, and to validate health literacy measures in the Italian language. *BMJ Open*, 7(11), e017812. 10.1136/bmjopen-2017-01781229138204

Mancaniello, M. R. (2018). *Per una pedagogia dell'adolescenza. Società complessa e paesaggi della metamorfosi identitaria*. Pensa Multimedia.

Marcum, J. (2008). Reflections on Humanizing Biomedicine. *Perspectives in Biology and Medicine*, 51(3), 392–405. 10.1353/pbm.0.002318723943

Masini, V. (2005). *Medicina narrativa. Comunicazione empatica ed interazione dinamica nella relazione medico-paziente*. Franco Angeli.

McConnell, E. A., Janulis, P., Phillips, G.II, Truong, R., & Birkett, M. (2018). Multiple Minority Stress and LGBT Community Resilience among Sexual Minority Men. *Psychology of Sexual Orientation and Gender Diversity*, 5(1), 1–12. https://psycnet.apa.org/doi/10.1037/sgd0000265. 10.1037/sgd000026529546228

McWhinney, I. (1986). Are We on the Brink of a Major Transformation in Clinical Method? *Canadian Medical Association Journal*, 35, 873–878.3756718

Menton, M., Larrea, C., Latorre, S., Martinez-Alier, J., Peck, M., Temper, L., & Walter, M. (2020). Environmental justice and the SDGs: From synergies to gaps and contradictions. *Sustainability Science*, 15(6), 1621–1636. 10.1007/s11625-020-00789-8

Merton, T. (1961). *The Behaviours of Titans*. New Directions.

Meyer, I. H. (1995). Minority Stress and Mental Health in Gay Men. *Journal of Health and Social Behavior*, 36(1), 38–56. 10.2307/21372867738327

Mezirow, J. (2003). *Apprendimento e trasformazione. Il significato dell'esperienza e il valore della riflessione nell'apprendimento degli adulti*. Raffaello Cortina.

Morin, E. (1988). *Il pensiero ecologico*. Hopefulmonster.

Mortari, L. (2006). *La pratica dell'aver cura*. Bruno Mondadori.

Mustanski, B., & Liu, R. T. (2013). A longitudinal study of predictors of suicide attempts among lesbian, gay, bisexual, and transgender youth. *Archives of Suicide Research*, 42(3), 437–448.23054258

Nutbeam, D. (2008). The evolving concept of health literacy. *Social Science & Medicine*, 67(12), 2072–2078. 10.1016/j.socscimed.2008.09.05018952344

Operario, D., & Fiske, S. T. (2001). Ethnic identity moderates perceptions of prejudice: Judgments of personal versus group discrimination and subtle versus blatant bias. *Personality and Social Psychology Bulletin*, 27(5), 550–561. 10.1177/0146167201275004

Patel, V., Saxena, S., Lund, C., Thornicroft, G., Baingana, F., Bolton, P., Chisholm, D., Collins, P.Y., Cooper, J.L., Eaton, J., Herrman, H., Herzallah, M.M., Huang, Y., Jordans, M.J.D., Kleinman, A., Medina-Mora, M.E., Morgan, E,, Niaz, U., Omigbodun, O., Prince, M., Rahman, A., Saraceno, B., Sarkar, B.K., De Silva, M., Singh, I., Stein, D.J., Sunkel, C., & UnÜtzer, J. (2018). The Lancet Commission on global mental health and sustainable development. *Lancet*, *392*(10157), 1553–1598. https://doi.org/.10.1016/S0140-6736(18)31612-X

Pattison, S. (2003). Medical Humanities: A vision and some cautionary notes. *Medical Humanities*, 29(1), 33–36. 10.1136/mh.29.1.3323671170

Prigogine, I., & Stengers, I. (1993). *La nuova alleanza*. Einaudi.

Refuge-Ed. (2024). *Effective practices in education, mental health and psychosocial support for the integration of refugee children (2021-2023).* Refuge-Ed. https://www.refuge-ed.eu/

Rivoltella, P. (2022). Crescere Onlife. L'Educazione civica digitale progettata da 74 insegnanti-autori. *Schole.*

Rosati, A. (2015). Educare alla riflessività. *Educational Reflective Practices*, 2(2), 67–74. 10.3280/ERP2015-002005

Ryan, C., Huebner, D., Diaz, R. M., & Sanchez, J. (2009). Family rejection as a predictor of negative health outcomes in white and Latino lesbian, gay, and bisexual young adults. *Pediatrics*, 123(1), 346–352. 10.1542/peds.2007-352419117902

Scandurra, C., Amodeo, A. L., Valerio, P., Bochicchio, V., & Frost, D. M. (2017). Minority stress, resilience, and mental health: A study of Italian transgender people. *The Journal of Social Issues*, 73(3), 563–585. 10.1111/josi.12232

Schön, D. A. (1993). *Il professionista riflessivo. Per una nuova epistemologia della pratica professionale*. Dedalo.

Selmi, G., & Roberti, V. (2019). *Una scuola arcobaleno. Dati e strumenti contro l'omobitransfobia in classe*. Settenove.

Sirignano, F. M. (2019). *La formazione pedagogica. Modelli e percorsi*. Liguori.

Smorti, A. (1994). *Il pensiero narrativo*. Giunti.

Soler-Gallart, M. (2017). *Achieving Social Impact. Sociology in the Public Sphere*. Springer.

Sordé-Martí, T., Ghani, A. A., Almobarak, B., Chiappelli, T., Flecha, A., Hristova, M., Krasteva, A., Kjellberg, F., McQuillan, K., Nixon, E., Qasemi, M., Serradell, O., Aiello, E., Swords, L., & Abdulrahman, H. T. (2023). The REFUGE-ED Dialogic Co-Creation Process: Working with and for REFUGE-ED children and minors. *Humanities & Social Sciences Communications*, 10(463), 463. 10.1057/s41599-023-01967-6

Sørensen, K., Van Den Broucke, S., Fullam, J., Doyle, G., Pelikan, J., Slonska, Z., & Brand, H. (2012). (HLS-EU) Consortium Health Literacy Project European. Health literacy and public health: A systematic reviewand integration of definitions and models. *BMC Public Health*, 12, 80. 10.1186/1471-2458-12-8022276600

Spinsanti, S. (2006). Una prospettiva storica. In Bucci, R. (Ed.), *Manuale di medical humanities*. Zadig.

Spinsanti, S. (2011). Critica della ragione medica. *Quaderni di Teoria*, terza serie VI/1, 23-38.

Striano, M. (2006). Processi conoscitivi e sviluppo professionale. Narrazione e sviluppo nei contesti di pratica. *Pedagogika.it*, *5*, 24-27.

Syse, K. L., & Mueller, M. L. (2015). *Sustainable Consumption and the Good Life. Interdisciplinary perspectives*. Routledge.

Turner, J. C., & Onorato, R. S. (1999). Social identity, personality, and the self-concept: A self-categorizing perspective. In Tyler, T. R., Kramer, R. M., & John, O. P. (Eds.), *The psychology of the social self* (pp. 11–46). Lawrence Erlbaum Associates Publishers.

UNICEF. (2021). *Gender in Adolescent Mental Health*. UNICEF. http://www.unicef.org/gender/files/Gender_Action_Plan_brochure-web.pdf

Veale, J.F., Peter, T., Travers, R., & Saewyc, E.M. (2017). Enacted Stigma, Mental Health, and Protective Factors Among Transgender Youth in Canada. *Transgender Health*, *2*(1), 207–216.

Venturini, B. (2020). *Come un romanzo. Viaggio nella libroterapia*. Transeuropa.

Villani, P. (2023). Per uno statuto narrativo della Medicina Narrativa. *Medical Humanities & Medicina Narrativa - MHMN, 7*(1), 19-37. 10.53136/97912218080872

Widman, L., Noar, S. M., Choukas-Bradley, S., & Francis, D. B. (2014). Adolescent sexual health communication and condom use: A meta-analysis. *Health Psychology*, 33(10), 1113–1124. 10.1037/hea000011225133828

World Health Organization. (1986). *Ottawa Charter for Health Promotion: First International Conference on Health Promotion Ottawa, 21 November.* WHO. https://www.healthpromotion.org.au/images/ottawa_charter_hp.pdf

Zannini, L. (Ed.). (2004). *Il corpo-paziente. Da oggetto delle cure a soggetto della relazione terapeutica*. Franco Angeli.

Zannini, L. (2008). *Medical humanities e medicina narrativa. Nuove prospettive nella formazione dei professionisti della cura*. Raffaello Cortina.

Zannini, L. (2009). Medicina Narrativa e Medical Humanities. In Gentile, A. E., Luzi, I., Razeto, S., Taruscio, D. (Eds.). *Convegno. Medicina narrativa e malattie rare. Istituto Superiore di Sanità*. Rapporti ISTISAN 09/50.

Zannini, L. (2021). Valutare gli effetti di interventi di medicina narrativa nella formazione dei professionisti della cura: esperienze e riflessioni. *Medical Humanities & Medicina Narrativa - MHMN, 3*(1), 21-38. https://doi.org/10.53136/97912599425172

Chapter 9
Narrative Medicine Practices:
Emotional Literacy and Inclusion Through Reading

Gianluca Amatori
https://orcid.org/0000-0002-2477-2422
European University of Rome, Italy

Maria Buccolo
European University of Rome, Italy

ABSTRACT

In narrative medicine practices, emotional education and reading represent two intrinsically connected elements for the countless reasons that describe the potential of reading in promoting well-being and quality of life, self-realization and planning of one's future. The chapter starts from some theoretical references that trace the reasons for the importance of reading from early childhood and takes a deliberately methodological turn when the discussion on emotions is addressed precisely to bring to light a possible educability and management of them to encourage well-being and interpersonal relationships. The contribution intends to reflect on the development of emotional education through the practice of reading to give a meaningful orientation to our human form, to our formation, to our taking care of ourselves to build together answers for the future starting from the reflection on the actions to be taken to re-plan existences from an inclusive and transformative perspective.

DOI: 10.4018/979-8-3693-4244-2.ch009

INTRODUCTION

Contemporary challenges have profoundly transformed the way childhood is understood, both culturally and pedagogically and in terms of welfare. In this circumstance, Early Childhood Education and Care (ECEC), defined by UNESCO as «provision for children from birth through to primary education that falls within a national regulatory framework, i.e., it has to comply with a set of rules, minimum standards and/or undergo accreditation procedures» (European Commission / EACEA / Euridyce / Eurostat 2014, p. 155), represents a more urgent issue than ever, insofar as, at the international level, the education policies promoted by the world's leading organisations have devoted profound efforts to the implementation of the fundamental right of every child to the best possible opportunities to develop their potential (European Commission/ EACEA/Eurydice, 2019). Over the past two decades, bodies such as the OECD and UNESCO have established specific departments and research groups for this purpose, confirming the importance of guaranteeing every child, including children with disabilities (Art. 23), «the best possible opportunities to develop their full potential» (Art. 6), as already widely recognised by the European Convention for the Protection of Human Rights and Fundamental Freedoms (Council of Europe, 1950) and the UNCRC (United Nations, 1989).

METHODS

Being able to enjoy positive, meaningful and quality experiences in the 0-6 age group can be an undoubtedly effective driver with respect to self-development, future educational and scholastic success as well as early support for learning processes, social inclusion and employability (Briceag, 2019; Bianquin, Giraldo, 2021). These benefits are even more relevant for children with disabilities, particularly when the key to understanding, in terms of potential development, becomes that of Quality of Life (Giaconi, 2015). Moreover, the positive effects derived from attending a nursery or pre-school also affect the strengthening of mnemonic skills, oral and written comprehension, numerical and calculation skills, inter- and intra-personal problem solving, sociability and physical and motor development, with an evident persistence of these aspects also during adolescence, reducing – therefore – the risk of early school leaving and the likelihood of repeating the school year (Save the Children, 2019). The progressive knowledge on inclusive early childhood education, with reference to disability, the explanatory hypotheses on learning, on cognitive processes, are increased by the fruitful fertilisation of interdisciplinary contaminations.

RESULTS

As indicated in international documents (Unesco-UIL, 2017), the explanatory hypotheses and guidelines aimed at the promotion of reading and writing have been expanded under the impetus of the new demands imposed by contemporary social contexts and the growth of advances in science. The International Board on Books for Young People in Norway has published a worldwide selection of quality picture books in order to promote the right of all children to read. Publishing with reference to disability, aimed at promoting inclusive education, has also increased considerably in Italy in recent years. These are books in which children and adults with disabilities are among the protagonists, in a key that enhances them and promotes their knowledge and rights. Different types of books are proposed by silent books, e-books, apps, touchscreens, game books, sound books, pop-up books, which are chosen from the general production of the International Children Digital Library for certain characteristics, and which may be useful and valuable because of the particular clarity of the illustrations and the graphic design, simple text and readable typography, or because they propose interesting content.

The promotion of reading, from this point of view, does not specifically concern the intentional action of the educator or teacher in preparing educational paths aimed at the individual; rather, it refers to the use of the book as a mediator of relationships and learning environments, capable of responding to the educational needs of all children in the age range from zero to six years. The book, following this direction, becomes a tool to promote amazement, curiosity, desire, and courage, because reading is also accessed out of wonder and not only out of "duty to read" (Pennac, 1993). In 0-6 educational and school services, it is also important to observe how books are displayed, paying attention to types, shapes and colours, through the careful guidance of the adult, which can become an opportunity to create the child's or section's personal book. This, in fact, can be constructed directly by the children, also involving the parents in collecting drawings, photos, stories, also social and with visual aids, made by the children themselves (also through the introduction of alternative augmentative communication systems), initiating creative activities to be shared during the growth path (Caliceti & Rivola, 2017). Such activities develop imagination and creativity, facilitate the acquisition of sensorimotor, cognitive, and socio-affective skills; they also promote the construction of a common vocabulary, teach how to organise and classify, preserve memories, organise sequences, and ritualise times and spaces, recognising their functions; lastly, they accustom children to a creative use of language, creating complicity and enhancing the potential of each one. In very early childhood, initial communication includes all the work necessary to involve the child, starting from his or her interests, the minimum spaces of engagement (a particularly important aspect in young children or children with difficulties), and to modify the environment so that it can better support communicative and relational development. Basic facilitation, which is useful at a very early stage in all situations where there is the slightest doubt of possible difficulties in the future development of communication, includes supporting partner-perceived communication, offering opportunities for choice and introducing 'tailor-made' books (Costantino, Marini, Bergamaschi & Lanzini, 2006;). For this reason, it is crucial to pay attention to the reading process from an early age in order to prepare the child for later formal learning.

DISCUSSION

According to Lonigan, and Shanahan, (2008) even before entering primary school and the last year of childhood, in everyday life situations, listening to reading, observing figures, shapes, musical and body games, facilitates the acquisition of the multiple ways in which human beings communicate. When a child is involved, for example, in reading a picture book, playing with a sound object, with a tactile book that he can also experience with his hands and mouth, he begins his first activities: cognitive, social, emotional, acquiring fundamental basic skills. Furthermore, a child's individual skills interact, especially in early childhood, with the family contexts by which it is surrounded, and the environment is vital for the development of reading. For a young child, before reading comes speech and before that comes voice, experienced within a relationship. There is a sound dialogue that begins before the child possesses words in full; Bateson calls them "proto-conversations", while for Stern they are sounds that represent the authentic expression of emotions, of intentions that enclose meanings and are at the basis of the construction of meaning that the child gives to the reality that surrounds it. The child takes its first steps into the world of reading from an early age, through sensory experiences: looking, touching, smelling is already experiencing the first forms of relationship with the book and reading. The actual reading process in the child develops later and comprises a series of very diverse and complex activities. Dehaene (2009) states: 'Being able to read means, first of all, being able to decode. The decoding of graphemes into phonemes is the transition from a visual to an auditory unit. In order to progress in reading, the child must know how to decode new sequences of characters by himself in order to recognise words whose pronunciation and meaning he already knows, and progressively automate the whole of this processing chain'. In addition, the environment within which reading takes place is fundamental (Aidan Chambers, 2015), since certain factors, fundamental to the development of learning and positive emotions, linked to the social context must be considered. Reading, therefore, contemplates places, habits, emotions, relationships with the adult, the reader and the book object. The creation of a favourable reading environment is crucial, in order to competently help children and young people to become passionate and thoughtful readers. Furthermore, it is necessary to make choices to facilitate the discovery of preferences and to propose a book only after having read it. The concept of the 'social context of reading' as proposed by Chambers is in line with the evidence that has emerged in recent years from numerous studies on the functioning of the brain in reading processes. The American neuroscientist and dyslexia expert, Maryanne Wolf (2012), in a study devoted to reading, states that there are no specific genes solely responsible for enabling human beings to read and write. In order to acquire this ability – which is not only natural – children need educational environments that support the connection (of structures related to vision and speech) of all those circuits, which need to be acquired, to enable the brain to read. The scientist draws attention to three fundamental factors - educational - that influence language learning and consequently, brain development during the reading process. The first relates to the availability of books and how a lack of them can adversely affect the knowledge of words and things, which should be formed in the very first years of life. The second, to the provision of environments in which plenty of time is devoted to the simple activity of dialogue, even at the table during meals, and to reading. The third, to support parenting, especially for those experiencing linguistic and cultural deprivation. The three factors highlighted by Wolf have also been incorporated in international documents on policy, literacy and inclusion processes (UNESCO, 2017). The right to read can be guaranteed, according to the UN Convention on the Rights of Persons with Disabilities (2006), through "reasonable accommodation", i.e.: "necessary and appropriate modifications and adaptations that do not impose a disproportionate or excessive burden, (...) to ensure that persons with disabilities enjoy and exercise, on an equal basis with others, all human rights and fundamental freedoms" (Art. 2, 'Definitions') among which is the right to read and the freedom to choose what to read from the widest possible range of proposals. These accommodations mediate a new arrangement in which everyone's needs meet, dialogue and contaminate each other through multiple forms of representation. They are, in practical terms, accommodations that make it possible to remove or circumvent the barriers currently present to the comprehension of a text by fragile subjects, guaranteeing access to the body of information it contains and, at the same time, favouring communication and comparison with others. The use of an inclusive language, therefore, is not an addition placed for the use and consumption of a few individuals with specific needs, but a choice that enriches the narrative for all. Reading or listening to a picture book frees one from the real condition of the 'here and now' and allows the reader to open up to the world of the possible. Exploring alternatives and safe places through metaphors, images and new, original, unexpected, unsettling or reassuring points of view. Indeed, illustrated books prove to be “silent educators” (Lepman 2018) capable of mediating not only between themselves and their own imagery, but also with others and the imagery of others, promoting identity construction in a privileged space such as that of shared reading. If reading, by its very nature, offers opportunities to meet with otherness, the best illustrated books can be the indispensable tools of educational work in different educational contexts. Particularly in places of care and health, they make it possible to erect 'bridges' for the transit and sharing of stories, emotions and hopes. Speaking of books aimed at children, we must not forget the mediation work of the adult - parent, educator, teacher, bookseller/librarian - in the proposal of quality books appropriate to the contexts within which we intend to promote reading and inclusion: the adult, in fact, has the primary responsibility to work for the right to read of each and every one, in the direction of building a vision of reality grasped in its richness and complexity. The adult, who is passionate about reading, will not fail in his task to make the child also discover this world of adventures, discoveries and fun. Bringing a child to a passion for reading benefits not only their enjoyment, but also the development of important areas, including linguistic, cognitive, emotional, and relational. There are many objectives that reading training and education set and for these reasons it must be widely valued. Reading helps the child, in a significant way, in the acquisition of new words; the book stimulates comprehension of the first words and in a completely natural way enables the child to learn the first words. Of course, all this is achievable if the text has a certain narrative style and if the reader is skilled at reading it in an expressive and emotionally engaging way. Reading stories together or telling them are modes of interaction with the child that are very rich in potential. They become opportunities for communicative exchanges and the circulation of information that are fundamental for the development of oral language and the emergence of the future reader, as well as for the child's cognitive and emotional growth. Through the reading of illustrated books, from early childhood onwards, the aim is to promote inclusion through the promotion of the value of diversity as wealth. For Emili, 'inclusion is above all a set of concrete practices (from the smallest to the largest), pedagogically based, that must be implemented every day and in every place. There are no breaks or exceptions. [...] Inclusion is certainly based on words, principles and reinforced by scientific evidence, but it is defined by our actions” (Emili, Macchia, 2020). A path to inclusion education in early childhood starts right here, from reading books, in which normality and speciality coexist and are enriched with/for each other. Precisely for this reason, children's book author Luigi Dal Cin has created splendid, illustrated books that succeed in explaining certain illnesses through storytelling. Among the titles, written by Dal Cin and illustrated by Chiara Carrer, are: 'The Flowering Desert: Angelmann's Syndrome Told to Children' (2015), 'Matthew's Puzzle: Prader Will's Syndrome Told to Children' (2015), 'The Fragile Gaze: Fragile X Chromosome Syndrome Told to Children' (2017) and 'Grab the Top!: Epilepsy Told to Children' (2018). The language that strikes the children, in this case, is not the clinical-adult language, but that of narration, because it allows them to activate the processes of projection and identification, triggering an emotional relationship with the character in the story and consequently also with the friend who has the same characteristics or the same disability. Children need honest words, truths explained in simple language, and storytelling is able to satisfy these needs. A valuable book for explaining diversity is 'What is a syndrome' (2019) by Giovanni Colaneri. This illustrated book explains with very few words and detailed illustrations how to approach the complex subject of syndromic pictures to young children. It provides some answers on a very delicate and complex subject, to which adults very often fail to find an adequate response. Through very short sentences, it explains to children the immense richness and all the facets that the many syndromes present. The syndrome, within the illustrated book, is represented through the metaphor of a climb, another world, a giant, a prejudice and as something unique. But above all something that concerns us. Because if disability became something that concerns everyone, we would certainly live in a world with less prejudice, where diversity can be recognised and valued. And this would benefit people with disabilities, because they would perceive that they live in a society that is more inclusive and more respectful of everyone's needs. If we continue to think that the disability or syndrome a person suffers from is something that does not concern us, "it would be like judging a book only by its cover and not by its content, by the story inside". And for those who experience the burden of a syndrome at first hand, it is seen as 'an ongoing struggle against discrimination so that inclusion can be won'. An ongoing struggle by many people with disabilities who try to make their voices heard. Making people understand that diversity is there and that it is part of the richness of the world is fundamental for a more inclusive world and to improve the lives of all those people who, forced to live with a condition they do not choose, still feel the prejudice of others. Another book that, in a veiled and delicate way, addresses the issue of diversity by explaining it to children, is the illustrated book 'As in a Garden' by Agata Vignes with illustrations by Antonio Boffa (2020). A bit like mankind, a garden is also colourful and full of different flowers. The protagonist of this extraordinary story is Michelino, a child who has high expectations of the seed he has just planted in his garden. When he discovers that the flower is not what he expected, he is deeply disappointed. But the other flowers in the garden make him reflect and he manages to realise that the flower he wanted to remove - because he thought it would make his garden ugly - actually makes it unique and special in the eyes of everyone. Before the protagonist convinces himself of the richness of his garden made up of flowers that are all different from each other, he is struck by these words, which the 'different' little flower pronounces: "Think how sad the world would be if we saw a rainbow made only of yellow or if there were an ice-cream truck only with lemon flavour or, even worse, if there were a world made up of people who are all the same: we would no longer be able to recognise our best friend, we would not be able to understand which are the good and which the bad, but above all we would no longer know who we are! An extraordinary message for children to grasp diversity as an indispensable richness. Reading these illustrated books allows children to discover that they are all different and this stimulates empathy towards all those people who appear different and special in our eyes. In recent decades, there has certainly been an increase in the number of illustrated books produced by the various publishing houses dealing with this topic. This has helped parents, educators and teachers to deal with a very often difficult subject: that of diversity linked to a disability. Reading and the language used in illustrated books is, in fact, the best way to answer the many questions, which would otherwise remain unanswered, without a clear answer to fully understand them. Dealing with such a complex and debated topic as inclusion, within illustrated children's books, makes it possible to raise more inclusive generations. Any quality reading is a valuable form that children can use to get to know the world and life around them; a book, however, also helps them to get to know themselves, because it guides them towards a path of newness and the construction of their own identity, different from all the others. In addition to deepening the sphere of the self, reading supports the child in becoming acquainted with the positive and negative events that he will encounter on his path, such as friendship, love of neighbour, but also facts that are often incomprehensible to the youngest, such as illness, death or war. Learning to read in early childhood - initiated through the unavoidable lens of inclusive education - ultimately suggests an integrated approach directed not only at children with disabilities, but at all subjects, seeking to respond to the human urge to 'inhabit' the world, i.e. allowing the full expression and sharing of thought and, before that, of emotional experiences. Understanding intentions and emotions allows one to empathise with the character in a narrative, helping the child towards the correct development and decoding of the real world, facilitating relationships, and laying the foundations for a conscious construction of well-being.

CONCLUSION

Over the last twenty years, the educational approach that has seemed more appropriate than others for developing and reinforcing skills on an emotional level is the one developed from the Medical Humanities model: this approach - which involves reading passages or parts of works from the liberal arts as powerful evokers of emotional experiences on which to stimulate reflection - has demonstrated the ability to enhance individuals' familiarity with their own emotions and at the same time their ability to recognise the emotions of others (Manus, 1995; Goleman, 2005; Gordon, 2005).

There are numerous studies that demonstrate and support the importance of the pleasure of reading (Beseghi, Grilli, 2011; Blezza Picherle, 1996, 2004, 2013; Bruner, 2006; Cambi, Cives, 1996; Campanile, Lovo, Musella, 2001; Catarsi, 2001; Frasnedi, Martari, Panzieri, 2005; Levorato, 2000; Merletti, 1996, 2006; Terrusi, 2012).

Reading improves language, enriching vocabulary and the ability to express one's emotions in children from an early age; it broadens attention and concentration time; it educates to silence and listening; it enables the creation of autonomous mental images; it increases the desire to learn to read independently; it makes it possible to highlight that language has a sound and a rhythm and narrative its own structure; allows the child to create a common territory of ideas, images and emotions; allows the child, from the age of just over a year, to know what a book looks like, how to hold it, how to turn the pages and which way to look at the pictures; allows the child, even if he or she does not yet say so, that stories amuse, comfort, keep one company, enchant, move and move to action.

Reading is a very important activity and promoting motivation to read leads a person to become a 'reader for life'. Reading, therefore, should be continuously nurtured, supported and stimulated. Expressive reading activities are not an attempt to teach reading, but children's books allow for enriching experiences, influencing feelings, behaviour and attitudes. Moreover, books allow the imagination to be stimulated. The encounter with the book, in fact, allows the 'little reader' to reach spaces of imagination denied by reality. The story has the great ability to take us where thought stops for fear of the unknown, thus enabling us to face fears, doubts and misunderstandings.

Reading is the result of a learning process that is initially pure decoding of signs to enable them to be given meaning. This definition, however, only partly answers what 'reading' stands for. In fact, it must be borne in mind that the activity of reading requires the subject to place himself actively in relation to the book, so as to construct the meanings it contains and compare them with his own experiences and knowledge. Therefore, a continuous interaction between reader and text is required, since the construction of hypotheses about the meaning of a text is made possible by the interconnection between visual information (the text in its graphic form and context) and non-visual information (the reader with his or her content knowledge, oral, bodily and emotional language skills, and readiness to receive information from the outside world) .

A text wants someone to help it work, a product whose interpretive fate must be part of its own generative mechanism. Thus Eco, in his essay 'Lector in fabula' (1986), emphasises that the formation of a literary text occurs in the encounter between author and reader. This union, between author and reader, brings with it the singularity of the encounter.

Reading, therefore, is a complex activity since it involves different areas of the person: the socio-affective area, the cognitive area and the communicative area. It calls for the development of critical and analytical skills, aesthetic taste and emotional expression. Reading also means acquiring knowledge, constructing meanings, satisfying curiosity, orienting oneself in the great themes of life and in the universe of values in order to learn respect for differences and a sense of responsibility.

In early childhood, reading has a complex meaning, since it does not denote the ability to decode and understand the text, but the activity of discovering reality through the book 'tool'. Reading is a complex activity, in which cognition (knowledge) and emotion (pleasure) are closely linked, and for this complexity it needs support and motivation (Boscolo, 2006; Dehaene, 2007, 2009; Longo, 2011; Merletti, 1996, 2006). Being a spontaneous activity, reading should not be imposed, but motivated by viewing reading as a source of pleasure. Therefore, one must have a reason to do it. In order to do this, first and foremost it is the educator in the nursery who must be convinced that reading is a pleasurable and exciting activity, presenting himself as a lover of reading and an emotionally involved subject in the stories he reads (Buccolo, 2019). Only in this way will the children with whom they establish a relationship receive the communicative emotional signals and process them. In this regard, it is useful to review some illustrated books that can help the child explore his or her inner world and try to tell it, through images and words. First among these - on the subject of early emotional literacy - we find the illustrated book "Che rabbia!" (d'Allancé, 2007) which, thanks to its skilfully chosen images, can be very useful for adults who want to relate to children to talk to them (and with them) about emotions and educate them to know how to recognise even the most complex and less pleasant ones, such as anger in this case. Every child can easily identify with the character of Roberto, a child who, after having had a bad day, is really furious, and at the height of his anger, this turns into a red monster, which throws everything up in the air! This reading is especially useful for children who find it hard to control themselves in moments of anger. This story helps them visualise what they do not yet understand, and the adults guiding them towards self-discovery, to learn to know and recognise their emotions and give them a name. Another reading for young children is about the moment when they have to give up the dummy, the illustrated book "Nina's Dummy" (Naumann-Villemin, 2003). A fun and surreal story with beautiful illustrations, it helps parents to deal with the problem in a less dramatic way, having faith in the sometimes unexpected abilities of children who know how to make important choices without impositions, but on the basis of their experience, with a bit of grit and courage just like in Nina's story. Children who are beginning their experience at the crèche and have difficulty detaching themselves from the parental figure are offered, on the other hand, the reading of the illustrated book entitled "A più tardi" (Ashbè, 2019) in which two small children are depicted during a day at the crèche. A reading that recounts through reassuring images and words the morning kisses, toys, companions, painting, feeding, peeing, naps, fights and cuddles, the tiredness of the evening and... the happiness of being reunited with their parents! Tender illustrations that speak sweetly of the detachment at the moment of entry to the daycare centre, of becoming part of a group of little friends, and of how young children cope with all the new things they experience in this situation. Negative emotions are also linked to the separation of parents, and to get through this difficult time, a very useful read is the illustrated book entitled 'My name is Nina and I live in two houses' (De Smet, Talsma, 2019), the aim of which is to give a representation of the often conflicting feelings that a separation brings with it. It does so with direct words that do not conceal the difficulty, nostalgia and resentment (but do not leave them alone) and with delicate illustrations that pay particular attention to the body and facial expressions of the characters that help the child recognise the emotions they feel along with those of their parents. A sensitive topic such as separation is treated in a natural and non-traumatic way for the child who is, in fact, reassured: "Mummy and Daddy live in two different houses, but in each of the two houses there is a lot of love for you"! The subject of death is one of those readings that solicit negative emotions, especially if it has to be tackled with a child, it is never easy; all the emotions that we carry within us, perhaps the result of past and very intense experiences, very often represent a subject that one tends not to want to propose to one's children, also having the spontaneous desire to protect them from the concept of death and mourning. One must first of all understand that, sooner or later, this confrontation will inexorably arrive and it is therefore very useful to be ready to answer questions that will be more than ever legitimate and normal. "Grandpa's Island" (Davies, 2016) is an illustrated book suitable for children aged 3 and up that tells the theme of separation due to death; the intention of the narration is to deal with such delicate topics with grace and feeling, adding that touch of melancholy that is inexorably linked to the concept of lack. The protagonists of the story are the child Syd and his grandfather who embark on a journey to an imaginary island, punctuated by moments of great amusement and amazement at all the wonders they find, so much so that the grandfather decides to stop there permanently, greeting his grandson with a strong embrace and heartening him that even if they are separated forever, their love will never cease. Also connected to this theme is the emptiness or absence that a person leaves behind after death and the big existential questions that four- and five-year-olds begin to ask their parents but also their teachers. A very useful read, then, is the illustrated book entitled 'the hole' (Llenas, 2016), which tells the story of Giulia who explains how each of us always needs to fill the void created by the absence of an object or a loved one. Little Giulia teaches us that the strength to deal with these bereavements lies within each of us and that we must always accept the 'holes' and fill them with memories and positive thoughts. Among the many transformations that took place during the Pandemic period, the most significant and incisive for the growth of children is undoubtedly the profound revolution in communication processes and the radical transformation of relations between people mediated by technology. The closure of educational services in the lockdown period, in fact, immediately called educators and teachers to question how to set up distance activities with the 0-6 age group. Since there are no specific guidelines concerning the use of media in early childhood, many approaches have been used. The most interesting aspect of this was certainly the common intention to establish a dialogue with families, forcing educators and teachers to reflect on what were the most appropriate ways to offer support to parents, to maintain educational continuity and, above all, not to lose contact with children. This led to the birth of the "Educational Distance Ties" (LEAD) as the educational aspect at this age is based on the affective bond with the educators and teachers of reference who must maintain or reconstruct that contact made up of emotions, glances, voices, closeness, sharing, complicity, with the children and their families. In this experience, expressive reading represented precisely that common strategy implemented to be able to communicate and reassure children in the face of the experience of isolation at home. Readings together with the parents and little brothers and sisters, but also readings with a live connection to the educators and teachers to keep the emotional and relational closeness with the children alive even at a distance. It was precisely during the Covid period that the story entitled 'Covid the Barbarian' was born, an unpublished, highly topical tale written by professional educator Sara Pizzoni to explain to the children the reason for isolating themselves at home in order to fight an enemy: Covid-19. The story is recommended for children from 3 to 7 years old and was illustrated by designer Elia Pizzoni; it is available among the read alouds made available by the 'Leggere: forte!' project of the Region of Tuscany in collaboration with the University of Perugia[1]. The Covid is a small monster that dreams of invading the world and dirtying the rest of the population with balls of dirt. The inhabitants realise, after being soiled, that if they did not wash their hands they would in turn infect other people. They then collectively decide to lock themselves indoors so as to leave Covid alone, forcing him to return to his dirty little house. Through this reading, the aim of the "Read Strong" project was to educate resilience in order to provide the children with resources with which they were able to direct their emotions constructively, without reacting impulsively and painfully to challenges and difficulties. Resilience in this experience did not lead to closing one's eyes in front of the obstacle to pretend it did not exist; on the contrary, it demonstrated an awareness of being able to manage it, to conceive of it as a natural change and not as an impediment to one's own growth and evolution. From this perspective, the shift from emergency teaching to resilience teaching is interpreted as 'the ability of a system to preserve its integrity and fundamental purpose in the face of a drastic change in circumstances'. Faced with this change, the challenge has been to stimulate educators and teachers to rediscover - even in this complex phase - the 'meaning' of educational work, placing training as a lever of human and social change at the centre.

A strong desire emerges from these experiences to promote motivation for expressive reading, so that it can constitute a very important educational and didactic action for the formation, in the subject, of a 'cognitive disposition' (Frasnedi, Poli, 1989) to be a 'reader for life', and this competence must be continually nurtured, supported and solicited. This is not easy and for this reason it is necessary for the educational agencies to offer support and motivation, organising themselves in an educational and cultural network that unites shared goals, objectives and tasks in a project. This does not mean considering the role of the family marginal; on the contrary, it becomes the great point of reference for a shared reading education project (Batini, 2023).

An early reading experience is not about trying to teach the child to read. On the contrary, the aim is to be able to create interest, motivation and preference for reading around the child, which will later be prerequisites for the evolution of language and cognitive skills related to it.

Reading to children is an activity that takes place regularly in families but also in kindergartens from an early age. Reading is often linked to routines (Bosi, 2002), such as sleep: 'bedtime stories' are a habit of many parents, even if they are not always aware of the importance of this activity in early childhood.

Various scientific studies highlight the importance of adults reading aloud to children from early infancy and in the pre-natal period (B. Sahakian, J. Feng et al. 2023).

In fact, the newborn baby is already able to recognise stories that the mother has read to him, particularly in the last period of pregnancy. Moreover, when a story is read or told to a newborn baby that he or she already knows from intrauterine life, it has a calming effect on him or her: this can also be a valuable aid for new parents in consoling and relaxing the baby when he or she is experiencing emotional tension accompanied by crying.

The relaxing effect is just one of the many benefits that expressive reading produces in very young children. On a relational level, reading fosters the consolidation of the relationship between reference adult and child.

Research in the field of childhood shows how a good attachment bond is correlated with the frequency with which the child is told and read to. Secure attachment (Bowlby, 1979) nurtures the child's sense of protection, well-being and feeling loved, from which healthy self-esteem, self-confidence and confidence in the world derive. On an emotional level, the child is calmed and reassured by the power of the voice and the physical closeness of the reference adult who may be the parent, the educator or the teacher, who favours expressive reading as an intimate instrument of emotional connection and relationship with the child. The child can be supported in the process of developing empathy: through stories and identifying with the protagonists, he or she can learn to "put him or herself in the shoes" of the different characters and also achieve valid emotional management tools by presenting each emotion through reading a story. This can be achieved above all thanks to the fact that books lend themselves to conversation with children on the most diverse topics, including, precisely, emotions. Adults can therefore involve the children in what is happening in the stories, making comments and examining what is happening in them, inviting them to interpret the images.

This dialogue helps children to analyse the book, talking about life, commenting on the various types of experiences and linking them to their own, clarifying their own ideas. Since most of the stories revolve around people or anthropomorphic animals, who experience emotions and feelings in what happens to them and what they do, these conversations prove to be perfect opportunities to stimulate children to talk about feelings and emotions in order to develop their empathic skills and emotional intelligence. Thus, while having fun and without effort, children can acquire emotional skills that are fundamental for their own harmonious growth. In terms of moral development, reading quality books can foster the acquisition of values, models and principles in children, avoiding a lot of abstract discourse that is often alien to their reality. The choice of books, therefore, from early childhood cannot be accidental, it is very important as they provide children with 'indications' and models of behaviour: stories propose, in one way or another, a world, possible and appropriate behaviour, emotions that can be felt in relation to certain encounters or events, they provide rules of conduct and morals (Batini, 2011).

In this sense, it can be useful to read stories that talk about play, sharing, friendship, acceptance of diversity, so as to facilitate the achievement of those principles that are important for personal and social well-being.

Reading with children in early childhood is, first and foremost, an enjoyable activity that contributes to the immediate psychophysical well-being of both the child and the adult reading with him/her. Listening to a story read aloud, leafing through a book, playing with a nursery rhyme, are all activities that aim to make children feel good, thanks to the contact, closeness, intimacy and complicity that attentive and helpful adults create around them. Early reading today represents a powerful means to renew and strengthen the relationship between adult and child. The quality of the relationship is fundamental to the child's development, because from birth the child is already a social and symbolic being rich in skills, with cognitive capacities for self-learning (Vygotsky,1973).

The relational approach is the methodological principle that is proposed in the expressive reading workshops to foster the development of emotional literacy in working with children in the 0-6 childhood education services. Being able to build a daily relationship between children and books is an operation that requires attention, curiosity, a desire to measure oneself against one's own abilities as an expressive reader and awareness of one's own choices. Precisely because of its characteristics, the crèche is a privileged place to propose the first books and readings, because it prepares dynamic and open contexts, supporting the child's learning phases linked to positive emotions. Alongside these emotional, affective and cognitive reasons, there are certainly others of an exquisitely evolutionary nature, which characterise the relationship between the child and the book. With very young children it is the narrative voice that supports and accompanies the important process of symbolisation that they initiate at a very early age. Working with and through symbols means, for the child, acquiring the ability to represent things, objects, people, situations, even in their absence, learning to replace them with signs and images that evoke them.

The stories told, read or invented and the images contained in books constitute the richest symbolic material in terms of possibilities and indirect experiences that can be offered to children. In the symbolic space created by expressive reading and the vision of images, children can move around with confidence, experiencing feelings and thoughts, recognising emotions (e.g. emotions such as anger, disgust, fear, sadness, joy) that do not guilt or hurt others; simulating conflicts and tensions that are resolved without drama, coming into contact with complex situations that activate new thoughts and new responses linked to their daily lives.

The process of symbolisation is fundamental for children, because transforming reality into symbols gives them control over their emotions, increasing their ability to assimilate knowledge and make generalisations. In other words, symbolising allows them to construct their own personal set of words, images and cognitive functions in interaction with other children and adults. Early books do an excellent job of initiating symbolisation, because they construct mental images that are the effective narrative representation of the object.

Reading, therefore, offers children models of life and styles of behaviour, social relationships with which to compare themselves, analogies with everyday problems, possible solutions or mediations with respect to strong emotions or conflictual situations and events. Territorial educational policies welcome social and cultural instances on reading, as a systematic and organised practice, from early childhood onwards, with institutional responses that are part of the evolution of services for children. Increasingly, activities such as Reading Centres - also called 'reading space', 'children's library', 'zerosei library' - are being set up to encourage the encounter between books and children between 0 and 6 years of age, accompanied by parents, educators and teachers. These projects, based on the experience of reading by the adult to the child, make it possible to initiate the process of cognitive and emotional literacy from an early age. The earliest possible introduction of children to reading is understood as a probability of success compared to late exposure, since the ability to read is the result of a long and articulated process of symbolisation that goes from drawing, to interpreting the drawing, to reading and understanding the text. It should be emphasised that in Reading Centre projects the main aim is not the teaching of reading technique, but the consolidation of motivation for reading and the building of the ability to grasp links between elements, both real and symbolic. In this regard, it is worth mentioning 'Nati per leggere', which is one of the Italian projects on reading conceived in 1999 (www.natiperleggere.it). It is promoted by the alliance between librarians and paediatricians. It has involved the following associations: the Associazione Culturale Pediatri (ACP), which brings together three thousand paediatricians with an exclusively cultural purpose; the Associazione Italiana Biblioteche (Italian Library Association), which brings together more than four thousand librarians, libraries, documentation centres, information services operating in the various environments of the profession; the Centro per la Salute del Bambino - ONLUS (CSB), which has training, research and solidarity activities for children as its statutory purposes. The alliance between librarians and paediatricians stems from society's need to concretely support the development of the habit of reading to children from pre-school age. The project is active throughout the country with around 400 local projects involving 1195 Italian municipalities. 'Born to read' aims to promote the child's encounter with books from the age of 6 months to 6 years using, among other strategies, expressive and emotional reading. The project starts from the idea that every child has the right to be protected: from illness, from violence, from the lack of adequate opportunities for affective and cognitive development. It has been documented by many studies how a continuous reading activity from the adult to the child, in pre-school age, has a benefit, or rather, has a positive influence both from a relational and cognitive point of view: from a relational point of view because it is an opportunity for a relationship between child and parent; from a cognitive point of view because it allows for earlier and better development of language comprehension and reading skills. In addition to these two positive influences, it helps to create the habit of reading, which lasts over time. Over the last few years, the project has had a remarkable spread, seeing the involvement of an increasing number of operators and services for children, including paediatricians, librarians, socio-cultural operators, educators, teachers, pedagogues, organisations and associations, educational centres and family centres. The experience of the 'Born to read' project has shown that reading contains many meanings linked to positive and affective communication patterns that have a significant influence on the emotional development of children. It is considered the most important activity for the acquisition of the skills necessary for success in reading and the development of positive emotions. Through reading, the child gradually takes possession of the mother tongue, its words, form and structure. This will enable him/her to build his/her own mental structures in order to be able to understand space-time relationships and distances. The project is rooted in studies on early literacy, the development of the conditions and skills for learning to read and the early ability to solve problems of increasing difficulty involving the comprehension of written texts. On the other hand, "Born to read" represents one of the most widespread projects in the world on the promotion of reading, involving health and cultural services in a cross-sectoral way, reading and health are intrinsically connected and in a non-explicit way, resilience is also developed, in the sense hypothesised and described by Walsh (2008). In fact, much research shows how 'Born to Read' is a project capable of promoting health and resilience with respect to the construction of informal networks, secure and multiple attachment, motor humour, the construction of meaningful relationships, emotional education, and the construction of a sense of coherence. The state of 'well-being', therefore, cannot disregard the dimension of the relationship with oneself and with others and its achievement is deeply linked to an emotional and empathic dimension that balances states of instability and uncertainty. We can affirm, from this perspective, that reading, despite causing fatigue, can become a source of well-being. Reading competence is a competence that heals. Reading can also be regarded as a resource for generating health, as intuited by Antonovsky (1996) in his salutogenic model.

Expressive and emotional reading - as a result of this reflection - has turned out to be a useful tool that can be applied at various times; even in the nursery and preschool, this awareness on the part of educators and teachers has prompted them to experiment with building a more meaningful relationship with children and families. The activity of reading to children can be proposed at different times such as during the reception, during educational activities or at bedtime. Reception has a fundamental function, since it is the moment that predisposes children to listening. The first contact with the children, the moment of picking them up from the section or dividing them into the groups that are going to read in the story corner, often called the reading corner, should be considered important. The most effective way of welcoming very young children consists of ritual actions, which make the reading activity into something extraordinary, an event that attracts their imagination, prepares them to take in and get involved. Rituals can be many other things, children can be invited to deposit something, such as their own shoes, outside the story place to sit on the soft mat that marks the transition from the ordinary environment of the nursery to the 'extraordinary' space dedicated to reading in order to attract their attention. When choosing the space to be used for reading in the crèche and kindergarten, and when setting up the story place, it is necessary to act with care and attention. Making shared choices and not letting decisions happen by chance is perhaps the most effective rule of conduct. For this it is useful to take a few criteria into account. Choose a venue that is easily accessible to all children and parents. It must be a strategic point for movement within the nursery, but also a visible point for families to be intrigued and stimulate attention towards reading. A good choice is a space that can be acoustically isolated, so that reading is not disturbed by calls between people and various noises. A room with large windows, where natural light can enter, is preferable to one that is artificially lit. The environment must convey quietness and tranquillity, emphasising the book and facilitating relationships. The shelves, bookcases and trolleys should be low, so that the books, preferably with their covers, are freely accessible to the children. Additional furniture is not necessary, because the children must be able to move freely in the space, crawl, lie down and read comfortably. The readings that take place in the story place take place systematically, i.e. they have defined times, according to the timetable and organisation laid down in the Educational Project of the individual 0-6 educational service. The most favourable part of the day must be chosen for the reading: away from tiredness, appetite, entering and leaving the nursery or pre-school, i.e. when the children are most relaxed and available, as for any other activity that requires a certain amount of effort. It is necessary for the educator or teacher to take into account the timing of the reception, the reading, the dialogue that must follow the listening and the time necessary for the children to 'read' independently, according to individual preferences and times, free among the books. The contribution presented here, with its articulations, demonstrates that children must be given the possibility of attention. And this attention is revealed precisely in participation in reading, in the discovery of the book that becomes a useful tool for learning about the world. Reading is therefore a fruitful tool for promoting individual and social well-being, it improves linguistic, logical and text comprehension skills. It increases knowledge of the world but also knowledge of oneself and others, keeps the cognitive functions of memory, attention and concentration, reasoning and critical capacity active. Stories provide access to the sphere of feelings and emotions of the protagonists and in this way increase emotional literacy. The emotional vocabulary becomes broader and this improves the definition, expression and understanding of one's own and others' emotions. Identifying with the characters in the stories allows one to develop the ability to feel the other's emotionality (what they are feeling and how), i.e. empathy. Mayer and Salovey (2004) call the letter “the first home of emotional intelligence”: assuming that books are the place where we practise our feelings, reflecting on the great potential of the letter in the formation of the individual and considering the fact that, through the actions, thoughts and emotions of fictional characters, children in particular can learn about themselves and the world, then it is possible to understand reading as a useful tool for acquiring good emotional competence. All these potentialities of reading are invaluable for children who, as they grow up, are constantly in search of reference points, they structure their own being, they build images with which to think, they learn to recognise and manage their emotions, and this is why it is possible to think of reading as a tool for educating emotions, hypothesising a real emotional literacy course in school through a selection of books. It is up to the educator and the teacher, in fact, to choose the materials through which to introduce children to reading, and certainly, by approaching children with a passion for reading, selecting suitable - and above all, interesting - books with which young readers can easily identify, and granting slightly more experienced readers all the 'rights' that we grant ourselves, the possibility of making them good readers for life is concrete. Only if one succeeds in transmitting a love of reading to children, will they become passionate readers and be able to benefit from the infinite advantages of this educational experience, first and foremost the possibility of practising the most important emotional and social skills, becoming emotionally aware subjects, able to put their inner world in order and maintain healthy interpersonal relationships throughout their lives.

REFERENCES

Amatori, G., & Maggiolini, S. (Eds.). (2021). *Pedagogia speciale per la prima infanzia. Politiche, famiglie, servizi*. Pearson.

Amatori, G., Maggiolini, S., Macchia, A (a cura di) (2021). *Pensare in Grande. L'educazione inclusiva per l'infanzia di oggi e di domani*. Pensa Multimedia.

Antonovsky, A. (1996). The salutogernic model as a theory to guide health promotion. *Health (San Francisco, Calif.)*.

Ashbè J., (2019). *A più tardi*. Babalibri. Trad.it Rocca F.

Batini, F. (2011). *Storie che crescono. Le storie al nido e alla scuola dell'infanzia*. Junior.

Batini, F. (Ed.). (2023). *La lettura ad alta voce condivisa. Un metodo in direzione dell'equità*. Il Mulino.

Beseghi, E., & Grilli, G. (2011). *La letteratura invisibile. Infanzia e libri per bambini*. Carocci.

Bianquin, N., & Giraldo, M. (2021). La qualità dell'inclusione nel sistema integrato 0-6: promozione e sostegno alla partecipazione. In Amatori, G., & Maggiolini, S. (Eds.), *Pedagogia speciale per la prima infanzia. Politiche, famiglie, servizi* (pp. 31–63). Pearson.

Blezza Picherle, S. (1996). *Leggere nella scuola materna*. La Scuola.

Blezza Picherle, S. (2004). *Libri bambini ragazzi. Incontri tra educazione e letteratura*. Vita e Pensiero.

Blezza Picherle, S. (2013). *Formare lettori, promuovere la lettura. Riflessioni e itinerari narrativi tra territorio e scuola*. Franco Angeli.

Boscolo, P. (2006). *Psicologia dell'apprendimento scolastico. Aspetti cognitive e motivazionali*. Utet.

Bosi, R. (2002). *Pedagogia al nido. Sentimenti e relazioni*. Carocci.

Bowlby, J. (1979). *Attaccamento e Perdita*. Bollati Boringhieri.

Bruner, J. (2006). *La fabbrica delle storie*. Laterza.

Buccolo, M. (2019). *L'educatore emozionale. Percorsi di alfabetizzazione emotiva per tutta la vita*. FrancoAngeli.

Caliceti, G., & Rivola, A. (2017). *Nel lontano regno di mongolfiera*. Sinnos.

Cambi, F. (2015). *La forza delle emozioni. Per la cura di sé*. Pacini.

Cambi, F., & Cives, G. (1996). *Il bambino e la lettura. Testi scolastici e libri per l'infanzia*. ETS.

Cambi, F., Di Bari, C., & Sarsini, D. (2012). *Il mondo dell'infanzia. Dalla scoperta al mito alla relazione di cura*. Apogeo.

Campagnaro, M. (2012). *Narrare per immagini. Uno strumento per l'indagine critica*. Pensa.

Campanile, S., Lovo, A., & Musella, M. (2001). *Il vizio di leggere*. Liguori.

Catarsi, E. (2001). *Lettura e narrazione nell'asilo nido*. Edizioni Junior.

Chambers, A. (2015). *Il lettore infinito. Educare alla lettura tra ragioni ed emozioni*. Equilibri.

Colaneri, G. (2019). *Che cos'è una sindrome*. Uovonero.

Corsi, M. (2006). *Il coraggio di Educare. Il valore della testimonianza*. Vita e Pensiero.

Costantino, M. A., Marini, M., Bergamaschi, E., & Lanzini, L. (2006). Dal "libro su misura" alla "biblioteca di tutti". *Quaderni ACP*, 13(5), 199–203.

D'Allancé M., (2007). *Che rabbia*. Babalibri. Trad.it Morpurgo A.

Dal Cin, L. (2015). *Il puzzle di Matteo: la sindrome di Prader Will raccontata ai bambini*. Uniti per Crescere.

Dal Cin, L. (2015). *Il deserto fiorito: La sindrome di Angelman raccontata ai bambini*. Uniti per Crescere.

Dal Cin, L. (2017). *Lo sguardo fragile: la sindrome del cromosoma X fragile raccontata ai bambini*. Lapis.

Dal Cin, L. (2018). *Afferra la cima!: l'epilessia raccontata ai ragazzi*. Brossura.

Davies B., (2016). *L'isola del nonno*. Giralangolo. Trad. It. Roveda A.

De Smet, M., & Talsma, N. (2019). *Mi chiamo Nina e vivo in due case*. Clavis.

Dehaene, S. (2007). Le basi cerebrali di un'acquisizione culturale: la lettura. In Changeux, J. P. (Ed.), *Geni e cultura*. Sellerio.

Dehaene, S. (2009). *I neuroni della lettura*. Raffaello Cortina.

Denham, S. A. (2001). *Lo sviluppo emotivo dei bambini*. Ubaldini.

Drigas, A. S., & Papoutsi, C. (2018). A new layered model on emotional intelligence. *Behavioral Sciences (Basel, Switzerland)*, 8(5), 45. 10.3390/bs805004529724021

Eco, U. (1986). *Lector in fabula. La cooperazione interpretativa nei testi narrativi*. Bompiani.

Emili, A. E., & Macchia, V. (Eds.). (2020). *Leggere l'inclusione. Albi illustrati e libri per tutti e per ciascuno*. Edizioni ETU.

European Commission/EACEA/Eurydice. (2019). Key data on Early Childhood Education and Care in Europe. *Eurydice Report*. Luxemburg. https://op.europa.eu/en/publicationdetail/-/ publication/5816a817-b72a-11e9-9d01-01aa75e d71a - 1/ language-en/format-PDF/source-102611557

European Commission/EACEA/Eurydice/Eurostat. (2014). Key data on Early Childhood Education and Care in Europe. *Eurydice and Eurostat Report* Luxemburg. https://ec.europa. eu/eurostat/documents/3217494/5785249/EC-01-14-484- EN .PDF/cbdf1804-a139-43a9-b8f1-ca5223eea2a1

Frasnedi, F., Martari, Y., & Panzieri, C. (Eds.). (2005). *La lingua per un maestro. "Vedere" la lingua per insegnare, per capire, per crescere*. FrancoAngeli.

Frasnedi, F., & Poli, L. (1989). *Lettura e azione cognitiva. Parole e immagini*. Thema.

Frauenfelder, E., & Santoianni, F. (Eds.), *A mente aperta. Ambienti di apprendimento. Contesti di formazione*. Pisanti.

Frauenfelder, E., Santoianni, F., & Striano, M. (2004). *Introduzione alle scienze bioeducative*. Laterza.

Freschi, E. (2013). *Il piacere delle storie. Per una "didattica" della lettura nel nido e nella scuola dell'infanzia*. Junior.

Giaconi, C. (2015). *Qualità della vita e adulti con disabilità*. FrancoAngeli.

Goleman, D. (2005). *Intelligenza emotiva*. Rizzoli.

Gordon, J. (2005). Medical humanities: To cure sometimes, to relieve often, to comfort always. *The Medical Journal of Australia*, 182(1), 5–8. 10.5694/j.1326-5377.2005. tb06543.x15651937

Gottschall, J. (2012). *L'istinto di narrare. Come le storie ci hanno resi umani*. Bollati Boringhieri.

Iavarone, M. L. (2008). *Educare al benessere*. Mondadori.

Iori, V. (Ed.). (2009). *Quaderno della vita emotiva. Strumenti per il lavoro di cura.* FrancoAngeli.

Izard, C. E. (1997). *Human emotions*. Plenum Pless.

LeDoux, J. (2003). *Il cervello emotivo. Alle origini delle emozioni.* Baldini Castoldi Dalai.

Lepman J., (2018). *Un ponte di libri*. Sinnos. Trad. It. A.P. Becchi.

Levorato, M. C. (2000). *Le emozioni della lettura.* il Mulino.

Llenas A., (2016). *Il buco*. Gribaudo Trad. it Gamba D.

Longo, G. (2011). *Cognizione ed emozione. Processi di interpretazione del testo letterario dalle neuroscienze cognitive all'educazione emotiva.* Pensa Multimedia.

Lonigan, C. J., & Shanahan, T. (2008). Developing Early Literacy: report of the national early literacy panel executive summary. A scientific synthesis of early literacy development and implications for intervention, *National Institute for Literacy*. https://files.eric.ed.gov/fulltext/ED508381.pdf

Mariani, A. (Ed.). (2018). *Educazione affettiva. L'impegno della scuola attuale.* Anicia.

Merletti, R. (1996). *Leggere ad alta voce*. Mondadori.

Merletti, R. (2001). *Libri e lettura da 0 a 6 anni*. Mondadori.

Merletti, R. (2006). *Leggimi forte. Accompagnare i bambini nel grande universo della lettura*. Sanali.

Naumann-Villemin C., (2003). *Il ciuccio di Nina*. Il castoro.

Nussbaum M. (2004). *L'intelligenza delle emozioni*. il Mulino.

Pennac, D. (1993). *Come un romanzo*. Feltrinelli.

Sahakian, J. Feng et al. (2023). Early-Initiated Childhood Reading for Pleasure: Associations with Better Cognitive Performance, Mental Well-being and Brain Structure in Young Adolescence. *Psychological Medicine*.https://www.cambridge.org/core/journals/psychological-medicine/article/earlyinitiated-childhood-reading-for-pleasure-associations-with-better-cognitive-performance-mental-wellbeing-and-brain-structure-in-young-adolescence/03FB342223A3896DB8C39F171659AE33

Salovey, P., Brackeyt, M., & Mayer, J. (2004). *Emotional Intelligence: Key Readings on the Mayer and Salovey Model*. Natl Professional Resources Inc.

Save the Children. (2019). *Il miglior inizio. Disuguaglianze e opportunità nei primi anni di vita*. Save The Children.

Sirignano, F. M. (2012). L'asilo nido come comunità educativa. Prospettive e riflessioni pedagogiche. In *L. Pati, M. Musello (Esd.), Pedagogia e didattica della prima infanzia*. Pensa Multimedia.

Sirignano, F. M. (2014). L'incontro educativo tra famiglia e servizi per l'infanzia. In Pati, L. (Ed.), *Pedagogia della famiglia*. La Scuola.

Terrusi, M. (2012). *Albi illustrati. Leggere, guardare, nominare il mondo nei libri per l'infanzia*. Carocci.

Terrusi, M. (2017). *Meraviglie mute. Silent book e letteratura per l'infanzia*. Carocci.

Toffano Martini, E. (2007). *Ripensare la relazione educativa*. Pensa Multimedia.

UN. (2006). *Convention on the Rights of Persons with Disabilities (CRPD)*. UN. https://www.un.org/development/desa/disabilities/convention-on-the-rights-of-persons-with-disabilities.html

UNESCO Institute for Lifelong Learning. (2017). *Engaging families in literacy and learning*. UNESCO. https://unesdoc.unesco.org/images/0024/002494/249463e.pdf

UNESCO. (2017). *Education 2030. Reading the past, writing the future, fifty years of promoting literacy*. UNESCO. https://unesdoc.unesco.org/images/0024/002475/247563e.pdf

United Nations. (1989). *Conventionon the Rights of the Child*. United Nation General Assembly. https://www. -ohchr.org /en/professionalinterest/pages/crc.aspx

Vignes, A., & Boffa, A. (2020). *Come in un giardino*. Saremo Alberi.

Vygotskij, L. S. (1972). *Immaginazione e creatività nell'età infantile*. Editori Riuniti.

Vygotskij, L. S. (1973). *Lo sviluppo psichico del bambino*. Editori Riuniti.

Walsh, F. (2008). *La resilienza Familiare*. Raffaello Cortina.

WHO - World Health Organization. (2001). *ICF. International Classification of Functioning, Disability and Health*. OMS Press.

ENDNOTE

1 For further information, see the dedicated special on the Regione Toscana website: https://www.regione.toscana.it/scuola/speciali/leggereforte

Chapter 10
The Aesthetic Dimension as a "Lost Paradigm" of Reading:
Education for Resilience Through Bibliotherapy

Maria Federica Paolozzi
https://orcid.org/0000-0002-0048-2340
Università degli Studi Suor Orsola Benincasa, Italy

Stefania Maddalena
https://orcid.org/0000-0002-5691-8158
University of Chieti-Pescara, Italy

ABSTRACT

In the twentieth century, aesthetics gained central importance in the philosophical debate. Croce viewed aesthetics as the first form of knowing, rooted in feeling and intuition. This challenges traditional methodologies that prioritize formalistic and intellectual aspects over intuition and aesthetics. Heidegger and Gadamer reinforced the significance of aesthetics in contrast to a technicist view of epistemology, emphasizing its intrinsic connection to truth, promoting a holistic understanding of art and expression. These ideas inform pedagogy's reflections on reading education, emphasizing narration as vital for education. Reading, storytelling, and writing are seen as tools that can enhance resilience and well-being, especially when approached within a narrative framework. Bibliotherapy and narrative based medicine are highlighted for their therapeutic and humanizing benefits in healthcare, emphasizing the importance of professional guidance for effective therapeutic results.

DOI: 10.4018/979-8-3693-4244-2.ch010

THE AESTHETIC DIMENSION IN PHILOSOPHICAL REFLECTION: LANGUAGE, NARRATIVE, POETIC EXPRESSION

Introduction

In this Chapter, the theme of reading is connected to the more general discourse on aesthetics as a specific dimension of human expression and life. In the twentieth century, in fact, the aesthetic dimension assumed a central position in the philosophical debate: in Benedetto Croce it represents a form, and in particular the first form, of knowing, that relating to feeling and the intuition of the particular, resembling history in this aspect. Only from the intuition of the 'particular', according to Croce, is it possible to begin the formation of the concept as the logical and universal form of knowing. This theoretical conception seems to invert and overturn a widespread teaching and learning methodology: the one in which the formalistic and intellectualistic aspect should predominate over the intuitive, aesthetic and poetic aspect. With the philosophers of the Hermeneutic Circle - Heidegger and Gadamer - the function of aesthetics is reaffirmed, and not merely accessory and secondary. In contrast to a technicist, instrumental and objectivist vision of twentieth-century epistemology, aesthetics is not a moment separate from truth, but an experience of truth in the broadest sense, an encounter with being and overcoming the presumed opposition between subject and object, which is functional to a vision that separates the human sciences from the natural sciences. These assumptions suggest a fundamental, ontological, epistemological and existential dimension of art and poetic expression that clears the field of limited, partial and erroneous visions of artistic expression and fruition. They thus indicate some perspective lines in the pedagogical sphere, in accordance with the scientific literature, regarding reading education. In fact, in a certain continuity with the assumptions that have historically dealt with the fundamental relationship between pedagogy and art - from Bildung to John Dewey - and taking their cue from the studies on narrative thought conducted by Jerome Bruner (1992), the element of narration is configured as an ontological dimension of education. The peculiar theme of reading from an educational and training point of view is then examined and some reflections on reading education are offered, highlighting, through the analysis of the literature on the subject, problematic aspects and methodological proposals from different approaches and reflections. In particular, a paradigm for reading, and for education in general, is highlighted and outlined through a narrative approach that, in accordance with the complexity paradigm, manages to challenge certain phenomena generated by the reductionist cultural model. Expressing themselves in the technologised society, these phenomena produce a dehumanisation at different levels, of the existential, individual and collective dimension.

Methodology

The invitation to reading and a narrative approach to reality - if we overcome certain methodological orientations to literary and artistic fruition present in many school and training systems - represent a privileged access route to the recomposition of a new complex humanism within which groups and individuals can trace that dimension of meaning that seems to be lost in the ganglions of practical living. The latter understood as the prevailing mode of our time, in which the most intimate and meaningful dimension of existence seems to lose meaning. The theme of reading - and the more general narrative dimension - is connected to the dimension of well-being and mental health, more specifically, through the 'lens' of resilience education. That is, of the subject's own capacity to become able to cope with adversity and produce positive development. In particular, it is believed possible that reading, listening, storytelling and writing can positively influence the ability to develop resilient behaviour in individuals who have experienced or are experiencing difficult experiences. Research on the subject of resilience, in psychology and pedagogy, highlights the multifactorial and processual dimension of the resilience construct, which is composed of aspects that can be generalised and indicated as resilience factors and others that are undeniably linked to each individual's history and experience. For these reasons, the narrative dimension succeeds in integrating - through the experiences and feelings narrated - characteristics that relate to human experience from a universal and individual point of view, tracing the transcultural cores of feelings that manifest and become visible in the particular experiences narrated.

The reading of novels and short stories, personal and autobiographical narration, and listening to stories (real or imagined) also make it possible to shape the dimension of suffering on which the process of transforming negative experience into a positive perspective is grafted. They can, then, generate that fusion and opening up of horizons that makes it possible to overcome, as some scholars affirm in the context of resilience reflections, the stigma and socio-cultural significance often attributed to stressful and traumatic situations. The practice of reading for therapeutic purposes - known as bibliotherapy or therapy through books - is certainly not a new concept. Since ancient times, people have found comfort, inspiration and support in the pages of books. Reading is not only a form of entertainment, but also a powerful tool for understanding and facing the challenges of everyday life. Through reading, people can explore ideas, viewpoints and solutions to their existential problems.

Furthermore, the act of reading creates a sense of community and connection between individuals who share the same experiences and concerns. Bibliotherapy is used in various fields of health and education. However, it is important to emphasise that the mere practice of reading, without the appropriate therapeutic support, does not result in bibliotherapy. This form of therapy requires a targeted encounter between the individual who is coping with a situation of emotional fragility and suffering and a specialised professional, known as a bibliotherapist. The bibliotherapist provides resources and personalised support to help the individual gain therapeutic benefits from reading. In this context, bibliotherapy becomes a guided and intentional process aimed at the individual's personal growth and emotional well-being. The link between resilience and cultural meanings shows how the dimension of Narrative Based Medicine (NBM) is of fundamental importance in building and promoting well-being and health. The NBM paradigm, as well as making a contribution in the direction of humanising medical care, is based on both defining and promoting wellbeing and health in a broader meaning in which other factors, not only biological and statistical ones, influence determining the causes of illness as well as the possibilities for recovery. NBM represents an important evolution in the field of patient care. Through this practice, it is possible not only to better identify the disease but also to communicate knowledge and show respect, to humbly collaborate among colleagues, and to accompany the patient and his or her family along the path of suffering. This approach not only allows for more ethical and effective care, but also contributes to a more empathetic and understanding care environment. NBM stems from the convergence of different disciplines, such as the humanities, narratology and research on the relationship between doctor and patient. It is a tangible field of knowledge that helps to understand the lived experience not only of patients, but also of healthcare professionals, thus improving the overall quality of the care pathway.

The title of the present effort reflects the notions and concepts expressed in its paragraphs and focuses on the lost paradigm Edgar Morin used as the title of a famous volume of his that can be considered the manifest of the transdisciplinary project of philosophy and anthropology of complexity.

This reference to Edgar Morin is the main thread of the preliminary considerations orienting the present contribution and the origin of the assumptions and questions. The aforesaid tenets do not necessarily ask for definite answers or exhaustive conclusions, but do require suggestive significance and future implementation with a view to identifying the major possible therapeutic effects of

1) reading in general and
2) sharing feelings and emotions

2a) through reading general text material and
2b) through reading poetry and prose.

If one wanted to describe briefly the paradigm Morin indicated and to try to identify the core of his research, one should say that the theoretical framework of complexity involves all aspects of the real world, as the main topics in the seven volumes of his *Method* show, and therefore argues for a new rationality that would enable us to interpret processes and phenomena. This new rationality must be able to integrate and bind all the aspects and dimensions of the real world, or to put it in technical terms, combine all factors concerning the phenomena and, at the same time, take into account all the interactions, even the non-linear ones, that the various dimensions entertain in an absolutely dynamic manner. Without going into great detail, for the sake of space, we might as well claim, as Morin himself does, that complex rationality, to start with, opposes a rationality which reduces multiple and variable aspects of different, sometimes even contradictory, facets and spheres of a phenomenon in the attempt to

a) mechanistically determine it as the effect of a cause;
b) reduce it and bring it back to only one of its aspects by separating it from all those other ones that could be called the terms of a piece of discourse.

Discourse here is nothing other than the fundamental dimension of thinking and of veritative thought, which Hannah Arendt (1958) explains with discourse and action as the modes whereby human beings appear to each other not as physical objects, but as human beings; at any rate, without being accompanied by discourse, not only the action, but also the actor, would lose its revelation potential - unlike humans who act, robots who perform would create something not humanly understandable. And we can agree on this to the full.

Starting from the aforesaid premises, the present work mainly aims at considering the elements and topics characterizing well-being, mental health, the contribution of bibliotherapy in putting them to the test of complexity in order to propose some theoretical and methodological perspectives.

As regards mental health, we are bound by the definition expressed in the first principle of the WHO Constitution, which refers to health as a state of total physical, mental and social well-being, not as confined to the mere absence of sickness and disease.

Being dynamically opened to all possible ways of understanding and building the meaning of health to include the myriad experiences which refer to the notions of health, mental health and well-being, as the numerous research works and considerations on this topics evince, does not mean

1. refusing to follow the tracks or to track some paths or even
2. thinking of solving the problem of so free an interpretation of its meaning by forcefully restricting it.

We can say that, as is the case with each and every era, our time is characterized by crises and peculiarities resulting from the further deterioration of long-standing problematic conditions which more or less differently affect and delineate the factors responsible for the individual and collective well-being or malaise of the people involved.

The present writer is sure that, yesterday and today, among the reasons for the unhappiness, malaise and suffering which have afflicted vast strata of the population as well as single individuals in their personal existence, there are, beside the social and political dimensions and peculiar discernable historical events, aspects strongly related to feelings and relationships, such as loneliness and despair. These sad perceptions might as well be affected by the far too common tendency for one person to misunderstand, fail to love, fear and discriminate against another, if you will. This is not to be ascribed solely to globalization, to meeting with diversity, nor to the dissolution of ethical coordinates one would otherwise have founded one's own existential values on. Albeit relevant, these aspects alone cannot justify the aforesaid attitudes without some factors deeply rooted in that mainstream culture that has lost sight of real data, which inevitably remain in a place that abstract taxonomic thought seems to have rendered inaccessible. Man today reflects and operates on a world that has lost hues, colours, odours, sounds; a world shredded and anatomized, forced into categorizations and locked in graphics and statistics; a mute world that is incapable of conveying emotions or move feelings and passions. Entrapped as he/she is in a binary dimension of the real world, man today fails to perceive the infinite palette where colours and tones fade into one another, the symphony of light and darkness and the infinite resonances" that seal each other in poetic imagery, the single and sole reality that discloses tragedy in comedy, tenderness in rigour, trepidation in courage, humility in boldness and so on and so forth. Man today still reflects and operates on the basis of a fundamental misunderstanding which places him/her right before an unreal world where tenderness is detached from rigour, as trepidation is from courage, humility from boldness, tragedy from comedy and individuality from the accidents determining its real essence - a world inhabited by numerous Hydes and rare Jekylls, all children of an experiment which is, right from the start, bound for tragic failure.

A famous painting by Rembrandt, *The Anatomy Lesson of Dr. Nicolaes Tulp*, can give the sense of what we want to say even better than a thousand words. the painting portrays the doctor engaged in dissecting a famous executioner's corpse right before his students. They stare not at the corpse at the centre, but at the anatomy book wide open in a corner of the room.

And it is right in this direction that we can borrow Morin's "poetic state" meaning that dimension which explains happiness, a quality/category of happiness, that which happiness largely depends upon. Morin (2021) also said that if man's aspiration towards individual fulfilment in a collective community is the first great human inspiration, the second one is leading a poetic life. If Morin considers prose the opposite of poetry, it does not mean that prose necessarily brings unhappiness or malaise, as it entails the absence of joy and unhappiness entails the presence of suffering. Suffering itself does not identify with a life of prose, or rather, as Achenbach (2000) puts it, a life of prose has eliminated the famous existential question "why do we suffer?" and replaced it with an explanation of the causes, thus banalizing it and making it ever more atrocious. A life of prose rather identifies with survival, which is, in and of itself, obviously necessary for living but not for pursuing a further and wider state of well-being that we could call happiness, momentary or lasting though it might be, and in which we could seriously consider our general wishes, goals and needs, not only the merely material ones.

Morin went on to point out that the overwhelming presence of prose to the detriment of poetry seems to characterize the western world and explains that the deterioration of the quality of life results from the primacy of quantity over quality in planning our society, and consequently our lives, where what counts the most is all that is human and, blind to anything individual, subjective and passionate, it can only see the gross internal product, statistics, surveys, economic growth.

The aforesaid premises strongly suggest that we should reconquer the aesthetic dimension, especially in education and in the pedagogic debate, which has long been related to art, poetry and the cult of beauty – as evinced in Schiller's Bildung, Dewey's 1934 essay *Art as Experience* and, going a few centuries back, instances of deep connection between aesthetics and training in each and every era can still be found, especially from Ancient Greece to the Renaissance. As Paolozzi (2016, 2023) maintains, however, it is in the 20th century that, in his *Estetica* [*Aesthetic as Science of Expression and General Linguistic*] (1902/1955), which celebrates his rise to international fame, Italian philosopher Benedetto Croce makes the Aesthetic dimension of life a substantial one, an ontological classification of the human being, a form of Spirit, featuring a logical status of its own and a specific function detached from the others concerning one's own life but still in some way or other connected to them within a concept of the real world which is articulated and standalone at the same time.

And even here, as is the case with what can still be read in Morin's texts, which is, in its turn, in line with a general tendency to oppose Positivism during its very heyday with the works of Husserl, Bergson, Heidegger and some other ones, the main result of the re-valorization of the aesthetic dimension was not only that of

a) *freeing* art, along with some sort of category of the human dimension, from its generally subordinate subjection to the central prominence of positive science and logical and intellectualistic abstraction, but also that of

b) *asserting* an idea of the real world as "Concrete Universal" that could not be reduced to the mere phenomena as conceived of by natural scientists, who select, schematize and abstract their quantifiable elements as the only aspects of an object that can be objectively and factually known.

It is worth our while providing the reader with an essential progression of Croce's thought to show how we could deduce from it a humanized and humanizing dimension of our world and time that we can use in a pedagogic perspective if we integrate it with interesting ideas and proposals.

In order to identify the function of poetry within Croce's system, it is useful to start from the assumption that there is no dichotomy between what could be considered a world outside the individual and his/er subjectivity that perceives it. Dialectic thinking is thinking of the unifying type, one which considers the real world a synthesis of opposites - subject and object, in this case. What we used to call external reality, for Croce, is nothing other than the product of some form of human activity which "creates" a world which is separate, immobile, "other" than the subject observing it. This activity typically severs, detaches, disrupts and dissects the throbbing real world, which is still a living being that is unique, single and sole in the elements it is made of and gives them all a separate existence which cannot find evidence of its essence within the eternal becoming of life in the world. In *Le due scienze mondane: l'Estetica e l'Economia* [*The Two Worldly Sciences:Aesthetics and Economics*] (1931/1963), Croce maintains that the only compact inseparable reality can be elaborated from time to time according to such notions as spirit, life, end, and those of matter, cause, mechanism (p.53).

In *L'arte come creazione e la creazione come fare* [*Art as creation and creation as making*] (1920/1969), on arguing against the concept of art as imitation of the real world, Croce wrote that an external world against or above spirit, exists neither for man the artist, nor for man in any other form and determination; there only exist feelings and volitions and representations and thoughts, and this is the circle of the real world itself, which is spirituality. So, art does not consist of things or ideas which have been made external, but man's feelings which art expresses in its images (p. 149).

If we wanted to identify a significant definition that could summarize Croce's view of art, we would choose one of his concepts from *Problemi di estetica* [*Problems of Aesthetics*] (1909/1954) whereby Art rests solely on imagination - it is only rich in images. Art does not classify objects, nor does it call them real or imaginary, qualify them, define them; it only feels them and represents them. Nothing more. So, as it is not abstract but concrete knowledge and such knowledge as captures the real without alterations or falsifications, art is intuition; and inasmuch as it presents the real in its immediacy, not yet mediated or freed from its own conception, it must be defined as being pure intuition (p.14).

In *New Essays on Aesthetic* Croce goes on to say that intuitions are as they are because they represent a feeling and only from it can they derive, and above it can they exist. They represent individual reality: not men or women, the young or the elderly, but that man, not just any man, that woman, not just any woman, that youth, not just any youth, that elderly person, not just any elderly person, with their own individual physical features, their own human peculiarities, their own existential issues. It must be pointed out, however, that the universe is not to be understood as a multiplicity of monads, but as a whole which needs to individualize itself in order to meaningfully live and exist - as Croce put it in *Conversazioni Critiche* [*Critical Conversations*] (1939/1951), the universal can take place solely as individuality and in no other way whatever (p. 342).

Talking about knowledge, which is something other than cold abstract classification, in his *Aesthetics*, Croce maintains that human knowledge "has two forms: it is either intuitive knowledge or logical knowledge; knowledge obtained through the imagination or knowledge obtained through the intellect; knowledge of the individual or knowledge of the universal; of individual things or of the relations between them: it is, in fact, productive either of images or of concepts". (p.1).

So the poetic world is one of multiplicity, i.e. individuality, one in which essence and existence coincide in a fantastic dimension and reach a state of peace even when tragedy, drama and horror set in. In his *Logic as the Science of the Pure Concept* (1905/1917) Croce asserts that logical activity derives from representations or intuitions. "If man had no representations, he would not think; were he not imaginative spirit, he would not be a logical spirit". (p.3).

As he said, without intuitions or images or representations, thought could not be thinking, because thought can never possess the real world conceived of as an external object; and it is so not because of its own impotence, but because of that object's impossibility to become the object of thinking, impossibility which is nothing other than its own unreality (Croce, 1920/1960, p.153).

So, instead of soaring above representations, thought is immersed in them as a concrete universal, which synthesizes thinking and imagination, not inert abstract separation. In these respects, in his *Commento a Croce* [*Commentary to Croce*], Carlo Antoni (1955) is right in saying that Croce's philosophy transcends the existence-value duality because it is just existence, the world of life and passions, the matter that art comes from as the dawn of knowledge, which turns experienced feeling into contemplated feeling by transporting it from the world of praxis to the world of intuition/representation that logical knowledge operates upon - as can be read in *The Two Worldly Sciences*, in Croce's thinking, sense becomes spirit and spirit becomes sense (p.49).

So, moving back to the poetic dimension, we hope we have explained how important it is. It is important because whenever this dimension is weakened, or undervalued or lost, the whole life suffers from this condition. Also historical knowledge, which moves volition, suffers from this situation, and praxis suffers as well, as Croce rightly says in *Nuove Pagine sparse* [*New Scattered Pages*] (1949/1966), whereby the lack of poetry, impoverishment and the barrenness of feeling cannot even generate anything new (p. 348).

Actually, as Croce put it in *The totality of artistic expression* (1917/1966), "In every utterance, every fanciful creation, of the poet, there lies the whole of human destiny, all human hopes, illusions, griefs, joy, human grandeurs and miseries, the whole drama of reality perpetually evolving and growing out of itself in suffering and joy" (p.263).

Croce always stressed the crucial role of the human being in the universe, which abstract science-oriented thinking actually expelled from the world. He also stressed the paramount importance of the emotional sphere not only in everyday life, but also in the theoretical dimension inevitably related to it.

After all, we cannot fail to see what happens when we listen to long series of data, numbers and percentages on immigration - grey sequences of numbers that move no feelings and tell no stories of life, hopes, fears, illusions until the image of a small corpse lying on the shore appears, to awaken our dormant hearts.

But Croce is not the only thinker who argued for the crucial role of Aesthetics in human existence. Also Hermeneutic philosophers such as Heidegger and Gadamer confirm and corroborate the primacy of Aesthetics which, unlike a technical, instrumental and positivistic view of the real, is a moment related to truth and an experience of truth in a wider sense, of meeting with the essence and of transcendence of the assumed opposition, which is functional to a dichotomy between human and social sciences and natural sciences, between subject and object.

At this point, we find it useful to integrate our observations with some suggestions on language which come from German Thinker Hans Georg Gadamer, who identifies language with the only place where subject and object, the interpreter and the real world meet and communicate in an act which is one of liberty and freedom.

In *Truth and Method*, Gadamer's analysis leads him to regard art as experience, experience of truth. Comprehension means interpretation and hermeneutics (in a cognitive sense, which is broader than purely philological hermeneutic sense). It is the very form of knowledge even compared to that of positive sciences, knowledge which expresses itself the most in art, in the interpretation of texts, v.i.z. in language. Meeting with a text entails what Gadamer calls "fusion of horizons" whereby "the interpreter's own horizon is decisive, yet not as a personal standpoint that he maintains or enforces, but more as an opinion and a possibility that one brings into play and puts at risk, and that helps one truly to make one's own what the text says. I have described this above as a "fusion of horizons." We can now see that this is what takes place in conversation, in which something is expressed that is not only mine or my author's, but common" (Gadamer, 1960/2004, p. 390). In Gadamer's Hermeneutics, the subject loses its granitic social self-referring substance which becomes similar to the player right when gaming, the subject of the game is not the players, but the game itself, which is produced by the players and represents an experience which modifies those who live it (p.103).

Through language, the world (which is not given, but giving itself, linguistically) gives itself. This means that it is language, with its plastic power, which enables the world to manifest and express itself - the world expresses itself in language. But world and language cannot exist without one another - they are not standalone entities, but coexist in the speech act, in dialogue, in language exchange, in the exertion of mutual understanding. So, language is that which relates, the essential medium, the meeting place of comprehension, liberty and freedom - language is the horizon of sense.

Gadamer goes on to say that the reading conscience is necessarily a historical one and it is in free communication with the historical tradition. A written tradition does not only teach us something in particular; in it we can also find a whole historical humanity with its general relationship with the world.

PERSPECTIVES ON READING EDUCATION

Findings

As Rossi (1997) would say, starting from this horizon of sense, we can trace a perspective of education to reading which would necessarily be designed as education to freedom. Still in the same direction, a book can and must be considered not a mere instrument, some sort of tool or support, for possible other aims outside reading itself, but as a fundamental means for the human being to be free inasmuch as he/she can recognize in it values that foster and support his/her inner experience, whereby he/she will be able to become a subjective protagonist of self-teaching and self-assessing dynamics, of meeting with dialogue, of a broadened and more in-depth knowledge, of a closer and closer approach to human culture, of opening and enlarging the horizons of space and time.

As Cambi (2014) pointed out the reading of a text can be associated with a particular liberating experience that interrupts practical everyday living.

In this perspective, we cannot fail to recall Niccolò Machiavelli's words in the description of a typical exile's day in his Letter to Francesco Vettori: "On the coming of evening, I return to my house and enter my study; and at the door I take off the day's clothing, covered with mud and dust, and put on garments regal and courtly; and reclothed appropriately, I enter the ancient courts of ancient men, where, received by them with affection, I feed on that food which only is mine and which I was born for, where I am not ashamed to speak with them and to ask them the reason for their actions; and they in their kindness answer me; and for four hours of time I do not feel boredom, I forget every trouble, I do not dread poverty, I am not frightened by death; entirely I give myself over to them."

Eugenio Garin (1953/1975), for that matter, rightly considers Humanism the philosophical, not only philological, matrix and criterion whereby Humanist scholars used to approach texts - what counts the most is starting a dialogue with those who expressed perfect types of humanity, with real masters, as for comprehending and in comprehending them we inevitably draw out the highest and topmost of us.

As Cambi (2016) puts it, reading does not make a reader the mere consumer of a product, but turns him/her into a producer. As Nobile (2004) pointed out, reading is some sort of rewriting, some sort of activation, which varies from one subject to another and also varies in the same reader, at different times and in successive reading sessions, of the multiple meanings underlying a literary work. Readers are not "operated on by the books", but they operate on the books. Readers actively make meanings relevant to their current lived experience and life challenges (Wilhelm, 2016, p. 37).

In his *American Lessons*, Calvino (1988) considered reading some sort of liberating experience opening towards the Imaginary or, to say it in a way so dear to Rossi (1997), that room of imagination where the projections of each and every man's real and ideal self can be created and stored - as it inhabits the language universe, reading specially and poignantly intercepts the core of the freeing dimension of education inasmuch as just language defines that potential of humanity which ensures and guarantees *that the human being can truly be educated.*

Even though the formative and self-formative value of reading is clearly recognized, a strictly functional, rational, intellectualistic way of reading books still prevails, especially at school or, at least, in those educational systems within standardized assessment systems.

The dramatic decrease in book reading could be ascribed to several factors, the most important ones being the spreading of new forms and media and the modern "an-aesthetic" cultural paradigm. Although a lot of specific action has been taken in Italy and many countries towards restoring the crucial role of Aesthetics to its primary role in the cultural scenario and promoting and supporting reading as a means for developing knowledge, spreading culture, fostering national civil, social and economic progress, the education and well-being of people (e.g: Italian Law No. 15 of 1st Feb 2020), the general book reading slump should be contrasted at least in those places, such as schools, where the latest education trends have at least not yet hurdled the studying of texts. Moreover, the pupils' ability to comprehend texts is still under the control of the national assessment systems, among others.

It must be said, however, that the above-mentioned systems have not always adopted non-Neo-Positivist assessment criteria. More often than not, a merely functional use of text that predominantly focuses on logical cognitive skills, formal schematic elements, the relevance of description, text analysis and the learning of lexical and communicative skills still prevails. The aforesaid aspects can partly be considered marginal and secondary elements external to such reading experience as has been conceived of so far. As can easily be inferred, literary texts and reading entail and express elements which are much richer than logical cognitive ones, evoke emotions, feelings interpretations transactive and formative, ethical, aesthetic, ludic (in an edifying and ennobling sense) experiences, thus revealing the formative meaning of reading which, as Mariani (2005, 2006) puts it, sits beyond literary textuality to intersect the realm of personal appreciation.

Mascia (2023) believes reading has something to do with motivation and identity, so much so that only *motivated readings*, as Giugni (1969) puts it, is one which leans on the youth's existential and spiritual needs and, in so doing, aims at making such changes in the system of his/her habits, thoughts, and feelings as would enrich, amplify and valorize his/her personality. The benefits of motivated reading are not only for one's intellect, but fall under the realm of those needs that "keep one on one's toes" (p. 142) towards an ideal goal.

In this direction, education to reading must necessarily follow individualized strategies that would have some grip on the learner's life. Rossi (1997) suggested that a prior analysis of each and every pupil's needs and skills be useful for obtaining a clear knowledge of their personality and aspirations so as to best motivate them. In a review of current research about Reading for Pleasure, indeed, the two most underlined notions in this regard refer to the importance of personalisation and to the acknowledgment of material and social dimension of reading (Vogrinčič Čepič et al., 2024). According to Spalviero (2015), in teaching and choosing school textbooks it would also be useful to "stretch the boundaries of literariness" in order to include in the choice even those young generations' tastes and references which are not typically literary and foster the students' discovery of their own "need for literature" as a need to tell and share human experience in its transcultural cores (love, friendship, emotions, feelings, death...) and find possible answers to the existential issues characterizing their adolescence (p. 49). Not coincidentally, in fact, recent research suggests the value in considering reading and reading for pleasure for studies that are interested in children's and adolescents' emotional and behavioural development (Mak & Fancourt, 2020, para.5).

As we consider reading an essential factor of human growth and development and do not want to demonize in any way whatever the totally unstoppable and not entirely foreseeable progressive combination of man's biocultural development and some sort of recognized creativity in technological evolution, we could definitely envisage some emerging perspectives in education to reading.

First of all, Mascia (2023) claims we have to acknowledge that the priority given to standardized testing has led facilitators to place greater emphasis on reading skill acquisition to the detriment of all due support to personal identity development and student motivation, thus influencing also education to reading at school. It does not seem impossible to assume that, in this direction, owing to the present reduction of education to the so-called "teach to test" formula, in their turn, standardized testing results have somewhat been affected by the lack of such free, motivated and in-depth knowledge as personal free reading or, more generally, regular book reading, can provide the student with.

Reading does not seem to be so different from the ability and form of thinking and thought. Reading meaningful and motivating texts trains the student to develop his/her own critical thinking and awareness, to perceive the diversity and variegatedness of the real world as well as the open character of possibilities and opportunities. As Rossi asserts, quitting reading can and does produce cultural deterioration, functional illiteracy, language standardization, spiritual impoverishment, conforming homogenization of behaviours and attitudes.

For all reasons described above, the education-to-reading paradigm is implemented with a view to making an *existential use of reading*, as Mariani (2005) puts it, to a Pedagogy of reading for pleasure, to a form of *off-school* reading, in Rossi's view. All these aspects do not deny in any way whatever our need for an education to reading within formal contexts, which must still be present, intentional and well-planned, also because, as research in neuroscience shows, *our brain is not made for reading*, i.e. reading does not seem to refer so much to biological evolution as to cultural evolution, as Crepaldi (2020) affirmed.

Another element to be taken into serious consideration is that, just for the above-mentioned reasons, it is the influence of a precocious education to reading that almost fully guarantees successful training for generations of readers. The validity of this assumption has been attested by a great number of international studies and by so many books on the subject. Moreover, as Kucirkova and Cremin (2018) and Mascia (2023) pointed out, the level of reading competence among children or teenagers and that of knowledge of children's or teenager's books by teachers and operators in preschool and primary school (if not in other schools) are determining factors for an efficient reading pedagogy.

THE THERAPEUTIC POWER OF LITERATURE BETWEEN BIBLIOTHERAPY AND NARRATIVE MEDICINE

Discussion

During the past few years, thanks to the power of reading as an instrument for mental and emotional wellbeing, we have witnessed the growth and formalization of bibliotherapy as a therapeutic and educational practice. Its evolution from a mere therapeutic tool to a scientific discipline has been supervised by the energy and determination of researchers, physicians, sociologists and pedagogists who have acknowledged the value of the written word in personal recovery and growth.

This approach actually dates back to far more remote eras, starting from Ancient Egypt, when the idea of libraries as spaces of knowledge and spirituality would reflect a deep connection between man's quest for knowledge and the care for the human soul. The fact that libraries were situated in temples, which were called 'houses of life', stresses the importance of the spiritual dimension in man's quest for knowledge. As Caldin (2001) and Alves (1982), pointed out, Pharaoh Ramesses II's phrase he had inscribed over the door of his library, "Medicine for the soul", enhances the high value of reading and knowledge as instruments of healing and spiritual growth.

Also in the Middle Ages, with libraries in monasteries and temples, this connection between the quest for knowledge and the religious dimension was kept. The choice of calling libraries "Treasures of the Medicine of the Soul" reflects the conviction that religious literature could function as spiritual guide and instrument of redemption.

These historical examples illustrate how various cultures and periods have recognized the power of libraries not only as knowledge bases, but also as places for spiritual wellbeing and inner growth.

In the 19th century, with the adoption of reading in treating the mentally-impaired and the recommendation to patients in general by Benjamin Rusch, an important step forward was taken in applying bibliotherapy as an instrument of therapeutic support. The view of reading as a therapeutic means to manage such emotional conflicts as depression, fear and phobia, as well as to improve old people's quality of life, has stressed the therapeutic power of literature.

The term "bibliotherapy" was coined by Samuel Crothers in 1916. This event has marked another official recognition of this practice. Originally limited to psychiatric hospitals in the 1930s, bibliotherapy has later spread to other institutions and showed satisfactory results in treating a variety of conditions.

The emerging role of bibliotherapy was considerable during WWI, mainly thanks to some lay librarians' contributions to the creation of libraries in army hospitals, which shows the crucial role of reading in conforting and morally supporting sick, hurt or wounded soldiers.

Bibliotherapy began to develop even further in 1920s and 1930s with articles and reports which promoted its use and explored its potential, thus contributing to the rise of bibliotherapy as a scientific discipline in contrast to a more artistic approach that had initially been ascribed to it.

Later on, some American researchers revised the bibliotherapy literature and isolated 4 main areas of professional applications, namely:

1) general medicine, where praxis is focused on the cooperation between hospital librarians and other medical professionals to give support through reading;
2) psychiatry, where bibliotherapy is integrated with other therapeutic techniques in hospital and clinical treatments;
3) education, where reading is used for educational aims at all levels; and
4) corrections, where books are used as instruments of support by researchers engaged in the rehabilitation of criminal offenders.

In the 1990s, John Pardeck stressed the fact that, as any other form of therapy, also bibliotherapy has its precautions and limitations and should be regarded as a complement to the other therapeutic modes available. He also stressed the need for accurate assessment of, and an integrated approach to, clinical treatment. When exploring bibliotherapy, a wide range of objectives can be found which go well beyond mere book-reading.

One of the key objectives of bibliotherapy is the production of beneficial effects on the mental health and general wellbeing of individuals, as it offers them an anchor of salvation, stability and comfort during periods of physical weakness or emotional stress. As it does not limit itself to offering temporary relief, but also fosters a sense of self-esteem and trust in oneself, bibliotherapy also acts as a powerful tool to alleviate daily tensions and provides a temporary escape from worries and oppressive thoughts. In doing all this, bibliotherapy fosters a more positive and resilient view of the individual. Through reading and analyzing narrations which reflect experience similar to one's own, one can find resources to manage emotions like rage and frustration, thus learning to constructively control them and to overcome one's hardships and vicissitudes. It can even have a positive impact on physical health.

The beauty of novels as bibliotherapy form rests in their ability to take us to alternative worlds and provide us with a temporary refuge from our daily thoughts and worries. When we immerge ourselves into a moving story, not only do we escape from reality, but we deeply connect with the characters and their experiences.

Novels enable and allow us to explore a wide range of emotions, face complex problems and life challenges through the main character's eyes. They show us new perspectives, help us become more empathetic and grow inside. In the end, when we read a novel, we are no longer alone in our own experience; we join a community of readers that share our emotions and our inner journeys. That is why, in those moments when we feel we need comfort and inspiration, a good novel can be our best ally. Through the pages of a book we find answers, hope, and sometimes even the strength to face the challenges that lie ahead. Novel-reading therapy is an ancient powerful art that still evinces its great value in the world today, by offering comfort, wisdom and a way towards emotional recovery, as E. Berthoud and S. Elderkin pointed out in 2013.

We might as well carry out all of the above by taking part in reading and discussion groups, which allow us to connect with the others through a shared reading experience. Bibliotherapy opens the door towards the world outside by offering a contact with the real through telling stories which reflect universal human experiences. This contact with the world outside can be an important stimulus for the individual to keep his/her mental and psychological health. What is more, bibliotherapy shows him/her new perspectives and encourages his/her personal growth and development.

As Ella Berthoud and Susan Elderkin (2017) maintain, one of the best strategies to help a child overcome difficult moments is to offer him/her a story that deals straight with his/her experience, be he/she a victim of school bullying, a first-time lover, or one who hasn't found the money the tooth fairy was supposed to leave for him/her under the pillow. Quality children's books can deal with complex issues and deep feelings with joyful bravery, as they aim at instilling strong emotions in the reader but also tranquillize him in the end. In this collection you will find a selection of the best children's books to give to (or read together with) the young protagonists of your lives, whether 3-year-olds or 13-year-olds, whether they love reading or skip reading, whether they are extroverted or introverted, whether they have suffered phobias or nightmares or seek independence. For many of us, our favourite children's books are inestimable treasures, and they are not mere editions, but our own personal copies, with the pages full of wax pastel marks and torn pop-ups. There is no foretelling which books will be part of our children's childhood memories, but they will most probably be physical tangible books. Tablet PCs and other devices do allow for the instant downloading of text, but getting touch and smell, along with sight, involved enriches one's experience with full immersion into history. When we turn yellowish pages over or smell book paper, we create an emotional bond with the book that goes beyond its mere narrative content.

Through reading and reflection, bibiotherapy appears like a powerful instrument to foster the overall wellbeing of individuals and give them an opportunity to explore their inner selves and connect with the world around them. Bibliotherapy goes beyond the mere reading and requires *ad-hoc* therapeutic supports to be effective. It involves professionals as well as bibliotherapists, psychologist, psychiatrists, educators and pedagogists who cooperate with the reader in order to provide adequate resources. The act of reading implies the construction of personal meanings, enabling and allowing readers to connect with the other people's life experiences and explore their own. The dialogue based on reading guides the therapeutic route by valorizing speakers as well as listeners. For dialogue to be effective, however, we must plan therapeutic routes very accurately, and propose each and every one of them according to the specificities, interests, notions, and health states of each and every sobject being dealt with. Choosing the techniques and materials most adequate to the specific situations is essential for achieving effective results.

The beauty of bibliotherapy resides in its universality: it can be applied to people of any age, social standing and cultural area without restrictions. As an innovative professional practise, not only does it contribute to healing the sick, but it can also prevent the insurgence of disease when it is integrated in public health schemes. This cooperation between librarians and other health professionals such as physicians, social assistants, nurses and psychologists evinces the versatility and effectiveness of bibliotherapy as a complementary approach to the patient's treatment and can have a positive impact on both their individual and collective wellbeing.

One of the most distinctive aspects of a traumatic experience is the crisis, which can engender irriversible ruptures at any moment during the life of the person involved, thus jeopardizing his/her ability to project himself/herself into the future. The road marked by a sudden destabilizing event characterized by pain and suffering can be so hard a path to tread as to appear insurmountable.

Even though it can have an objective cause which has determined it, a suffering condition is one that the subject involved experiences as something inexplicable. Questions like "Why just me?" often stay unanswered, thus augmenting the sense of total loss and disorientation of those who find themselves living such experiences.

If we go back to one of the most effective concepts Salvatore Natoli expressed about suffering in his now classic volume "The Experience of Pain. The Forms of Suffering in Western Culture", from a philosophical point of view, we must admit that the intrinsic quest for an answer to such a substantial question leads one to delve into a deeper dimension, which goes right to the bottom of ones's heart and mind and questions the ontology of human existence and life. Pain is nothing we can choose; it is something we suffer which, almost paradoxically in this case, if you will, denies our deepest essence - our own freedom. Nevertheless, it is a highly formative experience, thanks to which, one fortifies oneself and becomes capable of not only positively facing odds and adversities, but also developing empathy, and comprehension and solidarity along with it. In this sense, as Cyrulnik put it in 2000, the saying whereby one can learn from suffering can prove true. Such complex questions, however, can hardly "find" answers (which should, if any, be built in one's subjectivity and relational dimension, certainly not in the mechanistic cause-effect bonds of classic sciences), and one's ability to tread a path of transformation and positive development of one's existence cannot be left to mere chance.

The social, or even human, corresponsibility, if you will, of building the symbolic universes of expression and communication of pain requires the contribution of culture, art, and mainly the commitment of pedagogy. As Bruno Rossi pointed out in 2013, the dominant values and principles of the present era seem to be those of physical wellbeing, pleasure, self-gratification, disinvolvement, and people almost always tend to eliminate obstacles and difficulties, avoid efforts and sacrifices, cancel suffering by medicalizing life. A frequent orientation of the age is that of separating the ill from the illness, the diseased from the disease, thus reducing the person to a mere machine which treats medical disfunctions with pharmacologic remedies.

In the present social organization, which is all too often subjected to logics that are extra-human, Man's feelings and conditions occupy a lesser and lesser space, even within education systems. As Martha Nussbaum warns,

a) the need to adhere to economic models through the use of quantitative approaches and standardized evaluation measures, as well as
b) the view of knowledge as something more and more parallelized, extrinsic to human comprehension and aimed at the mere explanation of facts and
c) the subjection of training as an essential pedagogic category to the needs of technology and the job system, as Sirignano put it in 2019,

leave no place or time for the needs of a human soul that seems to plead for their fulfillment in vain. In fact, it is necessary to give more value to those pedagogic approaches that set great store by the deep, ethical, existential dimension of Man's growth and development.

Among the most "human-oriented" methodologic approaches today, it is worth our while mentioning the autobiographic one, which is used in pedagogy and enables and allows us to valorize the person holistically, in his/her entirety of mind, body, emotions, reason and feelings. Any autographically-based training route always implies a self-training route insofar as the person becomes more and more aware of those skills, abilities, competences and notions which have already been consolidated and of those which still want learning not only from himself/herself, but also from others and from his/her socio-cultural contexts.

THE AUTOBIOGRAPHICAL AND LIFE-STORY APPROACH

The narration of life stories is a device that enables and allows different dimensions of the individual to meet, so as to help him/her re-balance them and overcome frustrations and dissatisfactions. Even though they mainly address individual dimension of trainees, educational practises should not overlook their social dimension – they can be a stimulus for the trainee's inner world, but still with the explicit intention of fostering his/her shared participation in social life, which is the foundation of democracy. This task is a fundamental one inasmuch as it helps the subject to perceive his/her community as a pedagogic lab and a place where

a) relations could be humanized, and
b) networks of solidarity and dialogue, spaces for self-help and mutual help could be created,

which is made possible thanks to the facilitation of processes of collective responsibility and the growth and development of relationships. V.i.z., it is one occasion on which democratic responsibility could be exerted through the self-perception of a competent individual immersed in a social context. The narration taking place in meeting with the other is a creative activity which revitalizes something which would no longer exist otherwise – thanks to it we can protect images from the past, our life experience and our meetings from disappearance and oblivion by rooting them into the present. Narration as an experienee in and of itself enables and allows us to decompose and recompose words by relocating them from a cognitive, emotional, relational and experiential point of view. It is a sort of frame through which we filter our personal life experiences, the other people's' interpretations and the relations we entertain with the world around us.

As Bolzoni put it in 1999, even though present facts and situations are reported, the pivot of the story is still the past, which is just the reason why the narrator initially experiences some sort of estrangement in trying to give the events of his life a spatial and temporal order. The narrator overcomes the estrangement as he/she becomes aware that to list the events in precise chronological order (story, fable) is not so important as it is to focus on the salient happenings in his/her own life (plot, romance).

From this standpoint, self-narration becomes a trans-formative instrument that can be implemented by way of a proposal, as a process that facilitates the subject's resilience, particularly when he/she experiences odd circumstances. The traumatic event produces a short circuit which immobilizes the subject somewhere between a past that he/she cannot make sense of and a present that seems meaningless and inexorably projected into a future that he cannot imagine, never mind plan. Resilience is the ability to signify one's own life experience to re-sew the threads of the past, present and future by giving sense to the past in order to re-project into the future. In these respects, narrative methods right in their core, manage to activate the subject and make it the protagonist of his/her own change.

When we have to deal with disease, we often find ourselves in a state where we cannot express our autonomy of judgement, scared as we are of the specialist's knowledge, and in this sense, we feel forced into a double frustration and a condition of subjection. Autobiographic methods enable and allow the subject, especially an adult, to "take the floor", i.e. to liberate himself/herself. Thanks to the word, he/she becomes aware of his/her own life experience, of personal cognitive manners, of mental habits that have often stayed hidden. In this operation, his/her "taking the floor" is coupled with a quest for sense as an essential cognitive operation.

Conversely, when faced with his/her inability to give sense to our happenings, our feelings and emotions, the human being falls into total despair. In adult life, however, something paradoxical takes place - if, on the one hand, such a cognitive operation can rely on previous experience and knowledge, on the other there is an ever-growing tendency to resort to thinking stereotypes, to get used to commonplaces, because our curiosity to discover new perspectives, more typically associated with adolescence and youth, wanes.

Getting back to Laura Formenti's words, autobiographic tales and stories contain some "epistemic operations" that enable and allow the narrator to learn about reality and structure it; "taking the floor", searching for some sense, building theories, biographic structures coming up and taking over, inventing and interpreting texts, the interconnection of the various parts -and of the parts with the whole- (1998).

Some other observations must be made on the importance of narrative and autobiographic structure as self-treatment and support to the development of resilient personalities. As Robertson put it in 2015, resilience is also people's ability to face odds and adversities, adapt to and overcome traumas, threats or serious stress. So, being resilient does not mean experiencing no distress, emotional pain or difficulty when facing odds and adversities (the death of a person dear to us, a serious illness, job loss, financial problems, etc.). Resilience is combination of behaviors and ways of thinking that anyone can learn and develop within his/her own training, i.e. it can be trained and taught.

Even the philosophical reflection scenario can offer great teaching and learning opportunities. Aristotle, for instance, resumes the notion of "catharsis" from previous generations and enriches it, thus shaping one of the milestones of Western Aesthetic theory. In "Poetry", his immortal work, Aristotle traces an enlightening route on the cathartic power of Greek tragedy, stressing its ability to act as an instrument for the emotional purification of the human soul.

Aristotle did not see Greek tragedy as a mere exhibition of painful disastrous events; in fact, tragedy is such an emotional and intellectual experience as to induce spectators to explore and face the deepest human conflicts. Through the performances of tragically fallen protagonists like Oedipus or Prometheus, Ancient Greek tragedy instills emotions of piety and fear in the spectator, whose conscience is faced with the manifold facets of human fate. Aristotle's Catharsis emerges as a process of purification of human emotions through tragedy as aesthetic experience. Immersed as they are in the dramatic vicissitudes of the protagonists they are facing, the spectators find in them a mirror of their own inner conflicts and moral struggles. Comparing the difficulties and defeats of the tragic protagonists with their own enables and allows them to free and channel their own emotions, thus finding relief and comfort in sympathizing with the human condition and accepting it in the end.

Moreover, Aristotle ascribed an important educational and therapeutic function to Ancient Greek tragedy. By representing tragic events and the consequences of human actions, tragedy teaches the spectators a precious moral and philosophical lesson. Guided as they are by what they see of the tragic characters' disasters, the spectators are pushed to reflect on the meaning of virtue, justice, individual responsibility, thus paving the way for their spiritual growth and moral development. In sum, in Aristotle's view, the cathartic value of Ancient Greek tragedy resides in its ability to act as an instrument for the spectators' emotional purification and philosophical reflection. Through the active participation in the aesthetic experience of tragedy, the individuals are invited to explore the depths of the human soul, find comfort in the acceptance of their own emotions and learn precious lessons for their own lives. Masterpieces like "Oedipus The King", "Prometheus Bound" and "The Trojan Women", written by authors like Sophocles, Aeschylus and Euripides respectively, provide the spectators with the greatest opportunities for a full immersion into the most complex human emotions. Through iconic characters that face impossible challenges and personal disasters, these Ancient Greek tragedies give readers a way of exploring and comprehending their own experiences of pain and inner struggle. In this sense, the cathartic value of Ancient Greek tragedy in bibliotherapy and narrative medicine resides in its ability to provide fertile humus for narrative exploration and recovery. Through reading these ancient works and reflecting upon them, readers can find comfort, inspiration and a way towards resilience. Thus, Ancient Greek tragedy still evinces its own relevance and power in the world today inasmuch as it preciously contributes to healing one's body and soul.

After facing a wavering interest for the past six months, resilience has now become much more popular in a lot of research fields for several reasons. According to Masten (2015, 2021), one of these is the widespread alarm for the growing threats from natural an technological disasters, pandemics, terrorism and political struggle all over the world. The global COVID-19 pandemic in particular has made us realize day by day that crisis-overcoming and resilience attitudes in the face of this long dramatic condition help us manage and tackle it more effectively. What is more, as Cepero *et al.* put it in 2017, a resilient approach to critical situations has proved to be able to foster human experience in various fields, mainly art and culture, safe and secure public events and physical activity.

Up until today, however, these aspects have not been studied in-depth from the pedagogic point of view. What is more, for crisis operators in charge of fostering resilience in those subjects with particularly difficult life experiences, possession of the specific requirements has not been properly verified either.

Art, music and physical performances can trigger self-reflection, from the identification of the main emotions from listening to, watching or producing artistic or manufactured works to whatever else included, are somewhat immersive experiences that enable and allow the subject to acquire considerable self-awareness and identify the most adequate "strategies" to overcome all odds and adversities.

The aforesaid strategies are the result of a personal conquest and are therefore bound to last long. Only starting from the reflections on our life experiences of health and disease, thanks to a comparison of what happens when we find ourselves in either condition, can we enact adequate behaviors and strategies in order to be able to stay longer in the state we consider most in line with our psycho-physical wellbeing needs.

The narrative practice enables and allows us to reflect more upon ourselves, on our inner world, on those situations we often ignore because we are excessively *projected outside*. In fact, it is not an individual operation, because it is the other-than-us, the group, that enables and allows greater awareness, especially thanks to communication exchanges and what Bruner (1992), calls *narrative loans*. Thanks to the sharing of one's own life experiences of pain and to the listening of other people's experiences, one can understand, say, that suffering is a universal condition of mankind and even though pain will not extinguish itself to the full, we can still bear it better. As far as this latest statement is concerned, we should no doubt point out that there is no such thing as a general universal model valid for all to activate a resilience process - these aspects are too closely related to the individual's history, to his/her way to cope with odds and adversities to be defined in a stable categorical manner. And it is just for this reason that the importance of narration emerges even in a medical environment, where it is just a particular way of relating to one another and act therapeutically which actually makes the situation comprehensible. It is like a meaningful event in a person's life which also translates into an opportunity to authentically welcome the patient, especially in times of suffering that make him/her vulnerable and desperate for professional and human assistance. Narrative medicine embraces a complete integrated view of sickness and the sick which valorizes the patient's subjective experience and integrates medical knowledge with humanistic studies.

CONCLUSION

This approach aims at improving the effectiveness of treatments, restoring humanity in medical treatment and promoting the overall wellbeing of the patient. As Rita Charon claimed in 2006, patients do not need only a precise diagnosis or a therapy; they also need acceptance, comfort, hope, tenderness and support - illness and disease take something important from the patient, engender a deep inexpressible sadness, one must admit. Yet, if we understand him/her, identify his/her strong points in spite of his/her fear, walk him all the way down through his/her suffering, we will definitely go past the mere comprehension of his/her pathology. We suggest a real route towards recovery or the opportunity to live authentically even without one's health. We offer our presence to fight the patient's isolation, together with our encouraging confidence in his/her ability and power to face any trial.

A trauma specifically indicates that condition whereby, in order for recovery or resilience to be effective, the fracture that suddenly intervened in an individual's life requires that he/she retain the plots and threads of the times of his/her own existence that the situation engendering the trauma has irreversibly interrupted. The reconstruction of one's own biography, the recalling process in the complex mechanism of memory, the interpretation and significance of the development of one's own life and of its most salient moments give the present a new regenerated and unprecedented meaning that can enable and allow him/her to look into it differently and open the door to finding some sense to it.

With that said, there can no doubt be some elements that more than others foster resilient processes. We should never forget, however, the unavoidability of the relational space that gives body to narrative identities, which become able to face odds and adversities thanks to the trans-formative power of verbal listening and interaction.

Just because of this, the narration acquires great trans-formative value even in medicine, thus

a) enabling and allowing doctor and patient, first of all, to bridge the gaps deriving from their necessarily asymmetrical relationship,
b) turning the therapeutic relationship into a mutual-participation dance that both protagonists must be flexibly involved in,
c) keeping an adequate distance that varies according to the needs of ther relationship and, in so doing,
d) creating what we call the right distance.

As Bert pointed out in 2007, the asymmetry of a relationship defines the relational position implicit in that relation type: doctor-patient, but also master-pupil or parent-child. Equality, instead, entails the acceptance and respect that each part involved shows towards what the other part brings in: it is therefore the result of a continuous and continual negotiation between the parts in question. It requires, however, that the doctor initially take on responsibility – it is up to him to acquire, propose and/or keep a position of acceptance of, and respect for, the patient.

Empathy emerges as a fundamental instrument to keep one's optimal distance; unlike sympathy, which may lead us towards an excessive emotional identification, empathy operates in a more neutral manner, enables and allows us to comprehend the patient's experience without losing ourselves in it, but entering into a sort of emotional resonance that enriches communication. This scenario enables and allows the subjects involved (doctor and patient) to constantly adapt to the changing nuances of the relationship and of the shared objectives.

Numerous international studies, among which it is worth our while mentioning those of Rizzolatti and Sinigaglia (2005), have evinced the neurobiological roots of empathy, stressed their crucial role in the social dynamics and in interpersonal relations and also proposed a broader and more captivating view of empathy itself, which they called generosity. Frank (2001) maintains that generosity is not only an act of comprehending and behaving according to other people's lives, but also one of acknowledging and respecting their individuality and autonomy. It is a subtle balance between closeness and distance, which adapts to the changing dynamics of human relations. In this way, stories become the fabric through which we learn about generosity and put it into practice. As Bert wrote in 2007, listening to, witnessing or actively participating in other people's narration, we become actors of generosity, so we contribute to the construction of deeper and more meaningful bonds in the network of human relations.

Narration in the field of medicine could become the solution to a fundamental problem of mankind – how to communicate complex experiences in a universal comprehensible manner.

Doctor-patient dialogues inevitably evince cultural differences, especially when an experience of disease that can radically revolutionize the patient's inner world is dealt with, The narration, however, leaves a common ground for comprehending and facing these differences, thus fostering a deeper and more meaningful communication.

The patient's narration is much more generous than a mere accounting of his/her own life and the disease afflicting him/her. It reveals how the patient understands and interprets the world around him/her and relates with the others. The narration evinces the patient's unique language (idiolect), the deep meaning behind his/her words and concepts, and the emotions he/she experiences. The expression of one's own emotions can be a delicate and embarrassing moment, but in the narration all these emotions emerge quite naturally, often with metaphors that reveal the close intimacy of the patient's life experience, and play a crucial role in the way he/she perceives his/her life and disease.

As Giorgio Bert pointed out in 2007, the optimal use of this instrument would require deeper competences than are normally taught at Italian medical schools – for instance, communicative and counseling skills, philosophical, literary. ethical, pedagogic, anthropologic, sociologic, psychologic, literary, rhetoric, artistic knowledge … the medical humanities, all in all, obviously not in the sense of an impossible encyclopedic total knowledge, but knowing how to apply these disciplines in the medical practice.

Narration's small time space opens a singular unique world which orients later intervensions and transforms the dialogue with specialists of the treatment in an authentic relational meeting between individuals.

NOTE

The contribution is the result of collaborative work. For academic purposes only, the individual paragraphs are attributed as follows: Maria Federica Paolozzi: INTRODUCTION, METHODOLOGY, PERSPECTIVES ON READING EDUCATION FINDINGS; Stefania Maddalena: THE THERAPEUTIC POWER OF LITERATURE BETWEEN BIBLIOTHERAPY AND NARRATIVE MEDICINE, DISCUSSION, THE AUTOBIOGRAPHICAL AND LIFE-STORY APPROACH, THE AUTOBIOGRAPHICAL AND LIFE-STORY APPROACH. THE CONCLUSION ARE COMMON TO TWO AUTHORS.

REFERENCES

Achenbach, G. B. (2000). *Das kleine Buch der inneren Ruhe*. Herder.

Alves, M. H. H. (1982). L'applicazione della biblioterapia nel processo di reinserimento sociale. *Revista Brasileira de Biblioteconomia e Documentação*, 15(1/2), 54–61.

Antoni, C. (1955). *Commento a Croce*. Neri Pozza.

Arendt, H. (1958). *The Human Condition*. The University of Chigago Press.

Bert, G. (2007). *Medicina Narrativa. Storie e Parole nella relazione di cura*. Il Pensiero scientifico editore.

Berthoud, E., & Elderkin, S. (2013). *The Novel Cure: An A to Z of Literary Remedies*. Canongate Books.

Berthoud, E., & Elderkin, S. (2017). *Crescere con i libri. Rimedi letterari per mantenere i bambini sani, saggi e felici*. Sellerio.

Bolzoni, A. (1999). Oltre l'oralità. In Demetrio, D. (Ed.), *L'educatore (auto)biografo*. Unicopli.

Bruner, J. S. (1992). *La ricerca del significato. Per una psicologia culturale*. Bollati Boringhieri. (Original work published 1950)

Caldin, C. F. (2001) A leitura como função terapêutica: biblioterapia. *Encontros Bibli: revista eletrônica de biblioteconomia e ciência da informação*, [S. l.], *6*(12), 32–44. 10.5007/1518-2924.2001v6n12p32

Calvino, I. (1988). *Six Memos for the Next Millennium*. Harvard University Press.

Cambi, F. (2015). La bellezza ci "salva"! Osservazioni per una pedagogia estetica. *Studi Sulla Formazione/Open. Journal of Education*, 17(2), 7–11. 10.13128/Studi_Formaz-16171

Charon, R. (2006). *Narrative medicine: Honoring the stories of illness*. Oxford University Press. 10.1093/oso/9780195166750.001.0001

Crepaldi, D. (2020). *Neuropsicologia della lettura*. Carocci.

Croce, B. (1917). *Logic as the science of the pure concept* (Ainslie, D., Trans.). Macmillan and Co.

Croce, B. (1951). *Conversazioni critiche*. Laterza.

Croce, B. (1954). *Problemi di estetica*. Laterza.

Croce, B. (1955). *Aesthetic as Science of Expression and General Linguistic* (2nd ed.). (Ainslie, D., Trans.). Transaction Publishers.

Croce, B. (1963). *Le due scienze mondane: l'Estetica e l'Economia.* In B. Croce, *Ultimi Saggi*. (44-60). Laterza.

Croce, B. (1966). *Nuove pagine sparse*. Laterza.

Croce, B. (1966). *The totality of artistic expression*. In B. Croce, *Philosophy, Poetry, History: An Anthology of Essays*. (pp. 261 -273). Oxfrord University Press.

Croce, B. (1969). *L'arte come creazione e la creazione come fare*. In B. Croce, *Nuovi saggi di estetica*. (149- 156). Laterza.

Crothers, S. (1916). A literary clinic. *Atlantic Monthly*, 118(3), 291–302.

Cyrulnik, B. (2000). *Il dolore meraviglioso. Diventare adulti sereni superando i traumi dell'infanzia*. Frassinelli.

Dewey, J. (1934). *Art as experience*. Berkley Publishing Group.

Formenti, L. (1998). *La formazione autobiografica*. Guerini.

Frank, R. (2001). *Body of awareness: A somatic and developmental approach to psychotherapy*. GIC/Analytic Press.

Gadamer, H. G. (2004). *Truth and Method* (2nd ed.). (Weinsheimer, J., & Marshall, D. G., Trans.). Continuum Publishing.

Garin, E. (1975). *L'Educazione umanistica in Italia*. Laterza.

Giugni, G. (1969). *Pedagogia della lettura*. SEI.

Jedlowski, P. (2008). *Il sapere dell'esperienza. Fra l'abitudine e il dubbio*. Carocci.

Kucirkova, N., & Cremin, T. (2018). Personalised reading for pleasure with digital libraries: Towards a pedagogy of practice and design. *Cambridge Journal of Education*, 48(5), 571–589. 10.1080/0305764X.2017.1375458

Machiavelli, N. (2016). Letter to Francesco Vettori, December 10, 1513. In Connell, W. J. (Ed.), *The Prince with related documents* (2nd ed., pp. 130–136). Bedford/ St. Martin's.

Mak, H. W., & Fancourt, D. (2020). Longitudinal associations between reading for pleasure and child maladjustment: Results from a propensity score matching analysis. *Social Science & Medicine*, 253, 112971. 10.1016/j.socscimed.2020.11297132276184

Mariani, A. (2005). La lettura come formazione di sé. *MaGMa - Rivista internazionale di scienze umane e sociali, 3*(3).

Mariani, A. (2006). La cura di sé e la lettura. In Boffo, V. (Ed.), *La cura in pedagogia: linee di lettura* (pp. 159–168). Clueb.

Mascia, T. (2023). Pedagogia del leggere per piacere. Il ruolo della motivazione e l'identità del lettore. *Pedagogia più Didattica, 9*(1), 133-143. 10.14605/PD912309

Masten, A. S. (2015). *Ordinary Magic. Resilience in development.* Guildford Press.

Masten, A. S. (2021). Resilience of children in disasters: A multisystem perspective. *International Journal of Psychology*, 56(1), 1–11. 10.1002/ijop.1273733325580

Morin, E. (2021). *Lezioni da un secolo di vita* (S. Lazzari Trans.). Mimesis.

Natoli, S. (2016). *L'esperienza del dolore, Le forme del patire nella cultura occidentale.* Feltrinelli.

Nobile, A. (2004). *Lettura e formazione umana.* La Scuola Editrice.

Nussbaum, M. (2010). *Not for profit: why democracy needs the humanities.* Princeton University Press.

Olmo Extremera, M., Olmedo Moreno, E., Cepero González, M., Zurita Ortega, F., & Padial Ruz, R. (2017). Validation of Resilience Scale (CD-RISC) in elite athletes through a structural equation model. RETOS. Nuevas Tendencias en Educación Física. *Deporte y Recreación*, (32), 96–100.

Palozzi, E. (2023). *Lo storicismo ontologico e metodologico di Benedetto Croce.* Guida.

Paolozzi, E. (2016). *The Aesthetic of Benedetto Croce* (Paparella, E. L., Trans.). Ovi Magazine. (Original work published 2002)

Pardeck, J. T. (1990). Using bibliotherapy in clinical practice with children. *Psychological Reports*, 67(3, Pt 1), 1043–1049. 10.2466/PR0.67.7.1043-10492287656

Rizzolatti, G., & Sinigaglia, C. (2005). *So quel che fai. Il cervello che agisce e i neuroni specchio.* Raffaello Cortina Editore.

Rossi, B. (1997). *Ascoltare e leggere.* La Scuola Editrice.

Rossi, B. (2013). *Pedagogia Della Felicità.* FrancoAngeli.

Sirignano, F. M. (2019). *La formazione pedagogica.* Liguori.

Spalviero, C. (2015). L'educazione letteraria. Crisi e possibili vie d'uscita. *El.LE Educazione Linguistica. Language and Education*, 4(2), 41–57. 10.14277/2280-6792/136

Vogrinčič Čepič, A., Mascia, T., & Aerila, J. A. (2024). Reading for Pleasure: A Review of Current Research. *New Zealand Journal of Educational Studies*, 59(1), 49–71. Advance online publication. 10.1007/s40841-024-00313-x

Wilhelm, J. D. (2016). Recognising the power of pleasure: What engaged adolescent readers get from their free-choice reading, and how teachers can leverage this for all. *Australian Journal of Language and Literacy*, 39(1), 30–41. 10.1007/BF03651904

Chapter 11
Means and Tools of Bibliotherapy: The Help of Technology

Christos Lalos
University of Alicante, Greece

ABSTRACT

The burgeoning intersection of bibliotherapy and technology presents a dynamic frontier for mental health intervention and personal development. This chapter explores the evolving means and tools within bibliotherapy, emphasizing the integral role of technology in enhancing its accessibility, efficacy, and range. The authors delve into the foundations of bibliotherapy as a therapeutic modality, employing literature for emotional and psychological healing, and transition to a comprehensive examination of contemporary technological advancements that have transformed traditional practices. Key focal areas include digital platforms for literature access, such as e-books and audiobooks; online bibliotherapy sessions facilitated by professionals; and the utilization of algorithms for personalized reading recommendations based on psychological profiles. The chapter also highlights the importance of interactive applications that combine cognitive-behavioral techniques with literary exposure, offering users a multifaceted therapeutic tool.

LITERATURE AS A THERAPEUTIC TOOL

Literary texts were precursors to modern psychology as we know it. Works by Seneca, Montaigne, Wordsworth and Eliot contributed to the development of modern psychology. The contribution of Stoicism and specifically Seneca was significant

DOI: 10.4018/979-8-3693-4244-2.ch011

and especially in cognitive behavioral psychotherapy and therapeutic literature, as documented in the research of Kelda Green, University of Liverpool (Green, 2020).

Stoicism influenced many writers in different ways. Seneca's letters are known in the literature for their impact, as well as his philosophical works in the world of psychology (Shah, 2020b). Eis Eavton is the only written text left behind by the Roman emperor and great Stoic philosopher Marcus Aurelius, better known internationally as the Meditations. It is probably the first self-help book, which was not written to be published, but to guide the author in self-improvement and personal development. It mainly covers topics related to death, the universe as an entity, the importance of the present, and the necessity of a simple and benevolent life ("The Therapeutic Value of The Meditations of Marcus Aurelius" 2012).

The novel as we know it today appeared in the 19th century reflecting the socio-cultural changes and attitudes of the time by exploring the social, emotional and cognitive capacities of people through characters that were absent from literature until then. He represented psychology in a way that literature had not done before, penetrating the human characters. Until then literature consisted mainly of essays, poetry and the tragic plays of Shakespeare. This new form of literature presents conventional and unconventional perspectives on life and invites an in-depth look into human consciousness. It also allows for the exploration of expressions that would be painful or unbearable to explore in real life. It offers, from a safe distance, escape, new perspectives and connections even if they are imaginary (Shah, 2020a).

Mary Ann Evans (George Eliot), a Victorian author dealt with issues of psychology (when the latter was in its early stages) through the novel (Shah, 2020b). Thus, it paved the way for its use as a psychological tool that captures human complexity using modern psychological ideas (characteristic examples are her novels Silas Marner and Mill on the Floss) (Green, 2020).

The use of literature as therapy has many advantages such as low relapse rates, high patient acceptance, long-term benefits, low costs (Frude & Jandrić, 2015) and is apparently a very safe method of treatment (McKenna, Hevey, & Martin, 2010).). A trend in bibliotherapy practice today uses works of fiction, especially novels which are a literary genre that seems to be preferred by most readers. The novel helps the reader to identify with the characters to find analogies with his own problems, to gain a kind of "experience" that will help him face problems that concern him. This view is based on the healing power of reading and the interaction between text and reader.

Self-Help Books for Healing

Self-help books, the titles of which are multiplying at a rapid pace, are the best proof that man needs to find answers to everyday problems in a simple way and believes in his innate ability to help himself. From time immemorial, people have looked to religion and philosophy for advice on how to live (Neville, 2018). But today they seek guidance through psychology as well. There is an abundance of so-called "self-help" books, which contain printed guidance for every possible emotional problem and every life choice.

Modern bibliotherapy utilizes these books with terms and conditions of course. This means that these books are best used in a scientific context. In other words, a strict selection of the best quality books by a group of experts (mainly psychologists and psychiatrists) needs to be made and, on the other hand, each patient must use the appropriate book. The "Books on prescription" program, which we will refer to below, is a typical example. Certainly the relationship between therapist and client is an important factor in the effectiveness of therapy, and this element is obviously missing in self-help. In the scheme mentioned above, this relationship is restored, even partially (Wampold, 2001).

Starker (1988) cites four pragmatic factors that explain the success of self-help books (Starker, 1988):

- Cost: The cost of self-help books is low compared to a treatment with a psychologist.
- Accessibility: Books are easily available and can be read at any time (e.g. during a meal or overnight)
- Confidentiality: the patient is offered the opportunity to "work" on the problems that concern him, without being exposed or having to visit a psychologist.
- Enthusiasm: Self-help books often become best-sellers, and buying and reading such a book gives the client the opportunity to become part of a group.

There is no research data to answer the question of who prefers self-help books, but it seems that they began as a response to social perception based on what Thomas Jefferson in the Declaration of Independence called "the individual's pursuit of happiness."

Self-help books are unlikely to be effective if the topics they address have little relevance to most people's happiness. This can be tested by comparing self-development oriented books with empirical research findings on happiness. If a self-help writer attributes the pursuit of happiness to higher income, this advice is unlikely to work well for most readers, as research has found little relationship between happiness and income (Santos Laurie, n.d.). If, however, the advice is to improve one's personal relationships, an effective book has a chance of helping one improve one's quality of life and feel happier.

In self-help, the role of the reader is the most important. Perhaps self-help books work in a similar way to travel guides. Most readers will not follow the book's page order, but will study it piecemeal (Bergsma, 2008). In our country there are examples of self-help book series under the title "bibliotherapy" (Pataki publications) ("Books Practical Psychology Guides," n.d.).

Healing Through Poetry

"... I turn to you Art of Poetry, which somehow knows about medicines; narcotic of pain tests, in Fantasy and Reason...", wrote Konstantinos Cavafis in his poem "Melancholy of Jason Cleandros, poet in Kommagini 595 AD." (Cavafis, 2013).

Bibliotherapy includes therapy through poetry as part of its definition. Poets and philosophers have been aware of the healing nature of poetry for millennia. Hundreds of years ago there were poets and storytellers who helped people face their deepest fears by mirroring humanity's struggles in their poems, myths and stories (Harrower, 1972). So people did not feel that these problems were theirs alone, on the contrary, they affected others as well.

Aristotle discovered that through the process of creating poetry, people were able to turn their problems into strength (Furman, 2003). Specifically, in his poetics, the role of catharsis in effecting an emotional healing through reproduction of universal truths was discussed. Today, catharsis is considered an important aspect of psychotherapy, group therapy, and a central component of psychodrama. Emotional identification, a dominant and primary factor in cleansing, is taken seriously in the use of poetry in therapeutic processes (Mazza, 2016).

Nicholas Mazza in his book, *Poetry Therapy: Theory and Practice*, developed a practice model of poetry therapy that helped delineate its therapeutic elements. This model sets the stage for the types of exercises and interventions possible for the therapist who uses poetry in practice. The ways used in this are (Mazza, 2016):

1. The receptive / prescriptive. Existing poems are used, and the therapist encourages the client to respond. He then notes the person's verbal and non-verbal reactions which are then explored
2. The expressive / creative. Writing poetry for assessment and therapy purposes is encouraged. A group of therapists provides feedback to the client and
3. The symbolic / ritual. The therapist provokes discussion around the interpretation of poetic metaphors, stories, sayings, etc. trying to find relevance in their meaning to individual or group problems and experiences. Metaphors, which are essentially symbols, can help people explain complex emotions in a concise and meaningful way.

As Bijal Shah (Shah, n.d.) states, what makes a poem ideal for use in therapy is that it has the following characteristics:

- Concise: short but including details and able to convey the message to the reader
- Disciplined: discipline is required in the choice and number of words to create a clear and accurate snapshot of the author's feelings.
- Connection: Brevity and detail give access to the poet's mind and allow for meaningful connection with him.

One such poem used in therapy is Robert Frost's "The Road Not Taken," which is quoted translated:

In a yellowed forest there was a crossroads, and I was sorry that I could not take both roads, Because I was a traveler, I stood for a long time

And down I was looking at the one as far away

A point that sloped and disappeared into the undergrowth. Then, fair and fair, I took, resolute,

The other way, and maybe it was lucky

Since he was unfaithful, weedy;

Though there before me he was worn; In the beginning they were both alike.

The like lay before me that morning

In the leaves above, not a single step seemed to have been taken back. Oh! I left the first one for another day! Because

But I knew that one road leads to another

I doubted I could ever go back.

I will say it somewhere after some time

Sighing years and years later:

How in a forest there was a crossroads, and I - I took the road less traveled, and that Made all the difference.

The poem is addressed to everyone and to the choice that everyone makes when in a dilemma: does he choose the safe path or does he carve out a new path?

There are as many ways to read a poem as there are definitions of poetry. Often people are drawn to a poem when they connect with the poet, either feeling the same way as him or empathizing with his position (Shah, n.d.). Reading is active, not passive, and in poetry, this is even more true. Reading poetry is capable of expressing emotions and perhaps that is why it has been such a popular therapy since ancient times. Images and metaphors embedded in a poem with a rhythmic pattern create a similar effect to music: the poetic form allows the expression of feelings that would otherwise be difficult, for various reasons, to express (Curtin, 2013).

More and more psychotherapists in the UK, America and Europe are using poetry therapy as another weapon in the quiver of therapeutic practice (Shah, 2018). There is even an educational program for Bibliotherapy-Therapy through poetry provided by the international federation of the same name ("International Federation for Biblio/ Poetry Therapy," n.d.) as well as the quarterly scientific magazine Poetry Therapy ("NationalAssociationforPoetryTherapy" n.d.).

Writing Poetry as Therapy

Writing poetry for therapy requires that the person is willing to honestly record their thoughts and feelings. The recognition and acknowledgment of internal processes allows authentic communication with oneself and the enhancement of self-esteem. "Confessional Poetry" gives writers the opportunity to confess something personal that they could hardly express to a third party. It is a very good way to focus on the problem and after its completion, there is a sense of calmness. When thoughts become words and are recorded, their weight is immediately reduced and the person feels relief. It is a process that improves with practice and the essence lies in letting oneself be free to express oneself (Hasa, 2016). People usually write poetry when there is some difficulty in their life (Shah, n.d.). This method is particularly helpful in cases where the person faces difficult transitions such as a chronic illness, an unbearable situation that a loved one may be facing, a change of country and bereavement. The transition from a painful feeling to a lighter one, which follows the writing of the poem, is also the main reason that makes it an excellent tool (Hasa, 2016).

Treatment Through Graphic Novels

Graphic novels (books with comic content) are a good solution for adults and children struggling with literacy and communication issues, giving them access to literature in a different format. They are usually used to address physical and mental difficulties and assist in public health initiatives for children. They are very effective in treating a variety of issues such as depression, guilt-driven addictions, and post-traumatic stress disorders (McNicol, 2018).

The "Graphic Medicine" website ("Graphic Medicine", 2007), managed by a community of doctors, artists, writers and health professionals who evaluate and promote the valuable health outcomes of this underappreciated medium: bringing to life characters who tackle issues that many readers can identify and relate to, facilitating the discussion of difficult topics with friends / family / health professionals and offering catharsis. The site holds an annual conference on the use of graphic novels and comics in public health.

Additionally, graphic novels are a great solution for reluctant readers who typically have lower literacy skills and poorer vocabularies. Remarkable results have been seen in prisoners, people with dyslexia and other learning disabilities. These people usually also have psychological issues that show improvement by reading the appropriate graphic novels, under the supervision of a counselor, psychotherapist, book therapist, or teacher (Shah, n.d.).

Healing Through Horror Books

Recent studies have shown the value of horror books in various conditions such as bereavement, anxiety, depression and other mental disorders. People like to take someone else's journey, a journey of pain and suffering because that way they feel that someone else has been in their shoes and empathizes with them (Whitaker, 2020). When the protagonist with whom the reader identifies triumphs in the end and walks away from a negative experience stronger, the reader comes to terms with whatever negative happened in their life (Shah, n.d.).

Creative Writing as Therapy

Creative writing is characterized as an expressive therapy in which the person uses words to express what they are feeling and thinking. It can work on an individual and group level. It is an effective method for people dealing with anxiety (and difficulty expressing it), bereavement, depression, and abuse, as it helps reduce emotional trauma. This method involves writing letters that may or may not be sent to their intended recipients, combined with fictional responses or conversations with them. This helps with clear thinking and problem solving strategies. It can include writing poems, daily recording in a personal notebook (book journaling) or even voice recording.

The personal notebook is one of the best ways to effectively connect a client with their feelings and thoughts and create a sense of calm. It is a way of connecting with the deeper self. It consists of three phases:

1) Book selection: it can be a new one or one that has been re-read by the patient. In the second case, it must be something that affected him in some way.
2) Marking, recording and reflection: marking by the treated, passages that "resonate" within him and recording his feelings together with possible causes of this resonance.
3) Integration: the integration of the thoughts and feelings recorded, often bring to the surface themes-emotions-lessons that contributed to the formation of the person's personality consciously and unconsciously, focusing on a plan of action for the future.

The essential difference between recording and writing is that through the tone of voice and the way of expression, the emotion can be presented more effectively. The person, through the reproduction of the voice, feels that someone is listening to him, and thus he is validated and recognized. Thus, he is freed, both mentally and physically. It is an essential way of self-care as the "inner voice" gains expression.

Evaluation of the Therapeutic Methods of Bibliotherapy

In March 2021, a meta-study was published which examined "bibliotherapy as a non-pharmacological intervention to enhance mental health in response to the COVID-19 pandemic". For the research, 13 relevant studies were finally used which evaluate the effectiveness of bibliotherapy in different clinical settings (Monroy-Fraustro et al., 2021). We mention here some of the conclusions that emerged from this research:

Bibliotherapy is a comprehensive and interdisciplinary treatment that connects psychology, medicine, humanities and literature, works as a complement to clinical therapy and helps patients to cope with their condition, through books. An improvement in the clinical autonomy of the patients was observed as they participated more easily in their treatment, thus reducing any episodes of anxiety and also the emotional burden of the therapist. When the methodology of a bibliotherapy treatment is carefully followed, positive results can be observed, regardless of the diseases. For example, patients with psychosis who participated in a group reading program improved in their clinical symptomatology and cognitive and psychosocial functioning, compared to patients who did not attend such structured activities.

One of the advantages of bibliotherapy is that it can be widely available, can and should be taken into account when developing public policies for the mental health care of those affected by the COVID-19 pandemic. The most common method used in bibliotherapy is cognitive behavioral therapy, which uses self-help books, and it proves to be very effective as it helps to eliminate negative thoughts and create more productive ones for the patient, while it can be completed without the presence of a therapist. Accordingly, healing through books of fiction is achieved as readers recognize the similarities of their experiences with those of (the books') characters, and develop their own tools and gain better control over their lives. It can also help doctors, nurses and other healthcare professionals deal with the saturation of healthcare services during the COVID-19 pandemic.

APPLIED BIBLIOTHERAPY

Programs and Projects

Some typical efforts, small or large, public or private bibliotherapy projects are briefly presented below.

School of Life: Book Therapy Sessions ("The School of Life," n.d.)

The "School of Life" was founded in London in 2008 by the philosopher and writer Alain de Botton. It is a global organization that aims to promote emotional intelligence through teachings that utilize the humanities (literature, philosophy, psychoanalysis, history and art). There are branches all over the world and it offers books and courses for sale on the Internet. One of his services is bibliotherapy sessions. Book therapists Ella Berthoud, Simona Lyons and Susan Elderkin specialize in fiction therapy but also prescribe selected works of philosophy, poetry and other types of books.

Before each session, the participant is asked to complete a questionnaire that examines their reading habits in order to outline the unique "reader ID". This process leads to the selection of books that can open new perspectives, inspire, enrich the reader's thoughts. The full 'prescription' is given within a few days after the session, which can be done live in London or remotely by phone or internet. In addition, there is the possibility of purchasing a bibliotherapy session for a third party.

Kota Public Library, India

The Kota Public Library in India increased its online services by using bibliotherapy as a means of helping users in the midst of the pandemic crisis ("COVID-19 and the Global Library Field," 2020).

The idea was to soften the effects of confinement and avoid increasing stress. So a group was created on the Whats App app named "Knowledge at your doorstep". Dr. Deepak Srivastava, a librarian, created this group to connect people of all age groups. This is achieved through the ability to access digital content (e-books and magazines). In order to minimize the effect of the digital divide, the books provided as well as the rest of the reading material were decided to be in PDF format. In order to connect to this Whats App group one has to send some personal information (name, contact number, email address and others). In the digital collection, members can find e-newspapers, adult e-books, children's e-books, and there are also 10 websites on the following topics: career development, technical skill improvement, free online training and interview preparation (Shrivastava, 2020).

Reading Club Support Group, Mumbai

Sneha Rawlani and Apurupa Vatsalya started a book club named after the therapeutic practice of using books as part of treatment for psychological disorders. To create this group, they used their previous experience in the field of mental health and their shared love for books.

Every month, they organize therapy sessions with limited participation in Mumbai. While they plan to use literary books in these sessions in the future, for now, they are focusing on self-help books. They believe that books of this type are most useful for a mental health book club because they provide participants with information and tools they can use in their lives. While discussing concepts contained in each book, exercises are distributed so that participants can better understand these concepts. Rawlani and Vatsalya place bibliotherapy in the space between self-help and therapy, as an alternative for people who are not ready to expose themselves. in a group and given the tools to support themselves independently. In the future plans of the two therapists is to use a wider range of reading, from books to articles and even videos that they can discuss in their sessions (Agrawal, 2019).

"Words that Heal": Victoria, Australia

Words That Heal is a creative reading (book therapy) program that promotes the creation of a positive lifestyle. This program was created for use in Australia by Susan McLaine, a strong supporter of bibliotherapy in collaboration with a physiologist and a general practitioner. This program was developed and piloted in 2014. This creative book therapy program involves literary texts (fiction, inspirational stories, poetry) read aloud to a group by a trained facilitator, followed by discussion. Creative book therapy is supported by research in neuroscience, reading response, narrative, positive psychology, and the psychology of imagination. The emphasis is on improving well-being through building positivity and empathy (McLaine, n.d.).

In 2020, Susan McLaine created a series of book therapy podcasts for State Library Victoria. Each episode focuses on a different emotion or experience in order to use the healing power of literature to comfort during this difficult time of the pandemic. In this 9-episode series, selected literary texts and poems are read and discussed which focus on different aspects of 'well-being', using an easy-to-use, self-reflective approach. All texts are suitable for mature audiences and each episode is accompanied by a suggested action for the listener ("Bibliotherapy with State Library Victoria," n.d.).

Books on Prescription: United Kingdom

The program was created to provide self-supported psychological therapy. Its emergence as a scheme was prompted by increasing demands for psychological care that could not be met by current resources (Frude, 2004). Patient dissatisfaction caused by increased waiting times for psychotherapy was also a factor considered, in combined with the need for efficient, accessible, evidence-based care for mild to moderate mental health problems.

The first "Books on Prescription" (BoP) program was launched as the "Cardiff Book Prescription Scheme" in 2003 in Cardiff, United Kingdom. Subsequently, this program was followed by many regions of Wales, Scotland and England. In 2005, the Welsh Government decided to set up the first national scheme, 'Book Prescription Wales', which has been very successful and has made a significant contribution to supporting public mental health. It is essentially a scheme to make effective bibliotherapy books known to general practitioners and mental health professionals so that they can in turn recommend them to those who are likely to benefit from their use.

The program involves a familiar treatment strategy, the issuance of a prescription, except that the prescriptions issued are for books, not drugs, and so the prescriptions are distributed by the local public library. 'Book Prescription Wales' uses the library and public health system in a new way to enable large numbers of patients to access psychological treatment resources. The program uses books written by experts and readily available from publishers. Access to these books is facilitated by public libraries. Prescribing since 2005 has extended beyond GPs to include counsellors, nurses, psychologists, psychiatrists, health visitors, midwives etc. and began to be used in prisons, mental wards, drug addiction centers, job centers, voluntary organizations, etc.

The "Books on Prescription" program began to be implemented in New Zealand in 2011, in libraries in the Central Otago region. The program has since been rolled out across Otago and Southland and is now available in all public libraries in that region, as well as local University staff and students, through the Medical Library.

An extensive evaluation of the program was carried out by Wellsouth Primary Health Network in 2014, with very positive results. After the evaluation, mood-enhancing books were included in the program, as well as on other topics such as diabetes and heart disease, and smartphone apps and videos were added to the website.

Thus, the program consists of 3 parts:

- "Read Yourself Well" - a collection of books available at your local library. Reading has been shown to be an effective tool for self-management of a health problem.

- “T'App Yourself well” - a set of smartphone apps are available through this website. This tool can help the reader understand and manage a health problem. Applications are reviewed in collaboration with Health Navigator (“Health Navigator, New Zealand,” n.d.).
- - “Listen Yourself Well” - podcasts and videos available to borrow from libraries through this website that may help you understand and manage a health problem. Supported by Otago Access Radio 105.4FM and RadioSouthland 96.4FM.

Central European Bibliotherapy Program (Béres, 2016)

In 2016, a two-year program was created under the “Interreg Central Europe” program, which linked libraries with mental health and career counseling for young people. The project was aimed at youth and young adults, and its preparatory phase involved: librarians and bibliotherapists, social workers, Non-Profit Organizations (NGOs) and psychologists from partner universities.

The idea was to apply innovative techniques such as book consultation and self-help as key tools to create a learning system and database, which could be applied at regional level and give added value to youth libraries, universities and NGOs . Specifically, the goals were:

- Book counseling, applied to young people provided by libraries and NGOs with the aim of managing stress, preventing depression, enhancing creativity, better performance at work, with the help of reading lists, group reading, creative educational activities and events ” living” library.
- Careers guidance and skills training for youth in youth libraries, schools and NGOs to identify the profession that is 'best suited' for each
- Training and supervision guidelines: the ethical and effective use of bibliotherapy in the context of contributing to the development of readers requires education and training of professionals (workshops and tools from Finnish, British and Hungarian bibliotherapy)
- Creation of bibliotherapy database: Open access to knowledge for everyone in their national language. Preparation of annotated bibliographies, collection and translation of appropriate sources (full-text professional articles, case studies).

The World's First Virtual Book Therapy Project "InsidetheBookIsl@nd": Vilnius, Lithuania

In the year 2015-2016, an interactive bibliotherapy program in a digital environment, "Inside the Book Insl@nd", was run in the central library of the capital of Lithuania, Vilnius. Its purpose was to enable socially vulnerable children and young people to recognize their problems and talk openly about them. The fact that allowed them to have freedom of expression is that their participation in the activities was done through a digital image (avatar) and all communication was done in the digital world. (Glosaite & Jurgeleviciene, 2016).

Digital Bibliotherapy Tools

Bibliotherapy, the practice of using books and other reading materials as a therapeutic intervention, has been around for centuries. Traditionally, it involved the selection of specific texts for individuals to read, reflecting on their personal situations, challenges, and paths to healing or personal development. However, in the digital age, the means and tools of bibliotherapy have expanded significantly, incorporating various forms of technology to enhance accessibility, engagement, and effectiveness. Here's an overview of how technology has revolutionized bibliotherapy:

Digital Libraries and E-Books

Accessibility: Digital libraries and e-books have made it easier for individuals to access therapeutic materials anytime and anywhere, without the need for physical storage or visits to physical libraries.

Wide Range of Resources: There's an extensive range of digital books and articles available, covering numerous topics and therapeutic areas, making it easier to find materials that resonate with personal experiences or challenges.

Audiobooks and Podcasts

Auditory Learning: For those who prefer listening over reading, audiobooks and therapeutic podcasts offer a convenient way to engage with bibliotherapy. They can be particularly useful for individuals with visual impairments or those who find reading challenging.

Multitasking: Audiobooks and podcasts allow users to engage in therapy while performing other activities, such as commuting, exercising, or doing household chores.

Apps and Software

Interactive Platforms: Several apps and software are specifically designed for bibliotherapy, providing interactive reading experiences, self-help tools, mood tracking, and personalized recommendations based on users' emotional states or goals.

Confidentiality and Privacy: These tools often offer a private space for individuals to explore their feelings and challenges without the stigma or fear of judgment that can accompany traditional therapy settings.

Online Communities and Forums

Shared Experiences: Online forums and social media platforms allow individuals to share their reading experiences, insights, and progress with others, creating a sense of community and mutual support.

Guidance and Recommendations: These communities can also be a source of recommendations for therapeutic reading materials, as well as tips on how to engage with bibliotherapy effectively.

Virtual Reality (VR) and Augmented Reality (AR)

Immersive Experiences: VR and AR technologies can provide immersive reading or storytelling experiences that enhance emotional engagement and empathy, making bibliotherapy more impactful for some individuals.

Simulated Scenarios: They offer unique opportunities for exposure therapy, simulating real-life situations that individuals can navigate and learn from in a safe and controlled environment.

Data Analysis and AI

Personalization: Machine learning algorithms can analyze users' preferences, reading habits, and emotional responses to recommend the most relevant and helpful reading materials.

Therapeutic Insights: AI can also help in tracking progress and providing insights into users' emotional states or patterns, aiding in the therapeutic process.

In conclusion, technology has significantly broadened the scope and effectiveness of bibliotherapy, making therapeutic reading materials more accessible, engaging, and personalized than ever before. From digital libraries to VR experiences, the integration of technology into bibliotherapy offers promising avenues for mental health support and personal development.

CONCLUSION

Based on this research, we arrive at a number of basic conclusions that can form the basis of a study for the introduction of bibliotherapy in Greek libraries.

According to the answers we received and using definitions derived from previous research carried out in public libraries abroad, we can distinguish three concepts: a) creative bibliotherapy: the use of fiction and poetry in a formal format, with the aim of improving the mental health of individuals and groups b) informal bibliotherapy, that is, taking advantage of the development of readers' reading ability and the experience of librarians so as to connect (public) library users with books that may contribute to their well-being. c) self-help bibliotherapy: the use of expertly selected self-help books recommended by medical practitioners usually in a formal prescribed book format to provide practical help.

Bibliotherapy is applied with very good results at younger ages as it is linked to education but also for the social development of children and young people. It helps to form citizens capable of setting and achieving goals, as well as understanding themselves, others and the environment. Children today may be concerned with various issues as a pedagogical method (socio-cultural animation) such as adapting to the school environment, bullying, friendship, cooperation. Bibliotherapy helps them respond positively to these issues and helps to deal with fear, anxiety, anger and frustration. Many good children's books have a psychological (essentially bibliotherapeutic) dimension, while with the same logic and good results, literature is used as a pedagogical tool for socio-cultural animation.

From the results, it seems that reading is not just a leisure activity, but a way to deal with mental health problems. It is used to manage difficult emotions and facilitates the experience of catharsis and empathy.

REFERENCES

Bergsma, A. (2008). Do self-help books help? *Journal of Happiness Studies*, 9(3), 341–360. 10.1007/s10902-006-9041-2

Cavafis, K. P. (2013). *Cavafy: The Poems*. Metaichmium.

Frude, N., & Jandrić, P. (2015). The Intimate Machine: 30 years on. *E-Learning and Digital Media*, 12(3–4), 410–424. 10.1177/2042753015571830

Furman, R. (2003). Poetry Therapy and existential practice. *The Arts in Psychotherapy*, 30(4), 195–200. 10.1016/S0197-4556(03)00052-2

Green, K. (2020). *Rethinking Therapeutic Reading: lessons from Seneca Montaigne, Wordsworth and George Eliot*. In Anthem Press. 10.2307/j.ctvsn3p9x

Harrower, M. (1972). *The therapy of poetry*. Charles C Thomas.

Mazza, N. (2016). *Poetry Therapy: theory and practice*. Routledge. 10.4324/9781315748740

McKenna, G., Hevey, D., & Martin, E. (2010). Patients' and providers' perspectives on bibliotherapy in primary care. *Clinical Psychology & Psychotherapy*, 17(6), 497–509. 10.1002/cpp.67920146202

Monroy-Fraustro, D., Maldonado-Castellanos, I., Aboites-Molina, M., Rodríguez, S., Sueiras, P., Altamirano-Bustamante, N. F., de Hoyos-Bermea, A., & Altamirano-Bustamante, M. M. (2021, March 15). Bibliotherapy as a Non-pharmaceutical Intervention to Enhance Mental Health in Response to the COVID-19 Pandemic: A Mixed-Methods Systematic Review and Bioethical MetaAnalysis. [Frontiers Media S.A.]. *Frontiers in Public Health*, 9, 629872. 10.3389/fpubh.2021.62987233796496

Neville, R. (2018). Philosophy of religion and the big questions. *Palgrave Communications*, 4(1), 1–8. 10.1057/s41599-018-0182-9

Starker, S. (1988). Do-it-yourself therapy: The prescription of self-help books by psychologists. *Psychotherapy (Chicago, Ill.)*, 25(1), 142–146. 10.1037/h0085310

The Therapeutic Value of The Meditations of Marcus Aurelius. (2012). Tolstoy Therapy. https://www.tolstoytherapy.com/meditations-marcus-aurelius

Wampold, B. E. (2001). *The great psychotherapy debate: Models, methods, and findings*. Lawrence Erlbaum Associates Publishers.

Chapter 12
Creative Writing:
Creating Micro-Stories to Combat Ageism

Carles Cortés Orts
https://orcid.org/0000-0003-0647-5640
Universitat d'Alacant, Spain

ABSTRACT

This research addresses the therapeutic effects of creative writing for population segments aged over 50. In recent years, the author has taught story and micro-story writing workshops as part of the University of Alicante's training programmes for senior citizens, and this experience provides the starting point for the study. The study has focused on the creation of micro-stories (stories up to 10-12 lines in length), useful in developing writing skills due to the concision and precision needed to meet the length requirements. Thus, workshop participants of this age group have to be creative and innovative, improve their concentration and experiment with creative structures. With these objectives, several techniques have been employed to combat ageism: looking for diverse voices and experiences, exploring ageing-related issues, challenging standards of beauty and success, promoting empathy and understanding, and avoiding stereotypes and clichés.

INTRODUCTION

This research addresses the therapeutic effects of creative writing for population segments aged over 50. In recent years, the author has taught story and micro-story writing workshops as part of the University of Alicante's training programmes for senior citizens, and this experience provides the starting point for the study. Among others, the paper draws on psychological approaches proposed by such authors as

DOI: 10.4018/979-8-3693-4244-2.ch012

J. M. Smyth in "Written emotional expression: effect sizes, outcome types, and moderating variables" (1998), and especially on a book by A. Gaggioli et al., *Intergenerational group reminiscence: A potentially effective intervention to enhance elderly psychosocial wellbeing and to improve children's perception of aging* (2014). The aim is to highlight how creative writing can help overcome age stereotypes and encourage interaction across age groups through shared experiences.

The study has focused on the creation of micro-stories (stories up to 10-12 lines in length), useful in developing writing skills due to the concision and precision needed to meet the length requirements. Thus, workshop participants of this age group have to be creative and innovative, improve their concentration and experiment with creative structures. With these objectives, several techniques have been employed to combat ageism: looking for diverse voices and experiences, exploring ageing-related issues, challenging standards of beauty and success, promoting empathy and understanding, and avoiding stereotypes and clichés. A corpus of micro-stories written by workshop participants of this age group has been compiled, which will be analysed and from which examples will be taken.

BACKGROUND

The study has been conducted in the framework of the University of Alicante's Lifelong Learning Programme. Through scientific, cultural and social development, the programme seeks to support science, culture and intergenerational relations, improve the quality of life of older people and encourage them to play an active role in society. This is in line with principles of democratisation of knowledge, the fight against inequality and the promotion of social integration and participation; the specific objectives are stated on the programme's website.[1] The article focuses on a writing workshop targeted at people over 55 years of age. This population group can be subject to *ageism*, i.e. a form of social discrimination consisting of negative stereotypes, condescending attitudes and discriminatory practices that marginalise individuals exclusively on the ground of their chronological age. This term was defined by Robert. N. Butler in his study "Age-ism: Another form of bigotry" (1969, pp. 243-246). For Butler, ageism tends to underestimate the contributions and experiences of older people and to ignore or minimise their needs and rights.[2]

This theoretical background provided the basis for the creative writing workshop "El racó de l'escriptura" ("The writing corner"). The aim of the workshop was for participants to develop story writing skills as a way to enhance their enjoyment of reading and writing, and also to share their experiences in literary writing with others within the same generational group. As part of this annual course, the micro-stories written by the workshop participants were published as a book, *Microrrelatos. El racó de l'escriptura* ("Micro-stories. The writing corner," 2023), the corpus of analysis for this article.[3] The idea came about while re-reading and analysing a collection of stories by Isabel-Clara Simó that had been published for the first time in *L'inesperat i altres contes* ("The unexpected and other stories," 2022, p. 20). One of these stories was "El minotaure i jo" ("The minotaur and me"), which started with this striking sentence: "Segons el famosíssim conte d'Augusto Monterroso, *quan es va despertar, el minotaure encara era allà*, que ha fet vessar molta tinta. Estic malalt. De fet, m'estic morint, en un llit d'hospital i familiars cansats de la meva llarga agonia" ["Borrowing from Augusto Monterroso's widely known story, *when he awoke, the minotaur was still there* – much has been written about it. I am ill. In fact, I am dying, in a hospital bed, and my relatives are tired of my long agony"] (Simó, 2022, p. 20). The ending is quite clear: "no vaig poder evitar plagiar Monterroso, *vaig obrir els ulls i la realitat encara era allà*" ["I couldn't help but plagiarise Monterroso, *I opened my eyes and reality was still there*"]. By drawing inspiration from a story by Honduran writer Augusto Monterroso, Isabel-Clara Simó highlighted the importance of short stories or flash fiction, a new literary subgenre that has grown considerably in recent years. It should be noted, however, that new reading devices have emerged over the last few decades as a result of technological advances, and that these formats have in turn sparked interest in shorter literary forms.

Quick and easy to read (for instance, while commuting to work or during breaks), short stories are ideally suited for today's hectic lifestyle. This is also true in digital environments like social media, in which concision is a relevant factor due to length limitations. The rapid growth of this subgenre, then, has been boosted by easy-to-use platforms such as Twitter and Instagram. In an ever-faster world overloaded with information, micro-stories have become a popular, concise and effective form of storytelling.[4] The subgenre is in a stage of "strengthening and normalisation" that started in the 1980s, as pointed out by Irene Andrés-Suárez in *El microrrelato español. Una estética de la elipsis* ("The Spanish micro-story. An aesthetic of ellipsis," 2010, 47). Combined with new technologies, this kind of fiction is perfect for workshops targeted at older people, as it helps them overcome the obstacles posed by the *digital divide* and allows them to take an active part in social media by creating highly concise texts, in a subgenre that – unlike in the past – is now considered to be as prestigious as others. They accept a challenge that, according to some studies in ageing psychology,[5] can improve their digital skills and promote emerging technologies within this age group.

A MICRO-STORY WRITING WORKSHOP FOR OLDER PEOPLE

1. Analysis of micro-stories: elements of the subgenre

In the workshop, the main characteristics of story writing were explained, with special emphasis on the following: the story should focus on just a few characters, in a limited space and time period, to convey an impactful message or an intense emotion in as few words as possible. The subgenres of literary fiction (novel, novella, story, essay, monologue, prose poem, legend, folktale, short story, autobiography, and others) were analysed, after which the core elements of hyper-short or micro-stories were established: very short length (about 750 characters or 10 lines), concision and intensity of expression, condensing the story in a minimal number of words. Moreover, several examples were provided to highlight the importance of the title – to indicate how the story should be interpreted – and punctuation, as any deictic or prosodic element can alter the way readers understand it.

Based on the model proposed by Irene Andrés-Suárez (2010), two main categories were established: very short micro-stories, 200 to 1,000 words in length, and ultra-short stories, 1 to 200 words. José María Merino's classification is similar: "los microrrelatos, en su brevedad extrema, pueden clasificarse según su extensión, desde los llamados ultrabreves, que no exceden las cien palabras, hasta los de mayor extensión, que pueden ocupar dos o tres páginas" ["micro-stories, in their extreme brevity, can be classified according to length into ultra-short stories, not exceeding 100 words, and longer micro-stories of two or three pages"] (Merino, 2007, p. 20). The aim was also to observe what micro-stories have in common with other short genres, such as aphorisms, jokes, fables, or haikus. The conclusion was that, even if some of the parts of the traditional plot structure (exposition-complication -dénouement) are shortened or omitted, all three can be nevertheless present in intratextual elements like the title or omissions, as certain aspects of the underlying plot are not expressed.[6] Several micro-stories, in Spanish and Catalan, were provided as examples to be analysed prior to the creative process. The sample included, among others, the following texts:

"The Dinosaur," by Augusto Monterroso (1959)

When he awoke, the dinosaur was still there.

"Quality and Quantity," by Alejandro Jodorowsky (1995)

He did not fall in love with her, but with her shadow. He used to visit her at dawn, when his beloved was longer.

"A Dream," by Jorge Luis Borges (1981)

In a deserted place in Iran there is a not very tall stone tower that has neither door nor window. In the only room (with a dirt floor and shaped like a circle) there is a wooden table and a bench. In that circular cell, a man who looks like me is writing in letters I cannot understand a long poem about a man who in another circular cell is writing a poem about a man who in another circular cell... The process never ends and no one will be able to read what the prisoners write.

"Love 77," by Julio Cortázar (1979)

And after doing everything they do, they get up, take a bath, put on some powder, perfume themselves, get dressed, and thus gradually become again what they are not.

"The Letter," by Luis Mateo Díez (2001)

Every morning, I get to my office, sit down, switch on the lamp, open my briefcase and, before starting my tasks of the day, I write a line in the long letter where, for fourteen years, I have recorded in detail the reasons for my suicide.

"Curfew," by Omar Lara (2012)
-Stay, I told her.
And I touched her.

"Ghost," by Patricia Esteban Erlés (2009)

The man I once loved has become a ghost. I like to put a lot of fabric softener, steam iron him and use him as a fitted sheet the nights I have a promising date.

"She spoke on and on," by Max-Aub (1991)

She spoke on and on, and on and on and on and on. Speaking all the time. And I'm a home-loving woman. But that fat maid did nothing but speak on and on and on. Wherever I was, she came and started speaking. She spoke about everything and anything, she didn't care. Firing her because of that? I would have had to pay her three months' salary. And she would have been perfectly able to give me the evil eye. Even in the bathroom, always saying this and that. I stuffed the towel into her mouth to shut her up. She didn't die because of that, but because she couldn't speak: her words burst inside her.

"The Unexpected," by Isabel-Clara Simó (2022)

When a friend betrays you, it hurts a lot; when an enemy does something for you, we are perplexed. The unexpected is surprising, because we only feel at ease with the things we can expect in our routine, day-to-day life.

"The Minotaur and Me," by Isabel-Clara Simó (2022)

Borrowing from Augusto Monterroso's widely known story, when he awoke, the minotaur was still there – much has been written about it. I am ill. In fact, I am dying, in a hospital bed, and my relatives are tired of my long agony, coming and talking about my possessions in front of me, as if I had already died. How irritating it is to hear my daughter, who used to be so sweet, say to my wife, her mother, that when this guy is gone, we shouldn't fight over his shitty will; or when my wife asks the nurse, can't you give him something to speed up the process?

And at last, I died. I went down a hole where there was no conscience, I just felt I was falling deeper and deeper. Suddenly, an unfortunate cough brought me back to life. I couldn't help but plagiarise Monterroso: 'I opened my eyes and reality was still there.'

"IPAD," by Isabel-Clara Simó (2022)

The girl pushes the button to open the doors of the underground carriage: she has reached her stop. Once she has stepped down onto the platform and the train leaves, she feels someone tapping her back. She turns and sees a young man who tells her:

– Take this.

She instinctively takes what he gives her. The man darts away and she can no longer see him. The girl, at first terrified and then relieved, realises that the object he has given her is her iPad.

Standing still on the platform, she thinks: this guy has stolen my iPad, where I have absolutely everything, but he didn't like the model and returned it to me. Wow. How come this punk was rummaging in my bag and I didn't notice anything at all?

First, an overview of the stories was given. Next, they were read several times, so that students could fill in the gaps and silences – or, in other words, interpret the suggestions and omissions in the way the author intended.[7] Through Isabel-Clara Simó's "El minotaure i jo" ["The minotaur and me"], the topics of death and its proximity in the family environment were discussed, noting that, while the story is not autobiographical, it is still related to the author's situation when she wrote it, as she had a degenerative disease and knew that she would die soon. The fact that Simó had adapted Monterroso's "El dinosaurio" was also emphasised, as the students would have to do something similar. The objective was clear: anything in their environment could provide the starting point for a condensed story, a micro-story.

They could tap into their own experiences, using anecdotes or episodes that, like in Simó's posthumously published story, related specifically to older people.

2. Writing micro-stories: encouraging creativity
   a. In-class experience during the micro-story writing workshop

As stated in the introduction, 23 students contributed the micro-stories that were published online. Throughout the creative process, they had to consider the discursive, formal, thematic and pragmatic features outlined by David Roas in his article "El microrrelato y la teoría de los géneros" ("Micro-stories and genre theory," 2008, pp. 47-76):

- Discursive features: narrativity, hyper-brevity, concision and others.
- Formal features: simple structure, minimal characterisation (characters' physical or psychological traits are introduced indirectly), spaces are merely outlined, condensed time period and others.
- Pragmatic features: an active reader is required.

The most evident discursive feature is brevity, but there are others, as noted by Marcelo Gobo (2015, p. 96): "[la brevedad es una] condición absolutamente primaria de todo microrrelato, ésta es insuficiente por sí sola para establecer sus características" ["brevity is absolutely essential to every micro-story, but not sufficient by itself"]. Thus, micro-stories also depend on paratextual elements like the title, which often becomes part of the story and can even reveal the ending. Intertextuality is equally crucial in achieving concision; for instance, the intensive use of omissions allows the author to minimise the number of words – the process is similar to the one that led to the differentiation between novels and novellas (Andrés-Suárez, 2012, pp. 27-28). As for the pragmatic features, the most notable ones are those elements that encourage the reader to read again and discover aspects that would otherwise remain hidden.

To facilitate the cognitive process involved in writing a micro-story, the below steps have been followed:

- Choosing a specific idea. Each participant has selected a specific idea; although the story itself can be more complex, it should be encapsulated by the idea.
- Introducing the story in as few words as possible. The introduction of the characters, space and time period should be inferred from the general context or the title, which can serve as a preamble.

- Starting in the middle of the action. The author must be direct and to the point, describing only essential aspects; readers must be able to fill in the gaps.
- Focusing on an image. Through the image and its evocative elements, readers should imagine the space in which the story takes place.
- Building up the mystery. As the story unfolds, it should keep readers' attention until the end, encouraging them to be active readers. Unexpected and surprising elements can be added.

Based on the above guidelines, the 23 workshop participants created 120 micro-stories in total.[8] The stories reflected the diversity of the authors' interests and styles, as they were allowed to address any topic they wished. North American writer Natalie Goldberg says as follows in *Writing Down the Bones: Freeing the Writer Within*: "setting thematic limitations in creative writing is like locking a bird in a cage. True magic happens when imagination is allowed to fly unrestricted, exploring any topic that fills the writer's heart and mind" (Goldberg, 1986, p. 25). The objective was to see how many stories could be interpreted in terms of the fight against ageism – that is, how many of them addressed issues related to equal treatment for people of all ages. For the sake of creativity, participants were given no advice as to the ideas they should focus on. The resulting stories are therefore diverse, trying to reflect contemporary society from multiple perspectives (critical, ironic, comical, paradoxical), and can be perceived and interpreted in many ways.

During the workshop, each of the stories was shared with the rest of participants and, finally, evaluated on an individual basis. This was not intended to restrict the freedom of the creative process; rather, the aim was to encourage the students to be sincere and honest, as adults who, at this point in their lives, have made a major decision: to engage in literary creation as a shared experience. Because reading and writing have no age limit, but a starting point – the moment when the future writer feels the need to create something for others to read. North American author and journalist Joan Didion, in an autobiographical account about the period of mourning she went through after her husband's sudden death, explores how writing helped her come to terms with the new situation. Didion, who says nothing as to a possible desire to seek recognition from others, symbolically refers to her experience of writing as follows: "I did not grow old" (Didion, 2005, p. 167). This point accurately reflects the lasting nature of writing and the therapeutic effects of sharing experiences through literary creation.

b. Therapeutic effects of literary writing

Story writing generally involves a process of reflection and self-discovery, emerging as a powerful tool that can unlock forgotten memories, heal emotional wounds and strengthen one's sense of self and purpose. Creating a micro-story also forces writers to condense information; like word games, it sharpens the wits and reinforces the cognitive processes of older students. This is discussed by the psychologist Robert A. Wilson in "Effect of crossword puzzles on vocabulary knowledge and working memory in older adults: A randomized controlled trial" (2009, p. 159):

Word games, like crossword puzzles, can be an effective tool to stimulate vocabulary and working memory in older adults. Our study shows that regularly engaging in this kind of activities can have significant benefits for maintaining and improving cognitive functions in this population. (Wilson, 2009, p. 159)

If the story writing process is seen as some sort of word game, it becomes obvious how older people can benefit from developing an idea through their memories or experiences. Their lives offer a wealth of stories, whether shared with others or kept to themselves. On this journey of reflection and self-discovery, story writing is a powerful means of unlocking memories and reinforcing their individual identity within a group. With this in mind, it is not hard to understand the benefits involved in this form of creative expression and the therapeutic impact it has on the mental and emotional health of this age group. The ability to reflect on and share personal stories – of course, filtered through the creative process – can be a vital part of the emotional and psychological wellbeing of older people.

Story writing is a form of narrative therapy that allows older people to explore their past, process their experiences and give shape to the story of their lives. By creating characters, settings and plots, they have the opportunity to analyse their emotions, confront their fears and find meaning in their experiences, as noted by North American psychologist James W. Pennebaker in the study *Opening Up: The Healing Power of Expressing Emotions*: "story writing offers individuals a powerful way of exploring and processing their emotional experiences. By putting their thoughts and feelings into words, participants can shape their personal experiences in a way that promotes understanding, acceptance and healing" (1997, p. 213). As a means of creative expression, therefore, writing encourages self-exploration and emotional resilience, allowing participants to reinterpret their own experiences from a new, more insightful perspective. At the same time, they seek inspiration in and try to distance themselves from their personal stories, whether consciously (to hide the fact that the story is based on a true episode in the author's life) or unconsciously (without realising that the source of inspiration is something that actually happened to them).

As proposed by J. Cohen-Mansfield and A. Parpura-Gill in "Utilizing a structured reminiscence protocol: The effects on agitation and affect in nursing home residents with dementia" (2007, pp. 341-354), the therapeutic effects story writing has on older people are:

- Cognitive stimulation: story writing requires cognitive skills such as memory, attention and abstract thinking, increasing mental agility and activity.
- Emotional exploration: for older people, reflecting on their own emotions and experiences gives them clarity of mind and helps them find consolation when thinking about past and current problems.
- Traumatic therapy: story writing allows older people to process painful events and find healing through creative expression.
- Positive outlook: reimagining their own experiences from a new, positive perspective helps them develop effective strategies to face challenges in life.
- Social connection: sharing stories with others in a group environment strengthens their sense of belonging and social connection, which is a way to combat feelings of loneliness and isolation in older people.
- Sense of achievement: when authors finish writing a story or short story, they experience a sense of achievement that boosts their self-esteem and self-confidence.

Story writing, then, has a wide range of therapeutic benefits for older people, ranging from improved memory and cognitive processes to anxiety and stress control. They can explore their past, find meaning in the present and have better prospects for the future. Literary writing processes can also unlock the latent creativity of older adults for them to experiment with new ideas and approaches. In the study cited above, Natalie Goldberg states that "writing can be a form of meditation, a way of connecting with our innermost essence and releasing our inherent creativity" (Goldberg, 1986, p. 45). Through story writing, this age group can rekindle a sense of purpose and meaning after retiring or reducing their work responsibilities. In several studies, the psychologist Dan P. McAdams has highlighted the importance of consciously or unconsciously including autobiographical episodes in literary writing. For instance, in the article "Narrative Identity: What Is It? What Does It Do? How Do You Measure It?" (2018, pp. 359-372), he contends that storytelling can be essential in constructing personal identity throughout one's life. For older people, writing stories can be a means for them to look back on their experiences, achievements and relationships, to understand who they really are. The premise is evident: identity is constructed through stories that, when told, further strengthen that person's identity and values.

As for the therapeutic effects of social connection and empathy among older people, writer and therapist Anne Lamott points out in *Bird by Bird: Some Instructions on Writing and Life* that "sharing our stories connects us with others in a profound and significant way, reminding us that we are not alone in our struggles and triumphs" (Lamott, 1994, p. 72). Accordingly, participating in writing groups like the one discussed in the present study gives older adults a sense of community and belonging, a meeting point where they can share their own experiences and discover those of others. All in all, writing stories is an effective means of self-expression, self-reflection and connection within this age group. This form of narrative therapy can potentially transform the experience of ageing by offering a platform for personal growth, emotional healing and human connection.

3. Analysis of *micro-stories: overcoming* ageism[9]

The majority of prepared short stories become a therapeutic tool in the realization of the various elements that favor creativity in the indicated group. Thus, if we follow the previous systematization by J. Cohen-Mansfield and A. Parpura-Gill in "Utilizing a structured reminiscence protocol: The effects on agitation and affect in nursing home residents with dementia," we observe the sense of achievement achieved now to make the completion of texts a reality, which almost all of the students were experiencing for the first time. A job done that fosters self-esteem and self-confidence which have provoked a cognitive stimulation that represents the enhancement of the cognitive abilities of memory, attention and abstract thinking as a result of their imagination. This is a positive position; in that they have had to reimagine their own experiences from a new and active perspective in the face of the challenges of the new life stage. The difficulty of falling asleep and having sleep interrupted is the focus of a good number of stories. The insomnia or the difficulty of a deep sleep is the basis of Elvira Antón's short story "The Dead Hour": "It is 3 o'clock in the morning, as every day for some time, I wake up at the same time [...] What wakes us up?" (p. 14). A reality that is linked to another of the recurring themes of adults, death: "I return to bed again, and thinking that my time has not yet come" (p. 14). A final in which the loneliness of the deceased is raised, with the only company of a guide dog:

He knew no other life, no other company than his owner's and was happy, very happy. But the "glasses" his owner wore only allowed him to see a dark and sad life. And he took leave of the world leaving a note, with the luck that his dog guided him to the side of life. (Mila Belda, "The Guide Dog," p. 21)

An uncertainty before the existence in the present, the continuity of life the next day, when it dawns, governing the short story of Arturo Espinosa "The Adventure" (p. 25):

Short step, watchful eye. The night is coming and in the forest, everything becomes shadows. The sounds arc magnified and surround you, I don't know what they are or whose. The darkness is total. Everything is a threat.

Will I See Dawn?

The same author presents in "When I Woke Up" an overcoming of insomnia, with an alleged confirmation that older people can also sleep well. However, in the outcome we know, in a surprising way, that the well-being of the body is not the same as that of the soul, which cries after an apparently peaceful night: "without any sense of guilt. I had gained freedom! But why? How? When? I found it out easily. I saw my soul sitting in a chair in the kitchen, whimpering, it is all over now!" (p. 25). Insomnia also centers the story of Miguel García "The Silly Hours" (p. 28):

Immersed in a deep sleep, a sudden rumbling shook my consciousness. My mind, like a fragile building, convulsed before an internal earthquake. My thoughts shook violently, emotions collided like tectonic plates, and my emotions faded into tremors of anxiety. All my cells remained in a continuous quake. In the darkness of the night the silence was interrupted by an ominous echo. Sleep, an unattainable luxury.

Fucking insomnia.

As we see, the difficulty to fall asleep is recurrent in that anthology. "The Silence" by Victoria Ramos ends by highlighting the most characteristic element of the difficulty of sleeping: "Far away, three o'clock sounded. Darkness and serenity in the bedroom. I heard... and I listened. I heard... and I listened again. I listened once more, this time with my five senses... I recognized him. It was him: the Silence." (p. 58). An effect that is intensified in Raúl Sevilla's hyper-short story "Missed Call" with a powerful phrase contextualized by the title that delimits the action: "I called you. I never received an answer" (p. 65).

Among the effects of emotional exploration noted by Cohen-Mansfield and Parpura-Gill (2007), it is worth mentioning the reflection on the emotions and personal experiences of the past, so that clarity and comfort are fostered before the new situation of the present. Thus, the world of childhood, the updated memories, is also part of several stories. This is the case of Paqui Antón's "Full Moon": "Childhood innocence questions nuances that we as adults pass over" (p. 18). The protagonist of the micro-story reviews the image of the contemplation of the full moon and defends the development of the imagination of childhood in the present moment of the adult. A satellite that enhances the memory of childhood in the story "Tavira and Carminho" by Manel Soler:

Have you seen, Miquel, the times we've crossed paths in this seaside neighborhood full of stairs and the smell of fish? When I stop, I see you listening to the night, a night of round moon and shining stars, hearing the sound of a falling leaf, the flutter of fireflies and the monotonous chirping of crickets. (p. 67)

A childhood that is recreated in a positive sense from the distance of adulthood where problems have no solution: "He was the class nerd, always with good grades. But he grew up and life was more than academic concepts and when he had to face them, he could not decipher the enigma." (Mila Belda, "Spurred Clarity," p. 21). On the contrary, in a later account by the author herself, the passage of time and the coming of adulthood represents the consolidation of security in the face of the uncertainty of the world of children: "As we grow up, we imagine what we want to be as adults, we study, we take competitive exams or we start a business and when that comes we feel like on a throne that gives us security." (Mila Belda, "The Safe Throne," p. 22). A similar case is the memory that centers the story of Ramón García "The Child" where the child protagonist reaches maturity at the time he learns not to cry, something traditionally banished from adulthood in men. As we see, whether or not they have an autobiographical character, the fact of sharing stories or memories becomes a tool to reinforce the connection of the adult individual with the collective in which he or she interacts, as Anne Lamott pointed out *Bird by Bird: Some Instructions on Writing and Life* (Lamott, 1994, p. 72).

Within the group of childhood memories there are specific fragments that marked a generation, such as the confinement in a boarding school of the brother Ramón of the narrative voice built in "The boarding school" by Patricia de la Vega: "who was really aware of the impact that Miguel had of wearing a number embroidered on his bib as if he were a delinquent in a penitentiary" (p. 23). The author herself dedicates the story "Recuerdos" (Memories) to the evocation of childhood:

Until I was 12, I used to spend the summer in the country with my cousins. I keep very pleasant memories of everything I learned: riding a bike, riding a horse, caring for chickens, picking almonds, bagging grapes, washing our clothes and a long etcetera. Although the day-to-day life was not as comfortable as at home, we always said goodbye with plans for the following year.

From remembered images, the author intends to stop time, to leave a record in the present of the value of those scenes that are not erased and that offer personal satisfaction. The memory of a love of youth centers the story of Teo Molina's "Train crossings": "you were my youthful love that, for a reason I never understood, did not capture, did not take hold, and my beautiful illusion did not pass from my April" (p. 44). The awareness of the loss of human faculties in adulthood, such as the retention of memory, is the focus of Paqui Antón's story "Procrastinating" where the narrative voice sets herself the daily goal of "writing this down on a piece of paper and passing it to the notebook; even if it is a short sentence I will write it down" (p. 19), all to overcome the challenge "defying those ghosts that a blank piece of paper and a mute pen can turn into"" (p. 19).

The recreation of small everyday pleasures has a kind of pleasure effect, like drinking coffee every day: "It is 5.30 a.m. [...] I have been waiting almost half an hour to get up and prepare coffee. [...] I go back to bed with my precious and, for me, liquid gold between my hands, and drink it little by little lengthening the pleasure it gives me" ("The coffee at six in the morning, not one minute earlier, not one minute later," Elvira Antón, p. 15). In Victoria Ramos's story "And He Got Lost in Florence," the same drink is protagonist of the achievement of the pleasures of the protagonist who desires a change in her existence: "Saturday April 1st would be the first day of her new life. I had decided to wait for her with a coffee by the sea" (p. 59). Some satisfying actions that, from the experience of the workshop, are evidenced in the micro-story "Readings" of Patricia de la Vega: "Sometimes we wonder how the writer comes to express his ideas. And that's when we put ourselves before a blank sheet of paper". A new acquired habit that evidences the therapeutic effect of writing, as James W. Pennebaker (1997, p. 35) points out:

The act of putting words on a blank paper can be a liberating and therapeutic process. As we face the blank page, we give ourselves permission to explore our deepest thoughts, process complex emotions and shape our experience in the world.

The realization of dance, as an element of social connection, while promoting the collective sense, appears as a positive option for free time centers the story of Nuria Garrido "Hour of The Dance" (p. 35):

The moon dances contentedly waiting for its moment.
She has put on a new dress and dancing slippers.
But the jealous afternoon does not want to leave.
It scratches the hours with fingers of fire.
It does not want to see the moon dance.

A micro-story consisting of five separate sentences that acquires a style close to poetic prose to defend an activity that causes the well-being of the moon in full projection of a human activity that requires free time to carry it out. The fact of walking can also be understood as one of the daily pleasures of who sees spend life with more tranquility, as in the case of Arturo Espinosa's story "In a Park Bench" (p. 26):

Yes, every morning I would go for a long walk in the park. I liked to walk along the paths flanked by beautiful trees sheltering colorful and fragrant flowering shrubs. I would sit on a bench by the pond, where I would watch the swans and ducks sail and the golden fish jump and the frogs croak.

Until suddenly the monster of the pond emerged, grabbed me by the neck and dragged me to its shallow bottom. I held my breath as long as I could, but I drowned.

The supernatural element, the appearance of a monster, seems to break that harmony and provoke an implausible ending in which the protagonist dies. A way of calling the reader's attention and promoting, with subtle irony, the sensation that the joy of the peace of the moment lived can be broken precipitately. Similarly, "Original Monsters" by Josefina González provokes the recreation of new monsters that may represent a danger to the human species: "Look Sancho, we are surrounded. If you're afraid, pray, I plan to battle. My lord, I also see digital monsters that can kill human life" (p. 37). Along the lines of the unexpected, another of the thematic constants of the micro-stories of the anthology published with the students of the workshop is the desire for transformation and change. Thus, the short story of Paqui Antón "Reborn" offers the concretion of a metamorphosis with uncertain future:

I saw myself and I erased myself. I spoke to myself and I didn't hear myself. I looked in a closet for the most attractive outfit and I no longer liked it. Lost in the maelstrom of a different world my body is no longer my body. I am someone else. I am getting to know myself. I will tell you... (p. 18)

The desire for self-transformation involves reflection on the assumption of a passive role in the face of reality versus an active role that "when we are spectators of the lives of others, we feel safe and are critical of their actions" (Mila Belda, "The Stage Drama," p. 20). Relief comes "when we are spectators of the lives of others, we feel in a safe place and we are critical of their actions" (p. 20). We are before a kind of overcoming of the action of the passage of time that reminds us of the therapeutic effect of writing that Joan Didion pointed out in *The Year of Magical Thinking* (2005, p. 167). A tendency to propose the will to change, with the driving factor of love, which is the focus of Paqui Antón's short story "Primavera" (Spring): "Sorrows of love, winds of change arrive. Open your door and let spring come in" (p. 19). One of the factors that promotes awareness of the need to alter everyday life is the feeling of loneliness; this is how Mila Belda's story "Filling the void" is constructed:

We all know those moments when we feel lonely and to fill those voids there are those who collect things, others place pictures of family members around the house, others buy or acquire necessary or not necessary things. Others fill their emptiness with hobbies or learning or reading, others with additions. And there are those who paper the walls with books (p. 20).

In Ramón García's story "El niño isla" we know the isolation of a child who feels displaced from the world of adults: "there must be another world, but there is nothing in it for me" (p. 33). A feeling of incomprehension and separation from others that is projected through the short story. A perception of desolation that also governs Nuria Garrido's story "Lights and shadows" (p. 35) and that enhances the feeling of loneliness and isolation:

Under a lamppost I'm looking for my light.
You cast me into darkness.
I am a dark spirit begging for clarity.

A loneliness that is symbolized in the work of the undertaker, contrasted with the expired life of the flowers, an exemplification of the reality of death, in Jacinto Prieto's story "Fate" (p. 55): "In my work, very few people talk. People are crying all day, there are no tips, the only good thing is the flowers, but they are so ephemeral... said an undertaker." A story reduced to the minimum possible discourse to make understand, with the narrative force of the first person, the achievement of the reality of destiny: every life has an end. Perhaps that is why the recreation of sadness appears in several stories such as Leonor Reolid's "Identity" – "I have fallen in love with a sad man, or is he perhaps my reflection?" (p. 61) – and which is common to the two characters in "Shared Solitudes" (p. 66) by Raúl Sevilla. The scarcity of light at night, from the reflection of the stars, enhances this feeling in stories such as Manel Soler's "Towards the Sea": "A star without light sails in Gemini, the dawn limits the field of gray that goes or they come and sadly watch the olive groves at dawn." (p. 68).

Reading becomes, as we find in the text, a powerful tool to overcome the negative feeling of the narrative voice indicated in the title of the story. A remedy that even has its effect against the false decoration of books painted on the walls. Thus, Mila Belda, in "The light of a book," offers the figurative meaning of the light that a book gives off to the reader who thus escapes from reality itself: "The book is silent and immobile, it remains waiting for someone to light it, open it and read it" (p. 22). The empowerment of the adult person who flaunts his compulsive reading exclusively on digital support serves to break the prejudices that identify the older person with reading on paper and the young person with digital reading:

I love reading, in prose or verse, it doesn't matter to me. And I want the people around me to know it and say: he is a good reader, he reads everything.

The problem is that I can't stand it, I can't bear it, it makes me angry to read a book on paper, it's beyond my strength. I have long since replaced it with the e-book. And I have a large library in its memory. But as the good pedant that I am, I want people to see that I have a large library.

Solution: I have wallpapered the walls of my living room with paper printed with the spines of books that simulates being a library.

(Arturo Espinosa, “Una nueva biblioteca,” p. 26)

A recreation of reading that also focuses on Ramón García's micro-story “The Gold Mine” (p. 32) where we learn about the passion for reading continuously by a young man who begins his job as a scrap metal dealer's assistant. The act of reading and the fact of finding involuntary memories in the middle of the pages of library books is the creative basis of Dolores Ribera in “Between the Leaves”: “she smiled when she saw a beautiful hoopoe feather fall from the book she took from the shelf in the library. “She has picked up the feather and has carefully placed it in the center of the book to surprise other readers with the image of flying.” (p. 62).

The writing process is also presented as an action that becomes a challenge for the group of students in the workshop. In the micro-story by José Antonio Sánchez “The best story in the world” (p. 38) it becomes an enhancer of the escape from reality and, ironically, responsible for the protagonist's own madness:

I got into a creative writing workshop, with the ambition of writing the best story in the world.

I emptied myself. In the process I lost my friends and family. I reached the brink of madness looking for characters and situations never seen before, and yet, in the workshop my writings were kindly described as “logical” and “sensible.”

I couldn't have been offended in a worse way.

As a kind of hologram of the experience lived by this student body, with a dose of irony enhanced in the denouement of the micro-story, we find the story “Literary Bird” by Leonor Reolid: “The narrative teacher so elevated the creative spirit of his students who when he took flight (through the window) all followed him.” (p. 61). In general, the creative experience in the workshop offers texts that positively gloss the activity for the group of students, as we read in Dolores Ribera's micro-story “Stories”: “Surprises in books bring joy, even if they are sad. In stories, surprises are essential; even more so in good stories.” (p. 62).

CONCLUSION

From the analysis of the anthology of micro-stories written by the students of the narrative writing workshop, we have been able to observe how various elements of the stories show the generational group to which they belong. A concretion of themes that, unconsciously, having promoted the free creation of the plot, have been developed according to the style of each of the authors. Aspects such as the uncertainty of the continuity of life in the face of the unstoppable nature of the passage of time and the coming of the end of days, together with the memories of childhood as a lost space full of happiness, build sincere and direct stories that, beyond the option of some for the surprise effect, are intended to be a mosaic of memories and experiences that become more evident in adulthood. The approach to loneliness is also a recurring element and the desire to break with that feeling. The implementation of collective activities, such as the writing workshop itself, becomes a factor in overcoming this tendency of the elderly.

In view the evidence also of the progressive loss of faculties such as memory, several stories are constructed that represent a clear defense of the small daily pleasures that replace the possible shortcomings of the current moment. Thus, the contemplation of nature, the recreation of journeys or the habit of having a coffee become moments of shelter and fight against possible age discrimination. A fight against ageism that, beyond the creation of a workshop of these characteristics, more than permeates the stories told. The very fact of literary writing, as we have seen in several stories, becomes a plot motif, as a new tool for overcoming everyday life. The defense of reading as an individual act that also allows evasion also appears as an effective tool against feelings contrary to happiness in this group.

In short, we observed in our analysis, after the contextual reflection of the activities carried out and the bibliographical references on the subject, that the fact of writing short stories, which require an effective condensation of the stories that are to be told, is becomes an important element in age discrimination. Creative writing becomes a powerful way to challenge stereotypes, while reflecting one's own reality, and promote inclusion and empathy. Based on teaching experience, despite considering the different theoretical reflections included in this study, we can conclude with this list of recommendations that we can use in successive editions of this workshop:

- Challenge stereotypes: addressing the stereotypes associated with ageism and show older characters as complex and multifaceted people, with unique desires, challenges and hopes.

- Create diverse characters: include protagonists of different ages in stories that show their skills, experiences and contributions in a positive and realistic way.
- Encourage diversity: highlight the different life experiences and achievements of people of all ages, presenting how each stage of life has its own value and dignity.
- Explore relevant topics: address issues related to the passage of time, aging and possible age discrimination, such as social exclusion, retirement, reduction of physical activities and health care.
- Encourage reflection: encourage readers to reflect on their own prejudices about age, while questioning negative perceptions and promoting open and respectful dialogue on the subject. The realization of a final surprise in the micro-stories that addresses the incoherence of age assumptions can be a valid tool to attract the attention of the recipient of the text.
- Promote empathy: It is necessary to write from the perspective of people of different ages to foster understanding and empathy between generations.

Writing stories that challenge ageism can undoubtedly contribute to creating a more inclusive and compassionate narrative about aging and the diversity of experiences at all stages of life. This is the challenge that we set ourselves for future teaching experiences in the field and that can clearly reinforce the therapeutic sense of this initiative. We understand, therefore, that it is appropriate not to limit the topic in the creative writing workshop, as Natalie Goldberg pointed out in *Writing Down the Bones: Freeing the Writer Within* (1986, 25). Expressive freedom has provoked the drive and development of stories that, beyond portraying a specific generational group, have conveyed various situations of normalcy that contrast against various prejudices that constitute age discrimination. A confirmation of the therapeutic effect of creative writing in line with the recommendations outlined by James W. Pennebaker in *Opening Up: The Healing Power of Expressing Emotions* (1997, p. 213). In the case of our teaching and research experience, based on the stories created, we have seen how free writing in short texts has favored the processing of emotional experiences based on personal experiences or from personal imagination that has enhanced the understanding of oneself and its corresponding acceptance.

REFERENCES

AADD (2023). *Microrrelatos. El racó de l'escriptura.* AADD. [https://rua.ua.es/dspace/bitstream/10045/139266/1/Microrrelatos.pdf]

Andres-Suarés, I. (2010). *El microrrelato español. Una estética de la elipsis.* Menoscuarto.

Andres-Suárez, I. (2012). *Antología del microrrelato español (1906-2011). El cuarto género narrativo.* Madrid: Cátedra, 2017.

Arlés, E. Patricia (2009). *Por favor, sea breve 2.* Madrid: Páginas de Espuma.

Aub, M. (1991). *Crímenes ejemplares.* Calambur.

Borges, J. L. (1981). *La cifra.* Emecé.

Butler, R. N. (1969). Age-ism: Another form of bigotry. [https://doi.org/10.1093/geront/9.4_Part_1.243]. *The Gerontologist*, 9(4), 243–246. 10.1093/geront/9.4_Part_1.2435366225

Charness, N., Boot, W. R., Graesser, A. C., Sweller, J., & Salthouse, T. A. (2017). Ten challenges for making automation a "team player" in joint human-agent activity. *Theoretical Issues in Ergonomics Science*, 18(5), 489–508.

Cortázar, J. (1979). *Un tal Lucas.* Sudamericana.

Delafosse, É. (2013). Internet y el microrrelato español contemporáneo. *Letral*, 11, 70–82.

Didion, J. (2005). El año del pensamiento mágico. Barcelona: Random House, 2015.

Díez, M. Luis (2001). *Los males menores. Microrrelatos.* Madrid: Austral.

Espinós, J. (2000). *Literatura creativa.* Bullent.

Gaggioli, A., Morganti, L., Bonfiglio, S., Scaratti, Ch., Cipresso, P., Serino, S., & Riva, G. (2014). Intergenerational group reminiscence: A potentially effective intervention to enhance elderly psychosocial wellbeing and to improve children's perception of aging. *Educational Gerontology*, 40(7), 486–498. 10.1080/03601277.2013.844042

Gobbo, M. (2015). *Mini.* Vela al Viento Ediciones Patagónicas.

Goldberg, N. (1986). Writing Down the Bones: Freeing the Writer Within. Colorado (EEUU): Shambhala Publications.

Grau, I. (2001). *L'arquitectura del conte.* Octaedro – Accent.

Jodorowsky, A. (1995). *Sombras al mediodía*. Dolmén Ediciones.

Lamott, A. (1994). Bird by Bird: Some Instructions on Writing and Life. New York (EEUU): Pantheon Books.

Lara, O. (2012). *Voces de Portacaliu*. Ediciones La Cabra.

Mcadams. Dan P. (2018). Narrative identity: what is it? What does it do? How do you measure it? *Imagination, cognition and personality: consciousness in theory, research, and clinical practice, 37*(3), 359–372. .10.1177/0276236618756704

Merino, J. M. (2007). *Variaciones sobre el microrrelato*. Menoscuarto.

Monterroso, A. (1959). *Obras completas (y otros cuentos)*. Alianza Editorial.

Palmore, E. (1999). *Ageism: Negative and positive*. New York (EEUU): Springer Publishing Company.

Pennebaker, J. W. (1997). Opening Up: The Healing Power of Expressing Emotions. New York (EEUU): Guilford Press.

Roas, D. (2008). El microrrelato y la teoría de los géneros. *La era de la brevedad, el microrrelato hispánico: Actas del IV Congreso Internacional de Minificción, Universidad de Neuchâtel, 6-8 de noviembre de 2006*. Palencia: Menoscuarto Ediciones.

Simó, Isabel-Clara (2022). *L'inesperat i altres contes*. Alzira: Bromera.

Smyth, J. M. (1998). Written emotional expression: Effect sizes, outcome types, and moderating variables. [https://doi.org/10.1037/0022-006X.66.1.174]. *Journal of Consulting and Clinical Psychology*, 66(1), 174–184. 10.1037/0022-006X.66.1.1749489272

ENDNOTES

1 Link: https://web.ua.es/en/upua/studies/programme-description.html

2 Likewise, Erdman, in Ageism: Negative and positive (1999), stresses the need to raise awareness of ageism and promote a culture of respect and appreciation of all age groups, so as to build a more inclusive and equal society for people of all generations.

3 Link: https://rua.ua.es/dspace/bitstream/10045/139266/1/Microrrelatos.pdf

4 For an overview of how the subgenre has developed in today's technological world, see Emilie Delafosse's article "Internet y el microrrelato español contemporáneo" (2013).

5 This refers to an article by Neil Charness *et al.* "Ten challenges for making automation a team player in joint human-agent activity" (2017, pp. 489-508).

6 This refers to the general models of the structure of stories discussed in the relevant chapters of studies by Joaquim Espinós, *Literatura del conte* ("Literature of stories," 2000), or Isidre Grau, *L'arquitectura del conte* ("The architecture of stories," 2001).

7 With regard to the potential repercussions of the author's gender identity, see David Roas's article "El microrrelato y la teoría de los géneros" ("Micro-stories and gender theory," 2008, pp. 47-76), even if no differences by gender and age are established.

8 As stated in the source cited above, their names are: Elvira Antón, Paqui Antón, Mila Belda, Patricia de la Vega, Arturo Espinosa, Miguel García, Ramón García, Nuria Garrido, Josefina González, José A. Latorre, Rafaela Lillo, Teo Molina, Mar Muñoz, Ana Pascual, Ferran Pastor, Jacinto Prieto, Victoria Ramos, Leonor Reolid, Dolores Ribera, Raúl Sevila, Manel Soler, Beatriz Suárez and Rubén Vargas [https://rua.ua.es/dspace/bitstream/10045/139266/1/Microrrelatos.pdf].

9 *Microrrelatos. El rincón de la escritura: [*https://rua.ua.es/dspace/bitstream/10045/139266/1/Microrrelatos.pdf]

Chapter 13
An Oncology Patient's Reading:
Between Evasion and Knowledge

Flavia Amar
Universidad de Cádiz, Spain

Víctor Amar
https://orcid.org/0000-0001-9036-2651
Universidad de Cádiz, Spain

ABSTRACT

INTRODUCTION

Reading is, in the case we are going to show, not just running your eyes up and down a written or printed text with the intention of understanding it. Perhaps we seek enjoyment, evasion, training, or information. Others demand something more, because in reading they want to learn to understand or forget, to know more as personal satisfaction or with the desire to share. However, reading could also be about seeking enjoyment, finding the conjunction between evasion and knowledge. Barthes (1994, p. 38) defines reading as "making our body work". Something that is complemented by the action or the effect of evading, presenting a path to or from. In the same way, knowledge goes beyond the meaning that links it to knowing as discovery, as it becomes a path towards truth. The first verb, evade, serves for wandering through the magic of writing; in the second, discover, it is a need that, in many people, is treasured despite presenting them with a harsh reality. It is not fiction, it is the search for truth. Reading protects as well as brings out the need to discern, as it possesses powers (Cordón & Muñoz, 2023); thus, how we read and comprehension

DOI: 10.4018/979-8-3693-4244-2.ch013

skills have been diversified, with a book on paper or in digital format, acquired in a bookstore, in a library or on the Internet. With a contemporaneous result similar to transmedia reading "a type of inclusive, multimodal, diverse reading of all types of texts–written, visual, audio, fun–and supports, which in turn mixes and hybridises with the reader's production or prosumption practices" (Albarello, 2019, p. 166).

In the other possible area of this chapter, a sphere of interactions is shared, as an actor, which is presented in a quadripartite melting pot. That is, a) the one comprising literature itself and the act of reading; b) the reader with her need to delve into the story or the scientific text; c) the illness that would justify the two previous actions; and d) the therapeutic search of reading. Let us consider: a) literature is a result that aims to embellish her daily life, with the perspective that we want to share with the reader, as a long illness coexists with the participant of this narrative research. Where delving into the printed word immerses them in the refuge that is needed in the face of a lacerating reality. It is not that the pain disappears, however, it is diluted between the verb that makes the story acquire a routine-breaking dimension and, at the same time, presents itself as the prescribed medicine in the form of, for example, a novel. Fiction, in the case at hand, is not stranger than reality. However, whoever reads becomes submerged in the pertinent sleeping pill that allows them to wander between the letters, to flee in the arms of the protagonist. Here, the dosage is on demand and no contraindications or risk of abuse appear in the imaginary leaflet.

> *"At this point, it is unquestionable that the notion of fiction–in its various manifestations–has become part of the intellectual horizon of the last decades of the twentieth century and the beginning of the twenty-first century and is currently the object of study of several disciplines: Philosophy, Linguistics, Sociology, Neurology, Psychology, Anthropology, Evolutionism, Literary Theory, etc. This interest has undoubtedly been reinforced by some characteristic features or tendencies of the time in which we live, such as the crisis of the subject, the indistinction of boundaries between reality and fiction, the increasing virtualisation of the world as a result of the boom in communication technologies (especially the Internet), scepticism regarding the capacity of language to reflect the world, the influx of currents such as deconstruction, etc." (Garrido, 2011, p. 9).*

We interpret the reader and her need to read as a main clause with two subordinates. In other words, we already know the main clause as the participant in the research is an oncology patient. Subordinate clauses, on the other hand, are dependent and require additional information to make sense and subscribe to the fundamental idea. Therefore, the patient reads fiction or scientific literature related to her disease. In the first option, she obtains enjoyment, to get away from the routine; to know that it is possible to embark and leave behind that horizon of illness. However, likewise, the participant is required to read about her life situation, her prognosis, in order to know more or to share with others. In the first case, she sought to navigate; in the second, what she does not want is to be shipwrecked. For this reason, she subscribes to prestigious medical journals and has access to the best oncology databases. Nevertheless, the etymology of the sentence is anchored in the Latin "*oratio, -ōnis*" which we translate as discourse. And what she needs is to find that discourse that shows her the way, be it that of fiction or that of medical scientific literature.

"the so-called digital databases in which information is stored. Then, the problem of being able to consult scientifically reliable information is reduced to knowing and accessing the appropriate academic database, related to the research topic; But what is an academic or scientific database? Which are the most used academic databases? What characteristics differentiate them as a relevant factor for the research process? How are they structured? How do you access a database?" (Espinoza, 2019, p. 33).

The disease we have named becomes a nightmare. The *literato* would face it as an anti-hero, far from the Aristotelian behaviours of nobility or goodness necessary to establish them as an actor to be followed. Its wickedness seeps through the intent of the writing and the desire to read fades away. But in this case, it is real; it is seated in front of the protagonist of our narrative, it works as a concave mirror that deforms the gaze. It is not properly written, or even pleasantly described. The disease is a bad adjuvant that makes the story uncomfortable, invalidating it. But boldness makes one read and seek the possibility of disinhibition, like internal impulses that reach beyond the demands of the real or the conventional. And, in the reading chair, the other option fulfils the intention of knowing. She cannot remain in longing; she wants to find the answers. She turns to the scientific literature as an oracle that could explain it to her but, probably, not convince her. In it, an explanation of the inexplicable is sought and it becomes an experience of defiance of the myth, as from the incomprehension of what has happened and the need to understand it logically, this literature sometimes becomes both wonderful and spurious. The need to know, at times, becomes something to be forgotten. From the first literature, it could be acknowledged that it is pleasurable; while the patient in the second draws results and conclusions, yet overexposure can produce important reactions that are potentially serious for her emotional state.

"The question is to choose between the intoxicating consolation of art and of our ghosts and the restlessness of science. In other words, how should we live, in drunkenness or in knowledge? The ideal would be, by all accounts, to be able to enjoy both, drunkenness for leisure and science for knowledge. However, semi-culture

only leads to frustration: it gives us a state of semi-intoxication without teaching us anything. Due to this, it satisfies no one. (...).

Semi-culture is worse than ignorance because it deceives us. Its deception makes it possible to have us bound hand and foot, subjugated by chimaeras.

Semi-culture, in effect, is the illusion of knowing" (Rossellini, 1979, p. 113-116).

The therapeutic quest of reading acquires its own dimension due to the value it acquires and develops in the participant's need to read. That is, it possesses a personal sphere of well-being that is experienced in two moments. The reader approaches the immense window of reading, either for enjoyment or to satisfy the need to know. Pleasure is established in two ways, the first as a gift in the form of the written word that encourages getting away from the perverse reality and the second as a solace that alleviates the uncertainties of coexisting with the ailment. There are two ways of obtaining well-being: from amusement and in relation to the satisfaction that derives from knowing, which we assimilate to the concept of understanding based on the lucidity of the one who wants to know. Reading for pleasure derives from the need to achieve satisfaction in reading; however, reading to know promotes the urgency of responding to a dissatisfaction that could only be quelled by the action of enquiring. The former has an immediate result, in the latter, alacrity requires detachment from the imminent since it requires a different effort than delightful reading, inspired by reflection and analysis, understanding and discernment. A dialectical event (Luri, 2019) that arises from previous knowledge and continues with the need to know more; sometimes with inconclusive and unsatisfactory results (Adorno, 2005).

"Well, the most obvious definition comes from the very etymology of the word bibliotherapy, which would be "therapy or treatment through books." That is, as a first approximation, bibliotherapy consists in providing emotional support to an individual through reading and books. But expanding on this concept, for me bibliotherapy is a process of interaction with books and, by extension, with other texts that house a convening content, which allows a person to recreate and find in them content that affords meaning to their life or that works as mechanisms to heal psychic aspects" (Losada, 2020, p. 214).

Within this theoretical framework, presented as an introduction, lies the focus of this research: knowing and understanding reading modes manifested by an oncological patient. To this end, we establish five research questions based on the statements of:

What does reading mean at this time in your life?

What is the participant looking for in reading?

How many reading modes do you contemplate?

What role does the Internet play in this process?
How do you get answers to your demands as a reader and a patient?

METHODOLOGY

General

In the methodological area, it would be worth alluding to narrative as the path that has been traced to know and understand the feelings and modes of action of this reader patient. Likewise, the concept of participant is chosen rather than that of investigated or informant. In this sense, participating refers to a person who takes part in the research, since their story belongs to them and they desire to share it. On the other hand, rather than receiving a part, they intend to make their appreciation, their sensitivity, and their experience understood. However, the principle on which we base this methodological intention is "because if these subjects modify their vision of society based on reflection on their own lives, they are creating conditions to transform the world" (Rivas, 2009: p. 29). Likewise, it becomes feasible to "recognise the bonds we share as human beings" (Ettling, 1998, p. 177). In addition, the narrative nourishes the personal discourse, as it offers the participant's point of view and focuses on the "biographical details as narrated by those who live them" (Chase, 2015, p. 59). However, the option of telling it in the first person acquires a prominent value, for two reasons: a) the dimension acquired by the voice shared with the participant and b) the fact that the research is inspired by the strictest "respect for others" (Denzin, 2008, p. 189). Clearly, the choice of narrative methodology is inspired by Connelly and Clandinin (1995, p. 11) concerning the fact that:

"The main reason for the use of narrative in educational research is that human beings are story-telling organisms, organisms that, individually and socially, live related lives. The study of narrative, therefore, is the study of the way we human beings experience the world."

Phases and Procedure

A phase is understood as each of the different moments in which the research is going to be configured, as well as seeing the structural appearance with which the intentions of this work are to be understood. For this reason, we follow Silverman (2000), who is inclined to establish four successive moments that intertwine and give meaning to the research work: A) Formulation of the theoretical meaning of the research, even using other related works, with the aim of demonstrating an introductory framework and previous knowledge on which to build a solid and coherent discourse. B) Research design inspired by the research objectives and questions, as well as bearing in mind the selection of the participant; which makes it possible to approach the design of the interview, its administration, and its return after the transcription. C) This item focuses on the analysis of the results, being structured around various thematic cores, which organise and give meaning to the structure and analysis of the interview. D) Finally, the drafting of the research report is established; answering the reason for the research according to the research objectives and questions, as well as assessing the procedure and concluding the study.

In other areas and concerning the procedure, it should be noted that the results are organised based on various cores of meanings or themes, instead of the usual categories. These cores agglutinate and encourage "states of reflection and awareness about lived experiences" (Landín & Sánchez, 2019, p. 229). The value that the establishment of thematic cores acquires in the procedure is based on that stated by Misischia (2020, p. 72) as the aim is to "recover the meanings that emerge in them"; augmented with their pertinent analysis.

Informant, Technique, and Instrument

Selecting a specific participant gives the researcher and the procedure a purpose: the choice of that person who will make them opt for a specific preference, which will establish and set a path of sensitivity and militancy with respect to the object of study. In this case, the participant is a person with higher education who was a university professor. Currently, she is not working due to illness, but she has not lost the need to continue to know more about the contents of life and her ailment. She has access to databases of the most prestigious universities, as well as consulting manuals and specialised documents. For this reason, she is an extremely demanding person, who goes after the consultation of that data or medical report. However, the selection of this participant is also inspired by the degree of generosity in sharing her concerns at such a delicate moment in her life, as well as the accessibility and proximity to the field (McMillan and Schumacher, 2005).

As regards the technique and the instrument, it could be said that the semi-structured interview has been chosen given the value acquired by conversing based on the centres of interest that emanate from the participant herself and the course of the interview. Emphasis is placed on the previous preparation, the situation of the participant, and the approach to the subject. At the same time, a non-directive interviewer role is established, which, according to Sanjuán (2019, p. 13):

"As unmistakably qualitative interviews, the researcher establishes a strategy in which they allow the spontaneous flow of the conversation and respect the subject's discourse while being able to steer the conversation towards the topics of interest.

These are usually unstructured or semi-structured interviews, aimed at dealing with the topics in depth and supported by a loose script, which allows access to a wide variety and volume of information."

The instrument is the interview script, previously reviewed and commented on by three university professors, for improvement. The purpose is to understand the moment and issues that she presents and, equally, to attend to the nuances that derive from her exposition of something that she has lived or experienced as a reader and a cancer patient. An interview model inspired by the flexibility and openness of the interview, which arises from being able to rephrase the question with the possibility of reconsidering a particular issue or asking for it to be more carefully evaluated (Kvale, 2011).

Subjectivity and Code of Ethics

Subjectivity is conditioned as an essential factor in narrative research. In a way, Bolívar (2002, p. 4) likens it to "a necessary condition of social knowledge. (...). The play of subjectivities, in a dialogic process, becomes a privileged way of constructing knowledge." In addition to subjectivity being that which belongs to the participant, in:

"constituent social subjectivity, the subject should be observed as a process that can be specified, as far as its contents are concerned, in different snippets of observation; in other words, according to different parameters, so that the observation cannot be exhausted in a single moment, (...). Rather, it should be considered that it can recognise different planes to manifest itself, such as those of everyday life that are seen in the situation of life and work; or, the planes in which the memory-utopia relationship and the system of needs itself are manifested" (Zemelman, 2010, p. 3).

In the framework of qualitative research, ethical codes are extremely relevant based on the relationship and, sometimes, the close complicity that is established between participant and researcher. In this sense, Rivas *et. al.* (2021, p. 141) points out that "The ethical implications of this form of research are important since both investigated subjects and researchers are exposed as they put into play their lives, their trajectories, their particular voices, ... in short, their subjectivity." That is why the ethical code considered is anchored to three guidelines: a) those inspired by Denzin (2008, p. 189) by which emphasis is placed on "knowing how to listen", as well as on "caution"; b) the perspectives highlighted by Roth and Unger (2018) on anonymity and respect for the words of the participant; and, finally, c) what emerges from the BERA text (2019, p. 19) in terms of "being open and honest with the participants".

RESULTS

Thematic Core One: Reading

(Order of interview: first day. Date: 26 March 2024. Type: Semi-structured. Nuance: Focused: -Reading-. Place: Teacher's office. Duration: 15 minutes)

"For me, reading is an approach to information, to knowledge, to the intention of knowing more. But I also seek the pleasure of reading, of the narrative. Having said that, I'd like to differentiate two moments in my reading. One in which I read looking for information or knowledge and, another in which I need to be more relaxed and, therefore, I read novels or something that entertains me, amuses me, or makes me think of other times in history; that's why I like historical novels. However, since I've been an oncology patient, I haven't stopped reading; nonetheless, I've experienced several levels of approach to literature; I have never shied away from reading."

(Analysis). Reading is more than a pleasure, for the participant it forms part of her daily life. It is a way of evading but, equally, encountering reality, without avoiding it but with the intention of knowing it. This reveals that there are two modes in their reading practice, one more playful and the other more focused on the search for knowledge. Both provide answers to her demands, whether for entertainment or reality at a particular time in their life. All in all, reading is a sphere to grab onto, to refloat oneself from the soul or through knowledge.

Thematic Core Two: Reading Modes

(Order of interview: first day. Date: 26 March 2024. Type: Semi-structured. Nuance: Focused: -Modes-. Place: Teacher's office. Duration: 15 minutes)

"At first, and after the first diagnosis, I was looking for scientific or pseudoscientific information or scientific Google in which I could figure out or find what I wanted to hear as an oncology patient. That is, I read newspaper articles and, at the same time, I began to consult scientific portals, with the desire to have a deeper knowledge. And I began to differentiate which documents were pseudoscience, popular, or rigorous. That's how I started to lean towards medical portals: the Spanish Society of Medical Oncology, and the International Society of Medical Oncology. However, at that time, I was looking for information that was not too complex, because I wanted to know the prognosis of the disease and, I found, that it differed from what I wanted to hear; which is why I started to do some more research. Then, when I had the relapses, I started to filter that information more and

I leaned towards fully scientific portals and I started to sign up for very specific portals as an oncology patient."

(Analysis). The steps in the reading modes are based on the participant's own needs to relate to the disease. Searching is not the same as finding. And a first diagnosis is not the same as a relapse. The complications in her disease are paralleled by the complexity and demands of searching and finding. For this reason, the search factor is a requirement that is enriched by filtering and consulting scientific or oncologic portals, overcoming the stage of generic searches.

Thematic Core Three: Quality of Reading

(Order of interview: first day. Date: 26 March 2024. Type: Semi-structured. Nuance: Focused: -Quality-. Place: Teacher's office. Duration: 15 minutes)

"Not only did I become selective, but I read daily. And I refined my reading material because now I'm in a quality phase where I read about clinical trials, and I look for the relevant information that's being performed nationally or internationally. I seek research results and conclusions; however, always from an ignorant stance because I'm not a doctor, but I'm driven by the desire to know, to obtain answers as an oncology patient. Also, for some time now, I've been very interested in reading books about the experiences of other people who have gone through cancer, or books by scholars to know their results or opinions. I like to know their narratives, their life stories, or their experiences of overcoming even if, sometimes, they don't have a happy ending. However, I'm interested in their process, how they overcame those obstacles that appeared throughout the disease; in short, how they have experienced it and how they told it".

(Analysis). A step in the quantity and the quality of the search. With a concern of the participant: quality. Nevertheless, there is a tendency: to obtain results and conclusions from the studies. However, there is a challenge: to obtain answers through narratives or experiences of overcoming. Altogether, she retains the desire to know more and thus encounters the necessary quality of the process and the results. However, she does not lose lucidity, that she is not a specialist in medicine, but is persistent, persevering, and stubborn.

Thematic Core Four: Interpreting the Reading

(Order of interview: first day. Date: 26 March 2024. Type: Semi-structured. Nuance: Focused: -Interpreting-. Place: Teacher's office. Duration: 15 minutes)

"At first it was more difficult for me and what I did was look for the information that I lacked or didn't understand. Also, I asked my brother a lot, who is a doctor. But I do take advantage when I go to the oncology clinic to ask about the data that appear in my reports or that I've been able to read and don't know what it refers to, whether it's the type of cancer, liquid biopsies and what they have to do with the disease, how a certain study is interpreted, or what the treatments that emerge are like as current treatments are very different from those around when I started. Therefore, I ask, I search, and in this way, I keep on reading. Of course, there are data that I don't understand or that escape me, so what do I do? Well, I read the objectives or intentions of the research in depth and, then, the conclusions they reach. My reading is mainly focused on metastatic breast cancer. I need to be careful because the information is very extensive due to the number of cancers that exist, whether lung, prostate, ovarian, etc., and they have treatments that combine with those of breast cancers or are similar. That's where I concentrate, on the lines of treatment that are in the experimental phase that, later, could be tested in breast cancer. What I do is filter the information but, of course, as someone ignorant of medicine, since what I am is an oncology patient."

(Analysis). We are facing a long and difficult process. Coming face to face with medical reality must be a shocking event. Especially when one does not always have the training to understand everything. The feeling of knowing is diluted by the need to find the truth through interpretation, which is sometimes biased. Without forgetting a concept that will do her a world of good: knowing that you are ignorant of medicine, and, still recognising that there is a lot of information, where quantity and quality come together. Undoubtedly, asking is wise, and so is acknowledging one's own ignorance.

Thematic Core Five: The Benefit of Ignorance

(Order of interview: first day. Date: 26 March 2024. Type: Semi-structured. Nuance: Focused: -Benefit-. Place: Teacher's office. Duration: 15 minutes)

"There are times when being ignorant of medicine helps me because it makes me want to continue investigating and obtaining answers. However, so that ignorance is not a burden, I look for solutions. For this reason, there are specific portals on metastatic cancers that conduct in-depth interviews, for example, with professionals who explain everything very clearly and, sometimes, it helps me to read that there are treatments that are working, to know a certain line that's being started, and its results, or to know that they are working on the quality of life of patients. Nevertheless, sometimes, the news is not so positive and I try to accept it because

it's clear that anything can happen. From a fatal outcome to people getting better with these treatments, surviving and with quality of life."

(Analysis). Ignorance is more than just being an ignoramus or a lack of knowledge. In this case, it is the challenge to know more. It is the desire to shatter it. It is establishing strategies for enquiry. It is looking for explanations or the clarity that is needed to be able to live (survive) with the disease. It is what incentivises the search for answers. Of course, for the participant, who seeks understanding, at least, ignorance returns her to her reality or lucidity and her limitations. Ignorance, here and now, is not synonymous with a lack of knowledge but rather the catalyst for searching and finding.

Thematic Core Six: Asking Questions

(Order of interview: second day. Date: 27 March 2024. Type: Semi-structured. Nuance: Focused: -Asking-. Place: Teacher's office. Duration: 15 minutes)

"I ask my female oncologist a lot of questions. I say female oncologist because I've always had women doctors. In fact, with my last oncologist, who participates in many trials, studies, and research, when I know that she has returned from a conference, I ask her about the results relevant to my treatment, because I had read about it on the website of her hospital or research institute. Also, it leads me to ask myself questions about issues related to the durability of a treatment or what is expected of that treatment in a patient with characteristics like mine. So, if a study says, for instance, that the treatment lasts eight to twelve months, then I ask my doctor if it could last longer than indicated in the study. I also ask about side effects or quality of life. I try to be informed beforehand, and, in their office, I ask them about matters that concern me."

(Analysis). One of the ways to find knowledge is to ask questions. The act of enquiring is endowed with meaning. Where the synonyms for this action are grouped around qualification and the need to know. However, it is performed based on previous information and continuous questions to their oncologist; focusing their concerns, among other issues, on the durability, side effects, or quality of life of a certain line of treatment. This is asking questions to obtain wise answers.

Thematic Core Seven: The Need to Know

(Order of interview: second day. Date: 27 March 2024. Type: Semi-structured. Nuance: Focused: -Know-. Place: Teacher's office. Duration: 15 minutes)

"Whenever I read, I intend to learn something. I read for pleasure, I insist, the books I like the most are historical novels and I try to know how they lived in those times, how they solved day-to-day problems, but I'm aware that they are presented in a fictitious way. My incentive to read any text has always been with the idea of learning something; even from classical or contemporary poetry. That is, to take something with me. The same thing occurs with other books or magazine articles. And now, since I have this disease, I try to continue to learn from what I'm capable of achieving; even though I don't get everything and my way of interpreting it is also biased because I'm not a specialist. However, I try my best to understand as much as possible to understand my own process, if there are similarities with other processes. Perhaps, this comes from my scientific interest in researching, knowing, or learning. That's why I save my articles or interviews, I have folders on my computer for this and I resort to them when I need to or feel like it, and sometimes I even return to that article because I've seen something similar on another portal or I'm interested in reading it again. On occasion, I even compare the information; but, of course, with reading material supported by scientific endorsement".

(Analysis). The need to know is obtained by reading life. The need to know is achieved at the moment you want to learn something. In other words, we are talking about a profound motivation but, at the same time, the recognition of limitations as she is not a specialist, rather she is accompanied by specialists who guide her. Some reading material is scientific and some is about life experiences. Likewise, on the computer, she can organise this reading material into folders that respond to her demands. However, they are referenced by specialised portals that ensure their quality.

Thematic Core Eight: The Pleasure of Sharing

(Order of interview: second day. Date: 27 March 2024. Type: Semi-structured. Nuance: Focused: -Pleasure-. Place: Teacher's office. Duration: 15 minutes)

"And I keep all these documents, not just for myself but also to share them with other colleagues who are going through the same processes. And, based on what I or they read, we give our opinion and notify each other of news that appears on a certain portal, we even estimate the time it will take to reach our context since some of us are not receiving treatment in the same hospital as we are in different clinical trials. From this way of reading and dialoguing, I'm constantly learning or wanting to learn. Sharing is a very important thing. There are times when you share good news, and, other times, it's not so positive, but you have to know how to accept it. However, the fact that you can share it with people who are in a very similar situation to yours facilitates not having to translate things for them to understand

you. When I talk to my group, go to a conference, or read something in a forum, we all speak the same language. I don't have to explain that it's a constant struggle for me or that a particular treatment is very aggressive. I talk to them as equals."

(Analysis). The act of reading, informing and educating oneself, entails not only the result of searching and transforming oneself, but rather what they want is to project it onto their collective or circle of action. Other people are recipients of your need to share knowledge. Sharing with a group of peers, not only of doctors but mainly of people with the same characteristics, facilitates the work; they share in the need to fight, suffer, and the desire for improvement. Sharing becomes the best way to grow personally and as a group. But always with the watchword of establishing it through dialogue.

Thematic Core Nine: The Power of the Network

(Order of interview: second day. Date: 27 March 2024. Type: Semi-structured. Nuance: Focused: -Network-. Place: Teacher's office. Duration: 15 minutes)

"Forums and chats on the Internet are very important as you are constantly receiving information. For this reason, I highlight the moment of being able to share experiences, many of which are inspired by reading material. We even exchange, through social networks or the WhatsApp group, articles that may come to you from another portal or we share a link that shows the treatment you are receiving, or if there are certain therapies to improve a particular symptom. Sometimes, our conversations, which are very immediate, are directed to very specific questions about treatments, duration, treatment stage, etc. And all with bibliographic or hemerographic contributions. It is a way of enriching ourselves at all levels. In this sense, I'd like to say that I promote a lot of reading material and I believe that by doing so I help other people, and others help me."

(Analysis). The Internet is a true ally in terms of the search and transfer of information. It also makes it easier to set up discussion forums and access news or data in specialised databases or social networks. The act of providing answers is anchored to immediacy and, likewise, to answering that specific question. It is an enriching process that, according to the participant herself, through the Internet, she not only reads but also promotes reading material among her group.

Thematic Core Ten: Reading on Screens

(Order of interview: second day. Date: 27 March 2024. Type: Semi-structured. Nuance: Focused: -Screens-. Place: Teacher's office. Duration: 15 minutes)

"Even though it's enabling, we have to be careful with, what I call, Google kills. For the simple reason that you need to tune your search very finely so as not to get confused or suffer more than necessary. And the doctors tell us this, or when we go to oncology-related events, that everything that comes up on Google is worthless because, perhaps, the first things to appear are statistics that are fifteen years old and have hardly anything to do with today. You can also focus on survival, as this is what a patient usually searches for. In other words, they seek to answer the question: how long am I going to live with this type of cancer? It is presented as general information. The same specialists tell us that each patient is unique and they don't know exactly how a certain treatment will work. This type of search usually occurs until you start to be more selective and search on other more specialised portals."

(Analysis). Screens are allies, but they have their facets. They can help just as much as they can hinder. A hasty or desperate search can have the opposite effect to that desired because the information is not precisely understood. You have to refine the search, update it, and contrast it. Do not rely, exclusively, on that general information as it is not entirely accurate. The watchword is to become more selective and more specialised to avoid the risk of confusion or inappropriate answers.

Thematic Core Eleven: The Excess of Information

(Order of interview: second day. Date: 27 March 2024. Type: Semi-structured. Nuance: Focused: -Information-. Place: Teacher's office. Duration: 15 minutes)

"I have friends who are saturated with information and no longer look for anything more to read with search engines. No matter how much we send them, even if it's positive, they refuse to read. So, what I do is send them an audio explaining what I've been able to conclude from a particular reading material. It's a labour of assistance, of solidarity. But other people whom I meet, love to read, but we prefer to go to the primary sources of the study, even with the interest of getting to that specific trial and discovering, knowing first-hand, the conclusions. I even like to read the proceedings of national or international conferences to know the latest things that have been presented. In February, when Cancer Day is commemorated, the flow of information or studies at a national or international level increases, and we must be cautious, because the excess, too, can harm us. But reading, in my

case, enriches me. Perhaps, because I go to that specific and specialised source and, more or less, I know that I must select who posted it, which team carried out certain research, or the laboratory that's behind the research. Personally, this type of information through the screens makes me feel safe because I pay attention to the source of origin, they are official articles on official portals, which are filtered and are not just the result of an informative magazine."

(Analysis). We indeed sin by excess as by defect. The experience narrated by the participant, that there are colleagues who do not want to read anymore must be normal, especially when there is so much information that they can access or receive. On the other hand, easy access to information and different channels are something to celebrate, especially when they come from endorsed sources and are not merely informative contributions. The work of aid and solidarity is evident, facilitated by access to reliable sources.

Thematic Core Twelve: Audiobooks, Podcasts, and Round Tables

(Order of interview: second day. Date: 27 March 2024. Type: Semi-structured. Nuance: Focused: -Resources-. Place: Teacher's office. Duration: 15 minutes)

"I don't usually listen to audiobooks, but I listen to a lot of podcasts, especially interviews with researchers, doctors, etc. And I always like to ask myself why they asked them that particular question and not the other one that I'd ask. Now, what I love are the round tables that are periodically organised by some research groups that allow us to ask questions, sometimes live and, other times, they answer us, personally, asynchronously. They tell us who the interviewee is going to be and even who is going to answer if you ask questions. And, of course, most of the questions I ask myself or ask them arise from reading the documents I consult. In addition, everything we receive is in writing. It's a way of interacting with the doctor, the director, or the principal investigator of the research project. Another thing I'd highlight is that it's not just doctors who participate, it's also open to patients and their families; with answers through audio documents or via texts that remain active for a reasonable amount of time. Therefore, it's not a research group but rather, to us, it's a collaborative group."

(Analysis). The web diversifies the ways in which information is accessed. It is no longer just audiobooks or podcasts, but also round tables that facilitate the question and the answer. Beyond a simple interaction with doctors or specialists, it is nourished by the participation of other people in similar circumstances, in addition to their relatives. This converts it into a collaborative group, where cooperation becomes contributions, participation, or help from one to another.

Thematic Core Thirteen: Scientific Reading

(Order of interview: second day. Date: 27 March 2024. Type: Semi-structured. Nuance: Focused: -Scientific-. Place: Teacher's office. Duration: 15 minutes)

"I avoid the positivist scientific part of a study. I go to the results and conclusions. I'd be lost in the medical part because I'm not a specialist and I get lost with the methodology, the parameters, and such-and-such molecule or protein. But when they present the results, I find it more comprehensible because the information is more concise and I see it as more organised. However, where I set my focus is on the conclusions, where new lines of treatment and their characteristics or contraindications are opened. However, I also say that there are things that I don't understand, they are beyond me because they are very specific. There are sections that I have no training in, but with an effort, I can translate and understand the conclusions. Whether they refer to prognosis, tests in certain patients, quality of life, etc. What I don't read are the different phases of the study; that's where I get lost. What I consider to be important are the results and conclusions. I highlight this last section because it's where they open up avenues for other lines of research or therapies."

(Analysis). Scientific reading, after knowing her shortcomings, acquires meaning from the moment two parts are differentiated. One that she avoids, because she does not find it comprehensible or helpful because of the specificity of the data. And the other is more interesting because it focuses on the results and conclusions. Her priority is to find new lines or therapies that satisfy her need to know. And, always, with the purpose of finding answers to everything related to quality of life.

Thematic Core Fourteen: The Disease Changed Her Reading Material

(Order of interview: second day. Date: 27 March 2024. Type: Semi-structured. Nuance: Focused: -Disease-. Place: Teacher's office. Duration: 15 minutes)

"Never in my life would I have thought that I was going to read about cancer. Unfortunately, I've had family members who have suffered from it, but I hadn't read about it until it touched me. And that being active, because I receive emails as I'm registered in several portals where I verify that articles are published daily, makes me, forces me, to read continuously. Also, I have to say that I know medical per-

sonnel who have access to very specific documents and they send them to me; And, so far, I read it all. That's why I like to talk about a profound change in the mode and content of my reading material. I consulted databases, portals, institutes, etc., and always with a hunger to read and learn more. For the simple reason that some articles refer me to others and, therefore, the spiral is very large and you should have a lot of information and capacity. Now, sometimes, I find that there are documents that I can't access or are not uploaded. And, on occasion, I've gone so far as to request that document or report to read it. Yet I recognise that the information I can extract from is 10%. But it adds up because I'm understanding my process a little more and I have hope that, at some point, they will come up with something that can give us greater survival or, at least, quality of life."

(Analysis). The participant does not stop at the elementary or superfluous information. She goes to the sources, asks other people, or searches for or requests that specific document. She always wants to know and not leave gaps in her process, although she recognises that its usefulness may be little. For her, reading is a summation and is based on the desire that current and future research offer a greater degree of survival. She reads to satisfy the need to know in the present, but she also wishes for improvements in the quality of life for her and the many cancer patients in the future.

CONCLUSION

As per the objective and the research questions raised above, they have been answered with the idea of establishing some conclusions from the present research, recapitulating via the results obtained. Moving away from the final summary, the conclusions are understood as the starting point for the closure of the investigation, promoting an impression that prevails, far from being embellished, it must be considered as a section to convince the reader about the coherence, relevance, and validity of the results.

What does reading mean at this time in your life?

It is an enriching and valid act. There are two variants: a) reading for pleasure and b) scientific reading. The participant speaks of two moments, which go beyond brevity or instantaneity, as she seeks fun or evasion, in her case, by immersing herself in a historical novel. At the other end, there is reading about the knowledge of her illness, where she seeks therapeutic well-being or knowledge. By all accounts, she has never shied away from or experienced rejection of reading. Quite the opposite, in fact. And, likewise, she reads to share with her peer group.

What is the participant looking for in reading?

Let us say that it does not just provide distraction or education, depending on the reading model she chooses. She leads a group of people with whom she is fully committed to providing them with information on new advances and lines of treatment. With one search: improvement and quality of life. To do this, she uses whatever resources she can and even goes to congresses or takes part in medical initiatives (including cancer research institutes). Knowing that her knowledge of health issues is not very extensive, but to her satisfaction she reads the results and conclusions in journals or clinical trials.

How many reading modes do you contemplate?

Apparently, according to her account, there is a first stage resulting from the initial diagnosis where (pseudo) scientific information is sought in generic search engines and with a somewhat popular result. Her demands, also driven by the worsening of the disease, lead her to more demanding and specific reading material. In other words, she carries out more effective searches on specialised portals with a clear medical and oncological intention. In this way, the qualitative step of reading to obtain answers at various moments of the disease is explained.

What role does the Internet play in this process?

The Google search, from the beginning, was linked to her purposes. Then, she became more demanding and had the support of doctors who provided her with links to take part in forums or training initiatives. The singularity lies in the fact that her demands for knowledge, for knowing the latest in metastatic breast cancer issues were becoming greater and greater. Immediacy is an incentive for her demands, she would be even more distressed if it were the other way around. In addition, being able to share information online and receive it from other people is perhaps an equally therapeutic spur.

How do you get answers to your demands as a reader and a patient?

Undoubtedly, the disease changed the way she related to reading. She experienced different phases and, also, different ways to obtain answers. At first, she consulted a generic search engine or databases; Now, likewise, she leans towards the implications that are generated on the Internet or in social networks, as well as her predilection for reading the experiences of people who live or have lived through the same thing as her. This procedure is anchored on two actions: that of a very broad field of knowledge and that she is not a doctor. Her demands are met thanks to her background as a reader and the possibility of getting answers in chats or from her oncologist.

REFERENCES

Adorno, Th. (2005). *Dialéctica negativa. La jerga de la autenticidad*. Akal.

Albarello, F. (2019). Lectura transmedia, leer, escribir, conversar en el ecosistema de pantallas. *Ampersand (Oxford, UK)*.

Barthes, R. (1994). *El susurro del lenguaje. Más allá de la palabra y de la escritura*. Paidós.

BERA (Asociación Británica de Investigación Educativa). (2019). *Guía Ética para la Investigación Educativa*. BERA. https://www.bera.ac.uk/publication/guia-etica-para-la-investigacion-educativa

Bolívar, A. (2002). ¿De nobis ipsis silemus? Epistemología de la investigación biográfico-narrativa en educación. *Revista Electrónica de Investigación Educativa*, 4(1), 1–26. https://www.scielo.org.mx/pdf/redie/v4n1/v4n1a3.pdf

Chase, S. (2015). Investigación narrativa. Multiplicidad de enfoques, perspectivas y voces. En N. Denzin & Y. Lincoln (coords.). *Métodos de recolección y análisis de datos. Manual de investigación cualitativa*, (pp. 58-112). Gedisa.

Connelly, M., & Clandinin, J. (1995). Relatos de experiencia e investigación educativa. En J. Larrosa et al. (comps.). *Déjame que te cuente. Ensayos sobre narrativa y educación* (pp. 11-59). Laertes/Psicopedagogía.

Cordón, J., & Muñoz, M. (2023). *El poder de la lectura. Geografías del libro, el lector y la edición en el ensayo y la literatura*. Marcel Pons.

Denzin, N. (2008). La política y la ética de la representación pedagógica: Hacia una pedagogía de la esperanza. In McLaren, P., & Kincheloe, J. (Eds.), *Pedagogía crítica. De qué hablamos, dónde estamos* (pp. 181–200). Graó.

Espinoza, E. (2020). La búsqueda de información científica en las bases de datos académicas. *Revista Metropolitana de Ciencias Aplicadas, 3*(1), 31-35. https://remca.umet.edu.ec/index.php/REMCA/article/view/219/268

Ettling, D. (1998). Levels of listening. In W. Braud & R. Anderson (Eds.). *Transpersonal research methods for the Social Sciences* (pp. 176-179). Sage.

Garrido, A. (2011). *Narración y ficción. Literatura e invención de mundos*. Iberoamericana/Vervuert. 10.31819/9783954871049

Kvale, S. (2011). *Las entrevistas en investigación cualitativa*. Ediciones Morata.

Landín, M., & Sánchez, S. (2019). El método biográfico-narrativo. Una herramienta para la investigación educativa. *Educación (Lima)*, XXVIII(54), 227–242. 10.18800/educacion.201901.011

Losada, A. (2020). La biblioterapia como recurso terapéutico interdisciplinario. *Revista de Psicología*, 19(1), 210–221. 10.24215/2422572Xe057

Luri, G. (2019). *Sobre el arte de leer: 10 tesis sobre la educación y la lectura*. Plataforma editorial.

McMillan, J., & Schumacher, S. (2005). *Investigación educativa*. Pearson education.

Misischia, B. (2020). Formación y Narrativa. Núcleos de sentido a partir del recorrido autobiográfico. *Márgenes. Revista de Educación de la Universidad de Málaga*, 1(3), 63–77. 10.24310/mgnmar.v%vi%i.8355

Rivas, I. (2009). Narración, conocimiento y realidad. Un cambio de argumento en la investigación educativa. En I. Rivas & D. Herrera (Coords.). *Voz y educación. La narrativa como enfoque de interpretación de la realidad* (pp. 17-36) Octaedro.

Rivas, I., Prados, E., Leite, A., Pablo Cortés, P., & Márquez, J. (2021). Ética, responsabilidad y trabajo colectivo en la investigación narrativa. *New Trends in Qualitative Research*, 5, 139–151. 10.36367/ntqr.5.2021.139-151

Rossellini, R. (1979). *Un espíritu libre no debe aprender como esclavo: Escritos sobre cine y educación*. Gustavo Gili.

Roth, W., & Unger, H. (2018). Current Perspectives on Research Ethics. Qualitative Research. *Forum Qualitative Social Research*, 19(3). 10.17169/fqs-19.3.3155

Sanjuán, L. (2019). *La entrevista y la historia de vida*. Universidad Oberta de Catalunya.

Silverman, D. (2000). Doing Qualitative Research: A Practical Handbook. *Sage (Atlanta, Ga.)*.

Zemelman, H. (2010). Sujeto y subjetividad: La problemática de las alternativas como construcción posible. *Polis (Santiago)*, 27(27), 1–12. 10.4067/S0718-65682010000300016

Chapter 14
The Therapeutic Value of Reading Graphic Medicine:
Visual Narratives of Eating Disorders in Comics

María José Mompeán Mejías
University of Alicante, Spain

ABSTRACT

Traditionally, comics were undervalued and relegated to being childish and immature. This situation began to change in the 20th century, when they gradually gained more social prestige and had a place in new circles, among them medicine. This is partly because of the growth of graphic medicine, a form of bibliotherapy and an emerging area that challenges traditional methods and offers a more inclusive perspective on medicine. Consequently, comics are no longer considered as mere entertainment, but as mediums that allow a new approach to medicine and the construction of safe spaces to talk about what is never talked about. This chapter explores the ways in which comics can be used as an effective and empowering tool of therapeutic storytelling through the representation of eating disorders in comics from a cross-cultural perspective, thus contributing to the consolidation of Graphic Medicine.

DOI: 10.4018/979-8-3693-4244-2.ch014

(RE)DISCOVERING READING: WHEN MENTAL ILLNESS BECOMES ART THROUGH COMICS

In recent years, the focus has been placed on the importance of mental health, as evidenced by the numerous interventions, both at European and global level, which promote emotional well-being and mental health, such as the Sustainable Development Goals and the Comprehensive Mental Health Action Plan 2013-2030. However, mental health continues to be a major global problem. In fact, according to the World Health Organization (WHO), 970 million people globally were living with a mental disorder in 2019 (World Health Organization, 2022, p. 39). Special attention should be paid to eating disorders, from now on EDs, which is the focus of the present research.

On the one hand, there are too many people suffering from EDs. Worldwide, the number of cases has doubled in the last 18 years, as the global EDs prevalence "increased from 3.5% for 2000-2006 to 4.9% for 2007-2012 and 7-8% for the 2013-2018 period" (Galmiche et al., 2019, p. 1408). The estimated share of people living in the United States who have experienced an ED at some stage of their life is 6.0% for females (14.4 million people) and 4.07% for males (6.6 million people) (Deloitte Access Economics, 2020, p. 13). These figures are extremely worrying taking into account that EDs "are associated with the highest rates of cause-specific mortality among mental disorders" (Santomauro et al., 2021, p. 320). In fact, there are 10,200 deaths per year as a direct result of an ED, equating to 1 death every 52 minutes (Deloitte Access Economics, 2020, p. 14), data that have been further aggravated as a result of the COVID-19 pandemic, as "most individual with an eating disorder were likely to experience worsening of symptoms" (McLean et al., 2022, p. 8).

On the other hand, the fact that EDs are so common has not prevented the appearance of stigmas, false prejudices, stereotypes, and the resulting discrimination against people suffering from these illnesses, which are far more than just a weight loss and a food obsession. This has a serious impact on people suffering from these illnesses, who usually tend to stigmatize themselves, hindering their recovery process by avoiding treatment-seeking behaviors: "Stigmatization may therefore lead to self-stigma (e.g., people with EDs feeling they are responsible for their condition), which has been linked to negative emotions and reduced treatment-seeking (Brelet et al., 2021, p. 16). As it is confirmed in the scoping review of these authors, the stigma is usually associated with the existence of negative beliefs towards people suffering from anorexia nervosa, bulimia nervosa and binge eating disorder, generally perceived as being responsible for their disorder. Furthermore, people suffering from anorexia are generally perceived as childish and "as a way of garnering attention from others and considered easy to overcome" (Brelet et al., 2021, p. 14). For these reasons, it is necessary to avoid misinformation about EDs, to raise social awareness, and to face the lack of knowledge on the part of society.

It is in this context that Graphic Medicine becomes important, an emerging area that explores the intersection of the medium of comics and the discourse of healthcare and a movement that "challenges dominant methods of scholarship in healthcare, offering a more inclusive perspective of medicine, illness, disability, caregiving, and being cared for" (Czerwiec et al., 2015, p. 2). Graphic Medicine is a powerful tool for bringing scientific knowledge closer to society and making it more accessible. These stories convey to the reader rigorous information about diseases in an understandable way and the reader is able to learn about health subjects "El lector, en definitiva, se instruye sobre temas propios de las ciencias de la salud que algunos dibujantes de cómic explican con meticuloso detalle" (Mayor Serrano, 2018). As González Cabeza (2024) explains, it is a subdiscipline of the health humanities devoted to the study of the intersection between comics, which explores its visual affordances with the narrative medicine:

> *Subdisciplina de las humanidades sanitarias consagrada al estudio de la intersección del lenguaje del cómic y el discurso sanitario que combina los principios de la medicina narrativa [...] con la exploración de los sistemas visuales del cómic para estudiar la representación de síntomas clínicos tanto físicos como emocionales en este medio artístico (p. 44).*

This new approach to medicine is necessary because the modern Western health systems tend to treat the physical and purely scientific aspects of the illness, without paying attention to the more emotional side of the ill person and their relatives or caregivers. Consequently, some patients use art as a safe space to express an intimate reality that has had no place in the health systems so far (González Cabeza, 2024, p. 43).

That is why many people have found in Graphic Medicine a new way of bibliotherapy, both to share and read personal stories about different illnesses from a more realistic and empathic approach. For this reason, we consider that this informative genre, with an inclusive and empathetic approach, together with the visual systems that allow the multimodality of comics, make it the most effective way to bring medicine closer to society and to overcome the endemic stigmas about mental health eating disorders, as confirmed by McNicol who encourages the use of comics because they "have the potential to challenge the stigma associated with many types of illness" (McNicol, 2018, p. 63).

A PANORAMIC VIEW OF THE GRAPHIC MEDICINE DISCIPLINE AND WHERE CAN WE FIND IT

The medical field has recently discovered the therapeutic effects of comics as an effective form of bibliotherapy, ceasing to be considered a medium relegated to entertainment and demonstrating its potential as a health resource. This is partly because of the growth of the Graphic Medicine movement, born in 2007 in the Anglo-Saxon academic field, when its precursor Williams (2007), a comics artist and physician, created a website, called Graphic Medicine[2] to compile, register and catalog comics with medical content. Although the practice of graphic narrative for the divulgation of science is not a phenomenon of the 21st century (Mayor Serrano, 2023, p. 164), the coining of the term in 2007 by Ian Williams was crucial in the establishment of the discipline. From that moment on, there has been a take-off of works centered on comics and this movement has been joined by several academics and medical experts, such as Green and Myers (2010) who, under the name of *graphic patographies*, promoted this use of comics in the field of medicine. The consolidation of this discipline came in 2015 with the publication of the Graphic Medicine Manifesto (Czerwiec et al., 2015). According to this manifesto, Graphic Medicine is a combination of medical narratives and the multimodality of comics because it "combines the principles of narrative medicine with an exploration of the visual systems of comic art, interrogating the representation of physical and emotional signs and symptoms within the medium" (Czerwiec et al., 2015, p. 2).

The influence of this international movement arrived in Spain ten years later with some differences, with the birth of the web and collective called Medicina Gráfica[3] thanks to its precursor the doctor Mónica Lalanda (2017). Thereafter, even more scholars provided valuable contributions to the field, such as Anderson et al. (2016); Myers & Goldenberg (2018), Mayor Serrano (2012, 2013, 2016, 2019, 2021), Cobos López (2021), among others.

Healthcare comics had already been published before the birth of this movement, such as: *True Anxiety* (Porcellino, 1992), *Our Cancer Year* (Joyce & Pekar, 1994), *L'Ascension du Haut Mal* (David B., 1996), *7 Miles a Second* (Wojnarowicz & Romberger, 1996), and *Heavy Snow: My Father's Disappearance Into Alzheimer's* (Haugse, 1999), among others. The first graphic photography is considered to be *Binky Brown meets the Holy Virgin Mary* (1972), written by Justin Green, which we categorize within the mental health topic, as the fictional character Binky Brown (the author's alter ego) develops obsessive compulsive disorder (OCD) as a child. However, as already explained, it is in the first decade of the 21st century when there is a sharp increase in the interest in this discipline and when a great number of works and comics on various topics emerge, more and more of them being published to this day.

On the Graphic Medicine website, there are about 450 books reviewed, without including interviews or podcasts that discuss books nor spotlights on books which are descriptions of books or other projects, and there are over 400 books awaiting review; and on the Spanish website there are more than 200 comics reviewed. However, it is a relatively recent discipline and, although we can increasingly find more and more titles in libraries, as McNicol (2018) explains "few libraries have graphic medicine collections and the possibilities for both reading clubs and creative activities are only just starting to be explored" (p. 68). Among the libraries cited by this author (pp. 64-65) are the following[4]: Ypsilanti District Library's collection, which includes over 350 titles; the Bibliothèque de la Santé at the University of Montréal in Canada, which has a collection of over 190 titles; the Newcomb Library in the UK with a collection of over 30 graphic novels; and the Lamar Soutter Library at the University of Massachusetts Medical School in the US, which is one of the most sophisticated graphic medicine resources.

To these already mentioned, we would like to add the following collections: the Graphic Medicine Collection created in 2018 at the Countway Library of Harvard University; the Gerstein Graphic Medicine Collection at the University of Toronto; the MCPHS (Massachusetts College of Pharmacy and Health Sciences) Graphic Medicine collection; the Graphic Medicine collection of the McGoogan Health Sciences Library (University of Nebraska); the Graphic Medicine Collection at the Duke Medical Center Library & Archives; and the collection from the National Library of Medicine in Bethesda, Mayland (US).

In Spain, as it is still a more recent discipline, there are not so many collections as in other countries. However, it is beginning to emerge in some libraries, such as: the Graphic Medicine collection in the Biomedical library of the University of Zaragoza; the collection of health science comics that since 2020 has been located in the Library of the Faculty of Nursing, Physiotherapy and Podiatry of the Complutense University of Madrid; the Graphic Medicine collection at the Faculty of Nursing and Physiotherapy of the University of Salamanca; the Graphic Medicine section at the Library of Health Sciences of the University of Oviedo; and the Graphic Medicine collection of the Library of Medicine at the Autonomous University of Madrid.

Throughout this chapter, we shall prove that Graphic Medicine is a form of bibliotherapy and a breeding ground for a new approach that improves doctor-patient communication, decentralizes the perspective of modern healthcare systems, and fosters empathy, as well as the disappearance of stigmas.

BUILDING BRIDGES BETWEEN REAL AND IMAGINARY WORDS: THE THERAPEUTIC POWER OF COMICS

Graphic Medicine is a discipline deeply rooted in the field of health, but with a very marked communicative dimension. Specifically, the graphic narratives found in comics, which often connect real and imaginary words, have a powerful therapeutic effect on the writers and the readers. In this section, the therapeutic power of comics will be explored through the explanation of the main characteristics of Graphic Medicine as a form of bibliotherapy.

As it has already been mentioned, these narratives are based on a more inclusive perspective of the medical discourse. In other words, they do not only take into account the physical part of the illness, but also the psychological and emotional part of the ill person, as well as that of their relatives or caregivers, or even the emotional and psychological burden on healthcare professionals. As Ravi Kasthuri & Venkatesan (2015, p. 13) explain, these narratives challenge the monopoly of the medical knowledge by constituting a new form of knowledge based on the subjective experience of illness.

This makes comics become a means of expression of an intimate reality that does not usually have a place in the traditional medical discourse, which in turn can have therapeutic effects on both the writer and the reader. On the one hand, writing and drawing about an illness can have a cathartic effect for the sick body or mind and, therefore, can become a means of therapy for the writer: "it can help individuals in revisiting, confronting and externalizing the experience of bodily or psychological trauma" (Venkatesan & Peter, 2018, p. 114). In fact, bibliotherapy through comics as a form of self-restauration is particularly important for the writers' mental health because "they allow for expression of the self in terms of body image, verbal expression, physical action, and emotion" (Mulholland, 2004, p. 43). On the other hand, these stories also have therapeutical effects on the readers because they "create an emotional, bio-social community of individuals dealing with similar conditions of trauma" (Venkatesan & Peter, 2018, p. 114).

Healthcare comics are also an effective tool to foster empathy because apart from "visually foregrounding the illness experiences of a sick person", they also "effectuate an empathetic listener in the readers" (Ravi Kasthuri & Venkatesan, 2015, p. 16). This is explained by the fact that stories are usually told in the first person, which allows the reader to see the world through the sick person's eyes and, therefore, to empathize with them. In this sense, the reader not only "becomes a creator of meaning, but also a witness to the sufferings of the author" (Venkatesan & Peter, 2018, p. 106).

Some of these stories focus on the process and, therefore, on the author's experience with their disease from early symptoms to recovery, such as *Depresso or: How I learned To Stop Worrying And Embrace Being Bonkers* (Brick, 2010) and *My Degeneration: A Journey Through Parkinson's* (Dunlap-Shohl, 2015); others are more focused on the treatment(s) of the disease, such as *Relatively Indolent but Relentless: A Cancer Treatment Journal* (Freedman, 2014); and other stories are written as a tribute to the people, who should not be defined by their disease and are meant to, in terms of Green & Myers, universalize the illness experience, such as *Hoy No Es El Día* (Urrutia Asua, 2022). Specifically, comics about mental health are characterized by being written during the patient's recovery or remission phase and, as El Refaie (2019) explains "this is surely no coincidence, as full-blown depression would most likely dampen the creative impulse and diminish the self-discipline required to produce a graphic narrative" (p. 154).

It should be highlighted that these stories do not only foster empathy towards the sick person. They also foster the empathy that healthcare professionals develop towards their patients, a very necessary empathy aimed to improve the doctor-patient communication, taking into account that it begins to decline after the third year of medical school (Hojat et al., 2009). This empowerment of empathy has a very positive impact on mental health stigmas, since "a doctor/caregiver who approaches a patient suffering from OCD or schizophrenia with empathy alleviates the stigma associated with the illness" (Venkatesan & Saji, 2021, p. 94). Thus, the therapeutic potential of these narratives that can effectively portray actions and feelings is reaffirmed, as comics do not only inform about an illness, but intimate stories of the patient's feelings and are considered as a "reflective tool that attempts to bridge the gap between knowing about a disease and understanding the patient's experience of that disease" (Williams, 2012, p. 21).

Another defining feature of comics is the multimodality of this medium, characterized by the confluence of two semiotic modes: the textual and the visual language. On the one hand, this allows that "complex ideas can be quickly and easily digested as images or as a partnership of words and imagery" (Williams, 2012, p. 22); and, on the other hand, that the narrative force can come through different ways. As González (2017, p. 61) points out in some cases the text may have a greater weight than the image; other times it is in the image where all the narrative force lies and silence might be used, through the absence of text to create meanings; and in other cases, the meaning arises from the combination of both semiotic modes. All these possibilities of expression make the comic the best medium to relate the illness experience.

In El Refaie's terms (2012), these graphic narratives are characterized by their "performing authenticity". This means that most stories, in order to be considered as nonfiction, explicitly highlight their own authenticity. However, they also contain fictional elements, which we will call *irrealia*. In fact, one of its particularities in storytelling is to connect real and imaginary worlds, full of magic, imagination, creativity, and metaphors, allowing us to understand complex situations or processes concerning our minds and bodies in a different manner. Most of these irrealia elements are found in the visual code through symbolic scenarios and visual metaphors, represented by hyperboles, personifications and through the chromatic plane, as we should explore more deeply in the following section.

Finally, Graphic Medicine comics are also characterized, to a greater or lesser extent, by humor, a topic that has not yet been studied extensively in the field. This type of humor has a great therapeutic power for two main reasons: it helps to explain complex processes of the body with a more accessible language; and it allows to normalize situations in the daily life of the sick person, which in turn makes the person suffering from the disease feel identified and not feel guilty about situations that cannot control or prevent them from happening. This type of humor has been called by Fernando Balius and Mario Pellejer, the authors of the Spanish comic *Desmesura* (Balius & Pellejer Ruiz, 2018), "humor-salud" (health humor) to refer to that humor that sabotages all unhealthy ways of dealing with the world and makes us feel better and live life from another perspective, a therapeutic humor:

> *Hablo de otra cosa, del humor-salud. Del humor como arma en la conquista de la salud, del comentario que es una chispa que ilumina la habitación oscura o un vaso de agua fresca y cristalina que alguien te regala en medio de la sed (p. 39).*

This type of humor is also mentioned in other comics, as it is the case of the French comic *Dodue, ou comment j'ai vaincu la dictature de la minceur* (Hagimont & André, 2013), which emphasizes that laughter helps us to accept ourselves:

> *À noter que je ne suis pas médecin, je suis quelqu'un qui a décidé de s'accepter et de ne plus se forcer à maigrir pour être dans la norme et qui a fait un livre humoristique sur ce sujet. Car le rire aide à s'accepter (p. 7).*

IMAGES SPEAK LOUDER THAN WORDS: THE REPRESENTATION OF EATING DISORDERS IN COMICS AND ITS THERAPEUTIC EFFECT

This section explores the visual representation of EDs in comics from a cross-cultural perspective, as comics in English, Spanish, and French will be analyzed; and it sheds some light on how that representation can be an effective and empowering tool of therapeutic storytelling.

Our corpus is composed of a total of eleven comics, which are the following: *Ingobernable* (García Fernández, 2021), *Yo, Gorda* (Bosch Martínez, 2017), *Comiendo Con Miedo* (Karin Pavón Rymer-Rythén, 2022), *Yo También Quise Ser Como Ana y Mía: Una Historia de Superación* (Martín Curto, 2021), *Ink in Water: An Illustrated Memoir (Or, How I Kicked Anorexia's Ass and Embraced Body Positivity)* (Davis & Kettner, 2017), *Lighter Than My Shadow* (Green, 2013), *Tyranny* (Fairfield, 2009), *Lucille,* (Debeurme, 2006), *Je Prends Feu Trop Souvent* (Gosselin, 2023), *La Fille Invisible* (Villeneuve & Rocheleau, 2010), and *Dodue, ou Comment J'ai Vaincu la Dictature de la Minceur* (Hagimont & André, 2013). They are written by North American, Canadian, and European authors (four are in Spanish, three in English, and the four remaining in French), and most of them except *Lucille,* are written by female authors. This is surely no coincidence considering that EDs have more prevalence on women (Hoek, 2006). All stories are autobiographical, meaning that they deal with the author's own illness and are told from the sick person's perspective; except *Lucille* and *La fille invisible*, which are semi-fiction stories told from the sick person's and from the doctor's perspective, respectively.

The selected comics focus on three types of EDs: seven deal with anorexia nervosa, one with bulimia nervosa, another with both anorexia and bulimia nervosa, and the remaining two with anorexia nervosa and binge eating disorder. Although most of the stories are autobiographical and share many similarities, they adopt different approaches. Some stories are focused on the process of hospitalization, as in the case of *Ingobernable,* where the author narrates in the form of a personal diary the 42 days she was hospitalized in the psychiatric section of the University Clinical Hospital of Valladolid. Others focus on the process of recovery (from the beginning of the disease to the recovery), emphasizing the positive role of therapy, as it is the case for *Yo, Gorda, Comiendo Con Miedo, Yo También Quise Ser Como Ana y Mía: Una Historia de Superación, Ink in Water: An Illustrated Memoir, Lighter Than My Shadow, Tyranny,* and *Je Prends Feu Trop Souvent.* Furthermore, there are comics told both from the doctor and patient's perspective at the same time, as the Canadian comic *La fille invisible*. In this comic, two stories are told in parallel: the story of Flavia, a teenager who starts eating healthily and becomes obsessed with exercise, leading eventually to anorexia; and a journalist, who interviews a doctor specialized in EDs. Furthermore, in other stories the focus is not placed on recovery, but on the day-to-day life of the sick person, as with *Lucille,* which has a circular structure regarding recovery: Lucille, after having escaped with Arthur, at the end of the story returns home to the same exact initial situation and without having treated her anorexia. Finally, other stories take a more educational and socially critical approach, such as *Dodue, Ou Comment J'ai Vaincu la Dictature de la Minceur*, which devotes an entire chapter "La Minceaur dans L'histoire" (p. 27) to the canons of beauty throughout history and social pressure, and at the end of the book (p. 92) the author offers us her "boîte à outils anticomplexes" (anti-complex toolbox).

For the purposes of this study, an exhaustive analysis of the comics will be carried out, paying special attention to their therapeutic effect, use of color to express emotions, hyperboles, visual metaphors, and symbolic scenarios.

On the one hand, there are many symbolic scenarios, which are fictional scenarios that have not happened in real life and are often linked with the characters' imagination, to represent subjective projections of their emotional state. For instance, in the Spanish comic *Ingobernable* (p. 18) a stormy and rainy cloud appear above Adara's head to represent her sadness and anger for being hospitalized of anorexia nervosa; and in *Je Prends Feu Trop Souvent* (p. 50), a stormy sea is depicted to represent the character's emotions after self-harming. Another symbolic scenario is observed in *Yo, Gorda* (p. 136) when Meritxell, in the same way that flowers start to bloom after hibernation, feels reborn after having gone to psychological therapy, which helped her to get rid of her complexes and raise her self-esteem. This therapeutical picture could be based on Botticelli's famous painting called The Birth of Venus. In this case, the giant scallop shell on the sea on which Venus poses is replaced by a big pink daisy flower. In the same way that Botticelli's painting broke the barriers of censorship and the prejudices of the time, the author of this comic draws this image as a vindication of her having learned to love herself and overcame the canons of beauty imposed by society.

Apart from representing emotional states, symbolic scenarios are also drawn to raise awareness about EDs and to represent the obsessive thoughts of the sick characters. On the one hand, a marine scenario is depicted in *Comiendo Con Miedo* (p. 164) to spread awareness about EDs and its implications, and to make visible other problems associated with EDs that remain invisible in society. In this picture, Elisabeth metaphorically navigates across the sea of her illness and encounters both submerged obstacles in the form of fishes, and the only visible obstacle: Nore, a monster representing anorexia, at the tip of the iceberg, and above her head the following text can be read: "an ED is not a problem with food, but a problem that is reflected in food"[5]. This powerful image conveys the meaning that anorexia, a visible illness, is only the tip of the iceberg, but there are other invisible problems that go unnoticed, such as: insecurities, anxiety, low self-esteem, self-demand, and feelings of lack of control. Another example is found in *Yo También Quise Ser Como Ana y Mía: Una Historia de Superación* (p. 46), where the psychological impact of EDs on people, unable to see reality, is depicted through Ana, the monster that represents anorexia, promising Leire to turn her into a fairy tale princess. This symbolic scenario is therapeutic and powerful because it vindicates the canons of beauty and gender stereotypes imposed in traditional fairy tales: Ana turns Leire into a fairy princess, just like the Fairy Godmother does with Cinderella. On the other hand, in *Ink in Water: An Illustrated Memoir* (p. 31), Lacy loses herself in her own compulsive thoughts and goes into an endless loop, which is why in this symbolic scenario she falls into the void and sinks into a kind of sieve of thoughts. These intrusive and negative thoughts are also represented in the symbolic scenario of fire in *Je Prends Feu Trop Souvent* (p. 13), since the author draws fire around the bed in which she sleeps to represent those intrusive thoughts that consume her when in reality there is no fire in the room.

A recurring pattern in these comics is the use of hyperboles in the drawings, which represent mainly three experiences associated with these mental illnesses: the distorted perception of body image, a central element in EDs; body shaming, weather intrafamilial or self-shaming; and some symptoms and consequences of EDs perceived in the first person. On the one hand, body image distortion is depicted through unfaithful exaggerations of the dimensions of the sick person's body to represent their excessive fear of getting fat and the pseudo-perception associated with these illnesses. In order to represent how people with EDs think they are perceived by others, a distorted version of their body usually appears next to the characters when they look at themselves in the mirror. This false perception associated with EDs is very well explained in the French comic *Dodue, Ou Comment J'ai Vaincu la Dictature de la Minceur*, where the author narrates her own experience when looking herself at the mirror:

> *Regarder la vérité en face, ou se regarder dans le miroir, méthode qui consistait pour moi à me dégoûter de moi-même pour me motiver à maigrir. J'appris plus tard que je ne voyais pas mon reflet réel tellement je me haïssais (p. 65).*

On the other hand, hyperboles are also used to visually represent the power, influence and authority that certain characters have over the sick person. For instance, in *Yo, Gorda* (p. 103) the body of Meritxell's mother is drawn hyperbolically large to represent the body shaming she exerts against her daughter and makes her feel "the most pitiful and ugly being on earth" (p. 72). Other times the body shaming is not intrafamilial, but intrapersonal, as the obsessive thoughts are personified in the form of monsters that become bigger when they gain more authority over the sick person. For instance, in *Yo También Quise Ser Como Ana y Mía: Una Historia de Superación* (p. 156), Ana and Mía, monsters that represent anorexia and bulimia respectively (hence their name), are bigger and more powerful when they have complete authority over Leire. Finally, hyperboles used to capture some of the symptoms and consequences of EDs help readers understand some of the complex processes of these illnesses, something very important considering that knowledge means understanding and, therefore, empathy. In *Comiendo Con Miedo* there is an exaggerated visual representation of one of the consequences of EDs: alterations in the functioning of the gastrointestinal tract. As a survival response, the digestion and metabolism of the sick person slows down, as the body tries to maximize the utilization of nutrients and the time food spends in the stomach. For this reason, when a person is recovering from an ED, digestive symptoms such as abdominal bloating appear after eating. This process is excellently captured in *Comiendo Con Miedo* (p. 86), as the author draws a picture of a completely unchewed sandwich doing down the esophagus to the stomach and, consequently, Elisabeth has a very swollen belly and show feelings of pain, accompanying the words "adapting to the routine was easy. The hard part was eating again. Physically, since my stomach had shrunk so much that filling it with food was very painful"[6] (p. 86). Likewise, in the comic *Lighter Than My Shadow* (p. 350) binge eating disorder is represented through the drawing of a hyperbolically giant mouth inside her belly that represents the hunger she has during recurrent binge eating episodes.

Another visual technique that characterizes these narratives is the expressive use of color, since colors generally evoke feelings and, therefore, provide information about the characters' emotions. A recurring pattern in these comics is the use of black and different shades of gray to convey low moods and unbalanced emotional states of the sick people, usually experiencing difficult moments and critical episodes of their disease when this color emerges. In *Yo También Quise Ser Como Ana y Mía: Una Historia de Superación* Leire always wears a blue sweater until she begins to develop anorexia and bulimia and the sweater turns gray as a reflection of her mood, as the author explains in the comic "along with my mood also changed my way of dressing. The color black started to fill my closet and my life" (p. 34). She does not get the blue color back until Chapter 8 (p. 163), when she goes to therapy and starts recovering and feeling better. This can also be observed in *Yo, Gorda* when Meritxell, who usually dresses in a magenta color, begins to develop bulimia nervosa and compensatory behaviors through vomiting after binge eating, her hair and clothes stops being magenta and are colored in grayscale to reflect her altered psychic state. As González Cabeza (2024) explains, the use of magenta, a color traditionally associated with femininity, is not arbitrary and also has a purpose of meaning in the comic against the body shaming that Meritxell's mother does to her:

Esta decisión estilística no parece trivial, pues lo "femenino" es, precisamente, uno de los conceptos más conflictivos en la vida de Meri, cuya madre siempre le recrimina que salga a la calle sin "arreglarse" ni "maquillarse" (p. 72), con ropa de "machorra" (p. 68) o "marimacho" (p. 97), y realiza comentarios humillantes sobre su peso de forma constante (p. 76).

This expressive use of color is also found in *Comiendo Con Miedo,* when Elisabeth dyes her hair bright red when she begins to recover (p. 148), in contrast to the grayish hair she has when she experiences difficult moments with anorexia. Black color, associated with critical and difficult moments of the disease, is also found in *Je Prends Feu Trop Souvent* (p. 52), where the main character is drawn in white and grey tones, surrounded by a total black background. Although there is a total absence of text, this is a very powerful image, since this use of color represents her emotional instability, just after a self-harm crisis, which can be noticed of her thighs. However, despite the predominance of black and white drawings in this comic, there is a bit of yellow color in some strips. In the comic, this warm and bright color evokes positive feelings and is used in order to express the main character's fleeting feelings of well-being because of the joyful sun hitting her face (p. 130 and 131) and the act of sharing moments with her friends (p. 133). On some occasions, the negativity of black contrasts with the positivity of white, associated with bad and good in our Western culture respectively, as occurs in *Ink in water: An Illustrated Memoir* (p. 102) when Lacy highlights both the advantages, on a white background, and disadvantages, on a black background, of group therapy.

On the other hand, the use of color does not only evoke the characters' psychic state, but also indicates when the action occurs within the story. In *Lighter Than My Shadow* (p. 225) the color is used to differentiate the strips that occur in the past (painted with a light blue filter) from those in the present (painted in brown). Finally, in *Comiendo Con Miedo,* as González Cabeza (2024, p. 83) explains, each moment of Elisabeth's life has its own color filter:

- The present, time in which the story is told, is linked to warm colors with reddish and copper tones, reflecting positivity, emotional well-being, and the recovery of the disease.
- The past, when the disease takes place, is illustrated in cold colors with blue, gray and lilac tones that reflect the harshness of the disease, negativity, darkness, weakness, and sadness.
- Her time in the psychiatric hospital, which she calls the "white room" is illustrated entirely in white in order to express the hermetic nature of that space, far from her everyday life and its problems, including Nore, the monster that personifies her anorexia nervosa.[7]

These graphic stories are also rich in visual metaphors that convey visual depictions of illness. As Venkatesan & Saji (2021) explain, metaphors are developed through two dominant ways: "utilizing conventional patterns from the available image bank and generating new metaphors essential for conveying the singular experience of the illness" (p. 112). These means that some of the metaphors are conventionalized, being part of our image bank of metaphors; but others are more creative and innovative, drawn on the basis of the subjective experience of the ill's person, as "artists either modify/redraw existing metaphors or generate new ones that more succinctly encapsulate perspectives on their illness" (p. 112). These visual metaphors help the reader understand complex situations and processes concerning the sick person's mind, as well as their own experience and perception of the condition, thus fostering empathy.

On the one hand, one of the most known metaphors in our available image bank is the one that compares the disease with a fight. For instance, there are many references to the mental struggle of the sick person against their obsessive thoughts about food and losing weight, as in *Ingobernable* (p. 56), where the main character Aldara fights in her mind against the ghosts of her anorexia nervosa. In the epilogue of the comic *Comiendo Con Miedo* (p. 166), Elisabeth welcomes us to the "living room of her head" and she uses this metaphor when talking about recovery. She explains that each person needs different weapons, such as confidence, hope, self-love, self-knowledge, security and goals in order to "combat" eating disorders; and visually represents that her psychologist gave her the key weapon to cope with her disease. Finally, in *Yo También Quise Ser Como Ana y Mía: Una Historia de Superación* (p. 174) Leire is drawn boxing against the monsters representing her anorexia and bulimia.

Two other conventionalized metaphors can be found in *Yo También Quise Ser Como Ana y Mía: Una Historia de Superación* and are common in these narratives: the 'problems are a heavy burden' and 'the person in a hole' metaphor, which are therapeutic. On the one hand, the insecurities and problems experienced by Leire throughout her childhood are materialized in the form of a backpack that becomes heavier and heavier over time (p. 14). This metaphor is very conventionalized, and, in fact, in psychology it is known as the "emotional backpack" to refer to the weight we carry of experiences, memories, fears or worries that are not being adequately addressed. On the other hand, the 'person in a hole' metaphor is one of the core ACT (Acceptance and Commitment Therapy) intervention metaphors in the early phase therapy, hence its therapeutic power. In the comic, Leire is trying to get out of the black hole in which Ana and Mia, anorexia and bulimia respectively, had submerged her and there is a text that says "the road to recovery is not easy. To have relapses are normal, but we must not give up"[8] (p. 113).

Other conventionalized metaphors transfer a mood to a meteorological phenomenon, such as 'the rain is sadness' metaphor. Some examples can be seen in *Ingobernable* (p. 14 and p. 18), in *Lighter Than My Shadow* (p. 70), and in *Ink in Water: An Illustrated Memoir* (p. 105), where the main characters are depicted walking in the rain during difficult moments of their illness. However, in some comics rain can have a double association, and it is not only used to represent sadness, but hope, as it is the case for the latter comic, where Lacy reconsiders rain as something positive, therapeutic and hopeful: "But one thing I've learned…is that hope spreads too. Creating a positive dialogue for myself…Being a friend to myself…is like water in ink. It dilutes the bullshit and washed it away" (257).

Another recurrent metaphor in EDs comics is the disappearing body metaphor, used to refer to cachexia, a syndrome of progressive deterioration, resulting in the loss of lean body mass and body fat due to anorexia. This is captured through what El Refaie (2019) calls 'transformational metaphor', which is "the gradual transformation of one concrete entity into something different" (p. 116). For instance, in *Comiendo Con Miedo*, the author evokes metaphorical meaning by showing the gradual disappearance of the sick person's body, which turns into gunpowder (p. 47); and in *Lighter Than My Shadow*, when Katie appears, frozen with cold, walking down the street very thin and gradually disappearing in each drawing (p. 125).

On the other hand, another particularity in storytelling of these narratives is to connect real and imaginary worlds, full of magic, imagination, creativity and diverse creatures, allowing us to understand complex situations or processes concerning our minds. In these stories, the fear, obsessive thoughts and EDs are personified in the form of metaphorical monsters. In El Refaie's (2019) terms, these monsters are contextual metaphors, which are "the depiction of a concrete entity in a context where it appears in some way incongruous" (114). However, these contextual metaphors have a particularity in these narratives, as "it is quite common in graphic illness narratives for an object or creature to invite a metaphorical interpretation by appearing in some way out of place of incongruous in its context, but without it necessarily replacing a more expected, concrete item" (El Refaie, 2019, p. 96). In these comics, the monsters are an expression of the different types of EDs and obsessive thoughts, but they do not replace something else that would have been more congruous in this context. As we shall see below, the artists of these comics have found striking visual ways of representing EDs.

In *Ingobernable*, the obsessive and intrusive thoughts of anorexia are represented through ghosts around Aldara's head, while in *Tyranny,* Lesley's thoughts are materialized in the form of an omnipotent tyrant and torturing demon that strangles her with the ropes forming its body when Anna does not obey. In *Yo, Gorda* there is a great diversity of creatures representing bulimia and Meritxell's obsessive thoughts with food. On the one hand, there is a red monster shadow that follows Meritxell and represents her obsessive thoughts, complexes, insecurity, and low self-esteem (p. 88). This is also confirmed by González Cabeza, who states that her psychological condition and traumas are personified in a monstruous entity that the author draws with the main character, like an evil shadow that is projected when she tries to vomit (González Cabeza, 2024, p. 77). On the other hand, these intrusive thoughts are also personified in two dark shadows with snake teeth and tongues that appear next to the main character (p. 142). Finally, the thoughts of the compensatory behaviors of vomiting are materialized in the form of a skeleton, classic evocation of death, coming out of Meritxell's mouth (p. 111).

A recurrent pattern in these monsters is that, far from being terrifying, they are friendly at first and become frightening when they have absolute control over the sick person's mind. In *Comiendo con miedo,* the monster Nore, an expressive name formed from the word *anorexia*, is a very chatty and charming Monster who helps Elisabeth to think up plans to lose weight and who gets angry if she does not fulfil them. The author herself analyses Nore's physical appearance as follows:

Nore wears heels. And that's because the objective of these monsters is to attract you. They're friendly at first, the problem comes later when they get angry. Nore has human proportions, that is, one head, two arms, two legs. This is because it's a part of me, so I couldn't make her too inhuman. For that very reason, because it's a part of me, it's a girl, so I'm going to refer to it in feminine terms. Her bones are visible, she's very thin. That's because she doesn't depend on food to live. In fact, she doesn't depend on anything or anyone, she's totally independent, and that's why she doesn't wear clothes either. Her fingers are long and sharp because she also liked to hold me very tightly to feel me and to feel secure. Nore is very pointed and has very sharp angles. This is why she also had some very strong rules, which are written in the book she carries in her hand because, of course, that's what monsters do. They give you a manual for life, a book full of rules that tell you what to eat, what to say, what to do and basically how to live. It's much easier to think about what you can and can't eat than to tell your friend that you're upset with her, for example. These rules give you control, they give you security. And speaking of control, in color psychology, that control is symbolized by blue. Nore has a dark tone to hide in the shadows and take you with her without anyone seeing her [9] (TEDx Talks, 2022).

In *Yo También Quise Ser Como Ana y Mía: Una Historia de Superación*, the most important irrealia are two monsters called Ana and Mía, who personify her anorexia and bulimia, respectively. In this story, Leire narrates her personal experiences with both monsters, who are also charismatic and chatty, except when they get angry, which makes them terrifying and bossy.

On the other hand, there are other visual resources less conventionalized. In *Ink in Water: An Illustrated Memoir* there are black spots that represent fears. When Lacy, who suffers from anorexia nervosa, begins to have obsessive thoughts about food, black spots emerge around her head and sometimes all over her body. Finally, in *Je Prends Feu Trop Souvent*, the author uses the irrealia element of fire to represent anorexia, as she considers anorexia to be a fire that consumes her. This symbolic fire might refer to the unpredictability of her psychological condition, the difficulty of reconstructing herself, and to the marks of her body after self-harm.

Finally, it is worth highlighting the therapeutic power of these stories, both for the author and for the reader. On the one hand, these stories allow the reader to externalize their own experience with the illness, something that can be difficult to do in other traditional media which do not involve drawing. Drawing in many cases is part of the patient's recovery process in order to explore their perceptions of the disease. This becomes clear in *Comiendo con miedo* when Elisabeth, the author and the main character, tells her friend that she wanted to talk about her experience with the disease but did not know how until she found the comic format, a medium that allowed her to write and, above all, to draw (p. 9). In fact, the author reflects on the therapeutic powers of drawing, which in her experience has enabled her to understand what anorexia is (TEDx Talks, 2022)[10]:

It is incredible how many conclusions we can draw from a simple drawing. Drawing enables us to reflect, to analyze, to understand, whether it is a leaf on a tree or a mental disorder. Talking about your monsters can be very scary, making the invisible visible is not easy, but it's necessary. [...] In the almost 10 years that I was in treatment for eating disorders, I was barely able to understand or explain what anorexia was, until I started to draw it.

Externalizing the personal experience of illness is also therapeutic for the reader, who feels more hopeful and identified when reading that there are more people going through a similar situation and, therefore, understand they are not alone. For instance, in the prologue of *Ingobernable*, the author encourages readers to have hope and to "row" towards recovery (p. 8):

[...] maybe it is also my way of telling myself and telling you that this disease can be defeated. To convince myself and you that, with a lot of effort and help, it is possible to recover and live a life where food is no longer just a necessity for our body. It is hard, but there is a way back to happiness: I have walked this path myself and it is written on every page of the story. I have decided to share it in case they help other people like me – lost and dreamers – to row towards their recovery [...]. [11]

Furthermore, at the end of the comic *La fille invisible*, the author explains her reasons for writing this comic and encourages people to free themselves from the cage of their body (p. 48): "I also need to say to all those who read these lines and who are imprisoned in the cage of their body that there is a way to free themselves from it"[12]; and this is also reflected in the prologue of *Lighter Than My Shadow* where the author explains to the reader the reason for the creation of the comic and gives them hope (p. 5):

Dear Reader, you are holding the book I wish had been there for me. It exists because I wanted nobody else to feel as lost, confused and alone as I felt. I wanted to be honest about how hard recovery is, and how long it takes, at the same time proving that it is possible [...]. I hope that in sharing my experience, my choices -good and bad- that I might reach out to someone struggling on their own journey. This book is my promise that it can and does get better. To others, and to myself.

These stories also provide the reader with therapeutic tools to help them move forward and accept themselves. At the end of the comic *Dodue: Ou comment j'ai vaincu la dictature de la minceur* (p. 92), the author in collaboration with Christophe André, a psychiatrist at Sainte-Anne Hospital Center in Paris, offers the reader a gift in the form of an epilogue called 'ma boîte à outils anticomplexes' (my anti-complex toolbox). It is a pictorial manual containing what we could consider the '10 commandments for recovery', which focus on the reflection of our complexes, the acceptance and self-love for our body, and the construction of self-esteem. A very powerful picture is the one drawn in *Tyranny* (p. 64), where Anna, with the help of her psychologist, builds a pyramid with boxes that represent her therapeutic mantras, such as: "don't give up", "love of life", "accept what can't be changed; change things that can be changed", "trust your own thoughts", among others. These mantras can be therapeutic for the readers, as they transmit positivity, hope and can make the readers themselves reconsider and change behaviors of their life.

Another therapeutic power of these narratives is to help overcome misinformation and stigmas. In *La fille invisible* the doctor of the psychiatric hospital communicates with the reader through the character of the journalist, who interviews him to do a report on anorexia, and asked her to empty her mind and forget everything she knows about anorexia; and to avoid the false belief rooted in society that anorexics only have a problem with food (p. 8). Moreover, in *Yo también quise ser como Ana y Mía: Una historia de superación* Leire explains how she gradually came to accept her illness and learned to talk about it naturally without feeling ashamed and demystifying the stigmas of eating disorders. A powerful picture is found on page 172, where Leire is shouting with a megaphone "No more stigmas!". In fact, the epilogue of this comic underlines that stigmas are a serious problem for society, as they cause people suffering from these mental diseases not to externalize what is happening to them and to suffer in silence, which is why these stories are necessary:

[...] *These diseases are highly stigmatized, judged and treated as a taboo subject to be ashamed of. This makes sufferers feel alone, misunderstood and afraid to externalize what is happening to them. And they suffer in silence, lie or hide their actions from others, because these actions cover up, in reality, a suffering that is very difficult to transmit to the people around them. Without going any further, until I experienced it personally and accepted that I had an eating disorder, I thought that anorexia only affected people who wanted to lose weight and who stopped eating or vomited, or that bulimia affected people who had no control over food, binge ate and vomited when they felt guilty, not to mention other eating disorders that exist but I had no idea about them* [...] (p. 179).

This demonstrates the importance of comics for the divulgation of EDs. It is necessary to make the society aware of these mental illnesses in order to make early detections. This idea is reflected in the epilogue of *Ingobernable*, where the author and patient Aldara collaborates with Dr. Marta Saray Hernández García, who states that: "The high prevalence of this disease in our society and its health and functional impact should make us aware of the importance of identifying some clinical symptoms and signs that allow early diagnosis" [13](p. 99). Finally, these stories are also therapeutic because of their prevention strategies: they make the reader aware of the dangers of society in the development of eating disorders and educate them to have a more critical eye. For instance, in *Comiendo con miedo* the monster Nore talks to Elisabeth about the cultural forces behind the drive for thinness: *"From a young age you were raised to be careful about drugs. But were you brought up to be careful about the culture of thinness or dieting? No, we weren't taught that [...] you grew up surrounded by prompts to obsess"* (p. 143).[14]

Finally, these stories help to make the reader understand that the difficult moments of illness can be overcome. The last sentence appearing in *Je prends feu trop souvent* (p. 200) says "le feu est déjà pàssé par ici", a short but very powerful sentence acting as a hopeful testimony. In general, all these stories act as testimonials from cured patients about their experience with EDs, testimonials that are especially therapeutic and encouraging to readers who, by seeing that other people who have been in similar situations have overcome the disease, feel more hopeful.

...AND THAT'S (NOT) THE END OF THE STORY

Comics' multimodality fosters the expression of subjective experiences and emotions of an illness, which would be difficult to capture in other traditional media and which are expressed through a variety of visual resources. Our comprehensive analysis has led us to the conclusion that comics are the master art of expression of

EDs and mental health in general, and that Graphic Medicine is a potential form of bibliotherapy for different reasons.

Externalizing the feelings of the sick person through this medium is beneficial for healing both writers and readers. On the one hand, writing and drawing about an illness can have a cathartic effect for the sick mind and, therefore, can become a means of therapy for the writer. On the other hand, these stories help the reader, who suffers from EDs or knows someone close to them, understand that what happens to them also happens to other people, to identify with them and to realize they are not alone.

This medium can be particularly effective in fostering empathy, making knowledge accessible for society, allowing the expression of taboo topics of eating disorders, and demystifying stigmas deeply rooted in our society. Furthermore, it allows useful and creative visual depictions of illness that are difficult to capture in other media; and it enables the creation of safe spaces to address the disease, often with some doses of humor.

In short, comics are a powerful tool for communication, understanding and making visible the invisible. Because it is necessary to talk about your monsters in order to understand them and learn to live with them.

NOTE

This study was done at the Institut Superior d'Investigació Cooperativa IVITRA [ISIC-IVITRA] (Programa per a la Constitució i Acreditació d'Instituts Superiors d'Investigació Cooperativa d'Excel•lència de la Generalitat Valenciana, Ref. ISIC/012/042), within the following research projects and groups: MICINUN, Ref. PID2021-128381NB-I00; IEC, Ref. PRO2018-S04-MARTINES; Grup d'Investigació VIGROB-125 of the UA; and the Grup d'Investigació en Tecnologia Educativa en Història de la Cultura, Diacronia lingüística i Traducció (Universitat d'Alacant, Ref. GITE-09009-UA]).

REFERENCES

Anderson, P. F., Wescom, E., & Carlos, R. (2016). Difficult Doctors, Difficult Patients: Building Empathy. *Journal of the American College of Radiology*, 13(12), 1590–1598. 10.1016/j.jacr.2016.09.01527888946

Balius, F., & Pellejer Ruiz, M. (2018). *Desmesura*. BELLATERRA.

Bosch Martínez. (2017). *Yo, gorda*. La Cúpula.

Brelet, L., Flaudias, V., Désert, M., Guillaume, S., Llorca, P.-M., & Boirie, Y. (2021). Stigmatization toward People with Anorexia Nervosa, Bulimia Nervosa, and Binge Eating Disorder: A Scoping Review. *Nutrients*, 13(8), 2834. Advance online publication. 10.3390/nu1308283434444994

Brick. (2010). *Depression or: How I learned To Stop Worrying And Embrace Being Bonkers*. KNOCKABOUT.

Cobos López, I. (2021). La medicina gráfica como herramienta para la traducción y la adaptación de textos biosanitarios. *Mutatis Mutandis.Revista Latinoamericana de Traducción*, 14, 397–426.

Czerwiec, M., Williams, I., Merill Squier, S., Green, M. J., Kimberly Rena, M., & Smith, S. T. (2015). *Graphic Medicine Manifesto*. Pennsylvania State University Press.

David B. (1996). *L'Ascension du Haut Mal*. L'Association.

Davis, L. J., & Kettner, J. (2017). *Ink in Water: An Illustrated Memoir (Or, How I Kicked Anorexia's Ass and Embraced Body Positivity)*. New Harbinger Publications.

Debeurme, L. (2006). *Lucille*. Futuropolis.

Deloitte Access Economics. (2020). *Social and economic cost of eating disorders in the United States of America: A Report for the Strategic Training Initiative for the Prevention of Eating Disorders and the Academy for Eating Disorders*. HSPH. https://www.hsph.harvard.edu/striped/report-economic-costs-of-eating-disorders/

Dunlap-Shohl, P. (2015). *My Degeneration: A Journey Through Parkinson's*. Penn State University Press. 10.1515/9780271085791

El Refaie, E. (2019). *Visual Metaphor and Embodiment in Graphic Illness Narratives*. Oxford University Press. 10.1093/oso/9780190678173.001.0001

Fairfield, L. (2009). *Tyranny*. Tundra Books.

Freedman, M. (2014). *Relatively Indolent but Relentless: A Cancer Treatment Journal*. Seven Stories Press.

Galmiche, M., Déchelotte, P., Lambert, G., & Tavolacci, M. P. (2019). Prevalence of eating disorders over the 2000-2018 period: A systematic literature review. *The American Journal of Clinical Nutrition*, 109(5), 1402–1413. 10.1093/ajcn/nqy34231051507

García Fernández, A. (2021). *Ingobernable*. Rimpego.

González Cabeza, I. (2017). *Imágenes de la enfermedad en el cómic actual*. Eolas Ediciones.

González Cabeza, I. (2024). Poéticas de la autoficción en la patografía femenina en España. *Creneida. Anuario de Literaturas Hispánicas, 11 SE-Monográfico*, 41–87. 10.21071/calh.vi11.15733

Gosselin, C. (2023). *Je prends feu trop souvent*. Station T.

Green, J. (1972). *Binky Brown meets the Holy Virgin Mary*. Last Gasp Eco Funnies.

Green, M., & Myers, K. (2010). Graphic medicine: Use of comics in medical education and patient care. *BMJ (Clinical Research Ed.)*, 340(mar03 2), 574–577. 10.1136/bmj.c86320200064

Hagimont, O., & André, C. (2013). *Dodue ou comment j'ai vaincu la dictature de la minceur*. Editions Odile Jacob.

Haugse, J. E. (1999). *Heavy snow: My father's disappearance into Alzheimer's*. HEALTH COMMUNICATIONS.

Hoek, H. W. (2006). Incidence, prevalence and mortality of anorexia nervosa and other eating disorders. *Current Opinion in Psychiatry*, 19(4), 389–394. 10.1097/01.yco.0000228759.95237.7816721169

Hojat, M., Vergare, M. J., Maxwell, K., Brainard, G., Herrine, S. K., Isenberg, G. A., Veloski, J., & Gonnella, J. S. (2009). The devil is in the third year: A longitudinal study of erosion of empathy in medical school. *Academic Medicine*, 84(9), 1182–1191. 10.1097/ACM.0b013e3181b17e5519707055

Joyce, B., & Pekar, H. (1994). *Our Cancer Year*. Da Capo Press Inc.

Karin Pavón Rymer-Rythén, E. (2022). *Comiendo con Miedo*. astronave.

Katie Green. (2013). *Lighter Than My Shadow*. Jonathan Cape.

Lalanda, M. (2017). *Medicina gráfica*. https://medicinagrafica.blog/

Martín Curto, L. (2021). *Yo también quise ser como Ana y Mía: Una historia de superación*. Zenith.

Mayor Serrano, B. (2012). El lenguaje del cómic a disposición de la divulgación médico-sanitaria: Alzheimer. *¿Qué tiene el abuelo? 13*(35), 115–117.

Mayor Serrano, B. (2013). La historieta en la divulgación médico-sanitaria. *Translation Journal, 17*(2). https://translationjournal.net/journal/64historietas.htm

Mayor Serrano, B. (2016). *El cómic como recurso didáctico en los estudios de Medicina Manual con ejercicios*. Fundación Dr. Antonio Esteve.

Mayor Serrano, B. (2018). Qué es la medicina gráfica. *Tebeosfera, tercera época, 9*. https://www.tebeosfera.com/documentos/que_es_la_medicina_grafica.html

Mayor Serrano, B. (2019). Cómics, o cómo aprender lenguaje médico a golpe de viñetas. In *Comunicación, lenguaje y salud: Estrategias lingüísticas para mejorar la comunicación con el paciente* (Rosa Estopà, Girona, Documenta Universitaria y IULA (Institut de Lingüística Aplicada, Universitat Pompeu Fabra), pp. 109–122).

Mayor Serrano, B. (2021). Divulgación científica a través del lenguaje del cómic: La covid-19. *Medicina y Cine*. https://www.academia.edu/45388153/Divulgaci%C3%B3n_cient%C3%ADfica_a_trav%C3%A9s_del_lenguaje_del_c%C3%B3mic_la_covid_19

Mayor Serrano, B. (2023). Los precedesores del cómic de ciencia actual: Una aproximación. *CuCo, Cuadernos de Cómic*, 161–184. 10.37536/cuco.2023.21.2300

McLean, C. P., Utpala, R., & Sharp, G. (2022). The impacts of COVID-19 on eating disorders and disordered eating: A mixed studies systematic review and implications. *Frontiers in Psychology*, 13, 926709. 10.3389/fpsyg.2022.92670936148134

McNicol, S. (2018). Bibliotherapy and graphic medicine. In McNicol, S., & Brewster, L. (Eds.), *Bibliotherapy* (pp. 59–74). Facet. 10.29085/9781783303434.005

Mulholland, M. J. (2004). Comics as Art Therapy. *Art Therapy: Journal of the American Art Therapy Association*, 21(1), 42–43. 10.1080/07421656.2004.10129317

Myers, K., & Goldenberg, M. (2018). Graphic Pathographies and the Ethical Practice of Person-Centered Medicine. *AMA Journal of Ethics*, 20(2), 158–166. 10.1001/journalofethics.2018.20.2.medu2-180229460769

Porcellino, J. (1992). *True Anxiety*.

Ravi Kasthuri, R., & Venkatesan, S. (2015, May 31). Picturing Illness: History, Poetics, and Graphic Medicine. *Research and Humanities in Medical Education*, 2, 11–17.

Refaie, E. E. (2012). *Autobiographical Comics: Life Writing in Pictures*. Univ. Press of Mississippi. 10.14325/mississippi/9781617036132.001.0001

Santomauro, D. F., Melen, S., Mitchison, D., Vos, T., Whiteford, H., & Ferrari, A. J. (2021). The hidden burden of eating disorders: An extension of estimates from the Global Burden of Disease Study 2019. *The Lancet. Psychiatry*, 8(4), 320–328. 10.1016/S2215-0366(21)00040-733675688

Urrutia Asua, J. (2022). *Hoy no es el día*. Astiberri. https://www.astiberri.com/products/hoy-no-es-el-dia

Venkatesan, S., & Peter, A. M. (2018). 'I Want to Live, I Want to Draw': The Poetics of Drawing and Graphic Medicine. *Journal of Creative Communications*, 13(2), 104–116. 10.1177/0973258618761406

Venkatesan, S., & Saji, S. (2021). *Metaphors of Mental Illness in Graphic Medicine*. Routledge. https://www.academia.edu/58871491/_Graphic_Medicine_Book_Metaphors_of_Mental_Illness_in_Graphic_Medicine

Villeneuve, E., & Rocheleau, J. (2010). *La fille invisible*. Glénat Québec.

Williams, I. (2007). *Graphic Medicine*. Graphic Medicine. https://www.graphicmedicine.org/

Williams, I. (2012). Graphic medicine: Comics as medical narrative. *Medical Humanities*, 38(1), 21–27. 10.1136/medhum-2011-01009322282425

Wojnarowicz, D., & Romberger, J. (1996). *7 Miles a Second*. Fantagraphics Books.

World Health Organization. (2022). *World mental health report: Transforming mental health for all*. WHO. https://www.who.int/publications/i/item/9789240049338

ENDNOTES

1. Own translation from the comic Comiendo con miedo "Hablar de tus monstruos no es fácil. Te hace vulnerable. Pero también te hace fuerte" (p. 7)
2. https://www.graphicmedicine.org/
3. https://medicinagrafica.blog/
4. The data McNicol published in 2018 have been updated and enriched with supplementary information of our research.
5. Own translation from the original "Un TCA no es un problema con la comida. Es un problema que se refleja en la comida."
6. Own translation

7 Own translation
8 Own translation
9 Own translation
10 Own translation
11 Own translation
12 Own translation
13 Own translation
14 Own translation

Chapter 15 Poetry as a Vehicle to Support Social and Emotional Learning

Mary Napoli
https://orcid.org/0000-0003-4470-9137
Penn State University, Harrisburg, USA

Deanna Day
Washington State University, USA

ABSTRACT

This chapter describes how two teacher educators incorporated children's poetry in their undergraduate children's literature courses. The preservice teachers participated in course invitations that exposed them to well-written children's poetry that focused on tenets of the collaborative for academic, social, and emotional learning (CASEL) framework. Poetry can be read and enjoyed by everyone to help navigate complex emotions while developing empathy and understanding. This chapter also includes suggestions to incorporate social and emotional poetry with readers of all ages. Professionals from all fields can utilize poetry to facilitate social and emotional learning within their respective contexts.

INTRODUCTION

I never really thought about poetry as a way to support my students. I did not like poetry before this class. After reading poems that focus on social-emotional learning themes, poetry holds many benefits to support my students' learning and

DOI: 10.4018/979-8-3693-4244-2.ch015

can support their emotional intelligence while also appreciating the genre. For me, poetry helped to open my eyes to how words can really help shape my emotions. I will definitely be reading and sharing poetry with my future students. (Preservice teacher, Fall 2023)

As teacher educators, we work with preservice teachers who are often dealing with multiple stressors from academic workloads, family obligations, and part-time work commitments. We also observed the effects of the pandemic on their social interactions and communication skills (Fink, et al., 2015). Therefore, as a way to support ongoing conversations about social and emotional learning, we created an inviting classroom environment by fostering "participatory spaces" (hooks, 1994) and course engagements centered around poetry as a way to illuminate a spirit of introspection and provide joy.

Poetry is a powerful genre that has been utilized across disciplines, offering readers ways to express and convey their emotions, experiences, and perspectives. Poetry is not just confined to the classroom but is part of the greater human experience connecting all of us as human beings. Everyone experiences different emotions when they hear or read poetry such as sadness, anxiety, happiness, or hopefulness. Well-written poetry can capture our real feelings (Kiefer, et al., 2023). Poetry can be used to support emotional intelligence and social skills while also deepening critical thinking and empathy.

Despite the existing research about the positive effects of using poetry in the classroom, preservice teachers often lack confidence in their poetry knowledge (Certo, et al., 2010) which results in the unfortunate reluctance to teach it (Hughes & Dymoke, 2011). Many preservice teachers approach the study of poetry with negative attitudes largely based on how they were introduced to the genre as children or young adults (Certo, et al., 2012).

Social and emotional learning and poetry naturally fit together. Poetry is enjoyable for children and helps build language, decoding, fluency, phonics skills, and comprehension (Newsome, 2008; Nichols, et al., 2018; Rasinski, et al, 2008; Stickling, et al., 2011). Yet, when children are invited to share personal connections to poetry, they are forming emotional expressions and interpreting life which is part of social and emotional learning. When students engage with a poem, they also have the opportunity to connect with the emotions and experiences of the poet. Many of us are familiar with the adage that laughter is good medicine for all, so reading humorous poems has the potential to reduce stress. Poet Georgia Heard emphasized the connection between poetry and social and emotional learning, "Poetry and mindfulness are kindred spirits—they both invite us to slow down, pay attention and grow more compassionate towards ourselves as well as to others" (Day, et al., 2023, p. 127). As we shared this advice and the poems from Heard's collections, as well as many scholarly articles on the importance of integrating social and emotional competencies, the preservice teachers' perceptions began to change. We believe that poetry is an equalizer to break the barriers of the post-pandemic, but also to instill real possibilities for preservice teachers and their learners to find comfort and foster empathy and understanding. Social and emotional learning (SEL) teaches students to "acquire and effectively apply the knowledge, attitudes, and skills necessary to understand and manage emotions, set and achieve positive goals, feel and show empathy for others, establish and maintain positive relationships, and make responsible decisions" (CASEL, 2020, p.1). Literacy experiences enriched with social and emotional learning can also enhance relationships between teachers and children and among children by improving children's social competence and behaviors (Domitrovich, Cortes, & Greenberg, 2007). The infusion of SEL and children's poetry in teacher preparation is significant for leveraging curricular engagements that promote social awareness and community building. Furthermore, PreK-8 classroom teachers need to learn how to have thoughtful conversations around social and emotional learning with children to ensure academic success. There is existing research about the importance of using children's literature to support social and emotional learning (Alberton Gunn, et al., 2022; Peterkin & Grewal, 2018), but there remains a paucity of available studies that examine preservice teachers' awareness of the confluence of poetry and SEL as a potential way to support learners in their future classrooms.

Now, more than ever, teachers need to find innovative approaches to reach their learners. As teacher educators working on the front lines, we note the challenges that young people are facing today. Even though the 2021 declaration of a national emergency in child and adolescent mental health was issued by the American Academy of Pediatrics, American Academy of Child and Adolescent Psychiatry, and Children's Hospital Association, more work is required by all facets of professional fields to support the well-being of our young people. Teachers at all levels must navigate the challenges of promoting academic achievement while also attending to students' social and emotional well-being (Darling-Hammond, Wilhoit, & Pittenger, 2014). Therefore, as preservice teachers enter the teaching profession, we believe that using poetry as a form of bibliotherapy to support social and emotional learning needs has the potential to help all learners.

In this chapter, we describe how preservice teachers engaged in exploring and reading poetry and course assignments around children's poetry with social and emotional themes. Specifically, we explored the following questions: 1) How did children's poetry with social and emotional themes affect preservice teachers' beliefs about its use in PreK-8 classrooms? and 2) How can children's poetry be used as a vehicle to instill social and emotional learning in educational contexts? Finally, we provide examples of social and emotional poetry as well as response strategies that could be implemented in both classrooms and professional settings.

Creating a Poetry-Enriched Environment

This study took place at two research universities, one in the Eastern United States and the other in the Pacific Northwest. Both authors teach children's literature courses on an annual basis to preservice teachers and champion the interdisciplinary implications of poetry to support readers, especially as a vehicle to support social and emotional learning. We have both served on national poetry committees such as the NCTE Award for Excellence in Poetry for Children and the Lee Bennett Hopkins Poetry Award, so we are familiar with the criteria that reflect well-written poetry for children. In addition, we are committed to supporting the social and emotional needs of our preservice teachers and children's poetry is an approachable and viable genre to do so. Over the past two years, our children's literature courses consisted of a total of 93 preservice teachers in their third year of studies. There were 78 females and 15 males, and their ethnic backgrounds were diverse and represented Asian American, Hispanic, and African American, with the majority being Caucasian.

Before the start of the semester, the authors communicated and collaborated on common readings, projects, and possible poetry titles. Throughout the semester, to help foster a sense of community, we immersed students in poetry experiences such as a "daily dose of poetry" and responding to the poems in writing and/or artwork for their personal poetry anthologies. These shared literacy experiences united our students as part of collaborative groups where poetry helped them express their thoughts and feelings in creative and cohesive ways (Sekeres & Gregg, 2007). Each week we highlighted a children's poet such as Kwame Alexander, Georgia Heard, Nikki Grimes, Janet Wong, and others. Together, we listened to a poem read aloud by the poet, viewed a collection of their poetry books, brainstormed classroom connections, and read a short biography or interview found on their website.

Before we launched our poetry course engagements, we administered a brief Likert-scale survey to gauge our preservice teachers' interest in and familiarity with poetry. We discovered that our preservice teachers had limited exposure to reading children's poetry with 65% (n=93) indicating that they did not feel confident in their ability to read children's poetry aloud. In addition, only 32% (n=93) of our preservice teachers noted that they were familiar with children's poetry. The results revealed that 8% (n=93) of our preservice teachers felt confident in their ability to select quality children's poems for their classroom. These statistics are not surprising. The literature (Certo et al., 2012; Hughes et al., 2011) notes that the majority of teachers and adults have negative experiences and thoughts about poetry. Based on these initial findings though, we knew that we needed to provide intentional strategies to support their content knowledge and comfort level in using poetry in their future classroom.

We introduced the National Council of Teachers of English (NCTE) Award for Excellence in Poetry for Children or the Lee Bennett Hopkins Poetry Award. The NCTE Award for Excellence in Poetry honors a living American poet for their aggregate work for children ages 3-13. In addition, NCTE creates a yearly list entitled *Notable poetry books and verse novels,* which is available for educators, librarians, and anyone interested in finding well-written poetry. The Lee Bennett Hopkins poetry was named for the internationally renowned educator, poet, and anthologist of poetry for young people. This award is presented annually to an American poet or anthologist for the most outstanding new book of poetry published in the previous calendar year. Ensuring that preservice teachers are familiar with the criteria for selecting well-written poems and where to find titles was crucial to their ability to complete various projects.

Half of the preservice teachers were required to read and analyze five poetry books from the NCTE Poetry Award list and submit a reflection paper about poetry integration. Preservice teachers also presented poetry projects including "poetry breaks" where they read aloud exemplary selections of children's poetry with a social-emotional theme to the class. As a way to foster individual choice, preservice teachers had the option of submitting poetry projects such as poetry suitcases (Wong, n.d.), themed engagements, poetry boxes, or poetry anthologies. Essentially, they built an anthology of poems around a theme, topic, or issue that they could use with their future students. At the final class, we celebrated poetry where every preservice teacher shared their poetry projects and favorite poems in a "share chair" (Concannon-Gibney, 2019). Some students even reread some of their favorite poems that they had enjoyed during the 15-week semester.

Poetry as a Way of Healing

Teaching and learning from poetry can help students respect and understand the viewpoints of people across the world. In an age of increasing divisiveness, this is huge in education. Most importantly, poetry can have a positive impact on student's mental health. (Preservice Teacher, Fall 2023).

We believe that poetry can provide comfort and healing for readers. In this section, we share how one could teach social and emotional learning through poetry by highlighting some exemplary poems and poetry anthologies. We also provide several pedagogical approaches that could be used by PK-8 educators and other professionals.

Teaching Social and Emotional Learning Through Poetry

The Collaborative for Academic, Social, and Emotional Learning (CASEL) framework includes five core competencies in Social and Emotional Learning (SEL): self-awareness, self-management, social awareness, relationship skills, and responsible decision-making (CASEL, 2020; Gimbert et al., 2021; Kaufman et al., 2021). The social and emotional framework is described as a process "through which all young people and adults acquire and apply the knowledge, skills, and attitudes to develop healthy identities, manage emotions and achieve personal and collective goals, feel and show empathy for others, establish and maintain supportive relationships, and make responsible and caring decisions" (CASEL, p.2).

Wassiliwizky, et al. (2017) conducted a focused study using psychophysiology, neuroimaging, and behavioral responses that explored the impact of poetry recitations and emotional responses. These authors concluded that poetry had the potential to "provide aesthetic pleasure and foster profound emotional engagement" (p.1239) and recommended that educators and other professionals promote more awareness about poetry. Moreover, Xiang & Yi's (2020) review of poetry and healing, especially during the pandemic, noted that reading poetry can "remind the individual of a similar experience or emotion, creating a sense of belonging (p. 606). The application of these findings to education is significant and calls on educators to support social and emotional learning by bringing poetry into their classrooms.

Bibliotherapy has been researched as an approach that has the potential to help children learn how to interact with others (Maich & Kean, 2004). As noted in Strainbrook's (2011) case study findings, bibliotherapy can be used in classrooms to help children see similarities and recognize their individual feelings and personal responses to literature. Teachers can also partner with their school counselors to support further conversations to help children respond to challenges. Therefore, as teachers and professionals browse poetry, they can look for examples to support social and emotional learning. In the next section, we share some poetry suggestions that align with the different social and emotional learning competencies. Readers of this chapter are encouraged to visit the CASEL website at https://casel.org/ to learn more comprehensive information about each of the competencies and additional resources to incorporate the framework in educational settings.

Core Competency 1: Self-awareness is defined as an essential competency to support and affirm agency and identity. Reading aloud poetry that can reflect the reader's sense of identity will contribute to their self-awareness.

- Read "Today, I Feel" by Gervase Phinn from *It Takes One to Know One* by Gervase Phinn (2001) to support the wide range of emotions and moods that children experience. This poem also appears on page 79 in the anthology entitled *A Whale of a Time* (2023) selected by Lou Peacock and illustrated by Matt Hunt.

- Read "Give Yourself a Hug" by Grace Nichols from the collection entitled *Give Yourself a Hug* (1996) by Grace Nichols and illustrated by Kim Harley. This poem supports self-affirmation by simply helping readers to recognize that they are special. This poem also appears on page 27 of the anthology *A Whale of a Time* (2023) selected by Lou Peacock and illustrated by Matt Hunt.
- Read the poetry anthology entitled *Things We Feel* (2022) edited by Sylvia Vardell and Janet Wong to discuss emotions and feelings. Geared for younger readers, the poems are organized alphabetically with matching photographs for different emotions such as *upset, worried, or determined.* Teachers and professionals can discuss the poems and invite students to write individual poems based on their feelings.

Core Competency 2: Self-management includes one's capacity to manage emotions, thoughts, and behaviors. Reading the poems below can leverage conversations between educators and students to identify stressors and exhibit self-discipline.

- Read "Hurricane" by Sherilyn Howard which appears in the anthology entitled *What is Hope?* (Wong & Vardell, 2023) to support the first day of school anxieties and how friends can provide support.
- Before a test or quiz read aloud "Ode to My Stress Ball" by Kalli Dakos (2006, 2021) and invite students to think about other ways to reduce stress.
- Read "I Find Peace" by Joyce Sidman (2013) in her collection entitled *What the Heart Knows: Chants, charms, and Blessings* and discuss different activities or locations where they find peace. The poet, Joyce Sidman, provides a plethora of curricular suggestions and discussion questions to accompany the poems in this award-winning collection. Readers are encouraged to visit her website https://www.joycesidman.com/books/what-the-heart-knows

Core Competency 3: Social Awareness reflects one's ability to empathize with others and show compassion. After reading poems such as the ones noted below, teachers and students can discuss if the poem is related to kindness and respect for others. The poems can be read during morning meetings or circle time depending on the grade level.

- When a pet or a classmate dies during the school year, share the poem "On the Day My Dog Died" or "J.T. Never Will Be Ten" both by Kalli Dakos (2021). Invite students to freely write their thoughts in a journal.

- Read "Were You Ever Fat Like Me?" or "When They Call Me Bad Names" both by Kalli Dakos (2021) when children are bullied or called names and hold a whole group discussion about feelings and kindness. Students can provide resolutions and suggestions to support kindness in their classroom community and towards others.
- When a classmate or friend moves away, share one of the following poems "If You Have to Say Goodbye" or "When a Friend Moves Away" both by Kalli Dakos (2021). Invite students to write a poem or letter to their friend.

Core Competency 4: Relationship Skills reflect one's ability to "establish and maintain healthy and supportive relationships to effectively navigate settings with diverse individuals and groups" (CASEL, 2021). When reading poetry aloud, teachers and students build a sense of community and acceptance of varied viewpoints. The poems below can help students build relationships with people in their homes, classrooms, and communities.

- Molly Lorenz's "Lunch" about making friends with a new student can be found in the anthology *What is a Friend?* (edited by Janet Wong and Sylvia Vardell). After reading the poem, discuss how one act of kindness can form a friendship and invite students to write an individual friendship poem.
- Read Nikki Grimes' (2015) *Poems in the Attic* to foster conversations about gaining an appreciation for your family. In this collection, a young girl discovers a book of poems penned by her mother when she was young. The young girl learns more about her mother and is inspired to create a gift of her original poems.
- Read the collection entitled *My Daddy Rules the World: Poems about Dads* by Hope Anita Smith (2017) to facilitate conversations about the father figures in their lives. Students can write a poem about someone in their life that they admire. For example, after reading the poem, "My Daddy," the students could use similes to write their personalized simile poem and can change the subject of the poem from "my daddy" to another member of their family or to someone from their community, such as the mail carrier or dentist.

Core Competency 5: Responsible Decision-Making reflects one's ability to make well-informed choices based on their social interactions and personal actions.

- The poem "Now" by Georgia Heard (2021) appears in her collection entitled *My Thoughts Are Clouds: Poems for Mindfulness* to guide discussions on how the personal decision to focus on the "now" can support an individual's well-being.

- "We are Brave when We Say No" by Kyunghee Kim (2024) from her book entitled *See Us Bloom: Poems on Compassion, Acceptance, and Bravery.* This poem invites students to be mindful of their feelings and to say 'no' when they feel upset. The encouraging tone of the poem will help readers find the courage to speak up. The poems in this collection were inspired by the author's journey moving to the United States from South Korea when she was a young child, and this collection aligns with more than one of the social and emotional competencies.
- In the anthology *Seeing the Blue Between: Advice and Inspiration for Young Poets* (Janeczko, 2002) there are a couple of poems that could be read aloud for students to think about making responsible decisions. For example, teachers can read "Pick Up Your Room" by Mary Ann Hoberman or "Who Clogged up our School Bell with Bubblegum?" by J. Kennedy to engage in interesting discussions about responsibility.
- *Oh, How Sylvester Can Pester: And Other Poems More or Less About Manners* (Kinerk, 2011) contains humorous poems about everyday decision-making. For example, the poem "What will happen to you if you talk while you chew?" gives insight into what could occur if we decide to do this. Other poems such as "Sneezes" or "Brussels Sprouts" remind children to think and choose wisely.

Exemplary Poetry Collections

Teachers and professionals need a wide range of children's literature, including poetry, to immerse students in rich language and to promote creative expression. When curating a collection of poetry for social and emotional learning, it is necessary to consider how the poems can enhance SEL competencies while ensuring that the chosen poetry is of high quality. While there are many poetry collections for children available, the following titles are recommended for libraries, classrooms, and other professional spaces as a way to foster dialogue and address the social and emotional competencies described in the aforementioned section.

My Thoughts Are Clouds: Poems for Mindfulness by Georgia Heard and illustrated by Isabel Roxas (2021), includes 30 free-verse poems about mindfulness and affirmations to support readers of all ages. The first section entitled *Breathe In, Breathe Out* includes poems that invite readers to participate in breathing practices. Reading aloud poems such as "Counting Breaths" and "Ocean Breath" provided our preservice teachers with an opportunity to discuss the connection to support mindfulness for their students while also addressing the CASEL competency of self-management. Our preservice teachers noted that the poems in this anthology not only support literacy connections but also can help serve as entry points for their future PreK-8 students to practice breathing strategies that have the potential to feel calmer and focused. According to a recent medical study (Komariah, et al., 2023), "Mindfulness is said to be a complete therapy that can minimize stress levels and improve psychological well-being because it includes various components of therapy, such as yoga, deep breathing techniques, focusing attention, and acceptance without judgment" (p.3). As preservice teachers searched for poems that would foster social and emotional connections, their written reflections supported their dispositions and professional knowledge. For example, one preservice teacher wrote, "*In my future teaching, I like the idea of reading a poem every day during morning time as a way to help students focus, self-monitor and express their emotions. I did not recognize the possibilities of using poetry to address social and emotional learning.*"

Climbing Shadows by Shannon Bramer (2019) is a collection of free verse poems that highlight common themes in a child's life such as feeling reticent or having a difficult day at school. One preservice teacher noted additional topics: joys, worries and fears, and humor as important to support students' self-awareness. One particular poem, "[a]fter school" communicates the feelings of a child whose difficult day at school made them too sad and simply wanted to disappear. The child in the poem communicates to their family that they do not want to go back to school and would rather be "a puddle." This poem provides opportunities to discuss the importance of communicating their feelings, but to also remain hopeful in the face of challenges. After sharing this particular poem, one of our preservice teachers' reflections indicated a shift in their perceptions when asked how they would use poetry in their classrooms. They shared, *"It will help students develop new understandings and emotions, as well as vocabulary. They will also learn more about the human experience and how to express themselves.* "

When You Breathe by Diana Farid and illustrated by Billy Renkl (2020) is a narrative poem about breathing. When we are outside, we feel and smell the air, yet when we breathe in or inhale the air, this becomes breath. The gorgeous illustrations help readers visualize the various aspects of breathing from taking in air to breathing it back outside into our world. Air is not just important to us but also to animals and nature. Our lungs are compared to an "...upside-down tree / inside your rising chest." Later we learn that: "It just takes seconds / for a piece of the sky / to fill your heart." The accompanying illustration shows large lungs filled with limbs, leaves, and flowers with the heart hiding amongst the lungs–full of the night sky constellations. This title would be perfect to read aloud a couple of times to children and then complete breathing exercises which have been found to help with stress, anxiety, ADHD, and anger. Our preservice teachers' favorite breathing exercises included: soup breathing, bunny breathing, flower smelling, bubble breathing, and bumblebee breath. One preservice teacher wrote: "*This is an important book for any ELL student because there are lots of terms you have to learn in order to understand the complicated processes like breathing.*" Lastly, the backmatter of the book also includes a glossary of breathing words that could support health and literacy.

They Only See the Outside by Kalli Dakos and illustrated by Jimothy Oliver (2021) showcases 30 poems with black and white illustrations. The book summary on the title page notes that this is "A selection of poems on mental health topics including emotions, bullying, failure, illness, war, immigration, and goodbyes." There is a poem for every grade level with some that are eight lines long and others that are six pages long with 25 stanzas. The poem "Don't Tell Me" includes descriptive language and goes like this: Don't tell me / I won't fail, / for it might / not be true. / Just tell me / you'll still / love me / even if I do." (p. 2). There are many elements of poetry contained in this brief volume–onomatopoeia, rhyme, imagery, and poems in different shapes. This collection captured the interest of our preservice teachers and one of them noted: "*The intense hard-to-talk topics will open up conversations about these issues. I think kids would like this book because they will be able to dialogue, connect, and know they are not alone in their feelings.*"

Pedagogical Approaches for Professionals

As teacher educators, we strive to inspire and equip our preservice teachers with the pedagogical content knowledge that will guide them as they enter the classroom. We emphasize the importance of educational research that aligns with classroom practice, and we model how to plan evidence-based curricular engagements. Therefore, in this section, we provide pedagogical approaches that leverage poetry and SEL. The suggestions can be integrated into PreK-8 classroom settings and adapted for professionals to use in other disciplines.

- Rasinski (2014) states that poetry builds foundational reading skills for children. Reading poetry aloud supports oral language, fluency, vocabulary, phonics, phonemic awareness, and comprehension. All professionals working with children need to collect SEL poems to read aloud and share with students to support these literacy connections.
- Social and emotional learning research suggests that teachers begin each school day with a student check-in. Likewise, poets Laura Purdie Salas and Janet Wong (2018) encourage teachers to read aloud a poem every day. These two ideas could be combined where a poem is read aloud and then students choral read, sing, move, or dramatize the poem. Students then could share their individual feelings or thoughts about the poem or provide information about themselves.
- Poetry contains rhythm, rhyme, repetition, and melody. This musicality provides support and scaffolding for children as they read poetry, but also helps

them actively engage in the reading. Students can clap or move to the rhythmic beats, choral read the poem, or freeze when there is a pause–helping children successfully participate in reading. In addition, movement is an important part of keeping a healthy mind, spirit, and body.

- Conversing and talking is critical to building a caring classroom. Collect and choose poems around topics such as getting along or friendship to help children think critically. Students can learn how to ask open-ended questions, actively listen, and critically discuss poems. Just like books, poems can have different meanings and evoke strong emotions. Children can share their thoughts and feelings about poems and gain new understandings.
- Every educator or professional has one minute to make an instructional move and to teach with intention. A social and emotional learning poem can be read in less than a minute during transitions such as when students are walking to recess or lining up to go home at the end of the school day. These transition times are also perfect for a yoga pose or a stretch or combine both.
- Reflective writing is imperative in supporting social and emotional health. Incorporating poetry writing could be less intimidating for children because fewer words are used, and complete sentences are not necessary. Through modeling, teachers can encourage their students that there is no right or wrong way to draft a poem. One simple suggestion is to brainstorm a list of social-emotional vocabulary words and create an anchor poster or poetry word wall. Then, encourage children to choose a word or grouping of words to create a poem. For children who need further scaffolding, the following prompts may help them: "If you are scared you can…" Students could produce adjectives to describe scared or even ideas to conquer these feelings to finish the poem. Another is: "I thought I knew fear, but now…" Students could write a poem using their imagination, observations, or the found words on the anchor poster.
- Janet Wong's (n.d.) Poetry Suitcase could help children collect and write poems. Students could select a prop or a social-emotional word (e.g., happy, sad, distressed, etc.) from the suitcase and create a poem that matches the prop/word. They could also look for poems from various collections or anthologies to attach to their prop. If a prop does not exist, they could always make one with simple craft materials. The best poems contain many emotions so encouraging students to state all of their emotions: grateful, thankful, blessed, etc. would be beneficial. Learn more about Janet Wong's poetry suitcase by visiting her website https://janetwong.com/poetry-suitcase/
- Match a social and emotional learning fictional book on having a good relationship with others and a poem on the same topic. For example, partner *Each Kindness* (2012) by Jacqueline Woodson with poems from the following col-

lections: *I like being me: Poems about kindness, friendship, and making good choices* (Lalli, 2016), *Lend a Hand: Poems about giving* (London, 2014) or *Friends and foes: Poems about us all* (Florian, 2018) to facilitate conversations about kindness and friendship.

- Read aloud Paul Fleishman's (2019)*Joyful Noise: Poems for two Voices* illustrated by Eric Beddows and invite older students to collaborate and create a two-voice poem with different perspectives on a social-emotional topic or theme. Another idea is to have students write a two-voice poem with their inner critic voice (how they feel, think, or act), contrasting with positive self-talk. Writing from two different perspectives could teach empathy and resilience.
- Students love to be creative, and the arts can regulate stress and anxiety; therefore, teachers can integrate the arts with poetry to support cross-curricular objectives and connections. For example, children can listen to music and think about what feelings or emotions they hear and then write a poem. They can also respond to art through feelings and emotions. Children could also create collages and then determine what is speaking to them in the art to help them write a free verse poem. In the classroom, students can express a poem through dance, movement, or musical instruments.
- Teachers can use the rhythmic picture book entitled *Looking Like Me* (2009) by Walter Dean Myers and illustrated by Christopher Myers as a mentor text to invite students to create positive affirmation poems with the prompt "I am…" For example, "I am loved, I am honest, I am kind, I am positive, and I am creative."
- Making new friends is a lifelong skill. In classrooms we can discuss how to make and keep friends, what a healthy friendship looks like, random acts of kindness, and the value of our unique qualities. After these discussions, students could write a two-word poem for a special friend. "My friend, very considerate, always shares, stands up, for me."
- Poet Georgia Heard (2016) developed the heart map where children create a map of their hearts. Students open up their hearts and think of every emotion and feeling they might have through small sketches or pictures and words. When the heart maps are completed, invite them to write a free verse poem. This process could be healing for children who have experienced grief or trauma. Georgia Heard also provides a plethora of approaches to incorporate heart maps on her website https://www.georgiaheard.com/heart-maps
- A strategy that teachers often use to help ground or calm children is to think of five things that they see, four things that they think, three things that they hear, two things that they feel, and one thing that they taste. Students could use all of this information to write a poem using their senses.

- Dramatizing poetry is a powerful way for readers to interpret situations and feelings with motions and expression. In Medina's (2004) study on drama and multicultural literature, she discovered that weaving drama throughout the curriculum promotes critical discourse among students. For example, teachers can read aloud Gervase Phinn's (2001) poem "Today, I Feel" for choral reading and also invite students to co-create motions for dramatization. The poem includes many similes to describe the myriad of emotions and moods that people experience.

Concluding Findings and Final Thoughts

Poetry can play a valuable role in my future teaching by enhancing language skills, fostering creativity, and encouraging thoughtful expression. It can provide a unique way for students to explore emotions, diverse perspectives, and cultural experiences. Incorporating poetry into lessons can make learning more engaging and enjoyable while promoting critical thinking and communication skills." (Post-reflection, Preservice Teacher, Fall 2023).

The aforementioned quote from one of our preservice teachers underscores the importance of integrating poetry into the educational and professional setting. Moreover, our preservice teachers were asked to share their learning experiences and reflections on their growth and shifts in their perceptions at the end of the semester. Based on the post-survey data, there were significant gains in preservice teachers' confidence level in reading poetry aloud with 90% (n=93) indicating that they were more comfortable reading aloud poetry. Furthermore, based on the course engagements, 94% (n=93) of preservice teachers gained more confidence in their ability to select poems for their future classrooms. One preservice teacher wrote, "I have found a lot of useful resources, books, and poems to take with me to use in my future kindergarten classroom." (Post reflection, Preservice Teacher, Fall 2023).

As the authors reviewed the post-survey and written reflections, we noted the number of positive responses to the exposure to poetry throughout the semester. We were pleased to read that future teachers learned the guidelines to evaluate poetry and the tools to integrate poetry across their curriculum. While both authors intentionally carved out time in their semester to infuse poetry, it is important to note that this is not a standard practice. We would encourage teachers, teacher educators, and other professionals to set aside a few minutes to share poetry with students and to encourage them to discuss how poetry can be infused to support social and emotional learning.

By providing positive poetry experiences we believe learners of all ages can gain confidence in themselves as readers of poetry, and find joy and comfort in the words. This study was limited to a small subset of preservice teachers; however, the initial findings provide evidence that there was a shift in their dispositions especially when asked about incorporating poetry into their future classrooms. Given that preservice teachers will be working with PreK-8 learners, the opportunity to support and solidify their experiences to enjoy and use poetry to address social and emotional learning will assist their future teaching careers.

In this chapter, we described the positive outcome of infusing poetry and SEL into a children's literature course with preservice teachers. We also address the growing mental health concerns that are faced by individuals across various disciplines and suggest the utilization of poetry as a way to strengthen bibliotherapy and dialogue. We also recommend that educators and professionals curate a poetry collection with titles that would address the SEL competencies. Finally, we recommended evidence-based pedagogical approaches to integrate SEL-focused poetry across the curriculum. While future research is needed to investigate the effects of SEL children's poetry on PreK-8 learners' well-being in the classroom setting, this chapter provides one step forward to increasing awareness of children's poetry as a potential site of hope and healing.

REFERENCES

American Academy of Pediatrics, American Academy of Child and Adolescent Psychiatry, and Children's Hospital Association. (2021). *AAP-AACAP- CHA Declaration of a National Emergency in Child and Adolescent Mental Health.* American Academy of Pediatrics. https://www.aap.org/en/advocacy/child-and-adolescent-healthy-mental- development/aap-aacap-cha-declaration-of-a-national-emergency-in-child-and- adolescent-mental-health/

Bramer, S. (2019). *Climbing shadows: Poems for children.* (C. Derby, Illus.). House of Anansi Press and Groundwood Books.

CASEL's SEL framework: What are the core competence areas and where are they promoted? (2020). Collaborative for Academic, Social and Emotional Learning. https://casel.org/casel-sel-framework-11-2020/

Certo, J., Apol, L., Wibbens, E., & Yoon, S. (2010). Teaching poetry writing, PreK–12: A review of research and suggested directions for teacher practice and development. In G. Troia, R.Shankland, & A. Heinz (Eds.). *Writing Research in Classroom Practice* (pp. 93-115). Guilford Press.

Certo, J. L., Apol, L., Wibbens, E., & Hawkins, L. K. (2012). Living the poet's life: Using an aesthetic approach to poetry to enhance preservice teachers' poetry experiences and dispositions. *English Education*, 44(2), 102–146. 10.58680/ee201218436

Concannon-Gibney, T. (2019). Immersing first graders in poetry: A genre study approach. *The Reading Teacher*, 72(4), 431–443. 10.1002/trtr.1728

Dakos, K. (2006). *Put your eyes up here and other school poems. (G.B. Karas, Illus.).* Simon & Schuster.

Dakos, K. (2021). *They only see the outside. (J. Oliver, Illus.).* Magination Press.

Darling-Hammond, L., Wilhoit, G., & Pittenger, L. (2014). Accountability for college and career readiness: Developing a new paradigm. *Education Policy Analysis Archives*, 22(86), 1–38. 10.14507/epaa.v22n86.2014

Day, D., Colwell, R., Pizzo, J. S., Sableski, M., Sakoi, J., & Dotlich, R. K. (2023). Awakening poets: The heart of Georgia Heard. *Language Arts*, 101(2), 126–129. https://ezaccess.libraries.psu.edu/login?url=https://www.proquest.com/scholarly-journals/awakening-poets-heart-georgia-heard/docview/2902061353/se-2. 10.58680/la202332687

Domitrovich, C. E., Cortes, R. C., & Greenberg, M. T. (2007). Improving young children's social and emotional competence: A randomized trial of the preschool "PATHS" curriculum. *The Journal of Primary Prevention*, 28(2), 67–91. 10.1007/s10935-007-0081-017265130

Farid, D. (2020). *When you breathe. (B. Renkl, Illus.).* Cameron Kids.

Fink, E., Patalay, P., Sharpe, H., Holley, S., Deighton, J., & Wolpert, M. (2015). Mental health difficulties in early adolescence: A comparison of two cross-sectional studies in England from 2009 to 2014. *The Journal of Adolescent Health*, 56(5), 502–507. 10.1016/j.jadohealth.2015.01.02325907650

Fleishman, P. (2019). *Joyful noise: Poems for two voices. (E. Beddows, Illus.).* HarperCollins.

Florian, D. (2018). *Friends and foes: Poems about us all.* Simon and Schuster.

Frank, J. (2014). *Lend a hand: Poems about giving. (L. Ladd, Illus.).* Lee and Low Books.

Gimbert, M., Miller, D., Herman, E., Breedlove, M., & Molina, C. E. (2021). Social emotional learning in schools: The importance of educator competence. *Journal of Research on Leadership Education*, 18(1), 3–39. 10.1177/19427751211014920

Grimes, N. (2016). *Poems in the attic. (E. Zunon, Illus.).* Lee and Low Books.

Heard, G. (2016). *Heart maps: Helping students to create and craft authentic writing*. Heinemann.

Heard, G. (2021). *My thoughts are clouds: Poems for mindfulness. (I. Roxas, Illus.).* Roaring Brook Press.

hooks, b. (1994). *Teaching to transgress: Education as the practice of freedom.* Routledge.

Hughes, J., & Dymoke, S. (2011). "Wiki-Ed poetry": Transforming preservice teachers' preconceptions about poetry and poetry teaching. *Journal of Adolescent & Adult Literacy*, 55(1), 46–56. 10.1598/JAAL.55.1.5

Janeczko, P. B. (2002). *Seeing the blue between: Advice and inspiration for young poets*. Candlewick.

Kaufman, N., Kaufman, L., & Black, D. L. (2021). *Essentials of social emotional learning: The complete guide for schools and practitioners*. Wiley.

Kiefer, B., & Tyson, C. A. Parsons Barger-B., Patrick, L., & Reilly-Sanders, E. (2023). *Charlotte Huck's children's literature: A brief guide* (4th ed.). McGraw-Hill.

Kim, K. (2023). *See us bloom: Poems on compassion, acceptance, and bravery. (E. Paik, Illus.)*. Modern Marigold Books.

Kinerk, R. (2011). *Oh, how Sylvester can pester: And other poems more or less about manners. (D. Kozjan, Illus.)*. Simon and Schuster.

Komariah, M., Ibrahim, K., Pahria, T., Rahayuwati, L., & Somantri, I. (2022). Effect of Mindfulness Breathing Meditation on Depression, Anxiety, and Stress: A Randomized Controlled Trial among University Students. *Healthcare (Basel)*, 11(1), 26. 10.3390/healthcare1101002636611488

Lally, K. (2016). *I like being me: Poems about kindness, friendship, and making good choices*. Free Spirit Publishing.

Maich, K., & Kean, S. (2004). Read two books and write me in the morning! Bibliotherapy for social emotional intervention in the inclusive classroom. Teaching Exceptional Children Plus, 1(2). *Article*, 5, 1–13.

Medina, C. (2004). Drama wor(l)ds: Explorations of Latina/o realistic fiction through drama. *Language Arts*, 81(4), 272–282. 10.58680/la20042905

Myers, W. D. (2009). *Looking like me. (C. Myers, Illus.)*. Egmont.

Newsome, K. E. (2008). Using poetry to improve fluency and comprehension in third-grade students. *Georgia Educational Researcher*, 6(1), 1–21. 10.20429/ger.2008.060101

Peacock, L. (2023). *A whale of a time. (M. Hunt, Illus.)*. Nosy Crow.

Peterkin, A., & Grewal, S. (2018). Bibliotherapy: The therapeutic use of fiction and poetry in mental health. *International Journal of Person Centered Medicine*, 7(3), 175–181. 10.5750/ijpcm.v7i3.648

Phinn, G. (2001). *It takes one to know one*. Penguin.

Purdie Salas, L., & Wong, J. (2018). Empower your students with poetry: Insights from Laura Purdie Salas and Janet Wong. *Journal of Children's Literature*, 44(1), 33–39.

Rasinski, T. (2014). Tapping the power of poetry. *Educational Leadership*, 72(3), 30–34.

Rasinski, T., Rupley, W., & Nichols, W. D. (2008). Two essential ingredients: Phonics and fluency getting to know each other. *The Reading Teacher*, 62(3), 257–260. 10.1598/RT.62.3.7

Sekers, D. C., & Gregg, M. (2007). Poetry in third grade: Getting started. *The Reading Teacher*, 60(5), 466–475. 10.1598/RT.60.5.6

Sloan, G. (2003). *Give them poetry! A guide for sharing poetry with children K-8.* Teachers College Press.

Smith, H.A. (2017). *My daddy rules the world: Poems about dads.* Henry Holt and Company.

Stickling, S., Prasun, M., & Olsen, C. (2011). Poetry: What's the sense in teaching it? *Illinois Reading Council Journal*, 39(3), 31–40.

Wassiliwizky, E., Koelsch, S., Wagner, V., Jacobsen, T., & Menninghaus, W. (2017). The emotional power of poetry: Neural circuitry, psychophysiology, and compositional principles. *Social Cognitive and Affective Neuroscience*, 12(8), 1229–1240. 10.1093/scan/nsx06928460078

Wong, J. (n.d.). *What is a poetry suitcase?* Janet Wong. https://janetwong.com/poetry-suitcase/

Wong, J., & Vardell, S. (2022). *What is a friend?* Pomelo Books.

Wong, J., & Vardell, S. (2022). *Things we feel.* Pomelo Books.

Wong, J., & Vardell, S. (2023). *What is hope?* Pomelo Books.

Xiang, D. H., & Yi, A. M. (2020). A look back and a path forward: Poetry's healing power during the pandemic. *Journal of Medical Humanities, 41*, 603–608. https://doi- org.ezaccess.libraries.psu.edu/10.1007/s10912-020-09657-z

Compilation of References

AADD (2023). *Microrrelatos. El racó de l'escriptura.* AADD. [https://rua.ua.es/dspace/bitstream/10045/139266/1/Microrrelatos.pdf]

Achenbach, G. B. (2000). *Das kleine Buch der inneren Ruhe.* Herder.

Adorno, Th. (2005). *Dialéctica negativa. La jerga de la autenticidad.* Akal.

Agamben, G. (2010). *Medios sin fin. Notas sobre política.* Pre-textos.

Albarello, F. (2019). Lectura transmedia, leer, escribir, conversar en el ecosistema de pantallas. *Ampersand (Oxford, UK).*

Alheit, P. (1995). *The Biographical Approach in European Adult Education.* Volkshochschule.

Allport, G. W. (1954). *The nature of prejudice.* Addison-Wesley.

Alves, M. H. H. (1982). L'applicazione della biblioterapia nel processo di reinserimento sociale. *Revista Brasileira de Biblioteconomia e Documentação*, 15(1/2), 54–61.

Amatori, G., Maggiolini, S., Macchia, A (a cura di) (2021). *Pensare in Grande. L'educazione inclusiva per l'infanzia di oggi e di domani.* Pensa Multimedia.

Amatori, G., & Maggiolini, S. (Eds.). (2021). *Pedagogia speciale per la prima infanzia. Politiche, famiglie, servizi.* Pearson.

American Academy of Pediatrics, American Academy of Child and Adolescent Psychiatry, and Children's Hospital Association. (2021). *AAP-AACAP- CHA Declaration of a National Emergency in Child and Adolescent Mental Health.* American Academy of Pediatrics. https://www.aap.org/en/advocacy/child-and-adolescent-healthy-mental- development/aap-aacap-cha-declaration-of-a-national-emergency-in-child-and- adolescent-mental-health/

American Society for Bioethics & Humanities. (2011). *Core competencies for healthcare ethics consultation* (2nd ed.). Author.

Anastasija, M., & Jelena, M. (2021). The role of action research in teachers' professional development. *International Journal of Cognitive Research in Science. Engineering and Education*, 9(3), 301–317.

Anderson, P. F., Wescom, E., & Carlos, R. (2016). Difficult Doctors, Difficult Patients: Building Empathy. *Journal of the American College of Radiology*, 13(12), 1590–1598. 10.1016/j.jacr.2016.09.01527888946

Andres-Suarés, I. (2010). *El microrrelato español. Una estética de la elipsis*. Menoscuarto.

Andres-Suárez, I. (2012). *Antología del microrrelato español (1906-2011). El cuarto género narrativo*. Madrid: Cátedra, 2017.

Antoni, C. (1955). *Commento a Croce*. Neri Pozza.

Antonovsky, A. (1996). The salutogernic model as a theory to guide health promotion. *Health (San Francisco, Calif.)*.

Arendt, H. (1958). *The Human Condition*. The University of Chigago Press.

Arlés, E. Patricia (2009). *Por favor, sea breve 2*. Madrid: Páginas de Espuma.

Armgardt, M. (2008). Zur Bedingungsdogmatik im klassischen römischen Recht und zu ihren Grundlagen in der stoischen Logik. *TR, 76*, 219-235.

Arts and Humanities Research Council. (2017). *Exploring Mental Health and Wellbeing: The Role of Arts and Humanities Research*. Arts and Humanities Research Council.

Ashbè J., (2019). *A più tardi*. Babalibri. Trad.it Rocca F.

Atkinson, R. (2002). *L'intervista narrativa. Raccontare la storia di sé nella ricerca formativa, organizzativa e sociale*. Raffaello Cortina.

Atkinson, S., Macnaughton, J., & Richards, J. (Eds.). (2016). *The Edinburgh Companion to the Critical Medical Humanities*. Edinburgh University Press.

Aub, M. (1991). *Crímenes ejemplares*. Calambur.

Avenarius, M. (2005). Das pandektistische Rechtsstudium in St. Petersburg in den letzten Jahrzehnten der Zarenherrschaft. Wojciech Dajczak y Hans-Georg Knothe (eds.) *Deutsches Sachenrecht in polnischer Gerichtspraxis. Das BGB-Sachenrecht in derpolnischen höchstrichterlichen Rechtsprechung in den Jahren 1920-1939: Tradition und europäische Perspektive,* Berlin.

Babini, V. P., & Lama, L. (2010). *Una donna nuova. Il femminismo scientifico di Maria Montessori*. FrancoAngeli.

Badinter, E. (1981). *L'amore in più. Storia dell'amore materno*. Longanesi.

Bakhtin, M. (2010). *Marxism and Philosophy of Language*. HUCITEC.

Baldacci, M. (2019). *La scuola al bivio. Mercato o democrazia?* FrancoAngeli.

Balius, F., & Pellejer Ruiz, M. (2018). *Desmesura*. BELLATERRA.

Barthes, R. (1994). *El susurro del lenguaje. Más allá de la palabra y de la escritura*. Paidós.

Batini, F. (2011). *Storie che crescono. Le storie al nido e alla scuola dell'infanzia*. Junior.

Batini, F. (Ed.). (2023). *La lettura ad alta voce condivisa. Un metodo in direzione dell'equità*. Il Mulino.

Batini, F., & Bartolucci, M. (2016). Chi legge ragiona meglio? Abitudini di lettura e funzioni di ragionamento. *Ricerche Di Pedagogia E Didattica.Journal of Theories and Research in Education*, 11(3), 37–45. 10.6092/issn.1970-2221/6444

Bauman, Z. (2021). *Modernità liquida* [Liquid Modernity]. Laterza.

Benjamin, W. (1971). *«La tarea del traductor». AngelusNovus*. La Gaya Ciencia.

BERA (Asociación Británica de Investigación Educativa). (2019). *Guía Ética para la Investigación Educativa*. BERA. https://www.bera.ac.uk/publication/guia-etica-para-la-investigacion-educativa

Bergsma, A. (2008). Do self-help books help? *Journal of Happiness Studies*, 9(3), 341–360. 10.1007/s10902-006-9041-2

Bert, G. (2007). *Medicina Narrativa. Storie e Parole nella relazione di cura*. Il Pensiero scientifico editore.

Bert, G., & Quadrino, S. (2002). *Parole di medici, parole di pazienti. Counselling e narrativa in Medicina*. Il Pensiero Scientifico.

Berthoud, E., & Elderkin, S. (2013). *The Novel Cure: An A to Z of Literary Remedies*. Canongate Books.

Berthoud, E., & Elderkin, S. (2013). *The Novel Cure: An A-Z Of Literary Remedies*. Canongate Books.

Berthoud, E., & Elderkin, S. (2017). *Crescere con i libri. Rimedi letterari per mantenere i bambini sani, saggi e felici*. Sellerio.

Bertolini, G. (Ed.). (1994). *Diventare medici*. Guerini Studio.

Bertolini, G., & Massa, R. (Eds.). (2003). *Clinica della formazione medica*. FrancoAngeli.

Beseghi, E., & Grilli, G. (2011). *La letteratura invisibile. Infanzia e libri per bambini*. Carocci.

Bevilacqua, A. (2014). Implementing Medical Humanities in Italy: progress of a research. *Formazione & Insegnamento, 9*(2), 101–112. https://ojs.pensamultimedia.it/index.php/siref/article/view/1048

Bindi, R. (2019). *I libri che fanno la felicità*. Vallardi.

Bleakley, A. (2005). Stories as data, data as stories: Making sense of narrative inquiry in clinical education. *Medical Education*, 39(5), 534–540. 10.1111/j.1365-2929.2005.02126.x15842721

Bleakley, A. (2024). *Medical Humanities. Ethics, Aesthetics, Politics*. Taylor and Francis Group.

Bleakley, A. (Ed.). (2020). *Routledge Handbook of the Medical Humanities*. Routledge.

Blezza Picherle, S. (1996). *Leggere nella scuola materna*. La Scuola.

Blezza Picherle, S. (2004). *Libri bambini ragazzi. Incontri tra educazione e letteratura*. Vita e Pensiero.

Blezza Picherle, S. (2013). *Formare lettori, promuovere la lettura. Riflessioni e itinerari narrativi tra territorio e scuola*. Franco Angeli.

Boffo, V. (Ed.). (2006). *La cura in pedagogia*. CLUEB.

Bolívar, A. (2002). ¿De nobis ipsis silemus? Epistemología de la investigación biográfico-narrativa en educación. *Revista Electrónica de Investigación Educativa*, 4(1), 1–26. https://www.scielo.org.mx/pdf/redie/v4n1/v4n1a3.pdf

Bollmann, St. (2021). *Der Atem der Welt. J. W. Goethe und die Erfahrung der Natur*. Klett-Cotta.

Bolzoni, A. (1999). Oltre l'oralità. In Demetrio, D. (Ed.), *L'educatore (auto)biografo*. Unicopli.

Borges, J. L. (1981). *La cifra*. Emecé.

Borruso, F., Gallelli, R., & Seveso, G. (Eds.). (2022). Dai saperi negati alle avventure della conoscenza. *Esclusione ed emancipazione delle donne nei percorsi educativi tra storia e attualità*. Edizioni Unicopli.

Bosch Martínez. (2017). *Yo, gorda*. La Cúpula.

Boscolo, P. (2006). *Psicologia dell'apprendimento scolastico. Aspetti cognitive e motivazionali*. Utet.

Bosi, R. (2002). *Pedagogia al nido. Sentimenti e relazioni*. Carocci.

Bowlby, J. (1979). *Attaccamento e Perdita*. Bollati Boringhieri.

Bramer, S. (2019). *Climbing shadows: Poems for children*. (C. Derby, Illus.). House of Anansi Press and Groundwood Books.

Brelet, L., Flaudias, V., Désert, M., Guillaume, S., Llorca, P.-M., & Boirie, Y. (2021). Stigmatization toward People with Anorexia Nervosa, Bulimia Nervosa, and Binge Eating Disorder: A Scoping Review. *Nutrients*, 13(8), 2834. Advance online publication. 10.3390/nu1308283434444994

Brick. (2010). *Depression or: How I learned To Stop Worrying And Embrace Being Bonkers*. KNOCKABOUT.

Brisson, L. (1998). *Plato the myth maker*. University of Chicago Press.

Bruner, J. (1986). *Actual Minds, Possible Worlds*. Harvard University Press. 10.4159/9780674029019

Bruner, J. (1988). *La mente a più dimensioni*. Laterza.

Bruner, J. (1996). *The Culture of Education*. Harvard University Press. 10.4159/9780674251083

Bruner, J. (2006). *La fabbrica delle storie*. Laterza.

Bruner, J. S. (1992). *La ricerca del significato. Per una psicologia culturale*. Bollati Boringhieri. (Original work published 1950)

Bruzzone, D. (2012). *Farsi persona. Lo sguardo fenomenologico e l'enigma della formazione*. FrancoAngeli.

Bruzzone, D., & Musi, E. (Eds.). (2007). *Vissuti di cura. Competenze emotive e formazione nelle professioni sanitarie*. Guerini e Associati.

Bruzzone, D., & Zannini, L. (Eds.). (2014). Dossier su "Prospettive fenomenologiche della cura di sé nella formazione continua dei professionisti della salute". *Encyclopaideia.Journal of Phenomenology and Education*, 39, 3–5.

Buccolo, M. (2019). *L'educatore emozionale. Percorsi di alfabetizzazione emotiva per tutta la vita*. FrancoAngeli.

Bund, E. (1965). *Untersuchungen zur Methode Julians (Forschungen zum römischen Recht, 20. Abhandlung)*. Böhlau Köln-Graz.

Burbick, J. (1987). *Thoreau's alternative history: Changing perspectives on nature, culture, and language*. University of Pennsylvania Press. 10.9783/9781512819779

Burgio, G. (2019). Una violenza normale. Maschilità, adolescenza, omofobia. *Education Sciences & Society*, *2*, 222–237.

Burgio, G. (2012). Adolescenza e violenza. Il bullismo omofobico come costruzione della maschilità. *Mimesis*.

Butler, R. N. (1969). Age-ism: Another form of bigotry. [https://doi.org/10.1093/geront/9.4_Part_1.243]. *The Gerontologist*, 9(4), 243–246. 10.1093/geront/9.4_Part_1.2435366225

Cain, W. E. (Ed.). (2000). *A historical guide to Henry David Thoreau*. Oxford University Press. 10.1093/oso/9780195138627.001.0001

Calabrese, S., Conti, V., & Fioretti, V. (2022). *Che cos'è la medicina narrativa*. Carocci.

Caldin, C. F. (2001) A leitura como função terapêutica: biblioterapia. *Encontros Bibli: revista eletrônica de biblioteconomia e ciência da informação*, [S. l.], *6*(12), 32–44. 10.5007/1518-2924.2001v6n12p32

Caliceti, G., & Rivola, A. (2017). *Nel lontano regno di mongolfiera*. Sinnos.

Calvino, I. (1988). *Six Memos for the Next Millennium*. Harvard University Press.

Cambi, F. (2014). La formazione dell'insegnante oggi: la funzione della riflessività. In Mariani, A. (Ed.), *L'orientamento e la formazione degli insegnanti del futuro* (pp. 31–36). Firenze University Press.

Cambi, F. (2015). La bellezza ci "salva"! Osservazioni per una pedagogia estetica. *Studi Sulla Formazione/Open. Journal of Education*, 17(2), 7–11. 10.13128/Studi_Formaz-16171

Cambi, F. (2015). *La forza delle emozioni. Per la cura di sé*. Pacini.

Cambi, F., & Cives, G. (1996). *Il bambino e la lettura. Testi scolastici e libri per l'infanzia*. ETS.

Cambi, F., Di Bari, C., & Sarsini, D. (2012). *Il mondo dell'infanzia. Dalla scoperta al mito alla relazione di cura*. Apogeo.

Campagnaro, M. (2012). *Narrare per immagini. Uno strumento per l'indagine critica*. Pensa.

Campanile, S., Lovo, A., & Musella, M. (2001). *Il vizio di leggere*. Liguori.

Campo, R. (2005). The Medical Humanities, for lack of a better term. *Journal of the American Medical Association*, 294(9), 1009–1011. 10.1001/jama.294.9.100916145021

CASEL's SEL framework: What are the core competence areas and where are they promoted? (2020). Collaborative for Academic, Social and Emotional Learning. https://casel.org/casel-sel-framework-11-2020/

Cassel, E. (1982). The Nature of Suffering and the Goals of Medicine. *The New England Journal of Medicine*, 306(11), 639–645. 10.1056/NEJM1982031830611047057823

Catarsi, E. (2001). *Lettura e narrazione nell'asilo nido*. Edizioni Junior.

Cattorini, P. (2003). *Bioetica e cinema. Racconti di malattia e dilemmi morali*. Franco Angeli.

Cavafis, K. P. (2013). *Cavafy: The Poems*. Metaichmium.

Centonze, V., Palmieri, V. O., Addabbo, F., Palmiotti, G. P., Albano, M. G., Ribatti, D., & Portincasa, P. (2018). *Le nuove frontiere della terapia: la biblioterapia*. Il Pensiero Scientifico Editore.

Certini, R. (2001). Il metodo autobiografico e la storia dell'educazione. [Autobiographical method and history of education]. *Studium Educationis*, 2, 440–449.

Certo, J., Apol, L., Wibbens, E., & Yoon, S. (2010). Teaching poetry writing, PreK–12: A review of research and suggested directions for teacher practice and development. In G. Troia, R.Shankland, & A. Heinz (Eds.). *Writing Research in Classroom Practice* (pp. 93-115). Guilford Press.

Certo, J. L., Apol, L., Wibbens, E., & Hawkins, L. K. (2012). Living the poet's life: Using an aesthetic approach to poetry to enhance preservice teachers' poetry experiences and dispositions. *English Education*, 44(2), 102–146. 10.58680/ee201218436

Chambers, A. (2015). *Il lettore infinito. Educare alla lettura tra ragioni ed emozioni*. Equilibri.

Chambers, T. (1999). *The Fiction of Bioethics: Cases as Literary Texts*. Routledge.

Channing, W. E. (1902). *Thoreau: The poet-naturalist*. C.E. Goodspeed.

Charness, N., Boot, W. R., Graesser, A. C., Sweller, J., & Salthouse, T. A. (2017). Ten challenges for making automation a "team player" in joint human-agent activity. *Theoretical Issues in Ergonomics Science*, 18(5), 489–508.

Charon, R. (2006). *Narrative Medicine: Honoring the Stories of Illness*. Oxford University Press. 10.1093/oso/9780195166750.001.0001

Charon, R., Sayantani, D., Nellie, H., Craig, I., Eric, R. M., Edgar, R. C., Spencer, D., & Spiegel, M. (2016). *Principles and Practices of Narrative Medicine*. Oxford University Press. 10.1093/med/9780199360192.001.0001

Chase, S. (2015). Investigación narrativa. Multiplicidad de enfoques, perspectivas y voces. En N. Denzin & Y. Lincoln (coords.). *Métodos de recolección y análisis de datos. Manual de investigación cualitativa*, (pp. 58-112). Gedisa.

Clift, S., & Camic, P. (Eds.). (2016). *Oxford Textbook of Creative Arts, Health, and Wellbeing: International Perspectives on Practice, Policy, and Research*. Oxford University Press.

Cobos López, I. (2021). La medicina gráfica como herramienta para la traducción y la adaptación de textos biosanitarios. *Mutatis Mutandis.Revista Latinoamericana de Traducción*, 14, 397–426.

Colaneri, G. (2019). *Che cos'è una sindrome*. Uovonero.

Cole, T. R., Carlin, N. S., & Carson, R. (2015). *Medical Humanities*. Cambridge University Press.

Concannon-Gibney, T. (2019). Immersing first graders in poetry: A genre study approach. *The Reading Teacher*, 72(4), 431–443. 10.1002/trtr.1728

Connelly, M., & Clandinin, J. (1995). Relatos de experiencia e investigación educativa. En J. Larrosa et al. (comps.). *Déjame que te cuente. Ensayos sobre narrativa y educación* (pp. 11-59). Laertes/Psicopedagogía.

Connelly, F. M., & Clandinin, D. J. (1997). *Il curriculum come narrazione*. Loffredo.

Connolly, M. D., Zervos, M. J., Barone, C. J.II, Johnson, C. C., & Joseph, C. L. (2016). The Mental Health of Transgender Youth: Advances in Understanding. *The Journal of Adolescent Health*, 59(5), 489–495. 10.1016/j.jadohealth.2016.06.01227544457

Conti, F., & Silei, G. (2022). *Breve storia dello Stato sociale* [Short History of the Welfare State]. Carocci.

Contini, M., & Manini, M. (2007). *La cura in educazione. Tra famiglie e servizi*. Carocci.

Cordón, J., & Muñoz, M. (2023). *El poder de la lectura. Geografías del libro, el lector y la edición en el ensayo y la literatura*. Marcel Pons.

Corsi, M. (2006). *Il coraggio di Educare. Il valore della testimonianza*. Vita e Pensiero.

Cortázar, J. (1979). *Un tal Lucas*. Sudamericana.

Costantino, M. A., Marini, M., Bergamaschi, E., & Lanzini, L. (2006). Dal "libro su misura" alla "biblioteca di tutti". *Quaderni ACP*, 13(5), 199–203.

Covato, C. (2014). *Idoli di bontà: il genere come norma nella storia dell'educazione*. Unicopli.

Crawford, P., Brown, B., Baker, C., Tischler, V., & Abrams, B. (Eds.). (2015). *Health Humanities*. Palgrave.

Crawford, P., Brown, B., & Charise, C. (Eds.). (2020). *The Routledge Companion to Health Humanities*. Routledge. 10.4324/9780429469060

Crepaldi, D. (2020). *Neuropsicologia della lettura*. Carocci.

Crescenza, G. (2024). *Ritratti di maestri. Suggestioni pedagogiche sulla professione docente*. Ed. Conoscenza.

Crescenza, G., & Fiorucci, M. (2024). Enfoques innovadores, retos formativos y vías pedagógicas plurales en la educación contemporánea. Reflexiones introductorias sobre un texto coral. In Crescenza, G., & Fiorucci, M. (Eds.), *Educación e Innovación al servicio de la mejora del Conocimiento* (pp. 15–26). AulaMagna.

Croce, B. (1963). *Le due scienze mondane: l'Estetica e l'Economia*. In B. Croce, *Ultimi Saggi*. (44-60). Laterza.

Croce, B. (1966). *The totality of artistic expression*. In B. Croce, *Philosophy, Poetry, History: An Anthology of Essays*. (pp. 261 -273). Oxfrord University Press.

Croce, B. (1969). *L'arte come creazione e la creazione come fare*. In B. Croce, *Nuovi saggi di estetica*. (149- 156). Laterza.

Croce, B. (1917). *Logic as the science of the pure concept* (Ainslie, D., Trans.). Macmillan and Co.

Croce, B. (1951). *Conversazioni critiche*. Laterza.

Croce, B. (1954). *Problemi di estetica*. Laterza.

Croce, B. (1955). *Aesthetic as Science of Expression and General Linguistic* (2nd ed.). (Ainslie, D., Trans.). Transaction Publishers.

Croce, B. (1966). *Nuove pagine sparse*. Laterza.

Crothers, S. (1916). A literary clinic. *Atlantic Monthly*, 118(3), 291–302.

Cyrulnik, B. (2000). *Il dolore meraviglioso. Diventare adulti sereni superando i traumi dell'infanzia*. Frassinelli.

Czerwiec, M., Williams, I., Merill Squier, S., Green, M. J., Kimberly Rena, M., & Smith, S. T. (2015). *Graphic Medicine Manifesto*. Pennsylvania State University Press.

D'Addelfio, G. (2017). La nostra epoca tarda. In Bellingreri, A. (Ed.), *Lezioni di pedagogia fondamentale* (pp. 75–92). La Scuola.

D'Allancé M., (2007). *Che rabbia*. Babalibri. Trad.it Morpurgo A.

Dakos, K. (2006). *Put your eyes up here and other school poems. (G.B. Karas, Illus.)*. Simon & Schuster.

Dakos, K. (2021). *They only see the outside. (J. Oliver, Illus.)*. Magination Press.

Dal Cin, L. (2015). *Il deserto fiorito: La sindrome di Angelman raccontata ai bambini*. Uniti per Crescere.

Dal Cin, L. (2015). *Il puzzle di Matteo: la sindrome di Prader Will raccontata ai bambini*. Uniti per Crescere.

Dal Cin, L. (2017). *Lo sguardo fragile: la sindrome del cromosoma X fragile raccontata ai bambini*. Lapis.

Dal Cin, L. (2018). *Afferra la cima!: l'epilessia raccontata ai ragazzi*. Brossura.

Damasio, A. R. (1995). *L'errore di Cartesio*.

Darling-Hammond, L., Wilhoit, G., & Pittenger, L. (2014). Accountability for college and career readiness: Developing a new paradigm. *Education Policy Analysis Archives*, 22(86), 1–38. 10.14507/epaa.v22n86.2014

David B. (1996). *L'Ascension du Haut Mal*. L'Association.

Davies B., (2016). *L'isola del nonno*. Giralangolo. Trad. It. Roveda A.

Davis, L. J., & Kettner, J. (2017). *Ink in Water: An Illustrated Memoir (Or, How I Kicked Anorexia's Ass and Embraced Body Positivity)*. New Harbinger Publications.

Day, D., Colwell, R., Pizzo, J. S., Sableski, M., Sakoi, J., & Dotlich, R. K. (2023). Awakening poets: The heart of Georgia Heard. *Language Arts*, 101(2), 126–129. https://ezaccess.libraries.psu.edu/login?url=https://www.proquest.com/scholarly-journals/awakening-poets-heart-georgia-heard/docview/2902061353/se-2. 10.58680/la202332687

De Feo, A. (2023). La formazione dell'operatore sanitario: Dall'approccio biomedico alla 'cura narrativa' [The Training of the Healthcare Professional: from the Biomedical Approach to the 'Narrative Care']. *Medical Humanities & Medicina Narrativa*, 1, 225–234.

de Mennato, P. (1999). *La ricerca partigiana*. Liguori.

De Serio, B. (2014). Help to life. Education from birth. A reflection on early childhood starting from Maria Montessori. *RELAdEI - Revista Latinoamericana de Educación Infantil, 3*(3), 59-66.

De Serio, B., (2022). "Esiste la scienza della guerra, dov'è quella della pace?". Maria Montessori e la sublimazione del materno. (2022). *Medical Humanities & Medicina Narrativa - MHMN, 5*(1), 35-50. https://doi.org/10.53136/97912218007223

De Smet, M., & Talsma, N. (2019). *Mi chiamo Nina e vivo in due case*. Clavis.

Debeurme, L. (2006). *Lucille*. Futuropolis.

Dehaene, S. (2007). Le basi cerebrali di un'acquisizione culturale: la lettura. In Changeux, J. P. (Ed.), *Geni e cultura*. Sellerio.

Dehaene, S. (2009). *I neuroni della lettura*. Raffaello Cortina.

Delafosse, É. (2013). Internet y el microrrelato español contemporáneo. *Letral*, 11, 70–82.

Deloitte Access Economics. (2020). *Social and economic cost of eating disorders in the United States of America: A Report for the Strategic Training Initiative for the Prevention of Eating Disorders and the Academy for Eating Disorders*. HSPH. https://www.hsph.harvard.edu/striped/report-economic-costs-of-eating-disorders/

Deluigi, R., & Stramaglia, M. (2020). Projectuality and education, between learning objectives and political-cultural dynamics. *Form@ re-Open Journal per la formazione in rete, 20*(2), 103-116.

Demetrio, D. (1994). La ricerca autobiografica come cura di sé e processo cognitivo [The Autobiographical Research as cure for the self and cognitive process]. *Animazione sociale, 6/7,* 10-18.

Demetrio, D. (2000). *Raccontarsi. L'autobiografia come cura di sè[Telling the self. Autobiography as self-care]*. Raffaello Cortina.

Demetrio, D. (2013). Educare è narrare. Le teorie, le pratiche, la cura. *Mimesis*.

Denham, S. A. (2001). *Lo sviluppo emotivo dei bambini*. Ubaldini.

Denzin, N. (2008). La política y la ética de la representación pedagógica: Hacia una pedagogía de la esperanza. In McLaren, P., & Kincheloe, J. (Eds.), *Pedagogía crítica. De qué hablamos, dónde estamos* (pp. 181–200). Graó.

Dewey, J. (1933). How We Think: A Restatement of the Relation of Reflective Thinking to the Educative Process. In Boydston, J. (Ed.), *John Dewey: The Later Works, 1925-1953* (Vol. 8, pp. 105–352). Southern Illinois University Press.

Dewey, J. (1934). *Art as experience*. Berkley Publishing Group.

Di Grigoli, A. R. (2024). La pedagogia queer e il riconoscimento della non-linearità identitaria. Verso un modello critico della cis-normatività in educazione. In *La pedagogia di genere. Percorsi di ricerca contemporanei* (pp. 205–215). FrancoAngeli.

Didion, J. (2005). El año del pensamiento mágico. Barcelona: Random House, 2015.

Díez, M. Luis (2001). *Los males menores. Microrrelatos*. Madrid: Austral.

Dominicé, P. (2000). *Learning from our lives*. Jossey-Bass.

Domitrovich, C. E., Cortes, R. C., & Greenberg, M. T. (2007). Improving young children's social and emotional competence: A randomized trial of the preschool "PATHS" curriculum. *The Journal of Primary Prevention*, 28(2), 67–91. 10.1007/s10935-007-0081-017265130

Donnie, S. (1988). The pedagogy of two different approaches to humanistic medical education: Cognitive vs affective. *Theoretical Medicine*, 9(2), 227–236. 10.1007/BF004894143413709

Dostoievski, F. (2010). *El gran inquisidor y otros cuentos*. Siruela.

Drigas, A. S., & Papoutsi, C. (2018). A new layered model on emotional intelligence. *Behavioral Sciences (Basel, Switzerland)*, 8(5), 45. 10.3390/bs805004529724021

Dunlap-Shohl, P. (2015). *My Degeneration: A Journey Through Parkinson's*. Penn State University Press. 10.1515/9780271085791

Durkheim, E. (1951). *Suicide*. Free Press.

Eco, U. (1986). *Lector in fabula. La cooperazione interpretativa nei testi narrativi*. Bompiani.

El Refaie, E. (2019). *Visual Metaphor and Embodiment in Graphic Illness Narratives*. Oxford University Press. 10.1093/oso/9780190678173.001.0001

Emili, A. E., & Macchia, V. (Eds.). (2020). *Leggere l'inclusione. Albi illustrati e libri per tutti e per ciascuno*. Edizioni ETU.

Espinós, J. (2000). *Literatura creativa*. Bullent.

Espinoza, E. (2020). La búsqueda de información científica en las bases de datos académicas. *Revista Metropolitana de Ciencias Aplicadas, 3*(1), 31-35. https://remca.umet.edu.ec/index.php/REMCA/article/view/219/268

Ettling, D. (1998). Levels of listening. In W. Braud & R. Anderson (Eds.). *Transpersonal research methods for the Social Sciences* (pp. 176-179). Sage.

European Commission/EACEA/Eurydice. (2019). Key data on Early Childhood Education and Care in Europe. *Eurydice Report*. Luxemburg. https://op.europa.eu/en/publicationdetail/-/publication/5816a817-b72a-11e9-9d01-01aa75e d71a - 1/ language-en/format-PDF/source-102611557

European Commission/EACEA/Eurydice/Eurostat. (2014). Key data on Early Childhood Education and Care in Europe. *Eurydice and Eurostat Report* Luxemburg. https://ec.europa. eu/eurostat/documents/3217494/5785249/EC-01-14-484- EN.PDF/cbdf1804-a139-43a9-b8f1-ca5223eea2a1

Evans, M. (2002). Reflections on the humanities in medical education. *Medical Education*, 36(6), 508–513. 10.1046/j.1365-2923.2002.01225.x12047662

Evans, M., Arnott, R., Bolton, G., Finlay, I., Macnaughton, J., Meakin, R., & Reid, W. (2001). The medical humanities as a field of enquiry. Statement from the Association for Medical Humanities. *Journal of Medical Ethics*, 27(2), 104–105.11314152

Evans, M., & Greaves, D. (2010). Ten years of medical humanities: A decade in the life of a journal and a discipline. *Medical Humanities*, 36(2), 66–68. 10.1136/jmh.2010.00560321393283

Fairfield, L. (2009). *Tyranny*. Tundra Books.

Farid, D. (2020). *When you breathe. (B. Renkl, Illus.)*. Cameron Kids.

Fernández-Villardón, A., Valls-Carol, R., Alcantud, M., & Tellado, I. (2021). Enhancing literacy and communicative skills of students with disabilities in Special Schools through Dialogic Literary gatherings. *Frontiers in Psychology*, 12, 1–13. 10.3389/fpsyg.2021.66263933935921

Ferro Allodola, V. (2021). Costruire una salute sostenibile post Covid-19: verso la Health Literacy nella scuola italiana. *Mizar. Costellazione di pensieri*, 15, 141-149. http://doi.org/10.1285/i24995835v2021n15p141

Fieschi, L., Matarese, M., Vellone, E., Alvaro, R., & De Marinis, M. G. (•••). Medical humanities in healthcare education in Italy: A literature review. *Annali dell'Istituto Superiore di Sanita*, 49(1), 56–64.23535131

Fink, E., Patalay, P., Sharpe, H., Holley, S., Deighton, J., & Wolpert, M. (2015). Mental health difficulties in early adolescence: A comparison of two cross-sectional studies in England from 2009 to 2014. *The Journal of Adolescent Health*, 56(5), 502–507. 10.1016/j.jadohealth.2015.01.02325907650

Fiorucci, M. (2020). *Educazione, formazione e pedagogia in prospettiva interculturale*. FrancoAngeli.

Flecha, R. (2000). *Sharing Words: Theory and Practice of Dialogic Learning*. Rowman & Littlefield.

Flecha, R. (2015). *Successful Educational Actions for Inclusion and Social Cohesion in Europe*. Springer. 10.1007/978-3-319-11176-6

Fleishman, P. (2019). *Joyful noise: Poems for two voices. (E. Beddows, Illus.)*. HarperCollins.

Florian, D. (2018). *Friends and foes: Poems about us all*. Simon and Schuster.

Floridi, L. (2015). *Onlife Manifesto*. Springer. 10.1007/978-3-319-04093-6

Formenti, L. (1998). *La formazione autobiografica [The autobiographical training]*. Guerini Studio.

Frank, A. W. (1995). *The Wounded Storyteller: Body, Illness and Ethics*. University of Chicago Press. 10.7208/chicago/9780226260037.001.0001

Frank, J. (2014). *Lend a hand: Poems about giving. (L. Ladd, Illus.)*. Lee and Low Books.

Frank, R. (2001). *Body of awareness: A somatic and developmental approach to psychotherapy*. GIC/Analytic Press.

Frasnedi, F., Martari, Y., & Panzieri, C. (Eds.). (2005). *La lingua per un maestro. "Vedere" la lingua per insegnare, per capire, per crescere*. FrancoAngeli.

Frasnedi, F., & Poli, L. (1989). *Lettura e azione cognitiva. Parole e immagini*. Thema.

Frauenfelder, E. (1994). *Pedagogia e Biologia. «Una possibile alleanza»*. Liguori.

Frauenfelder, E., & Santoianni, F. (2002). *Le scienze bioeducative. Prospettive di ricerca*. Liguori.

Frauenfelder, E., & Santoianni, F. (Eds.), *A mente aperta. Ambienti di apprendimento. Contesti di formazione*. Pisanti.

Frauenfelder, E., Santoianni, F., & Striano, M. (2004). *Introduzione alle scienze bioeducative*. Laterza.

Freedman, M. (2014). *Relatively Indolent but Relentless: A Cancer Treatment Journal*. Seven Stories Press.

Freeman, M. (1993). *Rewriting the Self. History, Memory, Narrative*. Routledge.

Frege, G. (1884). *Die Grundlagen der Arithmetik*.

Freire, P. (1970). *Pedagogy of the Oppressed*. Seabury Press.

Freschi, E. (2013). *Il piacere delle storie. Per una "didattica" della lettura nel nido e nella scuola dell'infanzia*. Junior.

Friedrich, P. (2009). *The Gita within Walden*. SUNY Press.

Frude, N., & Jandrić, P. (2015). The Intimate Machine: 30 years on. *E-Learning and Digital Media*, 12(3–4), 410–424. 10.1177/2042753015571830

Furman, R. (2003). Poetry Therapy and existential practice. *The Arts in Psychotherapy*, 30(4), 195–200. 10.1016/S0197-4556(03)00052-2

Furtak, R. A., Ellsworth, J., & Reid, J. D. (Eds.). (2012). *Thoreau's importance for philosophy*. Fordham University Press. 10.5422/fordham/9780823239306.001.0001

Gadamer, H. G. (2004). *Truth and Method* (2nd ed.). (Weinsheimer, J., & Marshall, D. G., Trans.). Continuum Publishing.

Gaggioli, A., Morganti, L., Bonfiglio, S., Scaratti, Ch., Cipresso, P., Serino, S., & Riva, G. (2014). Intergenerational group reminiscence: A potentially effective intervention to enhance elderly psychosocial wellbeing and to improve children's perception of aging. *Educational Gerontology*, 40(7), 486–498. 10.1080/03601277.2013.844042

Galimberti, U. (1983). *Il corpo: antropologia, psicoanalisi, fenomenologia*. Feltrinelli.

Galmiche, M., Déchelotte, P., Lambert, G., & Tavolacci, M. P. (2019). Prevalence of eating disorders over the 2000-2018 period: A systematic literature review. *The American Journal of Clinical Nutrition*, 109(5), 1402–1413. 10.1093/ajcn/nqy34231051507

García Barrientos, J. L. (2011). El Holocausto en el teatro de Juan Mayorga. M. Brizuela (ed.), *Un espejo que se despliega. El teatro de Juan Mayorga*. Universidad Nacional de Córdoba, Argentina.

García Fernández, A. (2021). *Ingobernable*. Rimpego.

Gargani, A. (1990). *L'altra storia[The Other Story]*. Il Saggiatore.

Garin, E. (1975). *L'Educazione umanistica in Italia*. Laterza.

Garista, P. (2017). The Health Promoting Schools model. School as a pedagogical setting for generating wellbeing and learning. *Formazione & Insegnamento, 15*(3), 381-390. https://ojs.pensamultimedia.it/index.php/siref/article/view/2651

Garista, P. (2020). Health humanities. Generare salute attraverso le narrazioni in una prospettiva di life-long learning, *Medical Humanities & Medicina Narrativa - MHMN*, 1(1), 65-82. http://dx.doi.org/10.4399/97888255332625

Garofalo, K. "Kandinsky e il diritto romano", (2003) Labeo 49, 1 pp. 49-60.

Garrido, A. (2011). *Narración y ficción. Literatura e invención de mundos.* Iberoamericana/Vervuert. 10.31819/9783954871049

Gentilcore, D. (2008). *Malattia e guarigione. Ciarlatani, guaritori e seri professionisti.* Controluce.

Giaconi, C. (2015). *Qualità della vita e adulti con disabilità.* FrancoAngeli.

Giani, U. (2006). Enigma. Ragionamento Clinico e Narrative Personali. *Millennium.*

Giani, U. (Ed.). (2005). *Complessità, salute e malattia: Medicina Centrata sulla Persona.* Millennium.

Gianola, M. (2015). *Giovanotti Femmenelle e Signurine Masculone A ognuno la libertà di esprimere la propria identità Gender Nonconformity, ruoli e stereotipi di genere tra un gruppo di minori a rischio in un quartiere della periferia napoletana.* Fondazione Genere Identità Cultura.

Giarelli, G., Good, B. J., Del Vecchio Good, M.-J., Martini, M., & Ruozi, C. (Eds.). (2005). *Storie di cura. Medicina narrativa e medicina delle evidenze: l'integrazione possibile.* Franco Angeli.

Gibbs, J. J., & Goldbach, J. (2015). Religious Conflict, Sexual Identity, and Suicidal Behaviors among LGBT Young Adults. *Archives of Suicide Research*, 19(4), 472–488. 10.1080/13811118.2015.100447625763926

Gimbert, M., Miller, D., Herman, E., Breedlove, M., & Molina, C. E. (2021). Social emotional learning in schools: The importance of educator competence. *Journal of Research on Leadership Education*, 18(1), 3–39. 10.1177/19427751211014920

Giugni, G. (1969). *Pedagogia della lettura.* SEI.

Gobbo, M. (2015). *Mini.* Vela al Viento Ediciones Patagónicas.

Goedewaagen, T. (1971). Hegel und der Pantheismus. *Hegel-Studien*, 6, 171–187.

Goethe, J. W. v. (2011). *Italienische Reise.* Deutscher Klassikerverlag.

Goethe, J. W. v. (2016). *Maximen und Reflexionen.* Verlag der Contumax.

Goldberg, N. (1986). Writing Down the Bones: Freeing the Writer Within. Colorado (EEUU): Shambhala Publications.

Goleman, D. (2005). *Intelligenza emotiva.* Rizzoli.

González Cabeza, I. (2024). Poéticas de la autoficción en la patografía femenina en España. *Creneida. Anuario de Literaturas Hispánicas, 11 SE-Monográfico*, 41–87. 10.21071/calh.vi11.15733

González Cabeza, I. (2017). *Imágenes de la enfermedad en el cómic actual.* Eolas Ediciones.

Good, B. J. (1999). *Narrare la malattia. Lo sguardo antropologico sul rapporto medico-paziente*. Edizioni di Comunità. (Original work published 1994)

Gordon, J. (2005). Medical humanities: To cure sometimes, to relieve often, to comfort always. *The Medical Journal of Australia*, 182(1), 430–432. 10.5694/j.1326-5377.2005.tb06772.x15850446

Gosselin, C. (2023). *Je prends feu trop souvent*. Station T.

Gottschall, J. (2012). *L'istinto di narrare. Come le storie ci hanno resi umani*. Bollati Boringhieri.

Grau, I. (2001). *L'arquitectura del conte*. Octaedro – Accent.

Greaves, D. (2001). Two conceptions of medical humanities. *Nursing Philosophy*, 2(3), 270–271. 10.1046/j.1466-769X.2000.00070.x

Greaves, D., & Evans, M. (2000). Conceptions of medical humanities. *Medical Humanities*, 26(2), 65–66. 10.1136/mh.26.2.6512068906

Green, J. (1972). *Binky Brown meets the Holy Virgin Mary*. Last Gasp Eco Funnies.

Green, K. (2020). *Rethinking Therapeutic Reading: lessons from Seneca Montaigne, Wordsworth and George Eliot*. In Anthem Press. 10.2307/j.ctvsn3p9x

Green, M., & Myers, K. (2010). Graphic medicine: Use of comics in medical education and patient care. *BMJ (Clinical Research Ed.)*, 340(mar03 2), 574–577. 10.1136/bmj.c86320200064

Gregory, R. J., Canning, S. S., Lee, T. W., & Wise, J. C. (2004). Cognitive bibliotherapy for depression: A meta-analysis. *Professional Psychology, Research and Practice*, 35(3), 275–280. 10.1037/0735-7028.35.3.275

Grimes, N. (2016). *Poems in the attic. (E. Zunon, Illus.)*. Lee and Low Books.

Groppo, M., Ornaghi, V., Grazzani, I., & Carrubba, L. (1999). *La psicologia culturale di Bruner*. Raffaello Cortina.

Guzmán. (2010). Memoria y fantasía de la guerra civil española en *Siete hombres buenos* y *El jardín quemado* de Juan Mayorga. *Estreno*, 36(2), 82–97.

Hagimont, O., & André, C. (2013). *Dodue ou comment j'ai vaincu la dictature de la minceur*. Editions Odile Jacob.

Hamza, G. (2013). Derecho Romano y el desarrollo del Derecho privado en Europa del Este. *AFDUC, 17,* 595-604.

Han, B. C. (2015). *The burnout society*. Stanford University Press. 10.1515/9780804797504

Han, B. C. (2015). *The transparency society*. Stanford Briefs. 10.1515/9780804797511

Han, B. C. (2017). *In the swarm: Digital prospects*. MIT Press. 10.7551/mitpress/11055.001.0001

Han, B. C. (2017). *Psychopolitics: Neoliberalism and new technologies of power*. Verso Books.

Han, B. C. (2017). *The agony of Eros*. MIT Press. 10.7551/mitpress/11054.001.0001

Han, B. C. (2017). *The scent of time: A philosophical essay on the art of lingering*. Polity Press.

Han, B. C. (2018). *Topology of violence*. MIT Press. 10.7551/mitpress/11056.001.0001

Han, B. C. (2021). *Capitalism and the death drive*. Polity Press.

Han, B. C. (2021). *The palliative society: Pain today*. Polity Press.

Han, B. C. (2022). *Hyperculture: Culture and globalisation*. Polity Press.

Han, B. C. (2022). *Infocracy: Digitization and the crisis of democracy*. Polity Press.

Han, B. C. (2022). *Non-things: Upheaval in the lifeworld*. Polity Press.

Han, B. C. (2022). *The philosophy of Zen Buddhism*. Polity Press.

Harding, W. (1982). *The days of Henry Thoreau: A biography*.

Harding, W., & Bode, C. (Eds.). (1958). *The Correspondence of Henry David Thoreau*. New York University Press.

Harrower, M. (1972). *The therapy of poetry*. Charles C Thomas.

Haugse, J. E. (1999). *Heavy snow: My father's disappearance into Alzheimer's*. HEALTH COMMUNICATIONS.

Hawley, S. W., & Spillman, C. V. (2003). *Literacy and Learning: An Expeditionary Discovery Through Children's Literature*. Scarecrow Press.

Heard, G. (2016). *Heart maps: Helping students to create and craft authentic writing*. Heinemann.

Heard, G. (2021). *My thoughts are clouds: Poems for mindfulness. (I. Roxas, Illus.)*. Roaring Brook Press.

Heatherington, L., & Lavner, J. (2008). Coming to Terms With Coming Out: Review and Recommendations for Family Systems-Focused Research. *Journal of Family Psychology*, 22(3), 329–343. 10.1037/0893-3200.22.3.32918540762

Hebert, T. P., & Kent, R. (2000). Nurturing social and emotional development in gifted teenagers through young adult literature. *Roeper Review*, 22(3), 167–172. 10.1080/02783190009554027

Higgins, R. (2017). *Thoreau and the language of trees*. University of California Press. 10.1525/california/9780520294042.001.0001

Hoek, H. W. (2006). Incidence, prevalence and mortality of anorexia nervosa and other eating disorders. *Current Opinion in Psychiatry*, 19(4), 389–394. 10.1097/01.yco.0000228759.95237.7816721169

Hojat, M., Vergare, M. J., Maxwell, K., Brainard, G., Herrine, S. K., Isenberg, G. A., Veloski, J., & Gonnella, J. S. (2009). The devil is in the third year: A longitudinal study of erosion of empathy in medical school. *Academic Medicine*, 84(9), 1182–1191. 10.1097/ACM.0b013e3181b17e5519707055

hooks, b. (1994). *Teaching to transgress: Education as the practice of freedom*. Routledge.

Hughes, J., & Dymoke, S. (2011). "Wiki-Ed poetry": Transforming preservice teachers' preconceptions about poetry and poetry teaching. *Journal of Adolescent & Adult Literacy*, 55(1), 46–56. 10.1598/JAAL.55.1.5

Hunter, K. M. (1991). *Doctors' Stories: The Narrative Structure of Medical Knowledge*. Princeton University Press. 10.1515/9780691214726

IASC - Inter-Agency Standing Committee. (2024, April 05). *About*. IASC. https://interagencystandingcommittee.org/

Iavarone, M. L. (2008). *Educare al benessere*. Mondadori.

Iori, V. (2012), Pedagogia dell'invecchiamento e identità di genere [Pedagogy of aging and gender identity], in Corsi, M., Ulivieri, S., *Progetto generazioni. Bambini e anziani due strategie a confronto. [Generations Project. Children and the elderly two strategies compared]*, ETS.

Iori, V. (Ed.). (2009). *Quaderno della vita emotiva. Strumenti per il lavoro di cura*. FrancoAngeli.

Izard, C. E. (1997). *Human emotions*. Plenum Pless.

Janeczko, P. B. (2002). *Seeing the blue between: Advice and inspiration for young poets*. Candlewick.

Jedlowski, P. (2008). *Il sapere dell'esperienza. Fra l'abitudine e il dubbio*. Carocci.

Jodorowsky, A. (1995). *Sombras al mediodía*. Dolmén Ediciones.

Jones, L., & Ventevogel, P. (2021). From exception to the norm: How mental health interventions have become part and parcel of the humanitarian response. *World Psychiatry; Official Journal of the World Psychiatric Association (WPA)*, 20(1), 2–3. 10.1002/wps.2080833432770

Jones, T., Wear, D., & Friedman, L. (2014). *Health Humanities Reader*. Rutgers University Press.

Joyce, B., & Pekar, H. (1994). *Our Cancer Year*. Da Capo Press Inc.

Kandinsky, W. (1996). *De lo espiritual en el arte. Contribución al análisis de los elementos pictóricos*. Genoveva Dieterich, Barcelona.

Kandinsky, N. (1976). *Kandinsky und ich*. Kindler.

Kaneklin, C., & Scaratti, G. (Eds.). (1998). *Formazione e narrazione. Costruzione di significato e processi di cambiamento personale e organizzativo*. Raffaello Cortina.

Kanisza, S. (1994). *L'ascolto del malato*. Guerini e Associati.

Kanisza, S. (1996). *Apprendere nei servizi socio-sanitari*. NIS.

Kanisza, S. (2001). *Pedagogia ospedaliera*. Carocci.

Karin Pavón Rymer-Rythén, E. (2022). *Comiendo con Miedo*. astronave.

Katie Green. (2013). *Lighter Than My Shadow*. Jonathan Cape.

Kaufman, N., Kaufman, L., & Black, D. L. (2021). *Essentials of social emotional learning: The complete guide for schools and practitioners*. Wiley.

Kavafis, K. (n.d.). *Ithaka*. [trans. Edmund Keeley]. Poetry Foundation. [https://www.poetryfoundation.org/poems/51296/ithaka-56d22eef917ec]

Kiefer, B., & Tyson, C. A. Parsons Barger-B., Patrick, L., & Reilly-Sanders, E. (2023). *Charlotte Huck's children's literature: A brief guide* (4th ed.). McGraw-Hill.

Kim, K. (2023). *See us bloom: Poems on compassion, acceptance, and bravery. (E. Paik, Illus.)*. Modern Marigold Books.

Kinerk, R. (2011). *Oh, how Sylvester can pester: And other poems more or less about manners. (D. Kozjan, Illus.)*. Simon and Schuster.

Klee, P. (1957). *Tagebücher 1898-1918. Herausgegeben und eingeleitet von Felix Klee*. Cologne (M. Dumont).

Klee, P. (1976). Schriften: Rezensionen und Aufsätze. Colonia (M. Dumont).

Komariah, M., Ibrahim, K., Pahria, T., Rahayuwati, L., & Somantri, I. (2022). Effect of Mindfulness Breathing Meditation on Depression, Anxiety, and Stress: A Randomized Controlled Trial among University Students. *Healthcare (Basel)*, 11(1), 26. 10.3390/healthcare1101002636611488

Krüger, P. (1888). *Geschichte der Quellen und Litteratur des Römischen Rechts*.

Krutch, J. W. (1976). *Henry David Thoreau*. Greenwood Press.

Kucirkova, N., & Cremin, T. (2018). Personalised reading for pleasure with digital libraries: Towards a pedagogy of practice and design. *Cambridge Journal of Education*, 48(5), 571–589. 10.1080/0305764X.2017.1375458

Kvale, S. (2011). *Las entrevistas en investigación cualitativa*. Ediciones Morata.

Lalanda, M. (2017). *Medicina gráfica*. https://medicinagrafica.blog/

Lally, K. (2016). *I like being me: Poems about kindness, friendship, and making good choices*. Free Spirit Publishing.

Lamott, A. (1994). Bird by Bird: Some Instructions on Writing and Life. New York (EEUU): Pantheon Books.

Landín, M., & Sánchez, S. (2019). El método biográfico-narrativo. Una herramienta para la investigación educativa. *Educación (Lima)*, XXVIII(54), 227–242. 10.18800/educacion.201901.011

Laporta, R. (2001). *Avviamento alla pedagogia*. Carocci.

Lara, O. (2012). *Voces de Portacaliu*. Ediciones La Cabra.

Launer, J. (2002). *Narrative-Based Primary Care. A Practical Guide*. Radcliffe Medical Press.

Lazarus, R. S., & Folkman, S. (1984). *Stress, Apparaisal and Coping*. Springer.

LeDoux, J. (2003). *Il cervello emotivo. Alle origini delle emozioni*. Baldini Castoldi Dalai.

Lefevre, E. (1998). Humanismus und humanistische Bildung. In *Humanismus in Europa* (pp. 1–43). Heidbollmelberg.

Lepman J., (2018). *Un ponte di libri*. Sinnos. Trad. It. A.P. Becchi.

Lévinas, E. (1974). *Humanismo del otro hombre*. Siglo XXI.

Lévinas, E. (1980). *Totalità e infinito*. Jaca Book.

Levorato, M. C. (2000). *Le emozioni della lettura*. il Mulino.

Lingiardi, V. (2007). *Citizen Gay. Affetti e diritti*. Il Saggiatore.

Llenas A., (2016). *Il buco*. Gribaudo Trad. it Gamba D.

Loiodice, I. (2014). *Formazione di genere. Racconti, immagini, relazione di persone e famiglie*. FrancoAngeli.

Loiodice, I. (2023). Prevenire la violenza contro le donne attraverso l'educazione di genere. A partire dall'infanzia. *Civitas educationis. Education. Política y Cultura*, 12(1), 43–57.

Longo, G. (2011). *Cognizione ed emozione. Processi di interpretazione del testo letterario dalle neuroscienze cognitive all'educazione emotiva*. Pensa Multimedia.

Lonigan, C. J., & Shanahan, T. (2008). Developing Early Literacy: report of the national early literacy panel executive summary. A scientific synthesis of early literacy development and implications for intervention, *National Institute for Literacy*. https://files.eric.ed.gov/fulltext/ED508381.pdf

López Juan, A. (2024). *Amazonas, creación de una nueva iconografía a través de la computación actual*. In: *Carolina Flores Lueg and Marcos Gómez Puerta, Conocimiento compartido y educación*. Dykinson.

López Juan, A., López Martínez, M. P., & Navarro López, O. (2022b). 88. Cuentos griegos en papiro: Un nuevo tipo de aplicación didáctica de la investigación en Filología Griega. En R. Roig-Vila (Coord.), V. Martines y J. Antolí (Edd.), *Proceedings.I International Congress: Education and Knowledge I Congres* (p. 148). Octaedro, S.L.

López Juan, A., López Martínez, M.P., y Navarro López, O. (2022a). *Ficción en papiro: nuevas.*

López Juan, A., López Martínez, M. P., & Navarro López, O. (2022a). Ficción en papiro: nuevas aplicaciones didácticas de la investigación en humanidades. In *D. Gavilán Martín, y G. Merma Molina, Investigación e innovación en el contexto educativo desde una perspectiva colectiva* (pp. 171–179). Dykinson.

López Juan, A., López Martínez, M. P., & Navarro López, O. (2022c). *Parténope*. Editorial Turpin.

López Martínez, M. P. (2023c). Docere delectando: Las aventuras de Calígone y las amazonas. In: Rosabel Roig-Vila, Fabrizio Manuel Sirignano y Jordi M. Antolí Martínez Actas / *Proceedings 2nd International Congress: Education and Knowledge*. Octaedro.

López Martínez, M. P. (2021a). *Las aventuras de Calígone y las amazonas*. Editorial Turpin.

López Martínez, M. P. (2021b). *Nino, las aventuras del rey de Nínive*. Editorial Turpin.

López Martínez, M. P. (2022a). *El papiro del Marino Sinuhé*. Editorial Turpin.

López Martínez, M. P. (2023a). *El martirio de Santa Parténope*. Turpin Editores.

López Martínez, M. P. (2023b). Un tópos literario apto para todos los públicos: los nombres de los personajes de los papiros de novelas griegas perdidas. In *Esther Chiner e Iván Sánchez-López, Nuevas tendencias interdisciplinares en educación y conocimiento* (pp. 331–346). Editorial Tirant lo Blanch.

Lopez, A.G. (2018). *Pedagogia delle differenze. Intersezioni tra genere ed etnia*. ETS.

López, M. P. (Dir.). (2023d). *Ficción en papiro* (Fiction in Papyri). [Website]. [https://www.ficcionenpapiro.es/index.php/es/]

Lopez, A. G. (2017). *Decostruire l'immaginario femminile. Percorsi educativi per vecchie e nuove forme di condizionamento culturale*. ETS.

Lorenzoni, F. (2019). *Il dialogo euristico. Orientamenti operativi per una pedagogia dell'ascolto nella scuola*. Carocci.

Lorini, C., Caini, S., Ierardi, F., Bachini, L., Gemmi, F., & Bonaccorsi, G. (2020). Health Literacy as a Shared Capacity: Does the Health Literacy of a Country Influence the Health Disparities among Immigrants? *International Journal of Environmental Research and Public Health*, 17(4), 1149. 10.3390/ijerph1704114932059496

Lorini, C., Santomauro, F., Grazzini, M., Mantwill, S., Vettori, V., Lastrucci, V., Bechini, A., Boccalini, S., Bussotti, A., & Bonaccorsi, G. (2017). Health literacy in Italy: A cross-sectional study protocol to assess the health literacy level in a population-based sample, and to validate health literacy measures in the Italian language. *BMJ Open*, 7(11), e017812. 10.1136/bmjopen-2017-01781229138204

Losada, A. (2020). La biblioterapia como recurso terapéutico interdisciplinario. *Revista de Psicología*, 19(1), 210–221. 10.24215/2422572Xe057

Luri, G. (2019). *Sobre el arte de leer: 10 tesis sobre la educación y la lectura*. Plataforma editorial.

Machiavelli, N. (2016). Letter to Francesco Vettori, December 10, 1513. In Connell, W. J. (Ed.), *The Prince with related documents* (2nd ed., pp. 130–136). Bedford/St. Martin's.

Maddalena, S., & Paolozzi, F. (2023). Complessità, bioetica, resilienza: Tre dimensioni paradigmatiche all'approccio MH e MN nella prospettiva pedagogica [Complexity, Bioethics, Resilience: three paradigmatic dimentions to the MH and MN in a Pedagogical Perspective]. *Medical Humanities & Medicina Narrativa*, 1, 145–164.

Maich, K., & Kean, S. (2004). Read two books and write me in the morning! Bibliotherapy for social emotional intervention in the inclusive classroom. Teaching Exceptional Children Plus, 1(2). *Article*, 5, 1–13.

Mak, H. W., & Fancourt, D. (2020). Longitudinal associations between reading for pleasure and child maladjustment: Results from a propensity score matching analysis. *Social Science & Medicine*, 253, 112971. 10.1016/j.socscimed.2020.11297132276184

Mancaniello, M. R. (2018). *Per una pedagogia dell'adolescenza. Società complessa e paesaggi della metamorfosi identitaria.* Pensa Multimedia.

Manghi, S. (2004). *La conoscenza ecologica. Attualità di Gregory Bateson.* Raffaello Cortina.

Mantegazza, P. (1891). *Fisiologia della donna.* Treves.

March, R. & Martínez, M. Á. (2012). Poéticas de la ausencia en *El cartógrafo. Varsovia. Stichomythia, 13.*

March, R. (2014). *Memoria y desmemoria, pensamiento y poética en la dramaturgia de Juan Mayorga.* [Tesis Doctoral, Universitat de València].

March, R. (2019). La elipse, una figura para leer su dramaturgia. In Puertas, D. (Ed.), *Poliedro. Acerca de Juan Mayorga.* Antígona-Serie de Estudios Teatrales RESAD.

Marcum, J. (2008). Reflections on Humanizing Biomedicine. *Perspectives in Biology and Medicine*, 51(3), 392–405. 10.1353/pbm.0.002318723943

Mariani, A. (2005). La lettura come formazione di sé. *MaGMa - Rivista internazionale di scienze umane e sociali, 3*(3).

Mariani, A. (2006). La cura di sé e la lettura. In Boffo, V. (Ed.), *La cura in pedagogia: linee di lettura* (pp. 159–168). Clueb.

Mariani, A. (Ed.). (2018). *Educazione affettiva. L'impegno della scuola attuale.* Anicia.

Marini, L. (1879). *L'educazione conveniente della donna.* Paravia.

Marini, M. G. (2016). *Narrative Medicine. Bridging the Gap between Evidence-Based Care and Medical Humanities.* Springer. 10.1007/978-3-319-22090-1

Marone, F. (2023). Arte, cultural wellbeing e medical education [Art, Cultural Wellbeing and Medical Education]. *Medical Humanities & Medicina Narrativa*, 1, 77–88.

Martín Curto, L. (2021). *Yo también quise ser como Ana y Mía: Una historia de superación*. Zenith.

Martini, R. (1966). *Le definizioni dei giuristi romani*. Giuffrè.

Mascia, T. (2023). Pedagogia del leggere per piacere. Il ruolo della motivazione e l'identità del lettore. *Pedagogia più Didattica, 9*(1), 133-143. 10.14605/PD912309

Masini, V. (2005). *Medicina narrativa. Comunicazione empatica ed interazione dinamica nella relazione medico-paziente*. Franco Angeli.

Masten, A. S. (2015). *Ordinary Magic. Resilience in development*. Guildford Press.

Masten, A. S. (2021). Resilience of children in disasters: A multisystem perspective. *International Journal of Psychology*, 56(1), 1–11. 10.1002/ijop.1273733325580

Mate, R. (2009). Medianoche en la historia. Comentarios a las tesis de Walter Benjamín. In *Sobre el concepto de historia*. Ed. Trotta.

Mates, B. (1953). *Stoic Logic*. University of California Press.

Mayor Serrano, B. (2012). El lenguaje del cómic a disposición de la divulgación médico-sanitaria: Alzheimer. *¿Qué tiene el abuelo? 13*(35), 115–117.

Mayor Serrano, B. (2013). La historieta en la divulgación médico-sanitaria. *Translation Journal, 17*(2). https://translationjournal.net/journal/64historietas.htm

Mayor Serrano, B. (2018). Qué es la medicina gráfica. *Tebeosfera, tercera época, 9*. https://www.tebeosfera.com/documentos/que_es_la_medicina_grafica.html

Mayor Serrano, B. (2019). Cómics, o cómo aprender lenguaje médico a golpe de viñetas. In *Comunicación, lenguaje y salud: Estrategias lingüísticas para mejorar la comunicación con el paciente* (Rosa Estopà, Girona, Documenta Universitaria y IULA (Institut de Lingüística Aplicada, Universitat Pompeu Fabra), pp. 109–122).

Mayor Serrano, B. (2021). Divulgación científica a través del lenguaje del cómic: La covid-19. *Medicina y Cine*. https://www.academia.edu/45388153/Divulgaci%C3%B3n_cient%C3%ADfica_a_trav%C3%A9s_del_lenguaje_del_c%C3%B3mic_la_covid_19

Mayor Serrano, B. (2023). Los precedesores del cómic de ciencia actual: Una aproximación. *CuCo, Cuadernos de Cómic*, 161–184. 10.37536/cuco.2023.21.2300

Mayor Serrano, B. (2016). *El cómic como recurso didáctico en los estudios de Medicina Manual con ejercicios*. Fundación Dr. Antonio Esteve.

Mayorga, J. (2009). *Teatro para minutos*. Ñaque editora.

Mayorga, J. (2015). *Teatro 1989-2014*. Ediciones La uña rota.

Mayorga, J. (2016). *Elipses*. Ediciones La uña rota.

Mayorga, J. (2022). *Silencio. Razón del teatro*. Ediciones La uña rota.

Mazza, N. (2016). *Poetry Therapy: theory and practice*. Routledge. 10.4324/9781315748740

Mcadams. Dan P. (2018). Narrative identity: what is it? What does it do? How do you measure it? *Imagination, cognition and personality: consciousness in theory, research, and clinical practice*, *37*(3), 359–372. .10.1177/0276236618756704

McConnell, E. A., Janulis, P., Phillips, G.II, Truong, R., & Birkett, M. (2018). Multiple Minority Stress and LGBT Community Resilience among Sexual Minority Men. *Psychology of Sexual Orientation and Gender Diversity*, 5(1), 1–12. https://psycnet.apa.org/doi/10.1037/sgd0000265. 10.1037/sgd000026529546228

McIntosh, M. (2013). The state and the oppression of women. In *Feminism and Materialism (RLE Feminist Theory)*. Routledge.

McKenna, G., Hevey, D., & Martin, E. (2010). Patients' and providers' perspectives on bibliotherapy in primary care. *Clinical Psychology & Psychotherapy*, 17(6), 497–509. 10.1002/cpp.67920146202

McLean, C. P., Utpala, R., & Sharp, G. (2022). The impacts of COVID-19 on eating disorders and disordered eating: A mixed studies systematic review and implications. *Frontiers in Psychology*, 13, 926709. 10.3389/fpsyg.2022.92670936148134

McMillan, J., & Schumacher, S. (2005). *Investigación educativa*. Pearson education.

McNicol, S. (2018). Bibliotherapy and graphic medicine. In McNicol, S., & Brewster, L. (Eds.), *Bibliotherapy* (pp. 59–74). Facet. 10.29085/9781783303434.005

McWhinney, I. (1986). Are We on the Brink of a Major Transformation in Clinical Method? *Canadian Medical Association Journal*, 35, 873–878.3756718

Medina, C. (2004). Drama wor(l)ds: Explorations of Latina/o realistic fiction through drama. *Language Arts*, 81(4), 272–282. 10.58680/la20042905

Meijer, G., & Meijer, S. Y. (2002). Influence of the Code Civil in the Netherlands. *European Journal of Law and Economics*, 14(3), 227–236. 10.1023/A:1020780914470

Mèlich, J. C. (2004). *La lección de Auschwitz*. Herder.

Mental Health America. (2023). *The State of Mental Health in America*. Mental Health America. https://www.mhanational.org/issues/state-mental-health-america

Menton, M., Larrea, C., Latorre, S., Martinez-Alier, J., Peck, M., Temper, L., & Walter, M. (2020). Environmental justice and the SDGs: From synergies to gaps and contradictions. *Sustainability Science*, 15(6), 1621–1636. 10.1007/s11625-020-00789-8

Merino, J. M. (2007). *Variaciones sobre el microrrelato*. Menoscuarto.

Merletti, R. (1996). *Leggere ad alta voce*. Mondadori.

Merletti, R. (2001). *Libri e lettura da 0 a 6 anni*. Mondadori.

Merletti, R. (2006). *Leggimi forte. Accompagnare i bambini nel grande universo della lettura.* Sanali.

Merton, T. (1961). *The Behaviours of Titans.* New Directions.

Meyer, I. H. (1995). Minority Stress and Mental Health in Gay Men. *Journal of Health and Social Behavior*, 36(1), 38–56. 10.2307/21372867738327

Mezirow, J. (2003). *Apprendimento e trasformazione. Il significato dell'esperienza e il valore della riflessione nell'apprendimento degli adulti.* Raffaello Cortina.

Miquel, J. (1970). Stoische Logik und römische Jurisprudenz. *SZ, 87*, 85-122.

Misischia, B. (2020). Formación y Narrativa. Núcleos de sentido a partir del recorrido autobiográfico. *Márgenes. Revista de Educación de la Universidad de Málaga*, 1(3), 63–77. 10.24310/mgnmar.v%vi%i.8355

Monroy-Fraustro, D., Maldonado-Castellanos, I., Aboites-Molina, M., Rodríguez, S., Sueiras, P., Altamirano-Bustamante, N. F., de Hoyos-Bermea, A., & Altamirano-Bustamante, M. M. (2021). Bibliotherapy as a non-pharmaceutical intervention to enhance mental health in response to the COVID-19 pandemic: A mixed-methods systematic review and bioethical meta-analysis. *Frontiers in Public Health*, 9, 629872. 10.3389/fpubh.2021.62987233796496

Monterroso, A. (1959). *Obras completas (y otros cuentos).* Alianza Editorial.

Morin, E. (2021). *Lezioni da un secolo di vita* (S. Lazzari Trans.). Mimesis.

Morin, E. (1988). *Il pensiero ecologico.* Hopefulmonster.

Morin, E. (2000). *La testa ben fatta* [*The 'well-made' head*]. Raffaello Cortina.

Morin, E. (2001). *Il metodo. La natura della natura* [Method: The Nature of Nature]. Raffaello Cortina.

Mortara, C. C. (2023). La scrittura terapeutica nella Medicina Narrativa [Therapeutic writing in Narrative Medicine]. *Medical Humanities & Medicina Narrativa*, 1, 287–295.

Mortari, L. (2006). *La pratica dell'aver cura.* Bruno Mondadori.

Mulholland, M. J. (2004). Comics as Art Therapy. *Art Therapy: Journal of the American Art Therapy Association*, 21(1), 42–43. 10.1080/07421656.2004.10129317

Mustanski, B., & Liu, R. T. (2013). A longitudinal study of predictors of suicide attempts among lesbian, gay, bisexual, and transgender youth. *Archives of Suicide Research*, 42(3), 437–448.23054258

Myers, K., & Goldenberg, M. (2018). Graphic Pathographies and the Ethical Practice of Person-Centered Medicine. *AMA Journal of Ethics*, 20(2), 158–166. 10.1001/journalofethics.2018.20.2.medu2-180229460769

Myers, W. D. (2009). *Looking like me. (C. Myers, Illus.).* Egmont.

National Institute of Mental Health. (2023). *Transforming the understanding and treatment of mental illnesses*. NIMH. https://www.nimh.nih.gov/health/statistics

Natoli, S. (2016). *L'esperienza del dolore, Le forme del patire nella cultura occidentale*. Feltrinelli.

Naumann-Villemin C., (2003). *Il ciuccio di Nina*. Il castoro.

Navarro López, O. (2023). La lectura del cuento troquelado como instrumento de intercambio generacional. *Proceedings 2nd International Congress: Education and Knowledge*. Ediciones Octaedro.

Navarro López, O. (2024). La lectura compartida como espacio de intercambio generacional: a propósito de la página cuatro de «*Las aventuras de Calígone y las amazonas*». In: *Conocimiento compartido y educación*. Universidad de Alicante.

Neville, R. (2018). Philosophy of religion and the big questions. *Palgrave Communications*, 4(1), 1–8. 10.1057/s41599-018-0182-9

Newsome, K. E. (2008). Using poetry to improve fluency and comprehension in third-grade students. *Georgia Educational Researcher*, 6(1), 1–21. 10.20429/ger.2008.060101

NextStep Solutions. (2023). *The State of Mental Health in America 2023: Adult Prevalence and Access to Care*. NextStep Solutions. https://www.nssbehavioralhealth.com/nss-blog-the-state-of-mental-health-in-america-2023-adult-prevalence-and-access-to-care/

Nietzsche, F. (1980). Sobre verdad y mentira en sentido extramoral, Teorema. Levi, P. (2010). *Trilogía de Auschwitz*. Aleph Editores. Lévinas, E. (1974). *El humanismo del otro hombre*. Siglo XXI.

Nobile, A. (2004). *Lettura e formazione umana*. La Scuola Editrice.

Nussbaum M. (2004). *L'intelligenza delle emozioni*. il Mulino.

Nussbaum, M. (2010). *Not for profit: why democracy needs the humanities*. Princeton University Press.

Nussbaum, M. C. (2012). *Creare capacità. Liberarsi dalla dittatura del Pil*. Il Mulino.

Nussbaum, M. C. (2017). *Rabbia e perdono. La generosità come giustizia*. Il Mulino.

Nutbeam, D. (2008). The evolving concept of health literacy. *Social Science & Medicine*, 67(12), 2072–2078. 10.1016/j.socscimed.2008.09.05018952344

Obaizamomwan-Hamilton, E., Norris, A., Elsinbawi, M., Paley, M., & Cohen, A. (2024). Femmenoir pedagogies: Rescripting the reproduction of Black women's marginalization in education. *Race, Ethnicity and Education*, 1–23. 10.1080/13613324.2024.2327110

Oliva, C. (2004). *La última escena (Teatro español de 1975 a nuestros días)*. Cátedra.

Olmo Extremera, M., Olmedo Moreno, E., Cepero González, M., Zurita Ortega, F., & Padial Ruz, R. (2017). Validation of Resilience Scale (CD-RISC) in elite athletes through a structural equation model. RETOS. Nuevas Tendencias en Educación Física. *Deporte y Recreación*, (32), 96–100.

Operario, D., & Fiske, S. T. (2001). Ethnic identity moderates perceptions of prejudice: Judgments of personal versus group discrimination and subtle versus blatant bias. *Personality and Social Psychology Bulletin*, 27(5), 550–561. 10.1177/0146167201275004

Ouzts, D. (1991). The emergence of bibliotherapy as a discipline. *Reading Horizons*, 31(3), 199–206.

Palmore, E. (1999). *Ageism: Negative and positive.* New York (EEUU): Springer Publishing Company.

Palozzi, E. (2023). *Lo storicismo ontologico e metodologico di Benedetto Croce*. Guida.

Paolozzi, E. (2016). *The Aesthetic of Benedetto Croce* (Paparella, E. L., Trans.). Ovi Magazine. (Original work published 2002)

Pardeck, J. T. (1990). Using bibliotherapy in clinical practice with children. *Psychological Reports*, 67(3, Pt 1), 1043–1049. 10.2466/PR0.67.7.1043-10492287656

Paricio, J. (2003). Mirada al pasado. A propósito de Kandinsky y de un artículo de Luigi Garofalo. *Labeo*, 49(3), 323–328.

Pasta, S., & Rondonotti, M. (2020). Competenze mediaeducative e tecnologie di comunità. Nuove direzioni per il lavoro socioeducativo territoriale. *Rivista Italiana di Educazione Familiare*, 17(2), 377–398.

Patel, V., Saxena, S., Lund, C., Thornicroft, G., Baingana, F., Bolton, P., Chisholm, D., Collins, P.Y., Cooper, J.L., Eaton, J., Herrman, H., Herzallah, M.M., Huang, Y., Jordans, M.J.D., Kleinman, A., Medina-Mora, M.E., Morgan, E,, Niaz, U., Omigbodun, O., Prince, M., Rahman, A., Saraceno, B., Sarkar, B.K., De Silva, M., Singh, I., Stein, D.J., Sunkel, C., & UnÜtzer, J. (2018). The Lancet Commission on global mental health and sustainable development. *Lancet*, *392*(10157), 1553–1598. https://doi.org/.10.1016/S0140-6736(18)31612-X

Pattison, S. (2003). Medical Humanities: A vision and some cautionary notes. *Medical Humanities*, 29(1), 33–36. 10.1136/mh.29.1.3323671170

Peacock, L. (2023). *A whale of a time. (M. Hunt, Illus.).* Nosy Crow.

Pennac, D. (1993). *Come un romanzo*. Feltrinelli.

Pennebaker, J. W. (1997). Opening Up: The Healing Power of Expressing Emotions. New York (EEUU): Guilford Press.

Perkins, J. (2008). Childhood and Eros: Parallels between Klee and Freud. *Source (New York, N.Y.)*, 27(2/3), 32–39. 10.1086/sou.27.2_3.23208134

Peterkin, A., & Grewal, S. (2018). Bibliotherapy: The therapeutic use of fiction and poetry in mental health. *International Journal of Person Centered Medicine*, 7(3), 175–181. 10.5750/ijpcm.v7i3.648

Phinn, G. (2001). *It takes one to know one*. Penguin.

Pineau, G., & Marie-Michèle, M.-M. (1983). *Produire sa vie: autoformation et autobiographie* [Producing your life: self-training and autobiography]. Éditions Saint-Martin.

Pironi, T. (2010). *Percorsi di pedagogia al femminile. Dall'Unità d'Italia al secondo dopoguerra*. Carocci.

Porcellino, J. (1992). *True Anxiety*.

Prigogine, I., & Stengers, I. (1993). *La nuova alleanza*. Einaudi.

Purdie Salas, L., & Wong, J. (2018). Empower your students with poetry: Insights from Laura Purdie Salas and Janet Wong. *Journal of Children's Literature*, 44(1), 33–39.

Rasinski, T. (2014). Tapping the power of poetry. *Educational Leadership*, 72(3), 30–34.

Rasinski, T., Rupley, W., & Nichols, W. D. (2008). Two essential ingredients: Phonics and fluency getting to know each other. *The Reading Teacher*, 62(3), 257–260. 10.1598/RT.62.3.7

Ravi Kasthuri, R., & Venkatesan, S. (2015, May 31). Picturing Illness: History, Poetics, and Graphic Medicine. *Research and Humanities in Medical Education*, 2, 11–17.

Refaie, E. E. (2012). *Autobiographical Comics: Life Writing in Pictures*. Univ. Press of Mississippi. 10.14325/mississippi/9781617036132.001.0001

Refuge-Ed. (2024). *Effective practices in education, mental health and psychosocial support for the integration of refugee children (2021-2023)*. Refuge-Ed. https://www.refuge-ed.eu/

Richardson, R. D. (1988). *Henry Thoreau: A life of the mind*. University of California Press.

Ricouer, P. (1983). *Tempo e racconto[Time and Tale]*. Jaca Book.

Riva, M. G. (2013). The role of the traumatic 'transgenerational unsaid'-historical, social, educational, psychological-in life histories. *Pedagogia oggi, 2*, 51-79.

Rivas, I. (2009). Narración, conocimiento y realidad. Un cambio de argumento en la investigación educativa. En I. Rivas & D. Herrera (Coords.). *Voz y educación. La narrativa como enfoque de interpretación de la realidad* (pp. 17-36) Octaedro.

Rivas, I., Prados, E., Leite, A., Pablo Cortés, P., & Márquez, J. (2021). Ética, responsabilidad y trabajo colectivo en la investigación narrativa. *New Trends in Qualitative Research*, 5, 139–151. 10.36367/ntqr.5.2021.139-151

Rivoltella, P. (2022). Crescere Onlife. L'Educazione civica digitale progettata da 74 insegnanti-autori. *Schole*.

Rizzolatti, G., & Sinigaglia, C. (2005). *So quel che fai. Il cervello che agisce e i neuroni specchio*. Raffaello Cortina Editore.

Roas, D. (2008). El microrrelato y la teoría de los géneros. *La era de la brevedad, el microrrelato hispánico: Actas del IV Congreso Internacional de Minificción, Universidad de Neuchâtel, 6-8 de noviembre de 2006*. Palencia: Menoscuarto Ediciones.

Rosati, A. (2015). Educare alla riflessività. *Educational Reflective Practices*, 2(2), 67–74. 10.3280/ERP2015-002005

Rossellini, R. (1979). *Un espíritu libre no debe aprender como esclavo: Escritos sobre cine y educación*. Gustavo Gili.

Rossi, B. (1997). *Ascoltare e leggere*. La Scuola Editrice.

Rossi, B. (2006). *L'educazione dei sentimenti*. Unicopli.

Rossi, B. (2013). *Pedagogia Della Felicità*. FrancoAngeli.

Rossiello, M. C. (2016). Gli anziani si raccontano. Alcune riflessioni. [The Elders Tell. Some Thoughts]. *Metis*, 1/6, 322–330.

Rossi, W. (2000). Thoreau's Transcendental Ecocentrism. In Schneider, R. J. (Ed.), *Thoreau's*. 10.2307/j.ctt20q20hz.8

Roth, W., & Unger, H. (2018). Current Perspectives on Research Ethics. Qualitative Research. *Forum Qualitative Social Research*, 19(3). 10.17169/fqs-19.3.3155

Rousseau, J. J. (1969). *Emilio [1762]*. Armando.

Ryan, C., Huebner, D., Diaz, R. M., & Sanchez, J. (2009). Family rejection as a predictor of negative health outcomes in white and Latino lesbian, gay, and bisexual young adults. *Pediatrics*, 123(1), 346–352. 10.1542/peds.2007-352419117902

Sahakian, J. Feng et al. (2023). Early-Initiated Childhood Reading for Pleasure: Associations with Better Cognitive Performance, Mental Well-being and Brain Structure in Young Adolescence. *Psychological Medicine*.https://www.cambridge.org/core/journals/psychological-medicine/article/earlyinitiated-childhood-reading-for-pleasure-associations-with-better-cognitive-performance-mental-wellbeing-and-brain-structure-in-young-adolescence/03FB342223A3896DB8C39F171659AE33

Salovey, P., Brackeyt, M., & Mayer, J. (2004). *Emotional Intelligence: Key Readings on the Mayer and Salovey Model*. Natl Professional Resources Inc.

Sanborn, F. (1917). *The Life of Henry David Thoreau*. Houghton Mifflin & Co.

Sánchez-Moreno, C. (2013). *Law and Oratory. The Encyclopedia of Ancient History*. Editorial Biley Blackwell.

Sanjuán, L. (2019). *La entrevista y la historia de vida*. Universidad Oberta de Catalunya.

Santomauro, D. F., Melen, S., Mitchison, D., Vos, T., Whiteford, H., & Ferrari, A. J. (2021). The hidden burden of eating disorders: An extension of estimates from the Global Burden of Disease Study 2019. *The Lancet. Psychiatry*, 8(4), 320–328. 10.1016/S2215-0366(21)00040-733675688

Sarah, J. J., & Kevin, R. R. (2008). Bibliotherapy. Practice and research. *School Psychology International*, 29(2).

Sattelmeyer, R. (2000). Depopulation, Deforestation, and the Actual Walden Pond. In Schneider, R. J. (Ed.), *Thoreau's Sense of Place: Essays in American Environmental Writing* (pp. 235–243). University of Iowa Press. 10.2307/j.ctt20q20hz.22

Save the Children. (2019). *Il miglior inizio. Disuguaglianze e opportunità nei primi anni di vita.* Save The Children.

Scandurra, C., Amodeo, A. L., Valerio, P., Bochicchio, V., & Frost, D. M. (2017). Minority stress, resilience, and mental health: A study of Italian transgender people. *The Journal of Social Issues*, 73(3), 563–585. 10.1111/josi.12232

Schön, D. A. (1987). *Educating the Reflective Practitioner: Toward a new design for teaching and learning in the professions.* Jossey-Bass.

Schön, D. A. (1993). *Il professionista riflessivo. Per una nuova epistemologia della pratica professionale*. Dedalo.

Schulz, F. (1950). *History of Roman Legal Science.*

Schwarz, A. (1921). Zur Entstehung des modernen Pandektensystems. ZSS.

Secretan, P. (1969). *Autorité, pauvoir, puissance. Principes de philosophie politique réflexive.* L'Age d'Homme.

Sekers, D. C., & Gregg, M. (2007). Poetry in third grade: Getting started. *The Reading Teacher*, 60(5), 466–475. 10.1598/RT.60.5.6

Selmi, G., & Roberti, V. (2019). *Una scuola arcobaleno. Dati e strumenti contro l'omobitrans-fobia in classe*. Settenove.

Silverman, D. (2000). Doing Qualitative Research: A Practical Handbook. *Sage (Atlanta, Ga.).*

Simó, Isabel-Clara (2022). *L'inesperat i altres contes*. Alzira: Bromera.

Sirera, J. L. (2005). *«La memòria no té passat (Per a una contextualització del teatre històric català actual)». I Simposi Internacional sobre Teatre Català Contemporani (de la transició a l'actualitat).* Diputació de Barcelona-Institut del Teatre.

Sirignano, F. M. (2003). *La pedagogia della formazione. Teoria e storia[Pedagogy of training. Theory and history].* Liguori.

Sirignano, F. M. (2012). L'asilo nido come comunità educativa. Prospettive e riflessioni pedagogiche. In *L. Pati, M. Musello (Esd.), Pedagogia e didattica della prima infanzia*. Pensa Multimedia.

Sirignano, F. M. (2014). L'incontro educativo tra famiglia e servizi per l'infanzia. In Pati, L. (Ed.), *Pedagogia della famiglia*. La Scuola.

Sirignano, F. M. (2019). *La formazione pedagogica*. Liguori.

Sirignano, F. M. (2019). *La formazione pedagogica. Modelli e percorsi*. Liguori.

Sirignano, F. M., & Maddalena, S. (2023). L'arte del curare. Nuove prospettive pedagogiche. [The Art of Care. New Pedagogical Perspectives]. *Medical Humanities & Medicina Narrativa*, 1, 15–18.

Sloan, G. (2003). *Give them poetry! A guide for sharing poetry with children K-8*. Teachers College Press.

Smith, H.A. (2017). *My daddy rules the world: Poems about dads*. Henry Holt and Company.

Smorti, A. (1994). *Il pensiero narrativo*. Giunti.

Smyth, J. M. (1998). Written emotional expression: Effect sizes, outcome types, and moderating variables. [https://doi.org/10.1037/0022-006X.66.1.174]. *Journal of Consulting and Clinical Psychology*, 66(1), 174–184. 10.1037/0022-006X.66.1.1749489272

Soler-Gallart, M. (2017). *Achieving Social Impact. Sociology in the Public Sphere*. Springer.

Sopeña, F. (1974). El diario de Paul Klee: un pintor músico. In *Música y Literatura* (pp. 145–151). Rialp.

Sordé-Martí, T., Ghani, A. A., Almobarak, B., Chiappelli, T., Flecha, A., Hristova, M., Krasteva, A., Kjellberg, F., McQuillan, K., Nixon, E., Qasemi, M., Serradell, O., Aiello, E., Swords, L., & Abdulrahman, H. T. (2023). The REFUGE-ED Dialogic Co-Creation Process: Working with and for REFUGE-ED children and minors. *Humanities & Social Sciences Communications*, 10(463), 463. 10.1057/s41599-023-01967-6

Sørensen, K., Van Den Broucke, S., Fullam, J., Doyle, G., Pelikan, J., Slonska, Z., & Brand, H. (2012). (HLS-EU) Consortium Health Literacy Project European. Health literacy and public health: A systematic reviewand integration of definitions and models. *BMC Public Health*, 12, 80. 10.1186/1471-2458-12-8022276600

Spalviero, C. (2015). L'educazione letteraria. Crisi e possibili vie d'uscita. *El.LE Educazione Linguistica.Language and Education*, 4(2), 41–57. 10.14277/2280-6792/136

Spinsanti, S. (2011). Critica della ragione medica. *Quaderni di Teoria*, terza serie VI/1, 23-38.

Spinsanti, S. (2006). Una prospettiva storica. In Bucci, R. (Ed.), *Manuale di medical humanities*. Zadig.

Spooner, C. (2013). *Le théatre de Juan Mayorga: de la scèneau monde à travers le prisme du langage*. [Thèse doctorale de l'Université de Toulouse].

Starker, S. (1988). Do-it-yourself therapy: The prescription of self-help books by psychologists. *Psychotherapy (Chicago, Ill.)*, 25(1), 142–146. 10.1037/h0085310

Stickling, S., Prasun, M., & Olsen, C. (2011). Poetry: What's the sense in teaching it? *Illinois Reading Council Journal*, 39(3), 31–40.

Striano, M. (2006). Processi conoscitivi e sviluppo professionale. Narrazione e sviluppo nei contesti di pratica. *Pedagogika.it*, *5*, 24-27.

Striano, M. (2010). *Pratiche educative per l'inclusione sociale*. FrancoAngeli.

Sullivan, A. K., & Strang, H. R. (2002). Bibliotherapy in the classroom: Using literature to promote the development of emotional intelligence. *Childhood Education*, 79(2), 74–80. 10.1080/00094056.2003.10522773

Swartz, E. (1996). Emancipatory Pedagogy: A postcritical response to 'standard' school knowledge. *Journal of Curriculum Studies*, 28(4), 397–418. 10.1080/0022027980280402

Syse, K. L., & Mueller, M. L. (2015). *Sustainable Consumption and the Good Life. Interdisciplinary perspectives*. Routledge.

Tauber, A. J. (2012). Thoreau's Moral Epistemology and Its Contemporary Relevance. In Furtak, R. A. (ed.), *Thoreau's Importance for Philosophy* (pp. 127–142). Fordham University Press. 10.5422/fordham/9780823239306.003.0008

Terrusi, M. (2012). *Albi illustrati. Leggere, guardare, nominare il mondo nei libri per l'infanzia*. Carocci.

Terrusi, M. (2017). *Meraviglie mute. Silent book e letteratura per l'infanzia*. Carocci.

The Therapeutic Value of The Meditations of Marcus Aurelius. (2012). Tolstoy Therapy. https://www.tolstoytherapy.com/meditations-marcus-aurelius

Thoreau, H. D. (1906). *The Writings of Henry D. Thoreau (20 vol.)*. Houghton Mifflin & Co.

Thoreau, H. D. (2008). *Walden*. Oxford University Press. 10.1093/owc/9780199538065.001.0001

Toffano Martini, E. (2007). *Ripensare la relazione educativa*. Pensa Multimedia.

Torrent, A. (1996). *Zur Bedingungsdogmatik im klassischen römischen Recht und zu ihren Grundlagen in der stoischen Logik*. AHDE.

Torrent, A. (2007). *Fundamentos del Derecho europeo. Ciencia del Derecho: Derecho romano-Ius Commune-Derecho comparado*. Edisofer.

Torrent, A. (2015). La Pandectística del siglo XIX, último gran andamiaje teórico de los fundamentos del derecho europeo. *SDHI*, 8, 469–514.

Torrent, A. (2016). *El iusnaturalismo racionalista de los siglos XVII y XVIII. Precursor de los códigos en la secuencia de fundamentos del Derecho europeo, Madrid, Edisofer, Torrent, A. (2021), Retórica, dialéctica, lógica en Juliano. Liber Singularis de Ambiguitatibus, Madrid, Edisofer. Krampe, C. (1970), Proculi Epistulae. Eine frühklassische Juristenschrift*. C. F. Müller.

Turner, J. C., & Onorato, R. S. (1999). Social identity, personality, and the self-concept: A self-categorizing perspective. In Tyler, T. R., Kramer, R. M., & John, O. P. (Eds.), *The psychology of the social self* (pp. 11–46). Lawrence Erlbaum Associates Publishers.

Ulivieri, S. (2019). Il femminismo di Maria Montessori. Educazione, emancipazione per un nuovo modello di donna. In Baldacci, M., & Zabalza, M. A. (Eds.), *L'utopia montessoriana. Pace, diritti, libertà, ambiente* (pp. 137–152). Erickson.

Ulivieri, S. (2023). Identità di genere, femminismo e educazione. *Civitas educationis. Education. Política y Cultura*, 12(1), 109–122.

Ulivieri, S., & Biemmi, I. (Eds.). (2020). *Storie di donne. Autobiografie al femminile e narrazione identitaria*. Guerini Associati.

UN. (2006). *Convention on the Rights of Persons with Disabilities (CRPD).* UN. https://www.un.org/development/desa/disabilities/convention-on-the-rights-of-persons-with-disabilities.html

UNESCO Institute for Lifelong Learning. (2017). *Engaging families in literacy and learni*ng. UNESCO. https://unesdoc.unesco.org/images/0024/002494/249463e.pdf

UNESCO. (2017). *Education 2030. Reading the past, writing the future, fifty years of promoting literacy*. UNESCO. https://unesdoc.unesco.org/images/0024/002475/247563e.pdf

UNICEF. (2021). *Gender in Adolescent Mental Health.* UNICEF. http://www.unicef.org/gender/files/Gender_Action_Plan_brochure-web.pdf

United Nations. (1989). *Conventionon the Rights of the Child.* United Nation General Assembly. https://www. -ohchr.org /en/professionalinterest/pages/crc.aspx

Urrutia Asua, J. (2022). *Hoy no es el día*. Astiberri. https://www.astiberri.com/products/hoy-no-es-el-dia

Veale, J.F., Peter, T., Travers, R., & Saewyc, E.M. (2017). Enacted Stigma, Mental Health, and Protective Factors Among Transgender Youth in Canada. *Transgender Health*, *2*(1), 207–216.

Venkatesan, S., & Saji, S. (2021). *Metaphors of Mental Illness in Graphic Medicine.* Routledge. https://www.academia.edu/58871491/_Graphic_Medicine_Book_Metaphors_of_Mental_Illness_in_Graphic_Medicine

Venkatesan, S., & Peter, A. M. (2018). 'I Want to Live, I Want to Draw': The Poetics of Drawing and Graphic Medicine. *Journal of Creative Communications*, 13(2), 104–116. 10.1177/0973258618761406

Venturini, B. (2020). *Come un romanzo. Viaggio nella libroterapia.* Transeuropa.

Vignes, A., & Boffa, A. (2020). *Come in un giardino.* Saremo Alberi.

Vilar, R. & Artesero, S. (2010). Conversación con Juan Mayorga. *Pausa,* 32.

Villani, P. (2023). Per uno statuto narrativo della Medicina Narrativa. *Medical Humanities & Medicina Narrativa - MHMN, 7*(1), 19-37. 10.53136/97912218080872

Villeneuve, E., & Rocheleau, J. (2010). *La fille invisible*. Glénat Québec.

Vogrinčič Čepič, A., Mascia, T., & Aerila, J. A. (2024). Reading for Pleasure: A Review of Current Research. *New Zealand Journal of Educational Studies*, 59(1), 49–71. Advance online publication. 10.1007/s40841-024-00313-x

Volpicella, A. M. (2017). *L'aprirsi delle famiglie alla comunità. Mito-Realtà-Utopia*. Pensa Multimedia.

Vygotskij, L. S. (1972). *Immaginazione e creatività nell'età infantile*. Editori Riuniti.

Vygotskij, L. S. (1973). *Lo sviluppo psichico del bambino*. Editori Riuniti.

Walls, L. D. (1995). *Seeing new worlds: Henry David Thoreau and nineteenth-century natural science*. The University of Wisconsin Press.

Walls, L. D. (2013). Walking West, Gazing East: Planetarity on the Shores of Cape Cod. In Specq, F., (ed.), *Thoreauvian Modernities: Transatlantic Conversations on an American Icon* (pp. 21–42). University of Georgia Press.

Walls, L. D. (2017). *Henry David Thoreau: A Life*. The University of Chicago Press. 10.7208/chicago/9780226344720.001.0001

Walsh, F. (2008). *La resilienza Familiare*. Raffaello Cortina.

Wampold, B. E. (2001). *The great psychotherapy debate: Models, methods, and findings*. Lawrence Erlbaum Associates Publishers.

Wassiliwizky, E., Koelsch, S., Wagner, V., Jacobsen, T., & Menninghaus, W. (2017). The emotional power of poetry: Neural circuitry, psychophysiology, and compositional principles. *Social Cognitive and Affective Neuroscience*, 12(8), 1229–1240. 10.1093/scan/nsx06928460078

WHO - World Health Organization. (2001). *ICF. International Classification of Functioning, Disability and Health*. OMS Press.

Widman, L., Noar, S. M., Choukas-Bradley, S., & Francis, D. B. (2014). Adolescent sexual health communication and condom use: A meta-analysis. *Health Psychology*, 33(10), 1113–1124. 10.1037/hea000011225133828

Wilhelm, J. D. (2016). Recognising the power of pleasure: What engaged adolescent readers get from their free-choice reading, and how teachers can leverage this for all. *Australian Journal of Language and Literacy*, 39(1), 30–41. 10.1007/BF03651904

Williams, I. (2007). *Graphic Medicine*. Graphic Medicine. https://www.graphicmedicine.org/

Williams, I. (2012). Graphic medicine: Comics as medical narrative. *Medical Humanities*, 38(1), 21–27. 10.1136/medhum-2011-01009322282425

Wojnarowicz, D., & Romberger, J. (1996). *7 Miles a Second.* Fantagraphics Books.

Wong, J. (n.d.). *What is a poetry suitcase?* Janet Wong. https://janetwong.com/poetry-suitcase/

Wong, J., & Vardell, S. (2022). *Things we feel.* Pomelo Books.

Wong, J., & Vardell, S. (2022). *What is a friend?* Pomelo Books.

Wong, J., & Vardell, S. (2023). *What is hope?* Pomelo Books.

World Health Organization. (1986). *Ottawa Charter for Health Promotion: First International Conference on Health Promotion Ottawa, 21 November.* WHO. https://www.healthpromotion.org.au/images/ottawa_charter_hp.pdf

World Health Organization. (2022). *World mental health report: Transforming mental health for all.* WHO. https://www.who.int/publications/i/item/9789240049338

Xiang, D. H., & Yi, A. M. (2020). A look back and a path forward: Poetry's healing power during the pandemic. *Journal of Medical Humanities, 41*, 603–608. https://doi- org.ezaccess.libraries.psu.edu/10.1007/s10912-020-09657-z

Yiannopoulos, A. (1993). Historical Development., in K. D. Kerameus y P. J. Kozyris (eds), *Introduction to Greek Law*, (2nd ed), Kluwer/Sakkoulas, Deventer.

Zannini, L. (2009). Medicina Narrativa e Medical Humanities. In Gentile, A. E., Luzi, I., Razeto, S., Taruscio, D. (Eds.). *Convegno. Medicina narrativa e malattie rare. Istituto Superiore di Sanità.* Rapporti ISTISAN 09/50.

Zannini, L. (2021). Valutare gli effetti di interventi di medicina narrativa nella formazione dei professionisti della cura: esperienze e riflessioni. *Medical Humanities & Medicina Narrativa - MHMN, 3*(1), 21-38. https://doi.org/10.53136/97912599425172

Zannini, L. (2008). *Medical humanities e medicina narrativa. Nuove prospettive nella formazione dei professionisti della cura.* Raffaello Cortina.

Zannini, L. (Ed.). (2004). *Il corpo-paziente. Da oggetto delle cure a soggetto della relazione terapeutica.* Franco Angeli.

Zemelman, H. (2010). Sujeto y subjetividad: La problemática de las alternativas como construcción posible. *Polis (Santiago)*, 27(27), 1–12. 10.4067/S0718-65682010000300016

About the Contributors

Antonio Cortijo Ocaña is a Professor at the University of California, Santa Barbara. He analyzes in his research the ideological structures and tensions that have forged the Modern Period across the Atlantic and across the languages and cultures of the Iberian Peninsula. He deals with issues such as nation building, power and ideology, religion and economy in the late medieval through 18th centuries, as well as with the larger topic of the relevance of Humanism in the creation of the modern nations. He is the author of over 500 publications, founder of eHumanista, member of the Reial Acadèmia de Bones Lletres de Barcelona, member of over 50 editorial boards of journals, and recipient of Saverio Nitti Award (2017), Scripta Humanistica Award (2010), Diputación de Sevilla Award (2001).

Vicent Martines is a Professor at the University of Alicante. He is PI of ISIC-IVITRA and a member of the Reial Acadèmia de Bones Lletres de Barcelona, IEC, IULMA, IIFV. He is the Co-director of the Center For Catalan Studies (University of California at Santa Barbara [UCSB] / University of Alicante). He is the chief editor of Series IVITRA Research in Linguistics and Literature, John Benjamin (Amsterdam/ Philadelphia) and the eHumanista/IVITRA (UCSB) co-editor. He has received the following awards: Rei En Pere el Catòlic d´Investigació (IEC, 1988), Premi d´Investigació Ibn Al-Abbar (Generalitat Valenciana, Ajuntament d´Onda, 1990), Premio de Ensayo de Catalán, Gallego y Vasco de la Fundación Ortega y Gasset (Madrid, 1993), and Premio Internazionale Francesco Saverio Nitti (Centro Internazionale di Ricerca Francesco Saverio Nitti per il Mediterraneo, Suor Orsola Benincasa University, Napoli, Italy, 2023). He is the author of 280 publications.

Veronica Orazi (Florence 1966), PhD in Ibero-Romance Philology, has taught at the Ca' Foscari University of Venice, the University of Bologna and the University of Siena. She is Full Professor of Spanish Literature and Catalan Language and Literature at the University of Turin. She is the Director of the Rivista Italiana di Studi Catalani, co-director of the series 'Bibliotheca Iberica' and a corresponding member of the “Institut d'Estudis Catalans” in Barcelona. She was awarded the Premi crítica Serra d'Or de catalanística (2000) and the Premio Città di Monselice per la traduzione letteraria - Sezione Leone Traverso (2002). In 2015 she received the Menció de la Delegació del Govern de la Generalitat de Catalunya a Itàlia for her activity in promoting Catalan culture. Since 2015 he has directed the international project “Glocal Perspectives in Iberian Studies” and she actually directs the project “Identity Heritage and Cultural Memory. The elaboration of the past through the theatre of democratic Spain (1975 to the present)”. Her research interests focus on medieval and contemporary Spanish and Catalan literature and on the Italian translation of Spanish and Catalan literature

***

Gianluca Amatori is Associate Professor in Didactics, Special Pedagogy and Educational Research at the European University of Rome. He is Scientific Director of the International Research Centre for Inclusion and Teacher Training - IRCIT, an international inter-university research centre.

About the Contributors

Gabriele Borghese His research, starting from the thought of Antonio Labriola, is focused on the links between politics and education. He also studies the social impact of use of digital technology in the various fields of education (e.g. critical literacy, digital divide). Is member of the international research team of the Francesco Saverio Nitti International Research Centre for the Mediterranean.

Maria Buccolo is a Researcher in General and Social Pedagogy at the European University of Rome. She is a member of the research group of the International Research Center for Inclusion and Teacher Training (IRCIT), an international interuniversity research center. She has been a Visiting Professor at the Universidade do Estado da Bahia (Salvador de Bahia, Brazil), at the Universidad de San Carlos de Guatemala (Guatemala City), and at the University of Alicante (Spain).

Aránzazu Calzada is a Professor of Roman Law at the University of Alicante since 2002. Degree and PhD in Law from the University of Valladolid. She has carried out her teaching and research work at the Universities of Castilla-La Mancha, Complutense de Madrid, La Rioja, Valencia and León. She is at the moment Deputy Director of the International Journal of Roman Law (RIDROM), member of the Scientific Committee of the journal Cultura Giuridica e Diritto Vivente and member of the Editorial Board of the journal Derecho y Literatura. She is the author of several scientific publications, especially in the field of family and inheritance law, such as aditio nuda voluntate, agreements for the limitation of inheritance liability, consortium ercto non cito, quasi-delictual liability in family matters, ademptio legati and the category of lo pro non scripto in testamentary succession. Furthermore, it is worth mentioning her contribution concerning the study of Lex Atinia de rebus subreptis and the reversio in potestatem de las res furtivae et vi possessae. He has also carried out studies on urban legislation and citizenship in the Lex Irnitana. She has also co-directed the project Analysis and monitoring of digital rights and currently leads the Social Council projects linked to the Alicante Digital Intelligence Centre (CENID). She has held various management positions at her own University, including vice-president and general secretary. She has also held positions in various public and private foundations.

Carles Cortés is a Professor at the University of Alicante. He directs the Institut Interuniversitari de Filologia Valenciana at the University of Alicante. He is also a literary author, especially of fiction.

Giorgio Crescenza is a Ricercatore in General and Social Pedagogy at the University of Tuscia (M-PED/01), he also teaches at the University La Sapienza in Rome and is a member of the Doctoral College in "Theory and Research educational and social research' at the University of Roma Tre.

Deanna Day weaves her passions—art, children's literature and technology—into the literacy courses she teaches for Washington State University. Her research focuses on children's literature and teaching preservice teachers. She has served on numerous children's literature committees.

Antonio Raimondo Di Grigoli is a research fellow at the University of Florence. His research interests revolve around the deconstruction of hegemonic masculinities in both formal and informal education. In addition, he is interested in the construction of a pedagogical epistemology that considers the intersection of Critical Studies on Men and Masculinities, queer theories, postcolonial studies and popular culture.

Alfonso Fernández-Manso has a PhD in two specialties, Applied Physics (University of Valladolid) and Literature (University of Alicante) and is currently a Professor at the University of León. He is also a member of the research laboratory of Applied Ecology (GEAT). His main lines of research related to literature focus on (i) Literature and nature in the USA, (ii) Nature Writing and (iii) ecocriticism applied to literary creation and analysis. He is the author of 10 books and co-author of more than 100 articles published in JCR indexed journals and has participated in more than forty research projects, ten of which he is the principal investigator.

Valerio Ferro Allodola is Researcher in History of Pedagogy at the Mediterranea University of Reggio Calabria. He has furthered the study of reflective and transformative learning processes in professional contexts (especially in social and health services), publishing books and scientific articles. His research activity, in recent years, has focused on scientific pedagogy and Medical Humanities in a historical-theoretical perspective. He is member of the international research team of the Francesco Saverio Nitti International Research Centre for the Mediterranean. He is Co-Editor in Chief - with Prof. Fabrizio Manuel Sirignano - of the journal Medical Humanities & Medicina Narrativa – MHMN.

Christos Lalos was born in Athens. Graduate of Informatics in Management and Economics, holder of two Master's Degrees in Digital Systems and Business Administration, graduate of ASPAITE and adult trainer. He is a Doctor in the field of Informatics and Lifelong Learning. He has worked in various private companies in the field of Plirifics and education, while in recent years in the public sector.

Olimpia López teaches Linguistics at the University of Alicante. She studied a degree in English Studies at the UA, specialising in Clinical Linguistics (TFG "Alteraciones en la lectoescritura por daños cerebrales: reflexiones desde la Lingüística Clínica") and has also completed the Training Course for Teachers of Spanish as a Foreign Language (Centro Superior de Idiomas, University of Alicante) and the Master's Degree in Foreign Trade - Carlos III University of Madrid (October 2018 - June 2019). She has participated as a guest speaker in Seminars: "Salidas profesionales de la Lingüística Clínica: la logopedia" in the Department of Spanish Philology, General Linguistics and Theory of Literature of the UA (2018) and has presented communications and papers at conferences: Comins, P.M. Comins, L. and Navarro, O. "La comprensión lingüística en los problemas matemáticos: éxito o fracaso", XXXI Congreso Internacional de la Asociación, Española de Logopedia, Foniatría y Audiología e Iberoamericana de Fonoaudiología. Granada, June 2018. She has experience as a copy editor in private companies and as a linguist in speech therapy clinics. She has enjoyed stays in foreign universities such as Eduardo Mondlane University. Maputo (Mozambique). April 2022 and has participated in the organisation of seminars and academic meetings: Collaborating scholar at the 34th AESLA International Congress (Alicante, 2016), organiser and director of the XXIII Jornadas Internacionales de Estudios de Lingüística "Identidades y Lenguaje", held at the Aula Magna of the Faculty of Philosophy and Letters of the University of Alicante, from 30 March to 1 April 2022 and member of the organising committee of the III Seminario internacional de Sociolingüística "De la norma, el estándar y lo normativo", held on 18 May 2022.

María López Martínez is and Associated Professor in Classical Greek Philology at the University of Alicante. She has directed several research projects on papyrology and the origins of narrative.

Stefania Maddalena, PhD, is Researcher in General and Social Pedagogy at the Gabriele d'Annunzio University of Chieti-Pescara, where she teaches General Pedagogy and Intercultural Pedagogy. She is a member of the research group of the Francesco Saverio Nitti International Research Centre for the Mediterranean and has been a visiting researcher at the University of Alicante, the University of Granada and the University of Belgrade. Her research interests focus on innovative pedagogies for the development of democratic competences, pedagogy of socio-political engagement and education for cultural differences.

Robert March is an Assistant Professor at the University of Alacant. He is Degree in English Philology, Audio-visual Communicatio and Catalan Philology; Postgraduate in Catalan Linguistic Correction, and Master and Phd in Advanced Hispanic Studies and Phd in Catalan Philology. Besides, he is currently studying a Master's Degree in Medieval European Identity: «Languages and Literatures of the Middle Ages», at the University of Lleida. In addition, he has written articles in different indexed journals and book chapters. His interests include Medieval, Modern and Contemporary literature, the relationships between poetics, thought and memory. He is part of the research project «Traducció de clàssics valencians a llengües europees. Estudis literaris, lingüístics i traductològics comparats» (VIGROB 125) and collaborator in «Llengua, Literatura i Cultura Valenciana del Segle d'Or a la Renaixença» (LLICVALSOR). He is member of Institut Superior d'Investigació Cooperativa IVITRA and IIFV.

About the Contributors

María José Mompeán Mejías is a predoctoral researcher FPI (within the project PID2021-128381NB-I00 of the Ministry of Science and Innovation) in the Departament of Catalan Studies of the University of Alicante, and is member of the research groups VIGROB-125 and ISIC-IVITRA of the same university. Her research is mainly focused on Graphic Medicine, medical communication tools, doctor-patient communication, metaphor, and multimodality.

Mary Napoli is an Associate Professor of Reading and Children's Literature at Penn State Harrisburg where she teaches undergraduate literacy courses. She has published numerous books, articles, book chapters, and professional resource materials pertaining to children's literature. She has also served on national level book award committees.

Maria Federica Paolozzi is PhD in General Pedagogy and Social Pedagogy as part of the PhD program "On the areas of interaction and integration between the humanities and advanced technologies. Humanities and Technologies: an integrated research path" at the Suor Orsola Benincasa University of Naples.

Carlos Sánchez-Moreno Ellart was born in Barcelona and studied Law, Philosophy, and Classical Philology, from which he graduated and obtained his doctorate in Law. He was a Humboldt scholar in Trier (Germany) and a Fulbright scholar at Columbia University (NY). He has been a Professor of Roman Law at the University of Valencia since 2002.

Fabrizio Manuel Sirignano is Full Professor of General and Social Pedagogy at the University of Naples Suor Orsola Benincasa, is the Rector's Delegate for Lifelong Learning and President of the B.Sc in Primary Education. He is Scientific Director of the Francesco Saverio Nitti International Research Centre for the Mediterranean. He teaches at the Democritus University of Thrace, was Visiting Professor at the Universities of Alicanteand Sevilla and is Scientific Coordinator of the Elisa Frauenfelder International Prize.

Index

Symbols

A

B

C

E

G

H

I

J

K

L

M

N

P

R

S

T

W

www.ingramcontent.com/pod-product-compliance
Lightning Source LLC
LaVergne TN
LVHW080905300926
849162LV00003B/562
9798369342442